To Dale:

To Enjoy During Recuperation

From Bea & Norm Kaarre
8-15-90

THE WORLD'S
GREAT
CARS

Contents

House Editor Dorothea Hall
Editor Jeremy Coulter
Art Editor Gordon Robertson
Production Controller Craig Chubb

This edition published 1989 by Chartwell Books, Inc.
A division of Book Sales, Inc.
110 Enterprise Avenue
Secaucus, New Jersey 07094

© Marshall Cavendish Limited 1989

Original material 'The Car' © Orbis Publishing Limited
1984/1985

ISBN 1 55521 404 5

Printed in Italy

THE WORLD'S
GREAT
CARS

EDITOR
JEREMY COULTER

CHARTWELL
BOOKS, INC.

THE WORLD'S
GREAT
CARS

EDITOR
JEREMY COULTER

CHARTWELL
BOOKS, INC.

Contents

House Editor Dorothea Hall
Editor Jeremy Coulter
Art Editor Gordon Robertson
Production Controller Craig Chubb

This edition published 1989 by Chartwell Books, Inc.
A division of Book Sales, Inc.
110 Enterprise Avenue
Secaucus, New Jersey 07094

© Marshall Cavendish Limited 1989

Original material 'The Car' © Orbis Publishing Limited
1984/1985

ISBN 1 55521 404 5

Printed in Italy

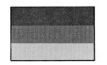

GERMANY

ITALY

FRANCE

AMERICA

Introduction

There is no widely accepted definition of what constitutes a 'Great Car' as can be seen by the considerable variety of vehicles within the pages of this book, which range from the humble Austin Seven to the regal Bugatti Royale. In making any selection of this type, personal opinion plays an important part and, unfortunately, some readers may find either that one or two of their favourites have been left out, or, conversely, that one or two of their pet hates have been included. However, this is hardly surprising when you consider that in Britain alone there are more than 300 one-make car clubs, and that one well-known encyclopedia of the motor car lists more than 4,000 makes of car built between 1885 and the present day.

In assessing merit, it should be remembered that a car does not automatically become 'great' simply by being of an impressive physical size, or by having an advanced technical specification, or even by having worn a very expensive price tag. Over the years there have been some interesting, costly and substantial white elephants that are, perhaps, best forgotten. On the other hand, there have been several modest, yet carefully crafted cars, such as the VW Beetle and the Austin Mini, which demand inclusion for the social and economic impact they have had on society; or those that have pioneered some technical or stylistic feature, as in the Citroën SM, Cord 810/812 the Lamborghini Miura or the Mercedes 540K.

In the way that it is impossible to make comparisons between the achievements of sportsmen of different generations, so it is equally impossible to compare the merits of cars from different decades. Who can assess the relative greatness of a Rolls-Royce Silver Ghost against that of a Ferrari GTO? When you consider that the average family car today will exceed 100 mph and would probably have won many a pre-war race, the relativity of speed, power and handling become extremely important factors and should be assessed in the context of the period before any judgement is made.

However, certain themes, such as performance, beauty of line, and exclusivity are common to many of the cars chosen. But perhaps the most prevalent observation to emerge is that few of the cars selected are the product of a design committee or a computer prediction of what will be a sure winner – made by feeding in parameters of all the elements that the buying public appears to want. In many cases there is just one talented person behind a 'great' car, be he Ettore Bugatti, Enzo Ferrari or Henry Royce – a man who has the strength to make an idea a reality.

At the same time, it is also important to point out that in their day, many of the cars now widely regarded as 'Great' or 'Classic' were often difficult to sell, or that they went through a trough of depression at some time in their history, when they were regarded merely as second-hand bangers, or, at best, as 'student transport'. As recently as the Sixties, for instance, it was often a fearful struggle for dealers to sell certain second-hand Ferraris. But, perhaps more surprisingly, during the Thirties, even Ettore Bugatti could not find a buyer for his last Royale and ended up keeping it himself. Rather perversely, the most recent Royale to come up for sale changed hands for comfortably more than five million pounds, and anyone lucky enough to own a Ferrari GTO knows he has an asset valued in the region of £2 million, and likely to become more valuable.

Whatever you may feel about the galloping inflation that has struck much of the older car market, one factor that works for the benefit of everyone is that if a car has survived to the present day, it will surely now survive for ever. This means that many of us will be able to examine and admire these great cars at first hand in museums or at car shows, even though we may never own them ourselves.

Great Britain

By virtue of its one-time prime economic position Britain has arguably been responsible for more well-known and widely admired cars than any other nation.

While British 'greats' may not have the grandeur of a German Mercedes 540K, the liveliness of an Italian 12-cylinder Ferrari or the sheer presence of an American Duesenberg, their individual greatness and significance is by no means diminished. The MGT series, for example, has epitomised the term 'sports car' for youthful generations the world over. Similarly, while glowing with success in the world's most famous motor race,

Le Mans, the Jaguar marque was universally admired and desired. Yet, neither range of these cars was marked by particular exclusivity or cost, but by sheer charisma and driver appeal. On the other hand, the stately appeal of the Bentley Continental is impossible to overlook; as is the massive power and speed of the superb GTs, the Aston Martin V8 and the DB series cars. The Austin Mini set the Sixties and Seventies motor industry on course for small front-wheel drive cars that not only changed the face of British motoring but that of motoring worldwide.

IT'S HARD TO BELIEVE now, but Jaguar's famous XK range of sports cars came about almost by accident. The first of the line, the XK 120, appeared on the motoring scene in October 1948 at the London Motor Show – but a few months before, hadn't even been thought of. Most new cars take years to emerge, but of the XK 120, the late Sir William Lyons told me that 'it was done more quickly than anything before or since, and I could compare weeks, almost days, with years'.

Up to a very short time before the show, Jaguar had no immediate plans for any sports car. Not that the company intended to ignore the sports car market permanently – the SS Jaguar 100 built before the war had proved how valuable it was for a manufacturer to make a high-performance car capable of winning important competitions and certainly the 100 elevated SS Cars' status out of all proportion to the numbers made. It had been Lyons' first true sports car, if you accept that the SS 90 which came before it in 1935 was really a pre-production prototype, and it had been made up to the outbreak of the war. Powered by the same (2½ or 3½ litre) overhead-valve engines used in the SS Jaguar saloons, it could achieve a genuine 100 mph (161 kph) in 3½ litre form and regularly wiped the board in the national road rallies of the late '30s.

Like nearly all subsequent Jaguar sports cars (the E-type was the major exception), the SS 100 used a modified, short-wheelbase version of the company's contemporary saloon – in this case, the SS 1, Lyons' first car which had made its own sensational appearance at the Motor Show back in 1931. Prior to that, Lyons and his partner William Walmsley had been coachbuilders, using Austin,

The spectacular six-cylinder twin-cam XKs combined speed, power and elegance at a price none of their rivals could match

Swallow, Swift and Standard chassis to produce very pretty cars which were bought by motorists who wanted something a little different.

The SS 100 (which with the handsome saloon of 1935 had brought the model name Jaguar into being) was a very traditional sports car with its four leaf springs, long bonnet and tail-mounted spare wheel, and achieved its results from the well-proven formula of light weight and a large, torquey engine. By then, however, independent

LEFT & BELOW *A 1954 Jaguar XK120 fixed-head coupé. The fixed-head appeared first in 1954 – initially all XK production was of the more spartan open roadster. Note the distinctive slim bumpers, changed for more robust items on the 140 and 150*

front suspension was being adopted by progressive car makers and by 1940, SS Cars were experimenting with it too – for what would have to be the post-war range of cars. Just as important, they were also developing a brand new engine… .

Williams Lyons had set his heart on an all-new luxury saloon capable of 100 mph (161 kph), and during those now-famous fire watching nights at the Foleshill factory he discussed how this might be achieved with his chief engineer Williams Heynes, his assistant Walter Hassan, and engineering draughtsman Claude Baily. Prototype engines and suspensions were built, and by 1945 the essential features of the new post-war range of cars had been finalised.

At the heart of the programme was a new engine, or family of engines. Of various capacities ranging from 2 litres to 3½ litres, they all had one feature in common – overhead camshafts. For William Heynes there was simply no other way to go, thanks to the impact made on him by twin-cam motorcycle engines during his youth and the high bhp figures produced by the successful racing cars of the '20s and '30s which used a similar layout.

When I asked William Heynes some time ago what the chief attraction of this configuration had been to him, he replied that cylinder filling was the key – with the valves set at an angle into a hemispherical combustion chamber, you can get a greater valve area than with valves set vertically as in a conventional overhead-valve engine. Certainly the new engine fulfilled its promise – in 3442 cc production form it gave 160 bhp on the test-bed, virtually matching the best that the old 3½-litre pushrod engine had given in

full competition tune before the war; it was exactly the output target Heynes had set himself at the design stage.

Meanwhile Heynes and Walter Hassan had arrived at an equally effective independent front suspension using torsion bars and wishbones, which Heynes freely acknowledged had been inspired by Andre Citroën's advanced front-wheel-drive saloon of 1934. The new suspension was mounted on an entirely new, very deep-section chassis frame of great rigidity, with the rear axle being carried by long, flexible leaf springs. So far, so good.

The real problems came with the bodyshell; Lyons was horrified by the long delivery date set by the Pressed Steel Co and decided that because of this enforced delay in the building of the new twin-cam saloon, they should produce an interim model which would utilize the new chassis and suspension. It would be powered by the old push-rod engine and clothed in a Foleshill-assembled body reminiscent of the pre-war saloons which had been put back into pro-

FAR LEFT *An XK 120 roadster*
TOP LEFT *The XK 140 of Walshaw and Bolton at Le Mans in 1956. The car suffered fuel problems and retired*
LEFT *The 'bubble top' XK 120 record breaker on the Jabbeke highway in Belgium in 1953*

EVOLUTION

The prototype XK120 was introduced at the 1948 Motor Show at Earls Court with aluminium body and the 3.4-litre twin-cam six-cylinder engine

1949 The first production XK left the factory in July

1950 Steel replaced aluminium for the bodies after 238 cars had been built

1951 The XK120 fixed-head coupé was introduced

1953 The third version of the XK120 was introduced, the drophead coupé with fixed screen and wind up windows

1954 The XK140 was announced in the same three versions as the 120 but with occasional rear seats in the fixed- and drophead coupés. Rack and pinion steering replaced the Burman box and telescopic dampers replaced the lever arm type on the rear.

1957 The last in the XK line, the 150, was introduced with the same chassis but restyled body. Disc brakes front and rear were standard

1958 A new Weslake-designed cylinder head was made available for the 150 which, with three rather than two SUs, produced an extra 30 bhp. The 150 was also available with the larger, 3.8-litre, version of the twin-cam to form the 150S

1961 The XK range was discontinued with the introduction of the E-type. XK120 production reached 12,078 and 140 production reached 8884. 9395 XK150s were built and total XK production betwen 1948 and 1961 was 30,357.

duction after the war. For some obscure reason this interim saloon was named the Mk V, and it was announced a little before the Motor Show in October 1948. Then, barely a few months before the Show, came the idea of producing a new sports car, using the new twin-cam XK engine. The proposal had a lot going for it too – such a car would undoubtedly be a show-stopper, and in any case building a couple of hundred would be a good way of testing the new power unit in the real world before it was installed in the all-important saloon.

Thus it was that the XK 120 came about; the chassis was almost pure Mk V, shortened and slightly modified, and of course as it had been designed with it in mind from the start, the frame readily accepted the 3.4-litre XK engine. Lyons set about designing the body, which as always evolved under his eye from a series of styling mock-ups at the back of the factory. A beautiful flowing body it was too, an almost faultless interpretation of the new streamlined post-war look which was banishing separate wings and headlights, along with big upright radiator grilles.

LEFT *Peter Walker's XK leads the similar car of Stirling Moss during a 1951 Silverstone production car race*
FAR LEFT *An XK 120 fixed-head*

Finished in metallic bronze with biscuit upholstery, the XK 120 Super Sports as it was called made its bow at Earls Court – and almost frightened Jaguar's production manager to death with the response! Virtually the whole of the first year's production was sold in the opening days of the show and Jaguar's American importers were hopping up and down in their anxiety to secure supplies. It quickly became obvious that building the new sports car as originally intended – by hand, using aluminium panels over an ash frame just like the SS 100 – would be ludicrously inadequate.

The Earls Court car was very much a one-off prototype, and the first XK 120 to be sold didn't leave the factory until July 1949; it and the next 238 cars were aluminium bodied, after which (from the spring of 1950) the bodyshells were in steel which allowed the production rate to be drastically increased. Virtually all the cars went overseas – export was mandatory in those days – and for a while it was only the press and a few privileged competition drivers who were able to sample the car on the roads of Britain.

Their experiences soon proved that the XK 120 was not just a pretty face – thanks to the magnificent new power unit, its performance was far in advance of almost anything else you could buy, with acceleration and top speed that had been available only from the most exotic and expensive of sports cars before the war. There was no penalty to pay either, no need for constant attention from a highly skilled mechanic. The XK engine might have had what was then the classic specification for a Grand Prix engine, but William Heynes had designed it solely as a production engine, more than able to take all the abuse that the average, unskilled driver could hand out, and well within the abilities of the average good mechanic to maintain.

Its performance was confirmed in 1949 when Jaguar arranged a demonstration run on the Jabbeke autoroute in Belgium before a party of journalists flown out from Britain to join their colleagues from the continent.

BELOW *In the foreground an XK 150, altogether more substantial than the XK 120 fixed-head behind it, although the closed car was still a most attractive creation*

409 AXT

ABOVE *Elegant and symmetrical – the dashboard of the XK 140*
LEFT *The famous XK twin-cam six*

Ron Sutton, the company's chief test driver, took the white roadster down the autoroute at a mean of 126.448 mph (203.58 kph) – and a resounding 132.596 mph (213.48 kph) with a screen removed and an undertray fitted. Those who speculated if the car handled had their doubts squashed when Leslie Johnson won the first *Daily Express* production car race at Silverstone in Ausust 1949.

During 1950 Jaguar embarked on a limited competition programme with selected private entrants; success didn't attend a brave attempt at Le Mans, but Stirling Moss gained a famous victory in the important Tourist Trophy event in Ireland and Ian Appleyard, (husband of Lyons' daughter Pat) gained a *Coupe des Alpes* by virtue of a penalty free run in the Alpine Rally. The next year, 1951, was the XK 120's peak year in competition but thereafter it was the C-type Jaguar, with its many XK 120 parts, that took over the job of promoting Jaguar's name on the track.

Meanwhile the XK 120 was settling down in its true role as a fast road sports car of great merit, complementing the new MK VII Jaguar (the 100 mph twin-cam saloon had arrived at last in 1950 – but not before Bentley had applied the MK VI designation

to their new car!). Export successes continued, and the XK became a favourite of film stars, building up a reputation for Jaguar in the United States that would benefit the company for years. In particular, its outstanding ride comfort and the quietness and docility of its engine endeared it to many who previously would have never have put up with the rigours of sports car motoring. In that respect, the XK 120 changed the concept of the sports car from an enthusiast's toy to a practical means of every-day transport.

While visually the two-seater XK 120 changed little, performance options gave greater speed (in Special Equipment form, a 0–60 mph time of 8.5 seconds and a top speed of 125 mph/201 kph were easily obtainable), and wire wheels became available. These helped a good deal with the XK 120's biggest failing – its brakes. A compara-

BELOW *An XK 150 roadster. The 150s could be distinguished from their predecessors by the far bigger waist line and other detail changes that gave a more modern appearance*

tively small, pressed-steel road wheel had meant an equally small brake drum, and fade was something familiar to all XK drivers; the extra ventilation from the spoked wheels helped considerably.

The appeal of the car was further widened when in 1951 the fixed-head coupé was announced. This very pretty car was soon labelled the 'business man's express' and it was joined by the last variant, the drop-head coupé, in April 1953. This had a non-detachable screen, a lined hood, and wind-up windows – all very civilised. The XK 120's reign came to an end in the last months of 1954 with the announcement of the XK 140. That never quite achieved the status of its forerunner but for all practical purposes it was a better car, many of the more primitive aspects of the XK 120 having been eradicated. All three body styles were continued – open-two-seater, fixed-head and drop-head – but the latter two now had occasional rear seats thanks to an enlarged cockpit. A rack and pinion replaced the XK 120's Burman steering box with a consequent improvement in precision, and telescopic dampers now controlled the rear axle.

While the same basic XK shape remained, the XK 140 was easily distinguished by its new bumpers. The XK 120 had possessed little more than overriders and these had proved totally inadequate, especially in North America where parking tended to be by feel. The new model was given massive protection front and rear in line with that of the Mk VII; this heavier look was continued by the radiator grille, the delicate 'continental' looking XK 120 item having been replaced by a bolder cast grille with thicker (and fewer) slats. The bootlid now boasted a chrome strip in which was incorporated a medallion celebrating the marque's Le Mans successes – two by that time.

On the road, most people agreed that the XK 140 handled better than the earlier car thanks to improved damping and an engine which had been moved a little further for-

RIGHT FROM TOP TO BOTTOM *An XK 150S, one of the last of the XKs and also one of the fastest, capable of 136 mph (219 kph). An XK 150 drophead with its engine, plain dashboard and interior*

An XK 150 roadster from 1960, the year before production ended to be replaced in due course by the legendary E-type which retained the same basic power unit

ward in the chassis – a change made to allow the cockpit to be lengthened but which also introduced a little more understeer. Long journeys were made even more pleasant if overdrive was specified; this new option considerably reduced rpm when engaged (on top only), and as I well remember from my own XK 140 drop-head so equipped, it was impossible to pull more than the permitted revs (5750 rpm) which meant that flat-out cruising – up to 135 mph (217 kph) according to wind and gradient – was feasible without inflicting mechanical cruelty. This was XK motoring at its best and only a handful of the world's most expensive cars – such as the Mercedes 300 SL – were quicker.

The XK 140 had a relatively brief lifespan, as it was replaced by the XK 150 in 1957. Again, the same basic chassis was employed although the body was very considerably altered – the sleek XK 120 lines were replaced by a much heavier-looking body with a higher wing and scuttle line. The interior had been modernised too and while the car still had its big speedometer and tachometer centrally mounted, the fixed-head and drop-head models no longer boasted walnut veneer cappings and dash. But at least an open-two-seater model remained (albeit arriving a little later), even if it did have real wind-up windows and a fixed windscreen.

In fact Lyons had planned a radically different look for the XK 150, but decided

the tooling costs could not be justified. Instead, much of the XK 120/140 body tooling was cleverly altered to produce a new look without a large capital expenditure. That and the new wrap-round windscreen did the job at a minimum of cost even if the final effect was not as dramatic as the XK 150 that never was.

Biggest news on the mechanical front was the disc brakes; these had been tested for years on Jaguar's competition models, but it was the XK 150 which was the first Jaguar to have them as standard, and all round too. It transformed the car in that now, all the performance could be used between corners without the dreaded fade intervening, and while the heavier XK 150 was not, on paper, faster than its Special Equipment forebears, in practical terms it was a quicker A–to–B car because of this factor. Many earlier XKs have subsequently been converted to disc brake specification, in recognition of the fact that the original drums were not really up to the level of performance that the power motor allowed.

Disc brakes had really hit the headlines in the mid Fifties, the system proving itself a critical factor in Jaguar success in the Le Mans 24 Hour race.

Attention had been paid to performance too and in March 1958, along with the introduction of the open-two-seater model, came the Weslake-developed straight-port cylinder head. This, fed by three instead of two SU carburettors, raised maximum power by some 30 bhp and cars so equipped were designated S models. Even more power came from a new 3.8-litre version of the XK engine which (with or without the new cylinder head) became optional in the XK 150.

Certainly, the 3.8 XK 150S was a very fast car, capable of achieving 100 mph (161 kph) in around 19 seconds – a formidable rate of acceleration even by today's standards. So when the XK 150's time was run in 1961, it could fairly be said that the XK left the scene on a high note, a note which was more than continued by the E-type.

The Jaguar XK was a remarkable car for a number of reasons; there was little that was innovative in its make-up, but the engineering behind it was of the highest quality. It was powered by what was probably the best high-performance engine in true series production, it had a properly designed front suspension (used by Jaguar in its essentials right up until the last E-type was built in 1975), and it was mechanically durable. It also cost approximately a third or even a half anything of comparable performance. Faults? Yes, it had some; the later cars in particular were a little too heavy, and the more powerful versions suffered from a rear suspension that was, by late 1950's standards, a little primitive. Also – and this has been an age-old failing of Jaguar – some of the secondary equipment was not as reliable as the major units.

In the context of what your money bought you, these minor failings were acceptable, and after all, no car built has ever been faultless. Today XKs are extremely popular and a cottage industry has been built up around the re-manufacture of parts and the restoration of the cars. They are still extremely usable too and while with its skinny tyres an XK doesn't corner like a modern car, you'd need something like an XJS to travel markedly faster and more comfortably from London to Birmingham on the M1!

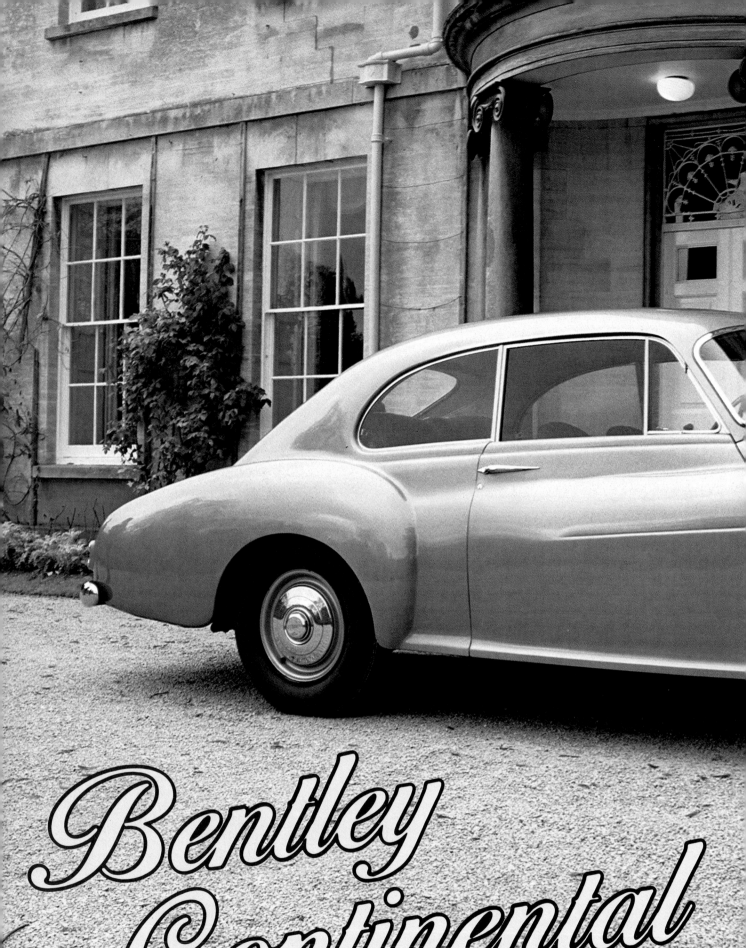

Bentley
Continental

ABOVE & TOP *The R-type Continental prototype Olga with its very traditional interior and inconvenient gearlever.*

Bentley Continental

In a time of austerity after World War II, the Bentley Continental offered an unrivalled standard of speed, luxury and refinement for the lucky few

'THE CONTINENTAL SPORTS SALOON is a new stage in the evolution of the post-war Bentley,' commented *The Autocar* in 1952, though in fact the Continental story had begun before the outbreak of hostilities, when a resident of Paris named Embiricos had commissioned a special Bentley, which was developed under the surveillance of Rolls-Royce development engineers, for it was intended that this vehicle would be the prototype of a new, limited production addition to the Bentley range.

With a raised compression ratio of 8:1, achieved by the use of taller pistons, and bigger SU carburettors, the 4257 cc engine of this special Bentley developed some 140 bhp, against 125 bhp for the standard power unit with its 6.5:1 compression. A close-ratio gearbox with overdrive fourth speed was fitted, but the most revolutionary aspect of the Bentley was its streamlined four-seat bodywork designed by Georges Paulin and developed through wind-tunnel testing of a scale model. It was unlike anything previously built on a British chassis, with a tapered fastback tail, virtually-flush glazing, fully enclosed rear wheels, faired-in handles, hinges and headlamps plus a streamlined radiator cowling which only

ABOVE *An R-type Continental from 1954*
ABOVE LEFT *An R-type with the rear wheel covers in place*
LEFT *Inspiration for the Continental came from pre-war designs such as this Airline*

revealed the familiar winged-B badge on careful examination. There were overtones of Philip Wright's streamlined Pierce Silver Arrow and some of Jaray's designs tailored by the high-speed motoring made possible by the newly-built autobahns of Hitler's Germany.

Despite its radical appearance, the car was endorsed by Walter Sleator, who ran the Paris branch of Bentley Motors; furthermore, it was built with the full co-operation of Rolls-Royce, who regarded it as the prototype of a new high-speed model, and stated that they were willing to supply replicas.

Early in February 1939, John Dugdale of *The Autocar* left the Paris showrooms of Rolls-Royce in the Avenue Georges Cinq aboard the streamlined Bentley bound for Germany, where the new autobahns gave the rare opportunity of trying a car flat out; running in convoy with the Paulin-bodied car was a second Bentley, this time with a more conventional Van Vooren four-door pillarless saloon body.

Fuelled with high-octane Azur petrol, the streamlined car, which was geared to 31 mph/1000 rpm in top, averaged 55 mph (88 kph) to the lunch-stop in La Ferté-sous-Jouarre, 38 miles (61 km) outside Paris, for a protracted meal prepared by hotelier Trucher, formerly *chef de cuisine* to General Joffre during the Great War. After this the Bentley covered the next 64 miles (103 km) in 50 minutes, an average of over 76 mph

(122 kph) an impressive achievement.

'This,' said Dugdale, 'is a new aspect of motoring; it is the nearest thing to flying…'.

The experimental Bentley was known as the Continental, a name previously applied to Rolls-Royce models designed for rapid Continental touring: in an extensive test covering over 1000 miles (1610 km), Dugdale took *La Streamline* to Ulm, in the foothills of the Bavarian Alps, and at one stage was averaging 96 mph (154 kph) over a 24-mile stretch of autobahn, reaching a peak speed of 118 mph (190 kph).

By July the Continental was in England, where George Eyston averaged 114.63 mph (184.55 kph) during an hour's run at Brooklands.

Plans were made to put the Continental into production – its attraction was shown by the fact that Lancefield built a similar streamline body for a Lagonda during 1939 – and Van Vooren built a prototype Corniche (the name was revived in 1971) with greater rear headroom than the Continental. Registered GRA 270, it was on test in France, with a special front end fitted to disguise the make, when war broke out in September 1939. Before the Bentley Corniche could be returned to England, it was destroyed by German bombing on the quayside at Dieppe (though the RAC port representative faithfully kept the ignition key throughout the war, after which he returned it to Rowbotham).

Less than twenty of the new MK V chassis intended for the Continental model were built, while Paulin, who had designed the streamlined body, was shot by the Germans for his activities in the Resistance.

In 1949, the streamlined 1939 Bentley Continental was driven by its then owner H.S.F. Hay and monocled motoring journalist Tommy Wisdom at Le Mans, finishing sixth at an average speed of 73.5 mph (118.33). The following year, with H. Hunter co-driving, the old Bentley averaged 78.6 mph (126.5 kph), but only managed to take fourteenth place.

raise the power output of the engine; in conformity with Rolls-Royce tradition the actual power and torque figures were not quoted. Judging by the performance of the pre-war streamliner, however, it seems likely that the new Continental's power unit was developing around 150 bhp, against a probably 130 bhp for a Bentley engine in standard tune.

Development of the new car began in 1951: Mulliner worked closely with Rolls-Royce stylist J.P. Blatchley in designing a lightweight, aerodynamic body for the new Continental. By using alloy panelling and other weight-saving devices, Mulliner kept the coachwork below 750 lb/340 kg (the standard steel saloon scaled approximately 1000 lb/454 kg) and the entire car weighed 3739 lb (1696 kg), against 4078 lb (1850 kg) for the standard Mark VI saloon.

It was still a massive car, but the increased power and better aerodynamics of its fastback two-door coachwork – quarter-scale models had been tested in the wind-tunnel of the Rolls-Royce Flight Establishment at Hucknall – allied to a higher final drive ratio, gave the new Continental impressive performance characteristics.

LEFT *An R-type from the first year of production, 1952. Initially all production was used for export only*

Walter Sleator had obviously kept the dream of putting a streamlined sports Bentley into production alive throughout the war, for he instigated a special project with Pinin Farina, the Bentley Cresta, which was shown at the 1948 Paris Salon and which abandoned the traditional ratiator design in favour of a wide grille; Crestas II and III (with vertical grilles) followed in due course. The Cresta III was unveiled at the Paris Salon in October 1951 by Facel-Metallon, who had also built the 1949 Farina-designed Cresta II in a limited series.

Jean Daninos, head of Facel, used the Facel-Metallon Bentley – which had the 4566 cc power unit introduced during 1951 – as his personal transport; its low lines were achieved by giving minimal headroom for the occupants, while the bonnet cleared the top of the engine by only a few millimetres.

The low, streamlined appearance of the Facel-Metallon Bentley was acclaimed by the press, though it obviously didn't please everyone; M.T.U. Collier, of Didcot, Berkshire, told *The Autocar* that the car 'had no merit from the angle of artistry and beauty of line'.

Mr Collier continued: 'I know that it is a wonderful example of body engineering, and that "beauty is in the eye of the beholder", but I contend that a car should look like a car, and not like a twin-boom aircraft. This Facel body apes the worst transatlantic tendencies, and surely the Franay body, exhibited on the same chassis at the 1950 Salon, was not only more beautiful but also – I suggest – a more efficient automobile.' *The Autocar* thought that the built-out wings of

EVOLUTION

The Bentley Continental could trace its origins back to 1938 when Georges Paulin designed a streamlined body for a Bentley chassis

1951 Development began on the Bentley Continental in conjunction with coachbuilders Mulliner

1952 The Continental entered production, initially for export only

1953 Changes to the Continental included a one-piece windscreen to replace the vee-shaped two-piece screen and a modified wing line. By this time the Continental was available on the home market. The compression ratio was changed to 7.2:1

1954 The fourth series of Continentals was introduced with the engine bored out to 4887 cc and the compression ratio increased again, to 7.25:1

1955 The S-type Bentley was introduced to replace the R-type after 207 R types had been built

the Franay Bentley made it look as though it had padded shoulders… .

But about the same time that Facel-Metallon was building its special Bentleys, Rolls-Royce Motors was talking to bodybuilder H.J. Mulliner about a planned performance model of the post-war Bentley Mark VI chassis, under development by H.I.F. Evernden, chief project engineer of Rolls-Royce. The 4566 cc engine was standardised, with modified carburation, inlet and exhaust manifolds and a higher compression ratio (7.0:1 instead of 6.4:1), all contributing to

When the prototype – code-named RBS 1287 – had been fitted with its bodywork in Mulliner's Chiswick works, it was given the Cheshire registration OLG 490 – which quickly earned the car the nickname Olga – in mid-1951.

Olga would be owned for many years by Bentley enthusiast and long-time Bentley Drivers Club stalwart Stanley Sedgwick who sold it in 1986, replacing it instead with a brand new Bentley Mulsanne Turbo. He feels that the modern car offers in many ways a similar driving experience to the legendary older Bentley that served him so well.

The project was closely followed by Walter Sleator, father of the Embiricos Bentley, who remarked to Evernden: 'Ev, if and when you produce the Continental Bentley, I will send you a case of champagne…'.

'Well,' recalled Evernden, I never received the champagne, but the success of Olga was adequate reward for me!'

That success began in the early days of development, when Olga was taken to France for testing: on the banked circuit at Montlhéry, observed by the Automobile Club de France, the Bentley còvered five laps at an average speed of 118.75 mph (191.2 kph), recording a best speed of 119.75 mph (192.79 kph).

It was noted that in the effort to maximise the aerodynamics of the new Continental, the lowered, slimmer radiator shell had neither radiator cap nor winged-B mascot. Aware that the performance of the Continental was equivalent to that of many contemporary two-seat open sports cars, and obviously alarmed by such escapades as Mr Hays's Le Mans entries with the pre-war car (racing driver Eddie Hall also took his prewar Derby Bentley, with a grafted-on streamlined nose and coupé top, to Le Mans in 1950), Rolls-Royce was reported to be asking owners of the new model to give an undertaking that they would not use the car in competition.

It was a concept that shocked at least one Bentley enthusiast: 'Here is a car with a magnificent performance and an unashamedly fantastic price, designed solely for export,' commented B. Joynson-Cork, of Pinner, Middlesex. 'Why, one cannot help but ask, should the fortunate man who is able to pay £7000 or so for a car have to submit to such conditions? Just what is supposed to happen if this new Bentley is entered for, shall we say, an Alpine rally? Do the makers fear it will fall to pieces, perform badly against foreign makes, or what?

'They should be reminded that they have the use of a name that gained by far the greater part of its lustre in the days when a man named W.O. Bentley was not apprehensive as to the show any of his cars would put up when matched against the best that other nations could produce.'

Sadly, those potential owners of the new Continental were not to be found in Britain, for, said *The Autocar*, 'The car is being produced in limited numbers, and is reserved for export only.'

That meant, particularly, for export to America, where the initial announcement was made that the Continental was going into production. The basic sterling price of the Bentley Continental was £4890, so that by the time the overseas buyer had paid delivery charges, import duties and local taxes, his car would have probably cost between £6000 and £7000, making the new Bentley the world's most costly production car – another measure of how much things have changed since the early 1950s!

It was also true, however, that the Bentley was probably the world's fastest production four/five seat saloon car in its day, capable of 120 mph (193.2 kph) 'Such a car is bound to be costly, and the British, who make it, cannot own it,' commented *The Autocar*, 'but it goes abroad as proof that a nation where the creators are constantly subjected to the debasement of their own living standards can still keep alive the ideal of perfection for others to enjoy.'

The 'ideal of perfection' was evident in the specification of the Continental: that Mulliner bodywork represented 'a combination of lightness and rigidity which may not be easy to emulate'. That meant, apart from the body panelling, that the window frames and bumpers were made of light alloy, and the seats were tubular-framed. The steering wheel carried hand throttle, starting mixture control, ride control (which modified the setting of the rear hydraulic dampers) and the main horn button, although there was a secondary horn button on the floor which could be operated by the left foot; another auxiliary pedal operated the one-shot chassis lubrication. An elaborate heating and ventilating system made provision for demisting both front and rear screens, there were two-speed wipers and a screen washer – all commonplace features in the 1980s, but very much the exception in 1952!

Certainly the performance of the Continental lived up to expectations; the servo-assisted brakes were singled out for particular comment by *The Autocar*, for they recorded 100 per cent efficiency on the Tapley meter. 'There are no better brakes on any car sold today, and they allow the Bentley's great performance to be enjoyed with complete confidence.'

And that 'great performance' was allied to utter refinement: 'Engine and gear box are slightly audible in first gear, but otherwise there is only that uncanny silence which

LEFT *The lovely lines of the Continental are still highly regarded today as a classic styling exercise. Well-preserved Continentals are now worth large sums*

FAR LEFT, LEFT & ABOVE *The prototype R-type which differed from the production cars in the windscreen and front wing. The controls on the steering-wheel boss are for the adjustable suspension dampers, starting mixture control and hand throttle. The interior was lavishly equipped with superb wood and leather, as might be expected of a car that was the most expensive of its day*

indicates long and careful attention to every detail of design and construction… There is no need to specify a cruising speed; progress seems as smooth, easy and effortless at 100 mph as at 50. Nor is there any imperative need for frequent gear changing. It is possible to make a smooth, easy start on top gear and accelerate relentlessly away to maximum speed without using the gearbox at all. This is hardly to be recommended as normal practice, however, especially as gear changing is such a pleasure for the Bentley owner with any appreciation of mechanical perfection… Hill-climbing is quite extraordinary, and main road hills can be climbed on top gear at speeds limited only by visibility and traffic conditions.'

Such outstanding performance appealed to wealthy enthusiasts overseas: the first two production Continentals were delivered to Bentley Drivers' Club members Briggs Cunningham and Bill Spear, while during 1953 former racing driver Raymond Mays, then heading the BRM project, borrowed Olga for a 2700-mile (4347 km) journey, with race and rally driver Ken Wharton as co-driver. Mays first tried the Continental round the BRM test track at Folkingham, and found 'a distinct affinity between the two vehicles… The vocabulary of motor racing being a lame and limited thing, it is difficult to put into words the gulf that separates a Continental

from the average car in all the qualities that have a bearing on safety at speed. In acceleration, in braking, in cornering power, in roadholding, in responsiveness to the controls, this Bentley is the equal of many modern racing cars, and superior to some.'

Wharton's comments, less fulsome, seemed no less sincere: 'This is the most perfect piece of road machinery I have ever driven; in particular, what fascinates me is the phenomenal restfulness of cruising at over 90 mph with the rev counter showing a mere 3000 rpm.'

The restrictions on UK sales had vanished by the time that *The Motor* took Olga to the Continent on test in July 1953: to the basic British price of £4890 had to be added £2038 12s 6d of purchase tax, making a total of £6928 12s 6d; modifications to the production model since the start of Continental production were the adoption of a one-piece windscreen in place of the slightly vee-d screen fitted to Olga, a modified wing line and a dummy radiator cap with flying-B badge.

Since each Continental was built to bespoke order, there was a diversity of equipment on each individual car, though of the 207 Continental chassis actually built (in five consecutive series) between 1952 and 1955, all but 16 were fitted with the well-known Mulliner coachwork. The principal modifications were the adoption of a 7.2:1 compression ratio in 1953 on the third series cars from chassis BC4C, and of a big-bore (95.25 mm) engine displacing 4887 cc and with a 7.25:1 compression ratio on the fourth series of Continentals in 1954.

The non-Mulliner bodies fitted to this exclusive chassis – distinguished, claimed its makers, by a 'pleasing hubble bubble exhaust note' – included a handsome drophead by Park Ward and a fixed-head coupé by Pinin Farina, though neither captured the sleek spirit of the Mulliner design, which was elegant enough for one of the last of the original A Series Continentals (BC24A) to be used as official transport by the British Ambassador in Paris. That particular car was subsequently fitted with the 4887 cc engine and tuned to produce a top speed in the region of 130 mph (209 kph) which, for a car nearly 4000 lb (1800 kg) in weight, was no mean achievement.

The Continental designation was continued on the S1 Bentley introduced during 1955, but the S Type Continentals were more ponderous vehicles than the original, more akin to the normal production model.

After many years in the ownership of Stanley Sedgwick, a prominent Bentley Drivers' Club member, Olga is now cared for by Victor Gauntlett, who heads Aston Martin-Lagonda. More than three decades after it was built, that first Bentley Continental still exemplifies *The Autocar's* 1952 verdict: 'The Bentley is a modern magic carpet which annihilates great distances and delivers the occupants well-nigh as fresh as when they started. It is a car Britain may well be proud of, and it is sure to add new lustre to the name it bears.'

Classless and unique, the Mini was one of the most revolutionary cars ever produced in Britain and is still in production 30 years after its introduction

IF IN THE PRESENT DAY, towards the end of the 1980s, you saw your first Austin Mini, your impression would almost certainly be of a very small, cramped, noisy, harsh-riding car with poorly designed controls and twitchy handling; and you would be right. On the other hand, nobody in Europe in the 1980s ever sees a Mini for the first time. The shape, and the whole character, of the car is essentially as it was when it was launched in August 1959, and well over four million have been built since then.

The Mini is inescapably associated with one man, Sir Alec Issigonis. He was born in Turkey but had British nationality, and this brought him to these shores in the 1920s when he decided to study engineering and join the motor industry. His first real triumph was the Morris Minor of 1948, and indeed it was in some senses out of the Minor that the Mini grew.

Issigonis rejoined BMC, the monolith that resulted from the 1952 merger of Austin and Morris, after a period at Alvis during which he had designed an advanced and ambitious sports saloon that was rejected by the management. His return to Longbridge occurred just before the 1956 Suez crisis, and it was the sudden shortage of petrol which this caused that led BMC chairman Sir Leonard Lord to postpone all other projects and set Issigonis the 'crash programme' task of de-

RIGHT *The 1275 GT was introduced in 1969 with the longer Clubman body but it did not prove as popular as the Cooper*
FAR RIGHT *A 997 cc version of the Mini Cooper, introduced in 1961*
BELOW *A Mini in the '64 Monte Carlo*

MINI

signing a completely new economy car, something which might hope to assume the mantle of the Austin Seven of the 1920s.

The Seven was regarded as a 'real' car in miniature as it had all the elements normally associated only with much more expensive cars and none of the rudimentary engineering of the normal 'cycle car,' that had hitherto been the most accessible form of transport to that growing band of people who were in a position to buy a vehicle.

Issigonis proceeded by using what has since become known as 'packaging'. He decided firstly the size of the smallest cabin which would accommodate four people in comfort, his chosen dimensions being 8 ft 9 in (267 cm) long, 4 ft 2 in (127 cm) wide and 4 ft 4 in (132 cm) high. Then, on the basis that the smallest and lightest – and therefore most economical – car would be arrived at by squeezing the engine, transmission and the rest of the mechanicals into the smallest possible extra box, he applied his undoubted engineering genius to finding the most compact arrangement. His task was complicated by having to use the existing A-series, overhead-valve engine which powered the Minor, since there was no time to develop a new one even if the money had been available. The decision to develop the Mini was taken early in 1957, and it says much for the speed of Issigonis' small engineering team that the car was in production and on sale within two and a half years. That, by the usual standards of the British motor industry in those days, would have been a remarkable achievement for a conventional model, let alone one which overturned as many cherished traditions as did the Mini.

The cornerstone of Issigonis' layout was the transverse engine and front-wheel drive. By setting the engine across the car he reduced the overall length; by driving the front wheels he retained interior space usually devoted to a propeller shaft and rear axle, which would in turn have meant enlarging his precious minimum-sized cabin. In essence the Mini consisted of a tightly-cowled driving pod trailing that cabin behind it, the rear supported as simply as possible on plain trailing arms with the simplest but most ingenious of springing: the rubber units developed by Alex Moulton. Another iconoclastic decision concerned the use of 10 in (25 cm) wheels,

EVOLUTION

Introduced in August 1959, the Mini, known as the Austin Seven and Morris Mini Minor, was available in basic and deluxe saloon versions, and was a highly compact four-seat saloon of integral construction powered by the 848 cc A – series four-cylinder engine

1960 The Mini Van, Countryman and Traveller estates were introduced, the latter two with ash-framed bodywork

1961 The Mini Super saloon was launched, fitted with an oil-pressure gauge, water temperature gauge, key-start ignition (instead of floor-mounted button) and Duotone paint scheme. The Mini Cooper was also launched, fitted with front disc brakes and, initially, a 997 cc version of the engine, later changed to 998 cc. The Riley Elf and Wolseley Hornet were introduced, with traditional radiator grilles, boots and wooden fascias

1962 The Austin model redesignated the Austin Mini. Deluxe and Super models replaced by Super Deluxe. A cheaper version of the estate car, without the wooden trim, also became avalable. The Riley Elf and Wolseley Hornet were fitted with the 998 cc engine

1963 The Mini Cooper S was launched, based on the Mini Cooper body but fitted with the 1071 cc engine, servo-assisted brakes and ventilated wheels

1964 The Mini Cooper S model's 1071 cc engine was replaced by the 1275 cc and 970 cc units. Improved gearboxes were introduced to the range, along with diaphragm spring clutch and Hydrolastic suspension on the saloons. Twin-leading-shoe front brakes were fitted to all but the Coopers. The Mini Moke was launched

1965 A four-speed automatic gearbox became optional (with uprated engine) on some models

1966 The Mk III Elf and Hornets were launched, with improved internal and external trim. All models were given a smoother clutch action

1967 The Mk II Mini Cooper, Standard and Super Deluxe saloons were launched, fitted with larger rear screens, larger grille and new exterior and internal trim. The new Cooper S model was fitted with an all-synchromesh gearbox. The Mini 1000 Super Deluxe was introduced, fitted with the 998 cc engine

1968 The Elf, Hornet and Mini Moke were discontinued. On other models the cable interior door-lock mechanism was replaced by handles. All-synchromesh gearboxes became standard. The Mk II models were replaced by a new series of saloons with wind-up windows, concealed hinges for the doors and dry-cone suspension

1969 The Mini Cooper Mk II was discontinued. Introduced were the Mini 1275 GT saloon with disc brakes and Hydrolastic suspension, the Mini Clubman saloon, with the 998 cc engine and Hydrolastic suspension, and the Clubman Estate, with dry cone suspension, replacing the 1000 Countryman and Traveller models

1970 Mini Cooper S Mk III introduced, fitted with wind-up windows, concealed hinges and new trim and seats

1971 Dry cone suspension fitted to the Mini Clubman. Cooper S discontinued

1973 Shorter-travel gearchange introduced

1974 Automatic gearbox only available on home market. Inertia-reel seat belts became a standard fitment

1975 The Mini 1000 Special (limited-edition) was announced, with distinctive interior and external trim. The Mini Clubman's 998 cc engine was replaced by the 1098 cc engine, except on the automatic versions

1979 Mini City 850 was launched, but then the 850 series was discontinued. Mini 1000 redesignated the Super. 1000 City introduced, with estate version, available in manual and automatic versions. The 848 cc pickup was discontinued

1980 The Mini Clubman was discontinued

1982 Mini 1000 estate discontinued, the City was renamed the Mini E, the HL the HLE, the HLE the Mini Mayfair. All van and pick-up versions were discontinued

1983 The limited-edition Mini Sprite was released, based on the City but with a special trim package

1984 The limited-edition Mini 25 was launched, commemorating a quarter of a century of Mini production.

1985 The Mini Ritz was announced, based on the City but with a special trim package.

1986 New, colour-matched interior for Mini Mayfair and City. The five-millionth Mini produced.

1988 Mini celebrates 30 years of continuous production.

TOP LEFT *Minis racing with typical gay abandon at Crystal Palace in 1962*
FAR LEFT *The Hopkirk/Liddon car from the '63 RAC Rally*
LEFT *Action from the 1969 British Saloon Car Championship*
BELOW LEFT *Years later and the Mini is still competitive. The year is 1978 and the venue Brands Hatch*

smaller than anything previously seen on a 'proper' car, for the sake of smaller wheel arches which helped preserve under-bonnet space at the front and seat width at the back.

In theory it would have been possible to add the engine and transmission package at the back; indeed it would have been much more fashionable since the increasingly successful Continental mass-manufacturers of the day – Fiat, Renault and Volkswagen – were churning out rear-engined cars which were much admired. Alec Issigonis chose his layout not because of concern for stability and handling, but because his studies showed that he could make the Mini far more compact that way than by trying to squeeze the tall A-series engine under or aft of the back seat. Of course, as soon as it became available, the Mini's handling qualities quickly made people realise how lacking the rear-engine layout was: it died a lingering death as Europe's car designers raced to climb on the front-drive band-

wagon. No car has ever been so flattered by imitation as the Mini.

It set the trend for the style and layout of so many modern cars with a transverse engine and front wheel drive. As more powerful derivatives were developed, so it became apparent that front-wheel drive was compatible with higher power outputs and did not necessarily make a vehicle that was impossible to steer in a straight line.

There have been arguments that the Mini layout was not original. Fiat's chief engineer recalled a pre-war paper in which he had sketched something similar in principle – yet when the Mini appeared, Fiat was building the 600 and preparing the directly competitive, rear-engined 850. Besides, Issigonis made no claims for originality as such but rather for the efficiency and logic of his engineering package. Not all of its features were brilliant, since the gearbox was packed into the sump – a clever piece of width-saving and a layout which permitted the use of a central differential and equal-length drive shafts, but which condemned the gears to run in engine oil and meant using a complicated transfer-gear system that caused insoluble noise problems (it also meant there was no prospect of the Mini or any derivative being given a fifth forward speed, but that was only to become a headache 20 years later). While the transverse engine layout has become well-nigh universal, few

engineers ever adopted Issigonis' transmission layout. Most found the room to put a conventional two-shaft gearbox on one end of the engine, even if it meant having one drive-shaft longer than the other.

The Mini was not an overnight success, surprising though it may seem today. When *The Autocar* first tested one, its conclusions were that 'the manufacturers are to be congratulated on producing, at a truly competitive price, an outstanding car providing unusual body space for its size, and one in which four persons can enjoy comfortable, safe and economical motoring. It is far from being an underpowered miniature, and has a very lively performance; it is certain to interest the sporting motorist because of its fine handling qualities. It scores in heavy traffic on account of its size, and its minimum overhang, front and rear, makes parking an easy matter in congested cities.' If that sounds like praise, remember that the motoring magazines of the 1950s were sparing indeed of outright criticism. Note the absence of any positive suggestion that this might be one of the epoch-making cars of the generation.

If there was initial caution, compounded by the almost simultaneous appearance of Ford's 105E Anglia with its more advanced engine and refined rear-drive chassis, there might almost have been worse to come. By the time the winter of 1959/60 was over, there were many stories of water leaks through the Mini's floor, of breakdown caused by a drowned distributor every time it rained, and of high oil consumption. People grumbled about the crudity of the interior with its slide windows, pull-string door handles and carpet dropped in more or less at random, and the osteopaths were crying about the driving position and control layout all the way to the bank.

Yet it transpired that these criticisms amounted to nothing. The Mini *was* a success and there appear to have been two reasons for it. The first was a social attitude, a matter of taste. While the 105E Anglia was kept firmly in its place by the unwillingness of the 'right' people of the early 1960s to be seen dead in a Ford, it appeared that you could take a Mini anywhere. It was soon enjoyed by shopping housewives and short-distance commuters, and then celebrities began to use Minis to arrive at Claridges functions – the interiors, of course, suitably treated by Hooper or Wood and Pickett to remove those cheap, but effective, pull-string door handles.

Why should the Mini have appealed in this classless way? That is probably where the second and very logical factor comes in. The Mini was extremely easy to drive to high limits of cornering and adhesion – and that mattered to people who didn't in the least think of themselves as budding rally drivers. It quickly gained the classic reputation of a 'nippy little car' (always high praise in British motoring circles), enhanced by superb visibility from the driving seat and those close dimensions which really did enable it to go where others could not: city parking, for example, ceased to be a problem for

Mini owners. Also, not to forget its original purpose, it was extremely economical to the extent where *The Autocar*'s lead-footed testers achieved an overall 40.1 mpg (against which the 105E Anglia returned 36.1 mpg and the 100E Popular, just 29.6 mpg).

What manner of car was it in engineering terms? The A-series engine had had its stroke shortened to reduce the standard 948 cc to 848 cc, giving a leisurely power output claimed to be 37 bhp gross (say 34 bhp DIN). However, the car was extremely light at just over 1300 lb (590 kg), justifying the Issigonis approach, and the main reason for the outstanding economy allied with reasonable performance. It would hardly seem reasonable by today's standards, for the first Press test cars crept past 70 mph (113 kph) and needed nearly half a minute to reach 60 mph, but it was enough in its day – and improvements were already in hand which would transform the situation. The lower gears of the four-speed gearbox took the Mini to roughly 25, 40 and 60 mph (40, 64 and 97 kph). Suspension was by double wishbones at the front, the drive shafts articulated by Mr Rzeppa's constant-velocity joints, another of the technical keys to the design. Moulton's rubber-cone springs were used here as well as for the rear trailing arms. The 10 in wheels were shod with 5.20 section cross-ply tyres – radials were then still in their formative years. Braking was by 7 in (18 cm) diameter Lockheed drums all round; discs were still for high-performance sports cars. The fuel tank was a mere 5.5 gallons (25 litres), then and for many years after. The battery was housed under the boot floor, causing a notable maintenance problem, for the sake of making the car a little less nose-heavy and the rear brakes less inclined to lock prematurely.

That was the Mini when first launched, but it soon began to sprout versions. Initially, to suit the BMC sales and dealership policy of the day, it was offered either as a Morris Mini-Minor or an Austin Seven, but

ABOVE *A Mini hydrolastic unit*
BELOW *The utilitarian Mini Moke was introduced in 1964 and proved popular in quite a different market*
It remains in small-scale production under license outside the UK

BELOW *With two engines this Moke had rather too much power but it was one way of giving this popular utility vehicle four-wheel drive, although it wasn't productionised*

ABOVE *The Wolsey Hornet, introduced in 1961, was more luxurious but rather pretentious, like its stablemate the Riley Elf* **ABOVE RIGHT** *which was mechanically identical*

the name Mini caught on and became universal more or less by public demand. An early extra model was the Mini Traveller with a miniature version of the then-classic BMC estate-car body style with exterior ash framing. A van version, without benefit of framing, had appeared a matter of months after the original launch and had proved a great success, making the estate-car conversion a simple matter. A year after that the Mini-Cooper arrived with its 997 cc engine, all of 55 bhp (net), disc front brakes, and capable of 85 mph (137 kph) or so, with 60 mph coming up in under 20 seconds! In 1961 such performance made the Cooper the first choice of every club rallyist until the Cortina GT came on the scene, and BMC trumped that particular Ford card with its 1963 launch of the Mini Cooper S, originally of 1071 cc but soon with a choice of 970 cc (rare) for 1-litre class events, and 1275 cc (far more popular) for the 1.3-litre class and for brisk motoring generally.

The Cooper S models quickly established a reputation second to none in top-class European rallying in the hands of drivers like Makinen, Aaltonen and Hopkirk, and in racing under the gentle urging of characters like Sir John Whitmore. One outcome of all this sporting activity was that the Mini's general sales success boomed in the mid-1960s, when, by normal motor industry logic, after six or seven years in production it should have been waning sufficiently to turn engineering minds towards its successor. There had been developments other than the purely sporting ones, of course. The 1961 arrival of the Cooper had been accompanied by the Riley Elf and Wolseley Hornet, with new radiator grilles and vestigial boots which added far less in the way of luggage space than they did in presumed distinction. Oddly, the public didn't seem to want the distinction nearly as much as the familiar, well-balanced but cheeky Mini shape, and neither the Riley nor the Wolseley enjoyed real success despite the fact that for some time they were the only non-Cooper ver-

sions (from 1962) with 1-litre rather than 848 cc engines and useful extra torque. Official BL figures quote production of less than 60,000 Rileys and Wolseleys, compared with over 100,000 for the Cooper and nearly 45,000 for the Cooper S. The 998 cc engine finally appeared in the Mini 1000 in 1967.

One of the more controversial moves in the Mini's history came in 1964 when the original 'dry' suspension was replaced by the Hydrolastic variety used with success in the bigger Austin/Morris 1100. The general consensus was that the Hydrolastic Minis traded a slightly more comfortable ride for slightly less crisp and predictable handling, but the overall value of the change was questionable. The following year the Mini formed the launching pad for the ingenious but largely ill-fated AP four-speed automatic transmission. Some customers may have bought this version because however much they loved the Mini, they had perpetual problems with the gearchange: throughout the 1960s there were detail changes to the synchromesh and the shift linkage, culminating in the adoption of an all-synchromesh box in 1968.

A major change in Mini policy became evident in 1969, following the Leyland merger with BMC that created the new British Leyland combine. By this time the Mini had been in production for 10 years and its shortcomings in some design areas were more than enough to cause speculation about its replacement. In the event, 1969 saw the appearance not of a replacement car but of a supposedly interim model, the Clubman, with a squared-off nose that added four inches to the famous 10 ft (305 cm) overall length, and a redesigned and updated in-

ABOVE, MIDDLE, LEFT *The Mini subframe was a cleverly engineered way of easing construction of the car, although subframe rust is a common problem on older examples of the model*

terior (the instruments were, wonder of wonders, in front of the driver!). The Clubman was offered in 998 and 1275 cc versions and supplanted the Riley Elf, the Wolseley Hornet and the Cooper. The 1275 Cooper S struggled on unchanged until 1971, but more significantly the original Mini shape also continued, in 850 and 1000 versions, with sufficient detail changes – like wind-up windows and flush door hinges – to warrant a change from the ADO15 designation to ADO20. Interestingly, the ADO20 also reverted to the original type of rubber-cone dry springing.

Partly because of BL's internal confusion about the future of individual marque names like Austin and Morris, there was a period during the 1970s when Mini became a marque in its own right, without any of the former badge distinction. This made some kind of sense as long as there were distinct basic and long-nosed Clubman models to form a range, but with the coming of the Metro (and the dropping of Morris) the Mini finally became an Austin again.

The question of a true Mini replacement was debated within BL throughout the 1970s, with various interesting prototypes like ADO74 and ADO88 failing on grounds of cost – or perhaps of lack of sufficient funds for development. The Mini and the Clubman soldiered on until at the end of the decade some 4.5 million Minis and derivatives had been made. By this time the Mini had become a legend, and there was no longer any question of replacing it directly.

Why so? In 1969, the Mini was 10 years old as a production model, rather elderly and fit for replacement by something better, but it was helped through the 1970s by two

great surges in demand for ultra-economy cars, after the 1973 Yom Kippur war and the 1978/79 Iranian crisis. By 1979 it was 20 years old, and cars which survive in production for that long, like the VW Beetle, the Citroën Traction Avant and 2CV, become motoring legends almost as of right, and so it was with the Mini.

Then again, the question of outright replacement hardly arose by the end of the 1970s. Had Issigonis sat down at his drawing board in 1977 rather than 1957, his minimum cabin would have been bigger, because people have, on average, become bigger. People's expectations of higher standards of comfort and equipment make life difficult for any car like the Mini, unless of course it has legendary status to back it up. In any event, the Mini replacements of the 1970s gradually grew into a car of the so-called 'supermini' class – the Metro, substantially bigger and heavier, built less to replace the Mini than to slog it out in the market with the Ford Fiesta, Fiat 127 and Renault 5. When the Metro arrived in 1980, the Mini Clubman models were dropped.

It is an interesting commentary on the pace of motoring development, and its direction, that the last Mini 850 to be tested by *Autocar*, just before the small engine was discontinued, managed a maximum speed of just 70 mph, actually slightly lower than that of the original. The overall fuel consumption was worse too, at 38.1 mpg, but six seconds had been carved off the 0–60 mph time giving the later 850 acceleration similar to that of the first Cooper!

Today, the Mini survives 30 years into production and likely at least to make its 30th birthday. In its current form it retains a 1-litre A-series engine, though now tuned for extreme economy with the help of modern technical developments under the 'A-plus' designation. The basic Mini City E remains cheap, although the man who paid £529 for a Mini de luxe in 1959 might look askance at £5,000, at least until he studied the price of the cheapest listed Ford which has more than kept pace.

Yet in a sense, the Metro *has* replaced the Mini. In 1979, the last complete sales year before the Metro became available, the evergreen Mini stood third in the British sales charts and took nearly 5 per cent of the British market. In 1981 it lay 10th, and took less than 2 per cent of sales, and by 1984 it had slumped to 16th, and 1.3 per cent, while the Metro was up there with the front-runners. The writing may be on the wall for the Mini, yet there seems no point in Austin-Rover handing 25,000 British sales a year, and a useful number of European customers, to their deadly rivals by simply consigning their legend to history.

LEFT *Where it all began, the original Mini introduced in 1959. This is a Morris Mini Minor version but the Austin Seven was identical*

FAR LEFT *The 848 cc A series engine produced just 37 bhp (gross)*
LEFT *The interiors were spartan indeed to begin with, but quite functional*

ROLLS ROYCE
SILVER GHOST

In 1907 the Silver Ghost began a journey that was to establish Rolls-Royce as builders of the undisputed 'best car in the world'

THE SOCIAL STANDING of Rolls, the engineering ability of Royce, and above all the commercial acumen of Johnson, had by 1905 made the Rolls-Royce company and its cars well enough respected. The 30 hp six-cylinder R-R was not as good as Johnson – a brilliant propagandist with a flair for telling lies in the most charming manner – maintained: like so many other early sixes, it suffered such severe torsional vibrations of the crankshaft that the miserable component too often broke. Something better was needed, and by 1907 it was ready – and so much better that it was kept in production, with periodic and rather reluctant changes, until 1925. Indeed it was so much better than anything else that it really earned its reputation of being the best car in the world. That accolade was originally bestowed by a journalist (not even Johnson would have had the nerve), and no other Rolls-Royce car ever deserved it. This one, the 40/50 horsepower model which later became known as the Silver Ghost, certainly did – at least until the advent of the new Hispano-Suiza in 1919. By that time, conditions were very different, and some of the factors influencing the original design were less important.

There was nothing superficially outstanding about the design; Royce deliberately avoided innovation whenever he could. What was outstanding was the attention to mechanical detail, the uncompromising search for constructional perfection. It was revealed in many beautiful felicities of design; it was backed by a quality control more stringent than any practised in the motor industry before or since.

The skills of the artisans at the factory could be taken for granted: Royce would summarily dismiss any worker seen mishandling a tool. That he understood tools and materials was beyond question: his designs proved it. For example, forgings were designed so that the grain flow of the finished machined piece should be most favourable. Thus a forging weighing 106 lb in its raw state ended up as a beautiful brake drum weighing 32 lb. Even more extreme was the connecting rod, finished at 2 lb from a raw forging weighing 8 lb, with only the perfect dense core remaining and the entire surface polished.

R-R claimed that every component of the car, if not machined, was filed and polished all over to find cracks or other flaws in the metal, and every highly stressed part was examined by magnifying glass to discover surface cracks. Flaw detection was in its infancy then, and in fact R-R were somewhat behind the times in their detection methods, as they still were 30 years later; but they were ahead of their time in the measures they took to prevent flaws.

ABOVE *The original Silver Ghost was actually the 13th car in the 40/50 series. Its name came from its silver paint finish and silver fittings and was soon adopted to refer to all 40/50s*
LEFT *Gear and brake levers were mounted outside, above the running-board*

LEFT *The 50 bhp 7-litre side-valve engine was a masterpiece of engineering and was produced to tolerances seldom seen before or since in the car industry*

35

Every hole, whether bored for clearance or for lightening, was carefully machined to a smooth finish lest any surface asperity act as a stress-raiser and start a fracture. The common practice of stamping the chassis number on one of the main frame members was shunned because the indentation might weaken the piece. Good stress distribution in the axle casing was sought by assembling it with a large number of small studs rather than a few big ones. Bolts had square heads above circular thrust faces, not the usual hexagonal heads; like their matching nuts, and everything else possible, they were made by Rolls-Royce themselves.

Royce was very distrustful of other people's methods. Every bolt-hole was checked for squareness with the abutment face, and all spring washers were tested and if necessary retempered; they were in any case only used for locking external nuts, internal ones always being castellated and locked with cotter pins or by similarly positive methods. All rotating parts were balanced, not just the wheels, crankshaft and flywheel but also all gearwheels and even the bevel gears in the final drive. Copper pipes were brazed, not merely soldered. Rods and tubes in tension were always straight. Everything ferrous was steel except the cast iron cylinders, piston rings and handbrake linings; and the steel parts were always rolled or forged, except for four pieces which could only be cast. In every little detail, masked or manifest, perfection was sought. The quality would still be appreciated, as Royce remarked, long

after the price had been forgotten.

The customer, who could certainly see the price, might not recognize such quality; but Royce appeased him with a superb and obviously durable finish. In particular, the nickel plating was unique in the motor industry, thanks to a Sheffield technique known as close plating: Royce despised the microscopically thin layer deposited by electroplating such as other firms used, instead employing craftsmen to cut to shape pure nickel sheet about 0.006 in (0.15 mm) thick and then soldering it onto the part to be plated. It kept its colour permanently, did not scrape off, and gave the impression that it would last forever.

Such standards were more necessary then than today. Most people were abysmally ignorant about machinery. Reliability had to be faultless because competent diagnosis

and repair of a fault was rare, and because the wealthy classes who bought such cars as these were intolerant of failure.

Because of these things, engine performance was best left mediocre; a good car had to be a gentle car. If it had any pretensions to performance, speed should be sought with a large engine rather than a notably efficient one. If it had any pretensions to elegance, it would probably have to carry a body custom-built by craftsmen still relying on horse-carriage methods, with no under-

ABOVE *The year is 1907 and the event the 15,000 mile trial. The rest stop is the Cat and Fiddle – near Buxton – and the original Silver Ghost is the car on the left. After the trial only the minutest wear was found in a handful of parts*

RIGHT *A 1912 Ghost, stately and solid but like many other examples of the model, still running well and reliably after the passing of more than 70 years and many miles*

standing of the interaction of high speeds, bad roads, coarse springs and flexible chassis. The body would be excessively heavy, structurally precarious, aerodynamically indefensible, and likely to promote or aggravate instability of the vehicle. It would provide little or no insulation against noise or vibration from engine or chassis, and its adverse effects on the behaviour of the car would be identified by most customers as the fault of the chassis manufacturer.

In this context the R-R 40/50 made very

BELOW *This Silver Ghost was built towards the end of Ghost production, in 1923. It was built by Rolls-Royce America Inc in Springfield, Massachusetts, with a body by Brewster. Although R-R America was shortlived, North American examples were often more elegant than the British*

good sense. Its chassis was broadly similar to that of the earlier 30 hp car, but the engine which gave it its title was completely new. The 40 was in round figures the horsepower according to the RAC taxation rating, determined according to piston area and thus the product of six cylinders each of 4½ inches (11.4 cm) bore, disregarding with splendid theoretical assurance the stroke which was also 4½ inches. The 50 was in ever rounder terms the actual output of the engine in brake horsepower, the product of 7036 cc running at a compression ratio of 3.2:1 and a brake mean effective pressure under 70 psi.

Unlike the earlier six-cylinder R-R, the 40/50 engine appeared as a brace of threes in line, rather than as three twins. The two cast iron blocks had integral heads, and were perched on a long aluminium-alloy crankcase within which the couples of two

mirror-image threes were lost in mutual cancellation, only the extra long centre main bearing testifying to the uneven distribution of loads typical of the type. There were altogether seven main bearings for the crankshaft, itself a particularly robust piece of work by the standards of the time although it was devoid of balance weights; Royce, who farmed out most of his mathematical tasks, never mastered the intricacies of engine balance. The old 30 hp problems were attacked first by adopting the basic layout just described, and then by making the main journals and crankpins nearly twice as thick as before. This entailed something better than the rudimentary lubrication system previously used: oil was fed under pressure through the hollow crankshaft of the 40/50, as Royce had done in his abortive V8 engines a little earlier.

The V8 format was not to reappear in a Rolls-Royce application until the Silver Cloud model of 1959, by which time the configuration was well-tried in many powerful applications. However, the intricacies of the design had proved too much for even the skill of Royce at that early stage of the development and refinement of the motor car.

Another change was in the valve apparatus. Royce discarded his overhead inlets and pushrods, preferring side valves. When compression ratios were perforce so low, when cam profiles were necessarily gentle, and when cylinder head gaskets were so treacherous, such a layout was attractive. Without those pushrods it was also quieter, especially because there was provision (not always to be found in those days) for adjusting the tappets which, like the valve springs, were exposed along the left-hand side of the

engine. The timing drive to camshaft and ignition was by gears, for Royce was utterly opposed to the use of chains; and only the cooling fan remained to be driven by a link belt from a pulley on the crankshaft.

It was in its ancillaries that the 40/50 displayed its class. The electrical apparatus was of outstanding quality, recalling the origins of the company. The distributor, trembler coils and magneto were Royce's own, abetted by 4V accumulators serving the coils. Two spark plugs served each cylinder: the drill then was to start on the coils and thereafter (to avoid draining the accumulators) run on the magneto. When running slowly both were kept switched on, for magnetos performed poorly at low rpm. When it could be deferred no longer (that is, in 1919) Royce grudgingly gave the car a dynamo so as to maintain the stored charge for lighting and starting; with the normal coils which then supplanted the tremblers, running with both ignition systems switched on became the normal practice.

Control mechanisms were as refined as the electrics. The governor system was often criticized as being too fancy, but those who

learned to use it appreciated that the complication and expense were justified by the pleasure and assurance it brought to driving. Very delicate and precise, the centrifugal governor was interlinked with the accelerator pedal so as to supplement it but be overridden by it; it was much more subtle than the simple constant-speed governor that some other engines borrowed from steam practice. It could control the tickover, or maintain a constant cruising speed regardless of gradient. Some drivers used it as an aid to achieving a smooth and silent gearchange without any need for skillful coordination of feet and hands; this trick was taught at the R-R drivers' school, to compensate for a rather difficult gearbox.

In fact the car was designed to be driven mostly in top gear, and in other respects was very forgiving of incompetence at the wheel, while rewarding skilled drivers with surprisingly high performance. It fared well in competitions such as the Alpine Trials, and in long-distance record-breaking over such routes as Monaco to London. First of all it distinguished itself in sundry officially-observed trials of roadworthiness, speed,

flexibility, reliability and economy, all organized for publicity by the ambitious Johnson. Thus is proved itself able to go from 3.5 to 53 mph (85 kph) in third (direct) gear, to 63 mph (101 kph) in overdrive fourth, and to average 17.8 mpg between London and Glasgow – repeating the trip until it had done 15,000 miles (24,150 km), when a complete strip-down revealed only the faintest wear in a handful of minor parts that could be replaced for £2 2s 7d.

The 4430 lb (2009 kg) car that did all this was the thirteenth chassis, fitted with a silver-painted touring body on which all appropriate metal fittings were silver-plated. On the scuttle gleamed a cast plate identifying this particular car as *Silver Ghost*; as it rapidly became famous, the car lent its name to the whole series, even the company eventually condescending to follow the public in adopting the model name. The fame was what mattered, and it was enough to encourage full production, four cars per week.

The rate was to grow, as was the fame. In the course of 18 years, R-R built 6173 examples, at an average of seven per week – including the war years, when the car did sterling service on the Western Front and quite amazing service (as armoured fighting vehicle, long-range reconnaissance intruder, staff car and dragoon-bearer) in the deserts of the Middle East. In all those years the design did not go unchanged, of course; the most notorious alteration was made within two years of production beginning.

It seemed logical to Royce to substitute a three-speed gearbox with direct top for the previous four-speeder. People expected to drive everywhere in top gear, and were incapable of understanding that direct third was to be treated as top, and that an overdrive fourth was something different. That indirect ratio could not be as quiet as the direct top, but they could not understand that either. To keep them quiet, they were given a three-speed box with revised ratios, while the engine was enlarged to 7428 cc by adding a quarter of an inch to the stroke.

Everybody was happy until one of the cars competing in the Austrian Alpine Trial of 1912 failed to restart on a 1 in 4 gradient. The high altitude and the high bottom gear were together too much for it: two passengers had to get out. It was a disgrace (if only to a Rolls-Royce) and so in 1913 a normal four-speed gearbox was installed, first in the so-called Continental model and later in the standard chassis.

Four cars were entered in the 1913 Austrian Alpine event, redeeming the firm's reputation by making mincemeat of all opposition. They were not perfectly standard (neither, presumably, were many of their rivals), for they had aluminium alloy

The 1910 Silver Ghost on these two pages has Roi des Belges bodywork, a style named after the coachwork the King of Belgium had built for him on his Panhard by the Paris company Rothschild & Fils in 1901. Seat elevation intimated status

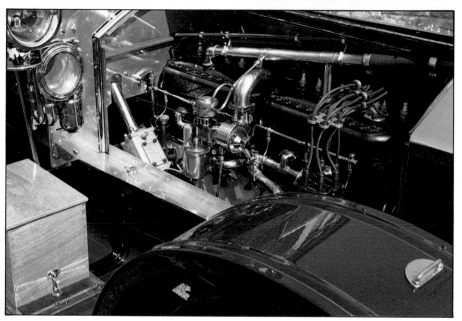

LEFT *The engine of this 1910 car has been superbly restored and shows clearly the quality of materials used in the construction of The World's Finest Car*

pistons, and they were sprung at the rear by the cantilevered half-elliptics that had been introduced on the London-Edinburgh cars.

The London-Edinburgh stunt grew from a challenge by Napier to drive from London to Edinburgh in top gear, then return to Brooklands for a speed test, fuel consumption also being measured. A Rolls-Royce with tapered bonnet, raised compression and larger carburettor as well as the new rear springs did 78.26 mph (125.9 kph) and 24.32 mpg, beating the Napier fair and square. It was then stripped and fitted with a higher axle ratio and a narrow single-seat racing body, in which it was timed at 101.8 mph (163.8 kph).

A few London-Edinburgh types were offered for sale, and it was from them that the Continental model was developed. This in turn became the standard model after the Great War ended in 1918. There was no time to prepare something new, least of all by the painstakingly slow R-R methods: people were avid for cars in the post-war euphoria, and would not wait. It was the same in the USA, where the firm was prompted to set up a satellite factory at Springfield: perversely the Americans wanted to buy the genuine English car, although the American one was made to the same standards and was often better bodied, but they managed to dispose of a further 1703 Ghosts, a respectable total when compared with the Derby figure quoted earlier.

By this time there had been some further changes. The adoption of relatively modern electrical gear – the dynamo, starter and revised ignition equipment – took place in 1919, rather a long time after most of the car's rivals had followed the example set in America by Cadillac. That the Ghost did have rivals was by this time beyond question, though Johnson always maintained the pretence that R-R were in a class of their own. He was always disappointed that he could never get the King to use one for personal travel, even though the Prince of Wales became an enthusiastic R-R owner. The King remained faithful to his silent sleeve-valve Daimlers (always extremely conservatively bodied, with the radiators painted instead of being plated), and many others thought that the Daimler offered superior ride comfort. Those who went abroad knew differently, however: on the roads of France, especially, the R-R was supreme (a result of extensive testing on that country's demanding highways) whereas the Daimler was grossly inferior. There were others to consider, too, but such debate should have ceased after the appearance of the Hispano-Suiza at the Paris Salon in 1919; Royce's limitations began to show more clearly.

There remained one more change, and this again was an example of R-R delaying the adoption of something modern until they had been able to make sure that it worked really well. This was the change, in 1923, to four-wheel brakes, accompanied by a brake servo of Hispano-Suiza type for which the necessary energy was derived from a power take-off at the gearbox. That servo was to remain a feature of Rolls-Royce brakes for no less than 42 years!

The firm did not like innovation. They did not even like modification, though sometimes a customer would force them to do it, and sometimes one of their own mistakes would be discovered and start a conscientious panic to get it righted. As such times it was convenient that customers had grown used to the idea of the travelling inspectors who would call from time to time to see that the car was still healthy: it was easy for modifications to be made during such visits without the customer ever knowing – and much less embarrassing than a recall!

Keeping the design up to date was a different matter. R-R simply never managed it, and the Ghost gradually ceased to be competitive. As it grew slower and heavier (as much the fault of the bodybuilders as of the unsympathetic customers) it was easier to dismiss. Finally came the inevitable day, in May 1925, when a successor was announced: the New Phantom was about the same size, but it had a long-stroke engine with overhead valves. It was faster and noisier, and it was much more popular among the Americans than the old side-valve car had been. It also gave the company an occasion on which to ratify the long-popular unofficial name for the old car: not until the New Phantom was on the market did Rolls-Royce themselves call the old model the Silver Ghost.

Such formality as only belatedly acknowledging a popular name is typical of the restraint with which Rolls-Royce have traditionally conducted themselves. By 1925 there can have been few people who were not aware of what a Silver Ghost was, such was its charisma and fame as transport for royalty and the famous all around the world.

The old car sired a long line of distinguished successors, even though none of

RIGHT *Silver Ghosts have been fitted with a wide variety of bodies by many British and overseas coachbuilders but few were more imposing than this Barker-clad example*

them was ever the best car in the world, as the Silver Ghost had for a while been. What might have succeeded it was a different matter: had the little 20 hp car, which was added to the catalogue in 1922, enjoyed the twin-overhead-camshaft specification originally intended for it when the design was begun in 1919, R-R history might have taken a very different course. As it happens, an overhead-camshaft version of the Ghost engine did put the firm on a new course, during the Great War: by copying the layout of the 1914 GP Mercedes cylinder head and the details of its single-camshaft valve gear, and superimposing this on the lower half of the Ghost engine, Royce made his first aero-engine (later to be very effective in the naval blimps used for submarine-hunting) and – very much against his will – started the firm on a new career in aviation. If it was any consolation, Rolls (killed in a flying accident at Bournemouth in 1910, a month after becoming the first Englishman to fly the Channel) would almost certainly have approved.

The Silver Ghost series lasted a long time, perhaps too long. By 1925 when it was replaced by the New Phantom, other manufacturers had improved on the 40/50 design. Nevertheless this 1921 Torpedo Tourer by Barker is a splendid device

PC 5553

The DB4 was announced in 1958 to a rapturous press reception, as the perfect Grand Tourer; the DB5 and DB6 proved even better...

THE ASTON MARTIN DB4 ARRIVED in 1958 and represented the finest contemporary British interpretation of the *Gran Turismo* theme. A magnificent synthesis of the talents at the firm's Feltham works and the Italian Touring styling house, the DB4 was, during its five years of production, a best-selling model which paved the way for the even more successful DB5 and DB6.

The story of the DB4's development really began in 1950 when John Wyer started at the Feltham works as competitions manager, moving from his post as managing director of sports-car specialists Monaco Engineering. Another 1950 recruit was design draughtsman Harold Beach, whose previous career had included spells at the Barker coachbuilding company and Garner Straussler Mechanisation, who built commercial vehicles and ancillary equipment.

It was in 1954 that Beach began work on a DB2 series replacement which was to be titled DB4, the DB3 having been one of the firm's sports racers. Known as Project 114 it had a perimeter chassis frame with a sophisticated de Dion rear axle employing parellel trailing links, the lower ones connected to laminated torsion bars. At the front of the car Beach introduced wishbone and coil independent front suspension where the DB2, by contrast, had a trailing arm system. A 3-litre version of the then current twin-cam six was employed and Frank Feeley designed a traditional, suitable closed body, not dissimilar to that of the DB2.

Significant changes were made to the specifications in 1956 with the appointment of John Wyer as general manager; he had also been made technical director during the previous year. Beach was later to remember Wyer's promotion as of the utmost significance in the DB4's development as then 'a true sense of direction and purpose decended on Feltham'. The first modification to the concept came with the decision to dispense with the Lagonda engine and replace it with a purpose-built Aston Martin unit. It perpetuated the twin-overhead-camshaft six-cylinder theme and in its production form had 'square' 92 mm × 92 mm

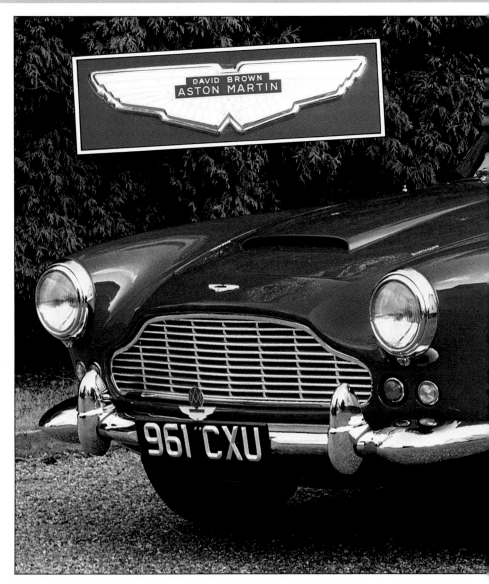

dimensions which gave a capacity of 3670 cc. In its original form designer Tadek Marek specified a cast-iron block but this was subsequently changed to aluminium with chrome vanadium wet cylinder liners. The head was of the same material with valves at an 80 degree included angle, while at the other end of the engine was a robust seven-bearing crankshaft. In this form the engine developed 240 bhp at 5700 rpm.

Wyer also decided, good as Feeley's styling had been, that he wanted the DB4 modelled by an Italian styling house. He decided on Carrozzeria Touring Superleggera of Milan, having been impressed by that firm's bodywork on the DB 2/4 chassis which the *Daily Mail* had offered as prizes at Motor Show time.

Harold Beach was therefore dispatched to Turin with drawings of the DB4 chassis, but after the Italians had examined the frame they informed Beach that it was not suitable for their Superleggera ('super lightweight') construction. That consisted of a substructure of small diameter tubes covered by an alloy skin, and resulted in a light but extremely rigid construction. What Touring required was a platform chassis which could be properly integrated with the body cage, and upon his return to Feltham, Beach sat down and designed one in six weeks flat! A chassis was soon built and dispatched, minus its engine and transmission, to Italy. On its return to Feltham the car, sprayed blue with matching upholstery, had its mechanics installed. The work was com-

The timeless elegance of Touring's styling combined with the punch of the Aston Martin engine made the DB4 a classic

pleted on a Saturday night in July 1957 and the following day Beach and John Wyer took the car down to David Brown's farm at Fulmer, Buckinghamshire. Brown was delighted with the performance of this prototype DB4 after putting it through its paces over the Chilterns on the Sunday morning.

Wyer subsequently took the car on a long Continental road test during August and September 1957. By then it had already covered 2500 miles (4023 km) and Wyer clocked up a further 2000 (3219 km). On his return he wrote a detailed report of his experiences with the car and summed up his impressions thus: 'While there remains a considerable amount of development work to be carried out, it is not too early to say that we have a car that can justly be described as "Grand Touring". The overall impression at the end of the test is that the car has magnificent performance and is full of promise. While faults are fairly numerous, as was to be expected, they were not fundamental and should not be too difficult to eradicate.'

He did, however, feel that the 3.27:1 rear axle ratio was too high and suggested that it should be replaced by a 3.54:1 unit. He was also critical of the amount of noise emanating from that source, and its elimination required that the de Dion rear axle be dispensed with. The problem was that Aston

43

Martin were unable to find a suitable chassis-mounted differential unit. Jaguar, for instance, had not yet gone to independent rear suspension, which ruled out a cross-pollenation of components, and Aston Martin decided to scrap the de Dion and employ a Salisbury live axle instead. The parallel trailing arms were retained but coil springs were introduced and a Watts linkage was used for location. This, of course, meant another chassis re-design, and consequently another prototype, this time painted green, was completed by Touring. After its return to Feltham for mechanical completion it was sent up to the Tickford factory at Newport Pagnell, Buckinghamshire, which Brown had purchased in 1955. Although Touring had produced the two prototype DB4s and the body tooling the model was to be built at the Tickford works, with the Feltham operation being progressively wound down and

only the competitions department left there until it was closed in 1963.

The DB4 was announced in October 1958 to a rapturous press reception. *Autosport* called it the 'Aston Marvel' and even the usually restrained pages of *The Autocar* spoke of a 'new and exciting car'. It cost £3976, which was considerably more than the DB Mark III which sold for £3076, and remained in production until July 1959. The really impressive aspect of the DB4 was its appearance, more than justifying Wyer's decision to opt for Touring's styling, and its performance. The 3-litre DB Mark III had been capable of 120 mph (193 kph) but the DB4 could nudge 140 mph (225 kph). Interior fittings were in keeping with the price, and Reutter reclining front seats were employed; both front and rear seats were upholstered in high quality Connolly hide. There was also pile carpeting throughout.

The DB4 looked the perfect Grand Tourer but, in truth, the model was plagued by unreliability for the first few years of its life.

These difficulties were mostly associated with engine overheating and associated lubrication problems. The former came to light on the Italian autostradas and were traced in part to a deficiency on the suction side of the

TOP LEFT *The Aston Martin straight-six twin-overhead-camshaft engine looks very similar to the Jaguar XK unit*
ABOVE *The stylish Aston Martin dashboard, here a left-hand-drive DB5 version*
BELOW *A 1964 example of the DB5 Volante which was one of the few true British 'supercars' of the early 1960s*

ABOVE *One of the rare estate conversions of the long-chassis DB6*
LEFT *The DB4 Vantage differed from the rest in having faired-in headlamps like the later DB5 and DB6 models*

oil pump which had not shown up during Aston Martin's own tests. There were also clutch problems and difficulties with the gearbox, which was built in-house by the parent David Brown organisation. These were caused by the synchromesh cones wearing badly, in extreme cases preventing gear engagement. Until about 1962 the engine also suffered from piston ring problems, resulting in excessive oil consumption. A number of modifications was introduced in 1960 when the DB4 was fitted with all-round servo-assisted Dunlop disc brakes, the front ones were enlarged and sump capacity was upped from 14 to 17 pints (7.9 to 9.6 litres). In April 1961 sump capacity was once again increased, this time to 21 pints (11.9 litres) and at the same time a Laycock overdrive unit became an optional extra. In September, a twin-plate clutch was introduced and an oil cooler added. Early in 1962 the DB4's headlights were faired in which greatly improved the appearance of the front end and followed the lines of the GT variant. Production lasted until June 1963, and sales were excellent.

There soon appeared some more powerful variations on the DB4 theme. There was the Vantage version with more potent engine and compression ratio raised from

8.25:1 to 9:1, which boosted output to 260 bhp. The offering of a higher performance version had been standard Aston Martin practice since the introduction of the DB2. A year after the DB4's announcement, in September 1959, a GT version appeared. This had lighter bodywork and turned the scales at 2800 lb (1270 kg) rather than the 2968 lb (1346 kg) of the mainstream model. Other weight-saving refinements included Borrani wheels, Girling instead of Dunlop discs and a 30-gallon (13.6-litre) fuel tank. The faired-in headlamps were subsequently transferred to DB4. These modifications all had the effect of pushing the GT's top speed beyond 150 mph (241 kph), and with 302 bhp available acceleration was also improved.

The ultimate expression of the GT model was the Zagato version, the rolling chassis of which were dispatched to Italy for bodying and then returned to Newport Pagnell for completion. The engines were similar to the GT's, but with a higher compression ratio produced 314 bhp.

Aston Martin's great racing days had been during the 1950s and competition activities were greatly reduced following the celebrated Le Mans victory in 1959. The DB4's engine had been run at Le Mans in 1957 under the bonnet of a DBR2 but broke its gearbox. The GT version, by contrast, enjoyed a successful competitive baptism in May 1959 when at the International Trophy meeting Stirling Moss enjoyed a runaway victory in the GT race. Moss also took the wheel of one of the Zagato-bodied versions at the Easter Goodwood meeting but had to content himself with third place. There were further clashes with Ferrari, with Maranello usually having the upper hand, but from then on Aston Martin GT 'Project' cars moved centre stage. These activities undoubtedly helped DB4 sales, and the final

production figure was an impressive endorsement of Wyer's stewardship of the project and the abilities of the Feltham design team. Until the arrival of the DB4 in 1958 the best selling post-war Aston Martin had been the DB2/4 with 565 sold. By contrast, the company sold 1110 DB4s including 70 drophead coupés, introduced in 1961. A further 75 GTs and 19 Zagato-bodied examples were also sold.

These special cars are now highly sought after with the Zagato examples in particular worth several hundred thousand pounds. Like all Astons, the 'ordinary' GTs went through a phase of being neglected but are now highly prized, not least because of their effectiveness in various forms of historic motor sport.

Once the mechanical maladies that had, to a limited extent, clouded the car's arrival were rectified, the DB5 which replaced it was destined to be a far more acceptable car. The principal difference between the two was the engine, the capacity of which was 3995 cc, attained by upping the DB5's bore from 92 mm to 96 mm. Power was accordingly increased from 240 bhp to 282 bhp. Top speed was up only marginally but acceleration was greatly improved. Other DB5 refinements included electric windows; air

conditioning and Borg-Warner automatic transmission were options, the latter having also been offered on the later DB4s. The gearbox problems were resolved by the replacement of the David Brown unit with a five-speed German ZF box, although a few early DB5s were fitted with the DB 'box. The company had gone abroad for its replacement gearbox because there was no British unit then available to cope with the torque developed by the DB5's engine. Maserati were using the ZF for the same reason and about the only problem to manifest itself was undue noise at tickover. Some clutch difficulties, however, persisted.

When *Road & Track* were introduced to the DB5 in 1964 they were suitably impressed, finding very little to complain about apart from the throttle action, 'which is awkward and tiring on long trips, and difficult to use with delicacy in traffic.' The live rear axle met with approval even in such an expensive car, '...by locating it with parallel trailing links (4) and transversely by Watt

ABOVE AND BELOW *The DB6 of 1966 featured a longer chassis, but is best identified by its flip-up rear spoiler*

linkage, they have achieved a rear suspension which is superior in road holding and adhesion to some of the independent arrangements we have encountered… At $13,000 it is beyond the reach of the majority, but for those who are able to beg, borrow or steal money in this quantity, and want the type of car which the French so aptly describe as a *voiture de grande luxe et de grande tourisme*, then the Aston Martin is hard to beat.'

The drophead coupé version also continued to be offered, known as the Volante when offered on the DB5, and there was a steel hardtop available. A prestigious estate car version was also produced by Harold Radford though only 12 were built. There was no separate GT version but the Vantage, with its Weber carburettors, gave 314 bhp. The DB5 sold slightly better than its predecessors with 1025 examples finding customers, 125 of them buying drophead versions. Sales were undoubtedly stimulated by the DB5's star billing in the James Bond film *Goldfinger*, in which one car proper and two replicas were used. The retractable machine guns, scythes and bullet-proof rear screen were peculiar to 007's requirements….

The DB5 was replaced in 1966 by the DB6, with a long wheelbase of 101.75 inches (258.5 cm) rather than the earlier model's 98 inches (249 cm) in response to demands for improved rear passenger accommodation. There was a distinctive spoilered tail included because the works team had experienced serious frontal lift problems during the model's evolution. Although mechanical-

LEFT AND ABOVE *Two examples of the lightweight Zagato version of the DB4, the car above owned by Nigel Dawes and the one on the left by Richard Williams*

47

EVOLUTION

1958 DB4 saloon and drophead introduced, fitted with Aston Martin twin-overhead-cam six-cylinder engine of 3670 cc, with aluminium block and head. Bodywork was hand-panelled aluminium over a Superleggera-type steel cage and boxed sheet steel platform chassis.

1959 DB4GT offered, with faired-in headlights and lightened bodywork. DB2/4 Mk III discontinued. Total production: 551

1960 Zagato-bodied version of DB4 offered

1961 The last DB4GT is built. Total production: 75

1963 DB5 saloon and drophead coupé introduced, with engine bored out to 3995 cc, producing 282 bhp, and fitted with ZF five-speed gearbox. DB4 discontinued. Total production: 1110, plus 19 Zagato versions

1965 DB6 and short-chassis Volante introduced, mechanically similar but the latter with new aerodynamic body with rear spoiler, and options of manual or automatic transmissions and Vantage engine. DB5 discontinued. Total production: (saloon) 896, (drophead) 125

1966 DB6 Volante drophead coupé introduced. Short-chassis Volante discontinued. Total production: 37

1969 DB6 Mk II introduced, with restyled interior, larger wheels and tyres and optional fuel injection. DB6 discontinued. Total production: 1327, (Volante) 140

1970 DB6 MkII and Volante discontinued

ly the car was almost identical to the DB5 the 6 was faster, due to its superior aerodynamics, with a top speed approaching 150 mph (241 kph). There was also an interior facelift, the first since 1958. The decision to lengthen the car was vindicated by the DB6 selling better than any of its predecessors.

Motor concluded that other cars may have had '…a more comfortable ride, higher ultimate cornering power or lighter controls, but for the fastidious driver whose machinery is an extension of himself (and not an enviable status symbol) the sheer masculinity of a car like the Aston has a very great appeal. You would be ashamed to be seen driving one badly.' The road testers liked the light gliding action of the ZF gearlever, the smooth and powerful clutch and the way in which the sensitive steering helped the driver maximise the car's roadholding: 'The steering has a superb sensitivity to variations of adhesion, which is essential if such handling is to be exploited; you can feel through the wheel when a surplus of power is starting to bring the tail around wider than the front and then balance the car's attitude with the throttle without any fear of sudden breakaway…'. They did go on to say that a lot of credit was

BELOW This DB4 illustrates well the lovely lines achieved by the Italian styling house of Touring using their steel tube and aluminium construction techniques

due to the Avon GT tyres but the chassis was obviously well balanced.

In July 1969 a Mark II version of the model was introduced but by this time the Superleggera type of construction had been dispensed with as Touring had ceased its body-building and styling activities in 1967. Changes included larger wheels and tyres, with the wheel arches flared accordingly to accommodate them. There were further trim changes with revisions to the rear seats while Brico electronic fuel injection was available as an optional extra. By the time production ceased in November 1970 a total of 1575 had been produced (1330 Mark Is, 245 Mark IIs), making the DB6 the most successful car of the range. The Volante really came into its own with the DB6. Fitted with a power-operated hood, 140 examples

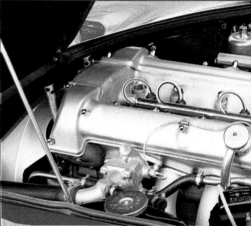

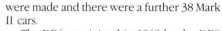

Unlike the later DB versions, the DB4 featured an engine of 3670 cc, but this was still enough to give the car a top speed approaching 140 mph (225 kph). This is a superbly restored 1962 Series 4

were made and there were a further 38 Mark II cars.

The DB6 was joined in 1968 by the DBS and for two years the models were produced side by side. Thoughts about the new car had gelled in 1966 when Touring followed in its DB4 wheel tracks by producing two prototypes titled DBS Cs, but with the Turin company's troubles it was decided to style the DB6's successor in-house. The job was undertaken by William Towns, who had initially joined the company to design interior trim, and the car was a worthy successor to the DB 4/5/6 range. The DBS was an altogether larger and heavier car having a 59-inch (150 cm) track as opposed to the 54-inch (137 cm) track of the earlier cars, and a 102.75-inch (261 cm) wheelbase, compared with the DB6's 101-inch (257 cm) wheelbase. These larger dimensions were demanded by the impending arrival of a new 5.3-litre V8 with twin overhead camshafts per bank which was then under development, but as it was not ready in time the company continued to use the DB6 engine. This powered the DBS from its introduction until 1970 when the V8 was at last ready. Mechanically the DBS was similar to the DB6 with the exception of the live rear axle, which was replaced, much to Harold Beach's delight, by a de Dion unit with high quality ball-spline drive-shafts. It proved itself the fastest four-seater of its day, capable of 171 mph (275 kph).

Despite the arrival of the DBS V8 in 1970 the six-cylinder DBS continued in production under this name until 1972. It was in that year that Sir David Brown, as he had become in 1968, decided that he could no longer carry the burden of a loss-making company and in February he sold the business to Company Developments. The new management continued to build the DBS, and renamed it the Vantage as the DB prefix no longer applied. This was made until July 1973. By this time 829 DBS sixes and 70 examples of the Vantage had been produced. This was the end of the line for the six and thereafter Aston Martin concentrated on its V8. It is this power unit that still powers the firm's V8 and Lagonda models, 15 years after it was introduced.

AC COBRA

AC COBRA

The Cobra, powered by mighty 4.2, 4.7 and 7-litre V8s, was the epitome of the muscle-bound sports car; with its beautiful shape and brutal performance, this AC has become a legend

ENTHUSIASTS DREAM about it and its drivers usually deplore it, but for those who feel that a beautiful car cannot be made unless the engine is at the front, the AC Cobra is perhaps the most attractive post-war sports car of all. Despite its excitingly stark mechanical specification – 4.2, 4.7 and 7-litre V8 engines, disc brakes all round, vast tyres and a weight of little more than a ton – it is the appearance which has elevated the Cobra to its high place in the motor car pantheon.

AC Cars started before the Great War, but first made a name for successful sporting cars when that well-known motoring character S.F. Edge took over the company in 1921. Under his aegis AC built the first 1½-litre car to exceed 100 mph (160 kph) and the first British car to win the Monte Carlo Rally. After World War II, using the same 2-litre aluminium alloy overhead-camshaft straight-six first built in 1919, they were making elegant, conventional two-door saloons when a builder of specials called John Tojeiro visited the AC factory at Thames Ditton in Surrey. He arrived in a one-off sports two-seater he had made for a London car dealer. It had a Bristol 2-litre engine, a simple ladder-like chassis made of two large diameter parallel steel tubes, and, at each end of the car, what was effectively double wishbone independent suspension using transverse leaf springs as the combined spring and top suspension member. Davis had raced it quite successfully, and by the standards of 1953 its design was advanced.

As a result of this visit, AC were sufficient-

BELOW *Innes Ireland driving a Cobra in the 1984 Targa Florio*
BOTTOM *The Bondurant/Neerpasch Cobra at the Nürburgring in 1965*

ly impressed to buy the design from Tojeiro on a royalty-per-car arrangement and use it as the basis for a new AC sports car.

The production version of Tojeiro's car was called the AC Ace, and followed its inspiration closely apart from the use of the AC power unit and Bishop worm and sector steering instead of rack and pinion. The venerable six, with its three SU carburettors and long stroke design (69 mm × 100 mm), was claimed to provide 85 bhp at 4500 rpm, good for an 18-second standing quarter-mile. Following one of the best dynamic characteristics of Edwardian and Vintage car design, the engine was mounted well behind the front wheel centre line, giving good balance and incidentally contributing to the car's gracefully long nose. The original Ace's combination of good handling, grip and speed was enough to draw enthusiastic approval from the motoring press.

Anything less than 20 seconds for the quarter-mile was good performance then, at any rate by normal standards, but it wasn't enough for true sports motoring. Tojeiro's special had the ex-BMW Bristol engine, a six-cylinder overhead-valve unit which could turn out between 100 bhp in road condition and more than 150 bhp when race-tuned, and it was not long before other enthusiasts began to fit this unit. Ken Rudd, an AC dealer at Worthing, on the South Coast, installed a tuned Bristol engine in his Ace and gave the car its debut at the 1956 Easter Monday Goodwood meeting, thus

beginning a season's domination by Ace-Bristols of British sports-car racing, and a similarly successful racing career in the USA. Ace-Bristols distinguished themselves in the Le Mans 24 Hour race, coming second in class and 10th overall in 1957, ninth overall in 1958 and seventh in 1959.

The road version was quick by contemporary standards, with a 115 mph (185 kph) top speed and a 16-second quarter-mile, but the Ace's original all-drum brake system was no match for the extra urge, so disc front brakes became optional in 1957.

Although the Bristol engine – and the

ABOVE A racing 289 cu in Cobra Mk II
BELOW A rare beast – one of the first
Cobras, a 260 cu in Mk I, of 1962. Note the
Shelby badge on the bonnet

much bigger power plants to come – were eventually to kill off the AC six in 1963, the Bristol unit's own future looked doubtful in 1961, when Bristol themselves were adopting a big American Chrysler V8 for their 407.

AC were investigating replacements when Ken Rudd showed what could be done with the 2553 cc Ford Zephyr straight-six, which in standard tune produced 90 bhp. Although a heavier lump to accommodate under the Ace's sleek nose, Rudd's attentions forced between 120 and 170 bhp from it. AC decided to use it, and strengthened the chassis, stiffened the springs and altered the nose to suit. As things turned out, the company made less than 40 Ace 2.6s between 1961 and 1963, and continued to look for something superior to the humble Ford unit.

AC had never been an inflexible mass

producer, and as was traditional with a specialist car builder, if a customer asked for something different and paid for it, AC would do their best to ensure he got it, even though their very successful mainstream engineering business meant that the car side was not vital to their survival. Thus when a burly Texan racing driver called Carroll Shelby wrote late in 1961 requesting an Ace chassis and body to take an American V8 engine, AC accepted the order.

Carroll Shelby had originally made a name for himself when he co-drove an Aston Martin to that company's long-sought-after and sole victory at Le Mans in 1959. He had then become involved with Ford USA, and it wasn't surprising that the V8 he wanted put into the Ace chassis was Ford's 260 cubic-inch (4261 cc) unit.

The Ace 2.6 was on the face of it well suited to the larger engine. The only modifications needed were the moving of the worm and sector steering box, to make room for the broader V8, and of the rear differential mounting to suit a Salisbury 4HA final drive, of the type used on independent-

EVOLUTION

AC Ace 2.6 introduced in 1961 with Rudd-tuned Ford Zephyr six-cylinder engine. It was based on a strengthened Ace frame which became the foundation for the V8 Cobra

1961 First AC Cobra built, with the 260 cu in (4.2-litre) Ford V8. A Salisbury final drive and inboard rear brakes were fitted. Production Cobras reverted to outboard rear discs.

1962 Production of 260 cu in Cobras ended

1963 Engine changed to the Ford 289 (4.7-litre) V8 which produced 11 bhp and 45 lb ft of torque more than the 260. Mk II Cobra introduced with rack and pinion steering, strengthened wishbones and the 289 engine

1965 Mk III Cobra introduced, powered by either the 427 cu in (6.9-litre) or the less sporting 428 cu in (7-litre) Ford V8. Chassis revisions included larger diameter main chassis members and coil spring rear suspension instead of transverse leaf. Cobra production ceased after around 1000 were built

ly rear-sprung Jaguars. This latter change was made partly because Shelby wanted inboard rear disc brakes, as used on some contemporary sports-racing cars (and the Jaguars). The Ace's 11.6 in (29 cm) diameter front discs and Girling calipers were retained, but wider offset wire wheels were used which demanded small sideways extensions of the wheel arches to keep the tyres decently covered. The original rearward position of the Ace engine was a help in preventing the extra mass of the V8 spoiling the balance too much.

This became the first AC Cobra and was unique in one comparatively small if important way: all subsequent Cobras had conventional outboard, wheel-mounted, rear disc brakes, for unless special measures are taken to provide a good flow of cool air, inboard brakes always tend to overheat and affect final-drive oil temperatures. In addi-

TOP A 7-litre Cobra engine with twin superchargers, built in the late '60s by Paxton for an ill-fated Shelby customer ABOVE and RIGHT Views of an immaculate 427 cu in Cobra. The chassis of the Mk III was strengthened and wider wheels necessitated flared wheel arches

tion, the benefits to ride and damping obtained with lower unsprung weight are offset by more difficult access for servicing.

A total of 75 260 cubic-inch Cobras were produced up to the end of 1962. The 96.52 mm × 73.03 mm bore and stroke 4.3-litre produced, in standard form, 260 bhp (gross) at 5800 rpm and 269 lb ft torque at 4800 rpm; with tuning up to 330 bhp was available. Early in 1963, Ford's better-known 289 cubic-inch (4736 cc, 101.6 mm × 72.9 mm bore and stroke) V8 was substituted, which in standard Cobra form was

claimed to give only 11 more horsepower at 6000 rpm, but obviously breathed much more easily, since the maximum torque went up by nearly 17 per cent to 314 lb ft at a usefully lower 3400 rpm. The kerb weight was 2020 lb (916 kg), virtually the same as the 260 cubic-inch model.

AC started work on an improved Cobra during 1962. The principle change was the replacement of the worm and sector box with a more precise rack and pinion unit. Although the transverse leaf springs were preserved, each front suspension lower wishbone member was made stronger.

This Mk II Cobra was originally built with the 4.7-litre (289 cubic-inch) V8, although as with many pre-1931 Bentleys, the engine

options list meant that in later life one could not always take that capacity for granted. All Mk I Cobras were left-hand drive, but the prototype Mk II was right-hand drive, as were a handful of subsequent examples.

It was not until November 1965 that a reliable British motoring journal managed to borrow a demonstrator Cobra for road test, a 4.7-litre Mk II whose engine was claimed to deliver 300 bhp (gross) at 5750 rpm, with a maximum torque of 285 lb ft at 4500 rpm, figures which suggest that this was a tuned engine with non-standard induction. The car had a measured kerb weight of only 2315 lb (1050 kg) with half-full tank, a 3.54:1 final drive gear ratio, Salisbury Powr-Lok clutch-type limited-slip

differential and 185-section 15 in tyres. This car could certainly accelerate: laden two-up, with an extra 50 lb of test equipment, it needed, on average, only 5.5 seconds to reach 60 mph (96 kph) – which it could do without having to change out of first, for that took the car to 64 mph – and 14 seconds to 100 mph (161 kph). It reached a mean maximum speed (the average of runs in opposite directions) of 138 mph (222 kph). One could reach 84 mph (135 kph) in second gear, and 116 mph (187 kph) in third. Left in top gear it was both ultra-flexible and shatteringly fast, as the times taken to cover each 20 mph (32 kph) interval between 20 and 120 mph showed: this Cobra never slowed into double figures. Going

up through the scale 20–40 mph, 30–50, 40–60 and so on, the car's times in seconds ran thus: 4.6, 4.3, 4.2, 4.1, 4.3, 4.8, 5.4, 6.1, and 8.3 – the last figure, for 100 to 120 mph, revealing how aerodynamic drag was just beginning to affect the Cobra.

Increasing a car's engine capacity has always been the best way to high performance, but usually there is one major problem, more difficult to overcome than obvious ones like improving the braking, and that's maintaining a good front/rear balance. More weight on the front wheels may improve stability in a straight line but rather negates the car's willingness to corner. Here

was a strength of the original Tojeiro design which, thanks to the shortness of the American power units, could be preserved in the Cobra. Weighing the Mk II car confirmed the advantage, showing that, most unusually for a front-engined sports cars, the unladen Cobra had 48.7 per cent of its mass on the front tyres.

The final production redesign of the Cobra was the Mk III, which began to emerge in January 1965 from Thames Ditton and Shelby's shop in Venice, California (where most drive units were fitted). Here was the most brutal of all Cobras, powered by the Ford 427 cubic-inch (6997 cc) or the

less powerful but cheaper 428 cubic-inch (7013 cc) V8s. The Mk III therefore had the most significantly altered chassis. Its twin parallel main chassis tubes were increased in diameter from 3 to 4 inches (7.6 to 10 cm) and were set further apart. Wheel location was improved by discarding the faithful transverse leaf springs – which, it will be recalled, acted as top suspension links – and replacing them with coil springs and full unequal-length double wishbones. These were still somewhat narrow by later competition standards, and although a circular section tube is torsionally the strongest of all section shapes, when even large diameter tubes are used as beams, (rather than struts and ties as in a true space-frame chassis) torsional stiffness suffers.

Such structural problems were compounded by the massive power outputs that were offered by the new 427 engine. Such a combination gave the biggest of all the Cobras handling that was, to say the least, interesting or, to be more precise, downright dangerous in inexperienced or disrespectful hands.

The body style was, depending on your taste, marvellously aggressive or a gross distortion of a once graceful original. The traditional wire wheels could be replaced with wider-rim cast aluminium alloy ones for big-section tyres (by 1965 roadgoing standards, the standard 8.15 × 15 in covers were wide) which necessitated wider wheel arches. The simple criss-cross grille of the previous car was removed and the main radiator air intake enlarged to provide the extra cooling, and an additional small scoop under the nose fed the oil cooler. With the

heavier chassis, bigger engine and the other changes, the weight had increased to around 2600 lb (1180 kg), but the 390 bhp at 5200 rpm and the meaty 475 lb ft of torque quoted for the 107.7 mm × 96.2 mm 427 engine more than compensated for this.

Seven-litre Cobras were rare beasts in Britain, and it isn't surprising that so few found their way into motoring journalists' hands. The one left-hand-drive example that the writer tested briefly was reputed to have nearly 500 bhp under its bulging bonnet, and it certainly went rather well: with two aboard we recorded 0-60 mph in 4.8 seconds, 0-100 mph in 11.7 seconds, 0-

120 mph in 17.9 seconds and the standing quarter-mile in 12.9 seconds. Other data gathering was suddenly curtailed when a back tyre burst at around 140 mph (225 kph), but thanks to the car's basic stability the only damage was to a wheel arch.

Cobras were raced to some extent, although not as much as one might expect. Fixed head bodies, in style faintly reminiscent of Italian Grand Touring cars, were built both by Shelby and by AC themselves, using a space-frame-like support on the old chassis. The AC-designed car was entered for the 1964 Le Mans – its race direction was in fact taken over by the official Cobra team

then – but was unluckily destroyed when a tyre burst at speed.

The Cobra's most successful exploit internationally was to win the 1965 GT category championship, with a team of open-top and Daytona coupés driven by people like John Whitmore, Jack Sears, Frank Gardner, Dan Gurney, Bob Bondurant, Dick Thompson and others, managed very ably by Alan Mann. The absence of real competition was a help, for unlike other cars which were being developed, the Cobra was not a scientifically designed race-winner. Nevertheless, through its drivers' skills and the shrewdness and experience of Alan Mann, the car did the job required in 1965. Then Ford USA cast the Cobra aside and channelled their efforts into the more promising GT40.

AC saw the warning lights, and after building a few of the dashing-looking Italian-styled (by Frua) 428 fixed-head coupés on a longer wheelbase Cobra chassis – they called it the AC 428, as Ford had by then given the Cobra name to a tarted-up Mustang – they stopped Cobra production. Experts believe that nearly 1000 Cobras were made.

By the mid-1960s the Cobra was an old-fashioned sports car. Its chassis was out of date, too flexible to compete successfully with better-designed cars which could be cornered and driven much more effectively and with a third of the effort. This applied both on the track and in the specialist road car market. Revivals have in one sense appeared of late – amazingly close replicas, with understandably high price tags, and these emphasise that the Cobra is an all-time great in sports-car shape if not sports car engineering.

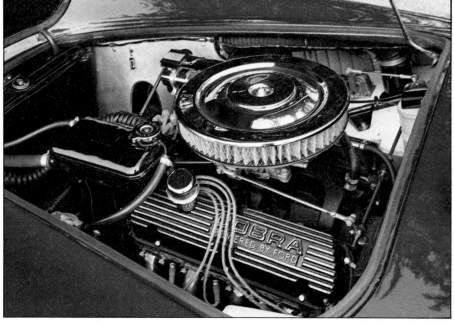

ABOVE *One of its eared wheel-spinners* **FAR LEFT** *The interior is both functional and attractive; instruments and controls are well positioned and seats and dashboard are leather-trimmed*

LEFT AND BELOW *A 1964 Cobra fitted with the 289 cu in (4736 cc) V8 engine. The 289 had more restrained styling than the later 427 cu in Cobras which sprouted wider wings and bigger wheels and tyres*

VAUXHALL 3

The 30/98 was a brilliantly
successful design, a car
equally at home on fast roads
and country lanes

LAURENCE HENRY POMEROY the Vauxhall designer (sometimes known as Pom Senior, to distinguish him from his son Laurence Evelyn or Pom Junior, the scarcely less famous motoring writer) was a very self-confident young man. His professional successes perhaps justified it: at the age of 30 (he was born in 1883) he became the youngest yet to be elected a full member of the Institution of Mechanical Engineers, a learned society which is still sufficiently august to be careful whom it honours. At any rate, Pom Senior, alias LHP, would happily engage in technical or intellectual arguments with that genius Dr Frederick Lanchester, and was no less eager to play the whippersnapper opposite Mr Frederick Henry Royce. On one occasion when the highly esteemed Rolls-Royce Silver Ghost particularly stimulated his pique, he observed that 'The Rolls-Royce represents the triumph of workmanship over design'.

He was jealous of that car's success, no doubt. Vauxhall in those days built definitely upper-class motorcars, but they were not made as meticulously as the Royce, they were not as expensive as the Royce, and they had not been introduced into high society by the Hon C.S. Rolls. True, they were popular in the Imperial Court of Russia, but so were Lagondas; it was left for Lenin to be a Rolls-Royce enthusiast. LHP could comfort himself with one fact, however: although the King's Messengers might have rushed around wartime France in a trio of Silver Ghosts, when HM King George V chose to be driven through the mud of Flanders to visit Vimy Ridge, he went in a 25 hp Vauxhall, Pomeroy's D-type.

LEFT *A 1923 Vauxhall 30/98 Velox*
BELOW *Despite its prosaic appearance the overhead-valve engine was very efficient*

That was a very highly esteemed staff car: Allenby drove into Jerusalem in one, and altogether a couple of thousand were made for the War Office during the 1914–1918 hostilities. It was very closely related to the E-type, the rare 30/98 sports car of which a dozen had been made after the issuance (in only a fortnight from when it was privately ordered!) of the prototype in 1913. It was also closely related to the Prince Henry Vauxhall, designed for the Austrian Alpine sporting trials of the late pre-war years; but it and these others were all derived from the first LHP Vauxhall, the one which deserved to be most famous of all, the 20 hp car built for the 1908 RAC 2000 Miles Trial.

Considering how much influence this car had upon Pomeroy's subsequent career, and upon Vauxhall's commercial fortunes – for both grew eminently successful – we can see how valuable was the young man's self-confidence in seizing the opportunity that

chance offered him. When the directors of the company decided to build a new car for the RAC Trial, LHP was assistant to their chief engineer, having joined the firm in 1906 after a youth spent in apprentice practice and academic qualification. However, the chief engineer was enjoying a long convalescent holiday in Egypt, and young LHP, freed from the constraints of his superior's rather heavy conservatism, happily assured the directors that he could do the job.

He was proved right. The Vauxhall was the first car in the world ever to complete 2000 stringently observed miles without a single involuntary stop. During the RAC Trial, which lasted for 13 days, it averaged 26 mpg (including 200 miles at high speed around the Brooklands track), it soundly beat every other car in its class on the several hill-climbs, and in the overall marks (which took fuel consumption and reliability into account) its loss of 77 points had to be

compared with the next best figure of 115 scored by...a Rolls-Royce Silver Ghost!

The car that LHP had created was based on a carefully studied engine, featuring monobloc construction for its four cylinders, a crankshaft running in five main bearings, and fully pressurised lubrication throughout. None of these features was yet a commonplace of design; nor did many others yet pay such attention as LHP did to free breathing through large ports and fluent manifolds. The result was a 90 mm × 120 mm engine giving 38 bhp at a rousing 2500 rpm, a yield which represented a 76 per cent increase in bhp per litre compared with the previous Vauxhall, and a 22 per cent increase in brake mean effective pressure – despite the fact that the engine was still an L-head side-valve type.

Having earned himself the respect, gratitude and confidence of his directors, LHP was promoted to works manager, with both the authority and the opportunity to develop his design further. Vauxhall found that suc-

cess in competition was commercially attractive, and that the costs of participation provided sufficient return to allow them a net profit of 10 per cent on the not-inconsiderable catalogue prices of their products. Accordingly the 3-litre car found itself entered in all manner of events, with appropriate preparation: as a low-drag single-seater, for example, it was the first car of its size to reach 100 mph (161 kph) at Brooklands.

Away in the Austro-Hungarian Empire, Prinz Heinrich had instituted a sporting team trial to be held on the mountain roads in his domain. Vauxhall sent a team of sharp-nosed 3-litre cars which became famous in Britain as the Prince Henry model, by now developing 60 bhp at 2800 rpm and

capable of 72 mph (116 kph). No match for the forceful 5.7-litre Austro-Daimler, a 90 mph (145 kph) four-seater which was perhaps the best thing that Ferdinand Porsche ever did, the Vauxhalls nevertheless had a trouble-free run and were by no means disgraced.

For his part, LHP was by no means dismayed: he knew what scope for development lay in his design. Bored out to 95 mm and stroked to 140 mm, the engine swelled to 4 litres displacement, giving the C-type Prince Henry model a more impressive urgency. Installed in a heavier chassis, and with the refinement of a Lanchester harmonic balancer (a counterweighted shaft driven at twice crankshaft speed to negate secondary vibrations) beneath its crankshaft, it made the D-type – known popularly by its RAC taxation rating of 25 hp – a wonderfully smooth and capable tourer.

These, then, were the cream of the Vauxhall range – fast and refined cars both comfortable and competent, cars admired by perceptive engineers and accepted in polite society – when, in 1913, LHP and Vauxhall were approached by one Joseph Higginson. This gentleman had been campaigning a La Buire in British hillclimbs with considerable success, but he now had cause to fear that his French car was no longer likely to enjoy its erstwhile supremacy. Could Vauxhall make him something appropriate, and make it soon?

They could; they did. Now 30 years old, the ambitious LHP had been a member of the Council of the Institution of Automobile Engineers for two years, and the recipient of the Crompton gold metal awarded by that body; his confidence knew no bounds, and his abilities had not yet approached theirs. In a fortnight, he created the fastest and most deservedly famous of all proper (that is pre-GM) Vauxhalls, the 30/98.

In an age when gearchanging was often a struggle that some drivers could never master, a car that could perform so competently and smoothly without recorse to shifting the ratios has an inbuilt advantage. Factors such as this, combined with the not inconsiderable style of the car made it appealing indeed.

No, it did not develop 98 bhp, only 90 – though in those days to use the word 'only' would have been thought scandalous. The 98 was the cylinder bore measurement in millimetres, which gave the engine an RAC rating of 30 hp and, with stroke elongated to 150 mm, a displacement of 4526 cc. Despite the lengthened stroke, it still ran up to 2800 rpm, the corresponding mean piston velocity not yet immoderate at 2756 ft/min (840 m/min). Because the dilated cylinders still breathed through existing porting, the low-speed torque and sheer flexibility were even better than before, and for hill-climbing that was worth as much as the extra power at the top of the range.

Hillclimbs and similar sprints call for a high ratio of power to weight. Since they invariably involved awkward corners, that ratio was better achieved by minimising the weight than by maximising the power, and the chassis for the 30/98 was schemed accordingly. Light and flexible, it had much in common with that of the 3-litre racers built by Vauxhall for the popular Coupe de l'Auto events accompanying the annual Grands Prix of the Automobile Club de France. What most distinguished it from these was its rear suspension, the usual live axle being carried at the extremities of fully cantilevered half-elliptic springs. Compared with conventional semi-elliptics, cantilever springs gave better ride and roadholding because less of their material counted as unsprung mass. The stressing of the spring leaves was better controlled, the lateral stiffness of their mountings ensured more precise location of the axle, and the self-damping characteristic inherent in multi-leaf springs was more consistent in its effect. At that time even Rolls-Royce only fitted such springs to the most rare and sporting of its 40/50 hp cars; LHP added them to his luxury tourers too, though in later years they were to disappear

from some models, including the 30/98.

The later cars were heavier anyway (the same blight afflicted all cars as the 1920s progressed) so ratios of sprung to unsprung masses were less problematic. The 1913 30/98 was very light indeed, however, with a slim but remarkably handsome body panelled in aluminium and looking very much like a roadgoing version of a contemporary GP car. It was entirely consonant with that spirit that the car had no brakes on its front wheels: no GP car yet had, and although the brakes at the rear had been made bigger than on the Prince Henry, it was widely known that vast brakes were not needed for a car designed to go fast up hills....

Mr Higginson demonstrated this quite conclusively. The car made its debut at the

BELOW & RIGHT *One of the last of the line, a 1927 30/98 with its spartan interior*

Waddington Fells event, where it made fastest time of day. Before the year was out, it had scored similar successes at Aston Clinton, Caerphilly and – most important of all venues in the British hillclimb calendar – at Shelsley Walsh, where it set a new record of 55.2 seconds (with four people aboard!) that was to be trimmed by less than ten seconds before Hans von Stuck brought his European Championship Austro-Daimler to the starting-line in 1930.

Lest it be thought that the 30/98 was fit only for climbing, it was entered for the speed trials held at Southport, Yorkshire, where car and motorcycle competitions were for many years run on the remarkably amenable sands of the beach. Over the flying kilometre, the 30/98 was the fastest vehicle there in 1913. In the following year, another finished second in the Russian Grand Prix.

Of the thirteen examples built before the Great War stopped production, some went to Australia where Vauxhall had a very enterprising agent named Bud Edkins. While the war was on, he used a 30/98 to break the existing records for the runs from Sydney to Melbourne and from Brisbane to Sydney, ensuring so brisk a demand for the car that two-thirds of post-war production went to Australia. Considering all that was involved – distances, surfaces, temperatures, and assorted other natural hazards, many of them mobile – the success of the car Down Under demonstrated that it was by no means a mere hillclimb special, but rather an exceptional high-speed roadster.

What made it really exceptional, particularly in its native English environment, was that the car was also a superb low-speed potterer, as much at ease meandering through Sussex lanes as hurtling up the Great North Road or charging across Alston Moor. It might not have much in the way of brakes, but their absence from the front axle left the steering deliciously light and accurate. The Hele-Shaw clutch (an expensive low-inertia multi-plate device) made light of the left foot's work, and the gearbox was a pleasant one despite its wide ratios – not that one often had recourse to it, so all-encompassing was the pulling power of that astonishingly flexible engine.

The recommended drill, according to the handbook, was to start off in first or second gear with the engine doing a lazy 250 rpm, and to move progressively into fourth gear with the least practicable variation in engine speed. Top gear acceleration was ample for most needs and adequate for all: one could positively romp up a long and fairly steep hill (the one from Stanmore up to Bentley Priory is the instance I recall), starting from the bottom at walking pace in top gear. With foot hard down, despite the 5:1 compression

TOP *This specially modified 30/98 covered 106.9 miles in the hour at Montlhéry in 1953, a major achievement for so old a car*

ratio and the mediocre fuel of the old days, one simply advanced the ignition lever as the speed rose.

There was none of the harshness and commotion typical of sports cars of the Vintage period, from the Great War to 1930. Bentleys and Aston Martins and the like were very solid and uncompromising adaptations of competition machinery, all thump and whine and crackle. The Vauxhall was quite different, having evolved from those lightly constructed, superbly balanced and moderately stressed high-performance supercars which were some of the noblest products of the Edwardian era, and which prompted Pom Junior to write that 'between 1885 and 1895, men contrived to make cars run; between 1895 and 1905 they made them run properly; and between 1905 and 1915 they made them run beautifully'.

The fact that the 30/98 did not have a dramatically successful competition career after the Great War does not imply that it was inferior to those cars which did. The fact is rather that competition had become so specialised that it called for purpose-built cars which were not always at ease on the public highway, in marked contrast to the similarly purpose-built 30/98 of 1913, which would be at ease there even now if it had adequate brakes. While Bentleys and Bugattis and such became race-famous cars to show off, the Vauxhall – like the race-shy Rolls-Royce and Hispano-Suiza – was a car to use.

Nevertheless it had to be developed as the times demanded. In 1919 it went back into production, at a price which could be as high as £1950, depending on the bodywork – but at least it now had full electrical equipment. About two hundred were made before the OE replaced the E-type, in the late summer of 1922. The O signified overhead valves, as it did in the OD 23/60 which replaced the D-type at the same time: pushrod-operated, they were accompanied by a reduction in engine dimensions to 4¼ litres, the combined effect being to allow the crankshaft to spin at 3500 rpm (as fast as the new 3-litre Bentley) and develop 110 bhp. The car could decently keep its Velox model-name: with a slightly lower axle ratio than the 3:1 of the E-type (to compensate for the higher rpm and also the greater weight of the OE car) it had better acceleration than before and could still do about 85 mph (137 kph), again according to bodywork. If asked, Vauxhall would readily prepare a car specially and guarantee that it would do 100 mph (161 khp) at Brooklands.

Being able to demonstrate such speed at Brooklands was a major sales feature for the influence of achievements at that Surrey circuit filtered through to all levels of the motoring public. Removed from the open sweeps of the Brooklands banking, reproducing such speeds on the open road might be a different matter, however!

More often they were asked to make it stop better, and soon the OE had four-wheel brakes, distinguished by a kidney-box on the front axle housing the cross-compensation device for the cables. Demand for the car

EVOLUTION

Prototype 30/98 introduced in 1913

1919 Vauxhall 30/98 E Type introduced. It was a sports tourer with a light ladder-frame chassis with a subframe to support the engine and gearbox. The four-cylinder 5425 cc engine was a fixed-head unit developing 90 bhp at 3000 rpm and suspension was non-independent with semi-elliptic leaf springs front and rear. The final drive was a straight-cut bevel gear and the car had rear-wheel drums and transmission brake. It was sold either as a chassis, for bespoke bodywork, or with the works-built Velox four-seat open tourer body. Top speed with the latter was 85 mph (137 kph). Total production: 274

1923 30/98 OE Type announced. The engine was fitted with overhead valves and the stroke was shortened to give a capacity of 4224 cc. Power output went up to 115 bhp at 3300 rpm, and the unit was both quieter and more flexible than that of the E Type. The chassis was made of heavier-gauge steel and a spiral-bevel rear axle was introduced. Towards the end of the year four-wheel braking arrived

1925 The engine was further improved with the addition of a balanced crankshaft and larger diameter main bearings. Power output was increased to 120 bhp at 3500 rpm

1926 Hydraulic brakes introduced

1927 30/98 discontinued. Total production (OE Type) 312

continued (especially from Australia) and rather more than three hundred of the OE model were built for people who recognised their superb qualities as fast road cars. Even their bodywork was envied: W.O. Bentley admitted having the utmost difficulty in making a body for his 3-litre which would be as light, as slim, and as good-looking, as the usual 30/98 body and still have practical seating for two passengers in the rear.

People have an unfortunate way of comparing the Velox with the 4½-litre Bentley, despite the fact that production of the former ceased as that of the latter began. They were very different cars. I have seen them matched at the Brighton speed trials: the Bentley overhauled the Vauxhall as the latter used up its intermediate gears, and then ran away from it with an almost insolent display of close-ratio gearchanging which carried it through most of the standing kilometre. On the other hand I have seen a 30/98 running quietly and serenely fast ahead of a whole bellowing field of Bentleys and other reput-

LEFT & BELOW *A 30/98 OE from the last year of production, 1927. By that stage the 30/98 had hydraulic rather than mechanical brakes and some had engines which produced up to 120 bhp*

able Vintage sports cars around the circuit at Gransden Lodge.

Maybe it was one of the very late 30/98 cars, the small batch built just before production ceased. They had balanced crankshafts making them smoother running, able to develop 120 bhp. They had a closer-ratio gearbox, taken from the recent sleeve-valved 25/70 S-type Vauxhall. They also had, likewise from that very heavy but otherwise admirable S-type, large and impressive-looking hydraulic brakes. What a pity that the car's production should have been stopped just when its reputation for being unstoppable looked like being corrected!

Many owners of the Velox in later years took their own measures to improve braking. Most popular was the substitution of a Delage front axle, with which it could be stopped quite well, but with which it did not steer nearly as nicely, even when wedges were packed under the spring-pads to increase the caster angle. One might have supposed that Vauxhall could have done better themselves, but there was a hint in their withdrawal from official competition in 1923 that all was no longer well with their fortunes. The wild fluctuations in the post-war market had left them less secure, and when General Motors came looking for

manufacturing facilities in England they encountered no great resistance to their offer to acquire all Vauxhall's ordinary shares, which they did in 1925. By 1927, with new designs readied to attract the volume sales that GM sought, the production of the OE and others of its ilk had to stop.

The new Vauxhalls were just not the same, but this old Vauxhall carried on as it always had. In 1953 a 29-years-old OE, owned and driven by Mr T.H. Plowman, went onto the rough concrete of the banked *piste de vitesse* at Montlhéry (where, not long earlier, Riley had been forced to spend a week binding springs and generally reinforcing their 2½-litre car before it could attempt the same sort of thing) and covered 107 miles (172 km) in one hour. Similar cars, now about 60 years old, continue to do well in Vintage competition, and continue to be enjoyed on the road. There is just no stopping them….

Vauxhall 30/98s continue to be sought after and successful cars in many spheres of the Vintage motoring scene in the UK, whether it is taking part in high-speed trials, autotests or shows. The 30/98 continues to prove itself a rugged and fast car capable of outperforming many more overtly sporting machines.

TRIUMPH TR 2/3

They were the models which established the TR line and proved that the company could make high-performance cars

SOME CARS ARE LUCKY, and some are not. Some succeed after a rather rocky start and others fail. The Triumph TR series undoubtedly falls into the first category, for its launch could not have been less favourable. Yet for nine years the same well-known range of sports cars sold strongly – more than 80,000 were built – and the car put the Triumph name firmly back on the motoring map.

It all started in the early 1950s, when Standard-Triumph's chairman, Sir John Black, was inspired to produce a sports car for export. Standard had bought the corporate remains of the bankrupt and bombed-out Triumph company in 1944, and in the first few post-war years had offered several undistinguished Triumphs such as the 1800/2000 Roadster, the Renown saloon and the quaint little Mayflower.

In the meantime, MG produced the TC and TD sports cars, and Jaguar produced the famous XK120. Both took the United States by storm, and consequently Sir John Black took the attitude that if they could succeed in the States, so could he – and that was the way it looked to his colleagues.

It couldn't be done overnight, however. First Sir John encouraged his chief styling engineer, Walter Belgrove, to produce a new Roadster (the TRX) on a Standard Vanguard chassis, but it had a bulbous shape, too many complicated electro-hydraulic controls and never got beyond the prototype stage. Next, Sir John tried to take over the Morgan company, but after being rebuffed at the end of 1951, he decided to have another attempt 'in house'.

Thus the real TR story began early in 1952, on a minimum-cost/minimum tooling basis. The engineers and chief designer Harry Webster were encouraged to use as many existing Standard components as possible, while Walter Belgrove was offered a mere £16,000 budget for body tooling, a ludicrously low figure even in 1952. The result was that the design used an obsolete

RIGHT *The interior of a 1960 Triumph TR3A, a model first introduced in 1958. It had a wide grille and front disc brakes*

1936–39 type of Standard Flying Nine chassis frame (of which more than 500 examples were in stock in the Spares department!) to which a Triumph Mayflower's coil-spring independent front suspension and live rear axle were grafted. The wet-liner Standard Vanguard engine was reduced in size from 2088 cc to 1991 cc by using smaller bore pistons, and was slightly tuned by the addition of twin SU carburettors, while the Vanguard's three-speed gearbox was converted to a four-speed with a central gear change.

Belgrove's style was surprisingly close to that finally used in production, except that there was a short, tucked-in tail, with an exposed spare wheel, and with the fuel tank's filler protruding through its centre.

Even Harry Webster now agrees that the original 20TS concept was not a success, and although the prototype shown at the 1952 Earls Court exhibition was one full step further advanced, it was still no beauty. That first car was built in just eight weeks, with an improved (though still not rigid enough) chassis frame, and with a remote-control change. Almost before it had run on the roads it was shown to the world, with a provisional price tag of £555 (basic), and a 75 bhp engine; its top speed was claimed (but not measured) to be 90 mph (145 kph).

Such claimed performance figures were quite impressive for the immediate post-war years and perhaps are as much as might have been expected from such an assemblage of everyday production items. However, any announcements of the car's price and performance were soon proved to have been a little premature.

Immediately after the show, a seasoned driver/tester/mechanic, Ken Richardson, who had long been involved with the V16 BRM project and who was a confidant of Raymond Mays, was invited to try the car and offer his opinions. This he did, and after a relatively short outing was so appalled by the car's behaviour that he returned and told the startled Standard directors: 'I think it's the most awful car I've ever driven in my life. It's a death trap!'

As *The Motor* wrote at a later date: 'At this point the Standard company might well have

thanked Richardson politely for his expert opinion, but pointed out that questions of production made it impossible to carry out any fundamental alterations to the design. And if they had done so, the TR would have died very soon after its birth…'.

However, the directors not only listened, but acted. Richardson was invited to join the company to develop a better TR, and Harry Webster's team was given a mere three months to transform its behaviour.

Thus it was that the definitive TR – the TR2 – was first seen at the Geneva Show of March 1953. The TR1, by the way, is a name retrospectively given to the original 20TS prototype.

The TR2, rapidly prepared for production, was a much more rugged car. The engineers had produced an entirely new box-section chassis frame, allied to an improved and tuned 90 bhp engine, and Belgrove's team had reworked the rear of the body, slotting the spare wheel away out of sight under the boot and squaring and lengthening the tail. Most important of all, Ken Richardson had put in many high-speed hours at the industry's MIRA proving ground, testing the components.

Thus, from its origins as an evil-handling 90 mph 'mongrel', the project had moved rapidly, so that the TR2's handling was much more predictable and the top speed was comfortably over 100 mph (161 kph). The development engineers were also delighted to discover that the engine was extremely fuel-efficient; if the optional Laycock de Normanville overdrive were fitted, the car could be driven hard and still over 30 mpg.

There was still, however, a major marketing problem. Whereas the MG, Jaguar and Healey sports cars already had established reputations, the Triumph TR2 had none. Sports car customers would sign an order for one of the aforementioned without even taking a test drive, because they knew and trusted the heritage. But what did they know about the TR2, and Triumph? Nothing – the car had no pedigree.

Standard-Triumph could, at least, prove a point by showing that the car was fast, so Ken Richardson took a prototype (MVC 575)

to the Jabbeke motor road in Belgium for speed trials. On 20 May 1953 he drove a mechanically standard car, with nothing but an aeroscreen and a full-length undershield to improve the aerodynamics, at 124.9 mph (201 kph). Even in full touring trim, with hood, screen, and side-screens erect (though still with the undershield in place) the car achieved 114.9 mph (185 kph).

Production of the TR2 got under way slowly in the summer of 1953 (the Austin-Healey 100, also previewed at the 1952 motor show, beat it to the showrooms by several months), and only 248 cars were actually delivered before the end of the year. Nevertheless, that did not disappoint the factory hierarchy, for the original plan had been to produce only 500 cars a year.

Things improved early in 1954, especially after *The Autocar* published a very favourable road test, in which their car achieved not only 103 mph (166 kph) and 0-60 mph (97 kph) in 11.9 seconds, but the quite remarkable fuel consumption figure of 32 mpg overall. Both at home and in the USA, the TR2 offered very good value for money. By mid-1954, when its reputation was becoming established, the TR2's all-in UK price of £887 compared very favourably with that of £780 for an MG TF, £1064 for an Austin-Healey 100 and £1602 for the Jaguar XK120.

Its pedigree, too, was rapidly refined, for not only did the TR2 establish itself as a

robust and reliable club rally car, but it achieved major competition successes. In March 1954, privately-owned TR2s took first, second and fifth places overall in the RAC International rally (John Wallwork driving the winning car, and Peter Cooper – now chief executive at the RAC's Motor Sport Association – runner up). In May, Ken Richardson and Maurice Gatsonides finished 27th overall in the Mille Miglia, at an average speed of 73 mph (117 kph). A month later Edgar Wadsworth's privately-owned car finished 15th (at 74.7 mph/120 kph in atrocious conditions) in the Le Mans 24 hours, while at the next big event in the calendar, the French Alpine rally, the TR2s won the manufacturers' team prize, and Gatsonides won a Coupe des Alpes for a clear run.

That did it. In Europe the TR2 had made its name as a strong, robust, 2-litre sports car, while in the USA it was rapidly being seen as an obvious alternative to MGs and

Austin-Healeys. Even though the MGA of 1955 was a vastly better car than the TF which it replaced, and the Austin-Healey was gradually improved, the TR family never looked back.

The TR2 had a very definite character, but not all of it was likeable. By the end of 1954 it could be ordered with overdrive, centre-lock wire wheels, and a removable hardtop, but less attractive was its very barky and boomy exhaust note, its hard and bumpy ride, its drum brakes which tended to grab when abused, and the way that the car would suddenly swop ends on slippery corners, especially if the optional Michelin X radial tyres were fitted.

But it was so reliable, and such good value, its owners seemed to forgive it anything. Spare parts were cheap and rarely seemed to be needed, and the engine was so rugged that it seemed to go on and on for years needing nothing more than routine

attention. It was surprisingly economical even when used for rallying, and unless you bent the chassis frame when crashing the car, it was quite cheap to repair.

From 1953 to the end of 1962, when the very last of this TR series was built, the cars were always recognisably the same. Badges changed, engines were slightly improved, grilles came, altered, and widened, but the TR went on and on. At its peak, in 1959, a total of 21,298 cars was delivered, the vast majority of them going overseas, and only 638 spared for the home market. The British sports car makers relied very much on the USA for sales, and the best year for TR sales in the UK was 1955, when 1730 were made available.

It is worth looking at the TRs specifications to see why they appealed so much to the enthusiasts of the day. At first the cars had what the aficionados now call 'long doors', but these were soon shortened so that they could, at least, be opened against a high kerb, and thereafter it was easy to get into or out of a TR2 or TR3. The seating position was low, necessitating a straight-legged posture. The gear-lever was short and stubby, with a quite delightful short-action change, and if the overdrive was fitted it was controlled by a switch on the instrument panel, close to the steering wheel rim. The handbrake, to the left of the transmission tunnel, had a fly-off action and was very powerful.

The Motor admitted that no '...pretence could be made that the chassis and suspension are at all advanced, and the result of orthodox layout is the expected compromise between comfort and road-holding.' They found that the TR3's back end would slide quite easily and was extremely sensitive to the type of tyres and their inflation pressures, finding that softer tyres at the front, '...serve to increase the understeering tendency which is inherent but not objectionable.' Overall the verdict was that the TR had '...shortcomings but no vices; the TR3 offers a great deal at a modest price...'.

very snug in winter. All these factors helped make it an extremely satisfactory rally car.

It was one of those cars which got better, season after season, because the changes all seemed to have been done with the enthusiast, and performance, in mind. All, that is, except the arrival of the full-width grill in 1958, which was strictly for American notions of taste....

By 1955, when it evolved into the TR3, the original TR2 had been much improved. The TR3 now had an egg-box grille in the nose instead of the open air-intake, while the engine power had been pushed up from 90 bhp to 95 bhp. That, incidentally, was the start of the process which showed that as the power went up, the fuel efficiency went down. The '56 was a good car, but the 1957

RIGHT AND BOTTOM RIGHT *Two racing TR3s, the first being that of Reg Woodcock who has enjoyed years of success with the car*

model was even better, for that particular TR3 became one of the first British series production car to be fitted with front-wheel disc brakes as standard.

Now that even the humble Metro, or Fiesta, has servo-assisted discs, it is difficult to recall just what a stir this innovation made. At a stroke, it seemed, the spectre of high-speed brake fade had gone for good, and the car which had been a good rally car now became a truly formidable machine.

In 1958 it became even more attractive. The TR3A (although the car was never actually badged as such) was given a new nose-panel with full-width grill, the 100 bhp engine recently phased in for TR3s was standardised and lockable handles were fitted to the doors and boot lid. American sales soared – over 300 cars were exported every week – and the TR3A became as typical a British sports car as any MG. This, by the way, made the Abingdon-traditionalists furious, and inter-marque rivalry intensified.

In the meantime, Triumph had set up a works competition team, which notched up more and more successes. In 1955 a trio of

The engine was extremely torquey, and most TR drivers learned to keep it booming away between about 3000 rpm and 5000 rpm. With overdrive they had no fewer than seven forward ratios, for overdrive was available on second, third and fourth gears.

It was even a joy to top up with fuel, for with 30 mpg (which dropped to about 26 mpg on later derivatives) the running costs were not high. Behind the cockpit, centrally located, was a fat, chrome-plated, snap-action filler cap, and nothing – not even the flow from modern electric pumps – could ever overload that amply-proportioned neck.

Most enthusiasts liked to drive their TRs with the hood down and the side-screens stowed, but even with all the weather-protection in place (especially if the optional hardtop was fitted), there was excellent all-round visibility. Heaters were not standard (but usually fitted), and made the interior

EVOLUTION

Introduced at the 1952 Earls Court Motor Show, the Triumph 20TS prototype (retrospectively known as the TR1) was an open two-seater based on a stiffened Standard Flying Nine chassis and fitted with a moderately tuned 75 bhp, 2-litre Standard Vanguard engine. Its top speed was claimed to be 90 mph (145 kph). When Ken Richardson, an experienced driver and engineer, test-drove the 20TS, he found it to be extremely dangerous, and the car underwent extensive modification

1953 The TR2 was unveiled at the Geneva Motor Show in March, an open two-seater with redesigned and smoother body, a new box-section chassis frame and the engine improved to produce 90 bhp. It had a maximum speed of 103 mph (166 kph), a 0-60 mph time of 12.6 seconds and an overall fuel consumption of 31 mpg

1954 The TR2 hard-top version became available (the roof was made of glassfibre), and other options included overdrive and wire wheels. Modifications included larger drum-brakes at the rear, stiffer sills and increased kerb-clearance for the doors

1955 The TR3 was announced, with its engine further tuned to produce 95 bhp, Girling disc brakes fitted to the front wheels and an egg-box grille. Maximum speed was 110 mph (177 kph) and the 0–60 mph time was reduced to 11.4 seconds. Average fuel consumption was 27 mpg

1958 The TR3A was announced, fitted with a new nose panel with full-width grille, and engine power was increased to 100 bhp

1961 The TR3B was built for the American market, fitted with the forthcoming TR4's all-synchromesh gearbox and a choice of its 2 and 2.2-litre engines

cars entered, and finished, at Le Mans, but in the main the works TR was a rally car. There were many stirring performances, and high-lights included five Coupes, the manufactur-er's team prize in the 1956 French Alpine rally, third overall in the gruelling Liège–Rome–Liège, victory in the Circuit of Ireland in 1958 and second in the 1959 Tulip rally.

The important feature of the 1958 French Alpine was not just that the works cars beat the works Austin-Healeys, but that they used the enlarged 2138 cc engines for the first time, a unit that soon became optional on production cars (although very few were built), and was later standard on the early '60s TRs.

The TR3A's production-line performance peaked in 1960 and tailed off rapidly thereaf-ter. From about 1957, Standard-Triumph had been casting around for a replacement style for the car, but it was not until the autumn of 1961 that the TR4 was ready to go on sale. That car retained the same basic chassis design, but the Michelotti-styled bodyshell was completely new.

When the American dealers first saw the TR4 they apparently commented that it looked too smooth, too modern and too comfortable, and asked that the TR3A be continued. This request was granted, for one more season, and explains why there was a special American-specification TR3B, effec-tively the same structure as the TR3A, but with the TR4's new all-synchromesh trans-mission, and a choice of 2- or 2.2-litre TR4 engines.

The death of the TR3B, however, was not the end of this type of Triumph sports car, for it was progressively changed and im-proved until 1976. In 1965 a new chassis was introduced, in 1967 a new engine and in 1969 a major facelift gave new life.

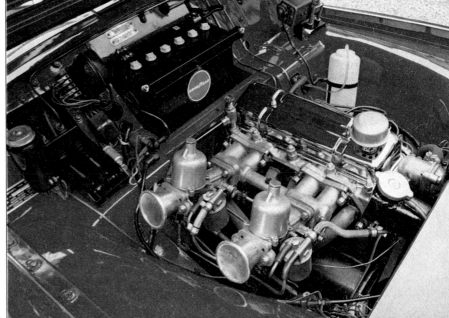

LEFT AND BELOW *Views of a 1960 TR3A, a car which was built to satisfy the enthusiast, being fast, attractive, reliable and relatively easy to maintain; the engine was very accessible and rarely gave trouble. The boot rack was a popular option, for boot space was limited, and with one the TR became a good tourer. Modest thirst for fuel was a major plus point of early TRs, with many miles possible between stops*

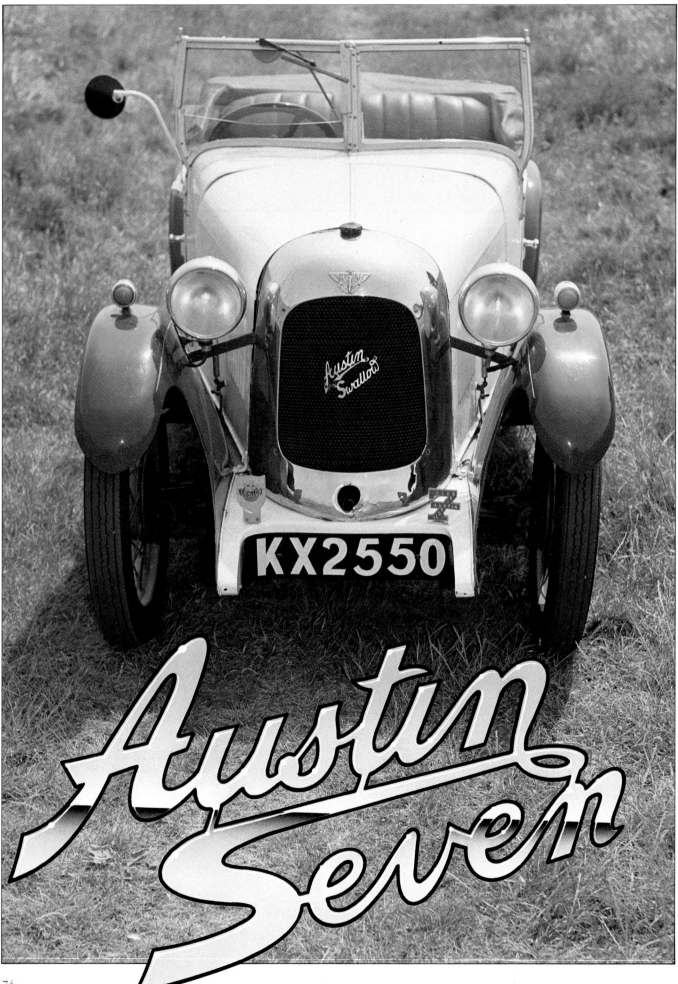

Austin Seven

WHEN AUSTIN ANNOUNCED its 696 cc Seven model in July 1922 it was the smallest capacity British made four-cylinder car on the market. It represented a considerable gamble by the Longbridge company which was just emerging from the most crucial financial period in its history and Sir Herbert Austin himself had personally financed the venture in the face of opposition from his co-directors.

In fact the Seven proved an outstanding success; it enjoyed a 17-year production run, from 1922 until 1939, and over 290,000 examples were built. The Seven was the best selling Austin model from 1926 until 1932 and production did not even peak until 1935. It also killed off the flimsy cycle car and provided transport for many families who might otherwise have gone by train.

Although Sir Herbert can be credited with the idea of producing a very small car, the concept of the diminutive four-cylinder engine, which was pivotal to the model's success, came from an 18-year-old draughtsman, Stanley Howard Edge.

Herbert Austin was 38 years old when he left the Wolseley company, where he was general manager, and established the Austin Motor Company in a former printing works at Longbridge, Birmingham in 1905. The coming of war in 1914 transformed the Longbridge works which, by the end of hostilities in 1918, had grown enormously. Sir Herbert, as he had become in 1917, decided to scrap his pre-war range and, like Henry Ford and his Model T, concentrate on just one model. That was the 3.6-litre Twenty, introduced at the end of 1919.

Although 4319 Twenties were built in 1920 demand fell off sharply at the end of the year when the post-war boom suddenly collapsed. Austin's problems were compounded when the so-called Horsepower Tax arrived in 1921 whereby a car's Road Fund Licence was dependent on the RAC horsepower rating. And at £1 per horse power, the Twenty rated at 22.4 hp, which meant the luckless owner would have to pay a £22 yearly tax.

This ill thought-out tax did a great deal to influence the development of the British car industry in those interwar years. To an extent it gave rise to a generation of tax-efficient cars, many of which were inappropriate to important overseas markets or just plain boring. Be that as it may, Austin needed a new car quickly..

The firm's finances suffered to such an extent that, in the April of 1921 (a year of ferocious depression throughout Britain) a receiver was appointed on behalf of the Midland Bank and the Eagle Star Insurance Company, Austin's principal creditors. What was required was a new, smaller car; Sir Herbert realised that with the Twenty he had introduced the wrong model at the wrong time. He took the large car's design and scaled it down to make a 1.6-litre version. Despite the commercial potential of such a model, the receiver would not sanction funds for its development, so Austin was forced to raise funds by selling unwanted

The Austin Seven of 1922 was the first civilised motor car of truly small proportions. It managed to breed contempt and inspire loyalty for nearly two decades

plant and stock. His fortitude was rewarded for after the new Twelve had arrived in 1921 it was soon outselling its larger brother, and remained in production until 1935; it was even produced in taxi form until the outbreak of World War II.

But Sir Herbert wanted another string to his bow. What was required, he felt, was a really small car, rather in the manner of the 8 hp air-cooled two-cylinder Rover, introduced in 1920. Yet although Austin was an accomplished stylist and possessed great drive and determination he was no innovator and was usually content to rely on other manufacturers to provide the inspiration for his designs. He needed someone well acquainted with current design trends who could be used as a foil for his ideas. Fortunately he had found such a person in the Austin drawing office – an 18-year-old draughtsman named Stanley Edge.

Stanley Edge, born in 1903, is a Black Countryman, who hails from Old Hill, Staffordshire. He had been attracted by engineering while at school and asked his father to see if there were any vacancies in the Longbridge drawing office. He did just that and took some examples of Stanley's engineering drawings to the chief draughtsman at the Austin works. This resulted in young Edge getting a job with the firm in August 1917. Soon he began attending the Austin technical college.

At this time aircraft were being produced at Longbridge and Stanley began in the aviation drawing office. But this was no more than a war-time interlude; he was advised to transfer to the car side of the

LEFT *A 1929 Austin Swallow – a conversion available with hood, detachable coupé or hard top*
ABOVE *A 1927 Austin Chummy*

business and this he did by the time the Armistice was signed in November 1918. However, as Stanley used to travel by train line between Old Hill and Longbridge he would arrive at work at 8 am on the only available train, and an hour earlier than the rest of the staff. The office was empty at this time with the exception of Sir Herbert Austin himself and as Edge later remembered: 'we began to discuss design together'.

When Stanley Edge returned from his summer holidays in August 1921, his boss A.J. Hancock wanted to see him 'and when he asked me to sit down I thought I was going to be asked to leave the company'. He asked Edge how he would feel about going to work with Sir Herbert Austin at his home, Lickey Grange. (This was because, although Edge did not know it at the time, Austin had been unable to get any support within the factory for his small car project, so was financing it out of his own pocket).

So, in September 1921, Stanley Edge began work at the Grange; all day Edge worked in the billiards room at the Grange and Austin would arrive in the evening to discuss what he had achieved.

Austin had already done some preliminary work on the design of his baby car. Not surprisingly his first thoughts for a small Austin closely followed the lines of the Tyseley-built air-cooled twin but the Rover was a noisy and crude contraption and Stanley wasted little time in pointing out its deficiencies. It says much for the youngster's direct and informed approach that he was able to get the 55-year-old Austin to abandon the idea of twin and adopt, instead, a small water-cooled four.

Even at this early stage, Stanley Edge was convinced of the need to make the new car every bit as appealing as the much larger, sophisticated machines. By that token, anything less than a four-cylinder engine would be second best. Similarly he saw the need to build the car well and solidly, and in no sense create a simple cyclecar.

Not that Sir Herbert gave up without a fight. For a time the pair wrestled with the pros and cons of a three-cylinder engine while a further excursion into unorthodoxy had a rear-mounted three-cylinder radial engine with the car's wheels set out in a diamond pattern. It was not until the early months of 1922 that these deliberations came to an end for Austin was convinced by Edge that a small four could be produced almost as cheaply as a two-cylinder motor. It would also be far smoother and more refined than the twin.

Edge had compiled a list of 26 small cars, the specifications of which he had culled from the pages of *Motor Trader* magazine. The one that really caught Austin's eye was the 668 cc Peugeot Quadrilette which at the time was the world's smallest production four. Peugeot had established a tradition for building such cars which dated back to 1912 when it introduced its Ettore Bugatti-designed Bébé but the 1920 Quadrilette, with its unusual tandem seating, was even smaller. Austin was sufficiently convinced

EVOLUTION

The Austin Seven was announced in July 1922 to become the smallest capacity British four-cylinder, with a displacement of just 696 cc

1923 Engine size was increased from 696 cc to 748 cc thanks to an increase in bore size. A fan was added to the engine and an electric starter introduced

1924 The Sports Tourer introduced

1926 The Seven Saloon was introduced

1927 A fabric-bodied version was introduced but only built until 1930

1928 The 'Top Hat' body style was introduced and a nickel-plated radiator replaced the painted type

1929 The lowered Ulster Seven was introduced with optional Cozette supercharger

1930 The brake system became entirely foot operated

1931 Wheelbase and rear track were increased

1933 A four-speed gearbox was introduced and the brakes and tyres uprated. The Opal two-seater was introduced, along with the lowered 65 Seven which had an engine tuned to produce 23 bhp at 4800 rpm

1934 The 65 was renamed the Nippy and the Speedy introduced. Synchromesh appeared on third and fourth gears and the Ruby was introduced along with the Pearl Cabriolet

1936 A central main bearing was added to the 748 cc engine along with a new cylinder head and different spark plugs. Power output was increased to 17 bhp. A twin-cam single seater was introduced for competition. Girling hydraulic brakes replaced the cable variety

1939 The final Austin Seven was built on 17 January

LEFT *Sevens from 1930 to 1934 illustrating the development of body styles of this popular little car*

for Edge to begin, 'I was the only man on this work and I made out arrangements of detail drawings of everything'. Although the Peugeot had provided the inspiration for the baby Austin for its detail design Edge was inspired by yet another European manufacturer. A keen motor cyclist, he had been much impressed by the four-cylinder Belgian FN and the lower half of the Seven's engine, with its two roller-bearing splash-lubricated crankshaft, were inspired by this motor cycle unit. The remainder of the design followed traditional Austin practice; a side-valve cylinder block, with detachable head, bolted directly on an aluminium crankcase. As designed by Edge, the Seven had a capacity of 696 cc (55 × 77 mm) and a 7.2 hp RAC rating. Edge was also responsible for calculating the ratios in the three-speed gearbox, the clutch dimensions and the transmission specifications. He was not, however, responsible for the rest of the car, as he was first and foremost an engine specialist.

The chassis, steering box and brakes, along with the designs for the coachwork can be regarded as Austin's contribution to the Seven. He adopted an A-frame chassis and it seems likely that the transverse leaf front and quarter-elliptic rear suspension were borrowed from the Peugeot as were the similar wire-spoked wheels. However, the Seven boasted four-wheel brakes, a revolutionary feature for a small car even though they could hardly be regarded as particularly efficient. All the design work was completed by the Easter of 1922 and on the Tuesday after the holiday, Stanley returned to Longbridge carrying the precious drawings of the Seven. A small section of the works was boarded off so the construction of the prototypes could proceed unimpeded. In addition to Stanley there was works superintendent McLellan, along with foreman Alf Depper, four mechanics and an apprentice. The intention was to have three cars completed by Whitsun.

The Midland Motor Cylinder Company

cast the tiny block and Edge can still recall the astonishment of the MMCC men when they first saw the drawings of the tiny block with 3/32 in between the cylinder walls and the eight minute valve chambers. The crankshafts and rods were machined from solid at Longbridge while Stirling Metals produced the aluminium crankcase, Zenith the carburettor and Watford the magneto.

All three cars were ready for a works gathering held at Longbridge at Whitsun. Although the design of the engine and gearbox had been resolved, each of the prototype Sevens had different transmission arrangements. One had an open propeller shaft, the second had the 'shaft contained within a torque tube while the third, which was adopted for production, had a half open shaft and a half closed one. Edge recalls that the example with an open shaft was particularly difficult to drive, 'It hopped like a kangaroo and Sir Herbert shot off like a rocket between the shop buildings'.

Soon afterwards Edge was present when Austin was familiarly addressed by a young man who arrived, unannounced, at the office, challenging Sir Herbert with 'so this is where you hide yourself away'. A rather stilted conversation followed and Edge produced the Seven's drawings, as they were required. The conversation ended with the young man telling Austin. 'My dear sir, the public will just not stand for this'. Austin responded with similar intransigence. 'My dear sir, I am educating the public'. After the visitor's departure, Austin told Edge his identity; he was William (Billy) Rootes, soon to head the country's largest car distributors and to co-found, with his brother Reginald, the Rootes Group in the 1930s.

Details of the new model were unveiled in the motoring press in July 1922. In the first instance it was only available in open form. It was a real four-seater although only children could be carried in the rear, so it was aimed foursquare at the family man and even though its top speed was around the 38 mph (61 kph) mark, it was a lion-hearted performer. Turning the scales at a mere 6.5 cwt (330 kg), it cost just £165 when it was introduced. On its launch *The Light Car and Cyclecar* commented, 'What more could a man of moderate means want for his money?'.

The public had the first real opportunity of viewing the Austin Seven at the 1922 Motor Show but the model got off to a slow start and only 1936 were built in 1923, the first year of production. By December a number of changes had been made to the original specification. The first came in March when the engine's capacity was increased from 696 cc to 748 cc, achieved by upping the bore size from 55 mm to 56 mm.

BOTTOM LEFT *Sir Herbert Austin posing with the Austin Seven racing team which enjoyed considerable success, particularly at Brooklands*

This resulted in the engine's RAC rating also increasing, to 7.8 hp. Then, in October, a fan was added to the engine. Originally it had not been included on cost grounds but the little unit overheated somewhat, so it was found necessary to fit one. This required that the position of the water outlet pipe be changed and Stanley Edge, who had by then returned to his job in the drawing office, accordingly made the alterations. In December another cost-conscious feature was discontinued. This was a mechanical starter positioned on top of the flywheel. The Seven's owner was intended to grasp the T-shaped handle and pull it smartly as if he were starting a motor mower. It was replaced by a conventional electric starter.

However, the performance of the starter, and, it should be said, the whole electrical system was not all it might be and the starting handle remained a prominent feature on the front of the car below the radiator, allowing the hapless driver to jump out and manually rotate the small, low compression engine, should the need arise.

Sales for 1924 were better at 4700 and the car also benefited from the fitment of a speedometer. That year an open Sports Tourer was introduced alongside the Chummy although as the two-seater with its distinctive pointed tail merely had standard mechanical parts it was no great performer. The really significant year for the Seven was 1926 when 14,000 left Longbridge making it the best selling Austin and justifying Sir Herbert's faith in the project. In addition the

ABOVE & RIGHT *A 1934 Austin Seven Box Saloon Deluxe – note the forward mounted lamps, deeper wings and plated radiator, developed from the 65 Seven*

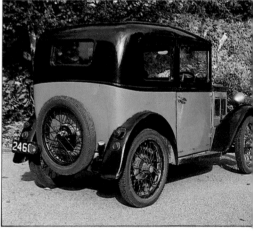

firm's board of directors had granted him a £2 royalty on each one built which must have given him great cause for satisfaction. A saloon version of the Seven arrived in May of the same year and in 1927 a fashionable fabric variant appeared. It proved popular for a time but was discontinued in 1930; the metal saloon was more enduring. The wide-door, so-called Top Hat arrived in 1928, the same year in which the painted radiator gave way to a nickel-finished one. Coil ignition replaced the magneto for 1929 while in 1930 came a much needed improvement to the braking system. Originally the cable operated brakes were uncoupled with the foot brake operating on the rear wheels and the handbrake responsible for the front ones. This endured until July 1930 when the entire system became foot operated although, it has to be said, it still left much to be desired!

It was in 1930 that the Austin Seven showed that it was just as effective on the race track as it was on the road when an example, driven by *The Autocar's* Sammy Davis and the Earl of March, gained a victory in the 500 Miles race held at Brooklands. This success represented the culmination of

eight years of development with the model. For, back in July 1922 just after Austin had announced the car, an example was placed third in its class in the Shelsley Walsh hill climb. Then, in March 1923 Austin's son-in-law, Arthur Waite won a Brooklands handicap event and the following month took a Seven to Monza, of all places, for the Cyclecar Grand Prix. Again the Seven proved victorious and lapped the Italian circuit at 55.86 mph (89.9 kph). E.C. Gordon England was then approached and began a spectacular racing career at Brooklands with the Seven breaking numerous long distance records. He also maintained the model's 1923 momentum by being placed second in the 1100 cc class in the 200 Miles Race at the same track.

In 1924 the Austin factory introduced its own Sports model which was good for around 50 mph (80 kph) but the same year Gordon England, who also owned a coachbuilding works, introduced his own Brooklands Super Sports, which was lower than the standard car and capable of 75 mph (120 kph). To prove his point he won the new 750 class in the 1924 200 Miles Race and to show that it was no flash in the pan he repeated the feat in 1925 and 1926. These successes culminated in Austin introducing its own lowered Ulster Seven in 1929 with optional Cozette supercharger.

In truth Austin had the 750 cc class very

much to itself until 1931 but that year MG introduced its 746 cc C-type Midget. Sir Herbert Austin's arch rival, Sir William Morris, had followed in the Seven's wheel tracks and introduced the 847 cc Minor in 1929, although its sophisticated overhead-cam engine was more at home in the M type MG introduced the same year. The smaller capacity C type was developed specifically for the class which the Sevens had dominated for so long and were immensely successful for the side-valvers were archaic by comparison. They trounced the Austins at the 1931 Double Twelve race; in addition, a continual ding-dong battle for record breaking resulted in the more modern cars from Abingdon having the upper hand, despite Sir Herbert having personally designed the bodywork for a supercharged single seater in 1931.

There was also the Rubber Duck team of Sevens but sadly the cars were plagued with cracked cylinder heads; despite this they managed a class win in the 1932 British Empire Trophy race. The Austin factory was impressed by the performance of an Ulster driven by young Tom Murray Jamieson and

LEFT AND BELOW *A 1934 Austin Seven Nippy; the Nippy was introduced in 1934 with an engine tuned to give 23 bhp, developed from the 65 Seven*

he was hired to sort out the works cars.

Jamieson was, alas, having to make the best of an ageing design although he produced an impressive streamlined single seater in 1935. Whenever Longbridge broke a record, however, MG got it back and Sir Herbert realised that if the Sevens were to make any real impact on the overhead-cam MGs, a completely new design a would be needed. So Jamieson was commissioned to design a new 744cc twin-cam single seater which appeared in 1936, but which falls outside the scope of this article. After some initial teething problems, the new cars found their form but the works MGs had disappeared from the racing circuits .because Leonard Lord, Morris's new managing director, had shut down the Abingdon racing department in 1935.

On the road-going Sevens bonnet louvres and trafficators arrived in 1931 and the following year interior accommodation was improved by the Seven's wheelbase being increased by 6 inches (15 cm) from 6 feet 3 inches (190 cm) while the rear track was upped from 3 feet 4 inches (101 cm) to 3 feet 7 inches (109 cm). For 1933 the gearbox received its first major revision since 1922 with the arrival of a crawler cog to make a four speed 'box. At the same time the petrol tank was removed from its traditional position beneath the scuttle, where it supplied the engine by gravity, to the rear. This meant that for the first time the Austin Seven boasted a petrol pump. There were larger

Although the Seven was powered by a diminutive 748 cc engine it was still strong enough to carry a van body, which was introduced in 1923 and continued until the war. The engine compartment of the first cars was even emptier, without even a cooling fan . . . which was added later in '23, along with an electric starter

brakes and wider tyres – Sir Herbert's baby was growing up. Another 1933 arrival was the Opal two seater which, in 1934, was offered in a £100 version. That year the traditional Austin radiator was replaced by a cowl, although the Opal was unique in that it perpetuated the original flat radiator design. Also new for 1933 was the open two-seater 65 Seven with lowered chassis and engine tuned and refined to give 23 bhp at 4800 rpm rather than the standard car's 12 bhp at 2600 rpm. This became the Nippy in 1934, the same year that the similar but more expensive Speedy arrived.

The Seven had benefited from synchromesh added to the third and top gears for 1934 and that year came the Ruby which perpetuated the precious stone theme of the Opal. This saloon boasted bumpers, recessed trafficators and the aforementioned cowled radiator. A Pearl Cabriolet arrived at the same time.

It was in 1935, when the Seven was 13 years old, that the model had its best ever production year when 27,280 cars left Longbridge. Then, in June of 1936, the first major revision to the Seven's engine appeared. Although the 748 cc engine remained inviolate, a central main bearing was introduced. Unlike the existing front and rear ones, which were of the roller variety, this was a plain bearing. A new cylinder head was introduced at the same time and 14 mm sparking plugs replaced the 18 mm ones that had been used hitherto. This resulted in output rising from 12 bhp at 3600 rpm to 17 at 3800. At the same time Girling brakes replaced the rather questionable cable-

operated drums that had sufficed until then. On a corporate front this was a big year for Sir Herbert Austin because he was made Baron Austin of Longbridge in Edward VII's one and only birthday honours.

For 1937 the long running Seven was replaced by the 900 cc Big Seven which was to outsell the older car by two to one in 1938. This was the last full year for the Seven but the model lasted into 1939 and the final car was built on 17 January. A van version, which had first appeared back in 1923, lasted about a month and a half longer and was made until 3 March.

Although the Seven had come to the end of the line, its engine continued for another 23 years under the bonnet of the Reliant van and subsequent car until it finally ceased production in 1962. Mention should also be made of the fact that the Seven was built under licence by the Dixi company in Germany from 1929 until 1932 by which time the firm had been taken over by BMW. Then there was a version by Lucien Rosengart in Paris though, perhaps inevitably, the American Austin Seven, the Bantam, never found its form. In Japan Datsun introduced its version of the design; there were significant mechanical changes although the 748 cc engine was retained.

Also it should not be forgotten that an Austin Seven formed the basis of the first car to be built by William Lyons, a young Blackpool coachbuilder, the stylish Swallow version being built between 1927 and 1932. It was to form the foundation of first the SS and so the Jaguar marque. Post-war, Colin Chapman's first Lotus cars sprang from a much modified Seven. One wonders what Lord Austin would have thought of that?

When an aircraft company sets out to make a car it should be superb – the six-cylinder Bristols were, and sophisticated and expensive

AT A CONCOURS IN THE AUTUMN of 1985 I met a man who had recently acquired a Bristol; it was a quarter of a century old, and he was amazed that a car with so many years behind it could put so much else behind it, with high-speed handling that was marvellous even by the standards of today. I knew the car, and was not surprised. I likewise knew a distinguished Norwegian motoring writer who was also present: he had lately bought an earlier model, over 30 years old, and had planned to take it back to Norway across the North Sea. When he began to drive it, he found it so delightful that he changed his plans and went home via Holland and Denmark so that he could enjoy the car more. Again, I was not surprised.

People who are not intimately familiar with Bristols are not exactly surprised either. *Suspicious* is more nearly the word, for *incredulous* is scarcely strong enough: their frank disbelief of the claims put forward for Bristols by those who know and love them may well be based on a proper disregard for the folly of enthusiasts, but these unbelievers invariably do not know, and therefore cannot be expected to know better.

Bristol themselves do nothing to help. They have consistently courted publicity less than any other motor manufacturer, in all the years they have been in business; and those years number as many as any car manufacturer outside the USA has been in continuous production. The origins of the firm are much older than that: today Bristol Cars is a little private company with premises on the edge of Filton aerodrome, but without tracing through to the old Bristol Tramways firm of the 19th century, it is easy enough to see the roots in the Bristol Aeroplane Company which had been busy at that airfield since 1910.

Before the outbreak of the World War in 1939, the Bristol Aeroplane Company was the largest single aircraft-manufacturing unit in the world, producing not only some remarkable 'planes but also some highly respected engines, the Jupiter radial for instance being licence-built in no fewer than 17 other countries as well. Bristol quality standards were the highest in the industry, and remained so: when the jets finally put high-powered piston engines out of aviation in the 1950s, the Bristol Centaurus sleeve-valve radial was left with the record for the longest certified overhaul life of any, ever.

Before that came about, even before the

RIGHT *A Bristol 405 made in late 1954. Its bodywork was surprisingly aerodynamic* **ABOVE** *The badge depicts the port of Bristol*

BRISTOL SIXES

93 EMG

ABOVE *The remarkable Bristol 450 racer shown here at Le Mans, on its way to its regular first-in-class finish in the famous race*

end of the war, the company's directors had begun to consider diversifying into car manufacture. Chief Engineer Sir Roy Fedden had some ideas on car design that he was keen to develop, although when his chance came they proved to be untenable. Frazer Nash manufacturer H.J. Aldington, who for some reason had been made a Bristol director, had on the other hand a lot of inside knowledge of what had been going on in the car department of BMW, and was instrumental in obtaining not only that firm's designs but also its engineer Dr. Fiedler very soon after the factory was liberated. Recognising the need to be quick in getting their first cars on the road and into the market, Bristol decided that they would make a start with their own version of the last BMW cars, combining the best features of the types 326 (chassis), 327 (styling) and 328 (engine) in a way that BMW themselves had never had the wit to try, and making the things far better than BMW or indeed anyone else could.

Very few men were deputed to do the work, but they were men blessed with the ability to get a lot of real engineering done without being hampered by paperwork, lack of facilities, or interference from the Board. Other assets included a handy little wind tunnel, ready advice from all the specialists in the other divisions, some prodigious runways (the 2-mile/3 km strip laid for the Brabazon airliner became particularly valuable) for special testing, and some test drivers of terrifying virtuosity who would habitually average 70 mph (113 kph) around the Gloucestershire lanes and hills without much exceeding 80 mph (129 kph).

What counted most, though, was the quality of the engineers posted to the new Cars Division. Thus, although dimensional changes to the BMW engine were subtle, the metallurgical improvements were tremendous: the cylinder liners, for example, were made of Brivadium, the austenitic alloy that had been evolved for aero-engine

sleeve-valves and which made Bristol bores paragons of durability for hundreds of thousands of miles. Again, the handful of outsiders who had occasion to inspect the internals of a Bristol gearbox and who actually knew anything about such things would shake their heads in astonishment over the quality of the aircraft-specification gears and bearings.

Bristol made almost everything themselves, except for tyres, wheels, electrics and carburettors – but these last were dismantled when they arrived from Solex so that the mating faces of disc valves in the enrichment circuits could be hand-lapped. That sort of attention to quality was everywhere: the ring nuts which held the two exhaust downpipes onto their respective (and efficient) three-branch manifolds looked ordinary enough, but were actually of phosphor-bronze with deliberately tight threads which were then matched with grinding-paste and elbow-grease to the manifolds' iron, producing a perfect joint.

Aircraft standards of inspection ensured such perfection in all components. For example, the entire front suspension assembly for each and every car was mounted (with steel discs in lieu of wheels) on a test jig for measurement of every dimension throughout the entire range of suspension and steering motions.

It was brilliantly contrived suspension, the work of Jack Channor who, when transferred to the Cars Division, set himself to study handling and roadholding and became one of the world's greatest experts. That was why the early Bristols had higher cornering limits than most contemporary racing cars, why the quality of their steering beggared comparison with anything else, and why the Type 400 with its Filton-made dampers gave so smooth a ride over stretches of frightful Belgian cobblestones, and faster than any other luxury car would dare.

The Bristol was a luxury car. It was made for small numbers of wealthy people who were accustomed to buying the best, and who also (which made their numbers even smaller) appreciated what was good in a car meant for serious use. Only a few were racing drivers, and then only incidentally; in those days, when civil aviation had not yet flowered and civilisation had not yet gone to

seed, it was not uncommon for the well-bred and the well-funded to undertake long and fast road journeys in discharge of avocational need or social obligation. These gentlemen knew what was meant by 'a driver's car' and recognised it in the Bristol.

They first saw it at the 1947 Geneva Show, though the prototype 400 first ran in the summer of 1946. The body, a confection of steel and aluminium, frankly acknowledged BMW ancestry; in everything else, the 400 set the pattern which was to endure for a very long time. Its six-cylinder long-stroke engine was exceptionally efficient, combining large valves in hemispherical combustion chambers with very fluent downdraught inlet ports entering vertically, between the banks of valves. With three carburettors, a camshaft that somehow combined flexibility with ample high-speed breathing, and a beautifully smooth-running crankshaft, it was both economical and responsive. The first one gave 85 bhp; by 1952 Mike Hawthorn's gave 150 bhp in the F2 Cooper which launched him to stardom and it was always open to a

TOP & FAR RIGHT *The Bristol 400 was closely based on pre-war BMWs, and was launched at the 1947 Geneva Motor Show* RIGHT & BELOW *The Bristol 401 of 1949 was mechanically identical to the 400, but its bodywork was extensively restyled*

customer to ask for a special state of tune, high or low, in one of the production saloons. Many an innocent-looking 2-litre saloon was factory-fitted with a sports engine giving as much as 140 bhp. Incidentally, Bristol power figures were always quoted for new engines: the output would improve steadily for the first 20,000 miles thereafter.

Since the cars invariably had low-drag bodies (even the 400 had a Cd of only 0.38) and were light for their size (between 2630 lb/1193 kg and 2700 lb/1225 kg) they had high top speeds and lively acceleration by the standards of the time. The 400 reached 80 mph (129 kph) faster than a 4-litre Lago-Talbot, for instance; it hardly made sense, until one realised how much more of the Bristol's power actually reached the back wheels because frictional losses in the driveline were so low. Quality shows in all sorts of ways . . . .

It showed in new ways in the 401 of 1949. Mechanically similar to the 400, it was clad in a beautiful new body, ultra-smooth and aerodynamically refined yet very roomy and practical. Nothing protruded from its smooth skin – the doors had flush buttons with aircraft locks, and all other hatches were opened from inside, making it burglar-proof – and the skin itself was varied in the thickness, hardness, and ductility of its aluminium alloy according to the loads (from mechanics' elbows around the engine bay, for example!) it might have to support. The bulkhead and floor panels were made of Paxolin, chemically and acoustically inert. The back window was bonded in flush with the surface, the bumpers carried on energy-absorbing mountings were integrated with the body contours, the steering wheel was

RIGHT AND INSET *The smooth balanced lines of a Bristol 404, a short-wheelbase, two-seat model introduced in 1954 and nowadays much sought after*

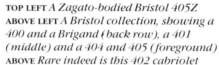

TOP LEFT *A Zagato-bodied Bristol 405Z*
ABOVE LEFT *A Bristol collection, showing a 400 and a Brigand (back row), a 401 (middle) and a 404 and 405 (foreground)*
ABOVE *Rare indeed is this 402 cabriolet*

also energy-absorbing. So was the body, and the immensely strong box-section chassis was confined within the wheelbase to leave long crumple zones fore and aft. It was extraordinary, a true safety-car built 20 years before the demand existed. When the TRRL (Transport Road and Research Laboratory) started its crash-tests in the late 1960s, it bought lots of old Bristols, finding they could be crashed three times more often than anything else before ceasing to be useful – and Bristol, who always kept in touch with their customers, could boast at the same time that nobody had ever been killed in one of their cars.

Italian and other bodybuilders tried their hands on Bristols, but the results were always inferior in quality and usually in looks, so after a nasty experience with some Farina cabriolets on the 401, Bristol made two dozen of their own drophead, the 402. The 403 looked almost identical to the 401, but there were bigger brakes to be seen through the properly-swaged holes of the wheels. It was a faster car, the standard engine now giving 100 bhp because in 1953 there was at last some decent petrol to be had. Amongst other refinements (dampers, heating, ventilation) there was a lovely new gearbox with closer ratios and Borg-Warner synchromesh. With the remote lever which came in 1954, this gave one of the most satisfying gearchanges of all time.

That remote lever was really part of the beautifully styled interior (featuring seven black-bezel dials binnacled before the driver) of the 404, the only short-wheelbase two-seater production car in Bristol history. The exterior styling was quite new: the

unadorned radiator intake was modelled on air-ducts perfected for the Brabazon, the twin vestigial tailfins echoed experience with the Le Mans type 450 racers. Offered with a choice of engines (105 or 125 bhp) and weighing only 2262 lb (1026 kg), it was still luxurious, and justified its 'Businessman's Express' soubriquet with very brisk performance, aided by huge front brakes.

With just two seats and a very hefty price tag, the Bristol 404 was never going to find a huge market but still there were sufficient discriminating and extremely wealthy buyers to account for the whole 40-strong production run. Survivors of this number are rare today and are among the most desirable of collectable Bristols.

Clearly related to it, the 405 reverted to the traditional 114-inch (289 cm) wheelbase and 1.2 ton (1219 kg) weight, but was distinguished in having an overdrive fifth gear and the only four-door body Bristol ever did. Bumpers and doorhandles spoiled the old smoothness, but the frontal area had been reduced (the 405 was lower than the 403) so overall drag remained the same. Stability was better than ever, for this car was supremely well balanced: as in the 404, the spare wheel was stored in a compartment behind the left front wheel, with brake servo, battery and a big terminal-board in a matching compartment on the right. With relocation of the 18-gallon fuel tank, the 405 had all its heavy masses within the wheelbase, reducing its moments of inertia in pitch and yaw and giving it incredibly good handling and ride.

Only two further refinements were needed, and both appeared in the 406 of 1958 (though a handful of 405s were also given the treatment). One was the use of a Watt linkage to locate the rear axle laterally and define a lower roll centre: this Bristol was the world's first to have this, perfecting a live-axle suspension (with torsion-bar springs) uncorrupted by any spurious steering effects caused by bump, rebound, or roll. The other refinement was disc brakes,

93 EMG

LEFT & BELOW *Views of an immaculate 405, a long-wheelbase, four-seat model designed for 'gentlemen drivers'. Its dashboard was remarkably informative, as one would expect from a company well used to making aircraft. The straight-six 2-litre engine was fed by three carburettors and produced between 105 and 125 bhp*

EVOLUTION

The Bristol 400 was introduced at the 1947 Geneva Motor Show with a 2-litre overhead-valve straight six based on the pre-war BMW

1949 The Bristol 401 was introduced. It was mechanically identical to the 400 but was clothed by a new and more aerodynamically efficient body. The 402 was introduced the same year; it was the drophead version of the 401 and built in even more limited numbers

1953 Visually almost identical to the 401, the 403 was introduced with larger brakes and a more powerful (100 bhp) version of the straight-six engine. The gearbox was new, with Borg-Warner synchromesh and close ratios

1954 The short-wheelbase, two-seater 404 was introduced with a choice of 105 bhp or 125 bhp engines and totally new styling. The remote gearchange was also introduced in '54

1955 The Bristol 405 was introduced, built on the traditional long wheelbase (114 in/289 cm). It was the first Bristol to have overdrive

1958 The Bristol 406 was announced with three major improvements over the 405 – the live rear axle was given extra location by Watt linkage, disc brakes were fitted and the engine displacement increased to 2.2 litres

1961 The ohc six-cylinder series came to an end with the introduction of the Chrysler V8-engined 407

on which the firm (familiar with them in aircraft) had been working for years: they were incidentally the first to identify the pad knock-back phenomenon, to the consternation of Dunlop.

Thanks to Channor's intense concern with such things, tyres enjoyed a lot of attention too. Michelin radials were offered as a standard option as early as the 401, though few other cars before the late 1960s could work well with either radials or high-speed bias-ply tyres. Few others (if any, indeed) also had the wit to employ aerodynamics as an aid to high-speed stability, but Bristol did this with distinction in their Type 450 sports-racers.

Nicknamed 'the fighter-pilot's delight', the 450 was based on the G-type ERA F2 chassis which had been developed with Bristol assistance and was further improved after they took it over. The main bodily feature was two big tail fins which extended as rails over the concave roof, to act as airflow fences maintaining attached flow over the roof and tail. The first cars of 1953 were untidy (due, it is believed, to the ingrained prejudices of the outside consultant hired as pit manager) but were soon smoothed out to minimise drag and frontal area. The engine had a special cylinder head

supporting six separate air intakes, could give about 160 bhp, could safely exceed 7000 rpm, and yet could endure being driven at 1300 rpm in top gear. A special crankshaft let it down at Le Mans in '53, but thereafter the 450 always won its class and the team award at Reims and Le Mans, finally as an open car (it was quieter for the driver!) at Le Mans in 1955 – where Bristol quietly gave all their winnings to the disaster fund and decided not to race again.

The Arnolt-Bristol was still racing effectively well into the 1960s. This was a two-seater bodied in steel by Bertone to the order of a Chicago businessman who just happened to be vice-president of the Italian firm. The basis was the 404 chassis, cheapened with 403 brakes and gearbox, but enlivened with one of the crisp and reliable sports engines which Bristol readily made available to specialist manufacturers galore – notably AC, Lister, Lotus, Tojeiro, Cooper and of course Frazer Nash. The last of 142 Arnolt-Bristols was delivered in 1964, 10 years after the first, and all of them in the USA; and it thus outlasted another interesting venture with Italy, the Zagato Bristol.

This began with recognition of the outstanding handling potential of the 406 chassis, despite the burden of its new and heavily luxurious body (which was actually to become the Chrysler-engined 407). Zagato was commissioned to build six lightweight GT bodies on six 406 chassis with tuned engines and Abarth exhausts, and although the quality was not up to Bristol standards the looks were very special and the behaviour prodigious. Several similar bodies were dropped onto old 400 or 401 chassis without being very convincing, but then Bristol built a brace of short-wheelbase 406 chassis: one they bodied themselves, as a sort of jazzy 404, and the other went to Zagato for a very light two-seater that still makes me envious whenever I visit the friend who owns it.

A lot has happened to Bristols since those days of the six-cylinder engines which ended when the 2.2-litre 406 gave way to the V8 407 in 1961. Why that happened is a story deriving most of its detail and impact from what was happening in the aviation industry in the late 1950s: at that time Bristol were developing a very promising all-independent 3½-litre twin-cam six, and a 170 bhp sloped version of the original engine for a spaceframed hyper-sports car, but all development had to be stopped, and all non-aviation activities had to be hived off.

That was how Bristol Cars came to be a private company without facilities for making its own engines any more, though fortunately it retained its staff, its premises, and its traditions. Today it still makes cars of the highest qualities for real drivers.

Running Bristol today is Anthony Crook, former racing driver and motor trader. With a head office and showroom in Kensington, London, and works in Bristol, the company addresses itself to the needs of owners of new Bristols as well as the requirements of enthusiasts for older models who recognise the cars' truly exceptional qualities.

LOTUS esprit

In the '70s, crisis-hit Lotus could only move one way – up market, to
Ferrari territory; the result was the Giugiaro-styled Esprit

DVG 40Y

THE ENIGMATIC ESPRIT has come a long way. It started as an impractical Giugiaro show car before becoming the Hethel firm's more upmarket replacement for the Europa Twin-Cam (and with just as many reliability and quality control problems). Nevertheless from these inauspicious beginnings greatness was to emerge. The wedge-shaped wonder gained a turbocharger, quality was improved and the Esprit became Lotus's first road-car to rival those of their long-time race-track protagonists, Ferrari. The buzzy sports car became a supercar, and since the Esprit Turbo first made its mark in 1980, Lotus's claim to be quality car makers has also come on in leaps and bounds.

Lotus is a firm well used to crises, and the Esprit was launched in the midst of their most difficult-ever period. In the early '70s, chairman Colin Chapman decided the only way the small company would survive – let alone prosper – was to move upmarket, for he knew that expensive cars were less susceptible to economic vicissitudes than cheap ones. A firm with Lotus's engineering excellence were capable, figured Chapman, of building a genuine British alternative to a Porsche or Ferrari – something no other UK company was doing. It was part pragmatism, part pride, and the consequence was that the type of car on which Lotus's reputation had rested for 15 years was ditched. Out went the Elan; out went the Europa. Instead of chasing people who aspired to a Porsche but couldn't afford one, Lotus went after people who could. The young, fast driving set which had formed the majority of Elan/Europa owners was ignored, and older, less impecunious buyers were sought.

The first stage was the four-seater Elite, launched in 1974. Thanks to its hefty price (£5749) and its introduction during the worst of the '70s oil crises, the Elite was never a great showroom success. The company's difficulties were exacerbated by the fact that at that point Lotus was only a one-product company, awaiting the launch of the Esprit, and the poor sales forced a decision to slash both production and workforce (the latter down from 830 in early '74 to less than 400 in '75). The change-over from being makers of cheap sports cars to makers of prestige cars was never going to be easy but in reality it was more difficult than Chapman ever imagined.

The Esprit helped, as he knew it would. The car was a spiritual successor to the Europa Twin-Cam, even though both its price-tag and equipment levels were always to be higher, but this was because the Esprit was really intended to be the car to lift Lotus into the Ferrari league. Code-named the M70, the mid-engined machine had first featured in Lotus's long range plans drawn

ABOVE *The now defunct Lotus badge*
LEFT *The distinctive lines of the Esprit Turbo which has now been updated with slightly softer lines*

up in 1970. The idea was to use as many parts from the yet-to-be-released Elite as possible, including the 16-valve four-cylinder engine then being developed, and a futuristic wedge-shaped body.

Chapman must have been wondering who was the best person to design that futuristic body for the M70 when, at the 1971 Geneva Motor Show, he as approached by Giorgetto Giugiaro. The master Italian stylist told Chapman that he wanted to do a show-car design based on a Lotus. With a background that included work for Bertone and Ghia – frequently on two-seater supercars – Giugiaro's qualifications were beyond dispute. Chapman agreed, and the Esprit's modern but simple lines took form.

A cut and reworked Europa chassis of intended M70 dimensions was delivered to Giugiaro's Torinese studio to be clothed, and in November 1972 a prototype was shown to the world at the Turin Show, a very angular wedge-shaped design with an extraordinary steeply raked windscreen. Lotus were enthusiastic about the shape but also bemused by what would be its inherent production problems. The Esprit theme had been set, but the practical 'productionising' of the car had yet to begin. Chapman was also suspicious of the car's aerodynamics, and soon asked for a second prototype to be made complete with interior and decent aerodynamics. He wanted a car capable of being produced in glassfibre (in line with Lotus tradition) rather than one merely to be ogled at. The second car would thus be built in glassfibre, the first time Giugiaro had worked with this substance. Long hours and late nights followed.

Some of the important Lotus executives moved to Turin to work close to Giugiaro, including stylist Oliver Winterbottom, who supervised the construction of the Esprit and who also designed the 1974 Elite. Others, including Chapman and Mike Kimberley (later to become chief engineer and managing director) made frequent private aircraft flights from Norfolk to Italy. A quarter-scale model of the original Giugiaro prototype was made and then taken to the MIRA wind tunnel in England. Tests there confirmed what Chapman had suspected – there were bad lift problems, which were as undesirable to a high-speed sports car as an ugly body. The changes effected during this period of development included decreasing the rake of the windscreen by three degrees to comply with US roll-over strength legislation and reducing the size of the rear opening door, which had been a full-length hatchback type on early designs. There were also numerous subtle styling differences, both to help Lotus build the body and to enable the car to penetrate the air with less

ABOVE & ABOVE RIGHT *Giugiaro's prototype was known, for obvious reasons, as 'the silver car'*

drag and lift. This second prototype almost identical with the production Esprit, was finished in 1973. Thus, two years before the Esprit made its world debut, the shape had nearly been finalised.

Lotus had always intended to use their new four-cylinder 16-valve engine in the Esprit, a unit which had been designed by former BRM engineer Tony Rudd, who had joined Lotus in 1969. This engine produced 140 bhp from 1973 cc, and was the first all-Lotus-designed production motor. It had been used first in the Jensen-Healey sports car, and as well as being high-revving and powerful, the all-alloy unit had a terrible thirst for oil – a characteristic which went down well neither with Jensen nor their customers – and it took Lotus some time to sort out this problem. Furthermore, the engine was inordinately harsh at high revs, the result of an inadequately stiff crankcase, and Lotus also had to do a lot of work on the motor's emission levels to make it acceptable in America, Japan and Australia.

The engineers had always anticipated that one of the most difficult problems with their new mid-engined car would be where to locate the rear-mounted transaxle. Lotus found an unlikely saviour: Citroën were about to discontinue production of their idiosyncratic Maserati-engined SM, a front-engined front-drive supercar. Nonetheless the French firm were able to guarantee Chapman a long-term supply of their five-speed gearboxes, and even production of tailor-made ratios. Fitting the transaxle, however, was not an easy task. It was mated to the engine via a Lotus-made bellhousing, which joined the centre line of the differential. The gearchange involved a rod to select the gears and a cable to work the across-the-gate movement, and was a complex fitting which 'broke every known engineering law,' according to one Lotus engineer. Nonethe-

RIGHT *The first version of the Esprit, the S1, looked rather different from the Giugiaro prototype but was clearly based upon it*

less, it worked. One of the priorities had been to give the Esprit a good gearchange, particularly after the atrocious cog-selection problems which had so blighted the Europa fitted with its Renault gearbox.

In between trying to get the new Elite ready for production and curing the problems inherent with the 16-valve engine, Lotus worked like Trojans in 1974 to get the Esprit developed for Chapman's Christmas deadline. Tony Rudd took overall responsibility, including specific engine and suspension work, Colin Spooner was responsible for the chassis and body and his brother Brian concentrated on adapting the Citroën gearbox. On Christmas Eve, one day ahead of the deadline, the team had a car to show the boss, although it was not a runner. The Esprit prototype's first real test in front of the boss was early in 1975, when Tony Rudd surprised Chapman by arriving to collect him in it at Heathrow Airport, after the first Grand Prix of the year. Chapman drove it part of the way back to Hethel before a hub carrier broke.

By early 1975 it really had to: the Elan and Europa were gone and Lotus's only model – the new Elite – was selling at the meagre rate of 20-25 cars a month, worldwide. It was just enough to carry Lotus through to the launch of the Esprit at the Paris Show in October 1975. That was when, according to *Motor Sport*, 'the most exciting, attractive, series-production British sports car since the E-type' was unveiled.

The Lotus twin-cam 2.0-litre engine, mounted longitudinally at 45 degrees to the horizontal, now developed 155 bhp at 6580 rpm in the Series 1 Esprit, and 140 lb ft of torque at 4800 rpm, breathing through twin Dellorto carburettors. The car's glassfibre reinforced plastic body was made in two halves and then bonded together at the prominent waist-line, riding on a steel back-boned tubular frame, partly sheet-braced. The front suspension used Opel Ascona double wishbones with integrated coil spring/damper units, and an Ascona anti-roll bar. Ascona front discs were also borrowed, and the steering rack was from the Elite.

At the back, the suspension was simple, unusual and flawed. The Esprit used its fixed-length driveshafts to form what was, in effect, its upper suspension links (Elite driveshafts and hubs were used). There were also box-framed trailing arms, a lower

RIGHT The turbo installation on the Esprit is one of the finest around. It is shown here under test in 1980. Note the massive heat build up in the exhaust system

LEFT *Lotus were always quick to capitalise on their great Grand Prix success, adorning their road cars, such as this S2, with 'World Champion' decals*
ABOVE *The exterior styling was far more agreeable than that of the early interiors, which have dated badly*

lateral link and integral coil spring/damper units. The rear disc brakes were inboard.

Inside, the Esprit was a mixture of good news and bad. The dash consisted of a futuristic wrap-around facia which contained the main gauges (which were hard to read) and the switchgear, and in between this and the driver was a cheap plastic two-spoke steering wheel. The interior ventilation was terrible, as it still is on the Esprit, and rear three-quarter vision was almost non-existent, but all these problems notwithstanding, the Esprit got a deservedly good reception at its world debut, and when it went on sale in June 1976 it looked like Lotus had built a winner. Its success came not a moment too soon.

The Series 1 was in production for two years before being superseded by the Series 2 in May 1978. Some of the S1 problems

were solved with the new S2; many were not. Lotus already knew that their rear suspension layout was inadequate for a car of this performance (even though it had worked adequately on the Elite), and they knew that the chassis had to be made stiffer. They reworked neither, however, for the S2. What they did do was improve the 16-valve engine and give it more mid-range pull (an improvement effected on some late S1 models, too) and better economy. New alloy wheels, made specially for Lotus by the Italian makers Speedline, replaced the off-the-shelf Wolfrace wheels which had looked so prosaic on the S1. A front wraparound spoiler was used, as were wider Rover 3500-borrowed tail lamps (subsequently used on all Lotuses).

The vague Veglia instruments were replaced by sensible Smiths ones, and the standard of interior trim was massively improved. Mind you, the trim should have been revised, for with the launch of the S2, the price of the Esprit had rocketed to £11,124. The one-time kit car makers were now selling, truly, a Porsche-priced car, but they still weren't building cars as well as Porsche. The S1 had had many teething problems, and Tony Rudd later said, 'I reckon we solved 90 per cent of the problems before manufacture, but there were others who reckoned I solved 10 per cent and they did the rest trying to put it into production'.

Lotus also didn't do the Guigiaro shape any favours by some of the 'limited edition' styling kits they offered. The company are renowned for their tasteless decals, but the nadir probably came with their awful 1978 'World Champion' edition, to commemorate the Team Lotus World Championship title.

BELOW *The Esprit production line at the modern well-equipped Lotus factory at Hethel, Norfolk. Quality of Esprits has improved steadily over the years*

Painted black with thick gold striping and big 'World Champion' lettering down the side, the styling pack was a salient reminder of the intrinsic differences in quality and taste between Ferrari and Porsche (could either ever produce such a kit?) and Lotus. Unfortunately, when the excellent Esprit Turbo was first launched, in 1980, its body was similarly spoilt by its garish Essex livery.

Despite its initial paint-job, the Esprit Turbo marked the long-awaited turning point for Lotus. At last here was a car that was good enough to take on – and beat – a Ferrari 308GTB. The high-speed Esprit variant had been originally scheduled to have a V8 engine, rather than a turbo four-cylinder. If one looks at the chassis' engine cradle in the Esprit, one can see plainly that there is room for an engine with two banks of four cylinders. Nonetheless, powertrain engineering manager Graham Atkin favoured the idea of a turbo four, largely on the grounds of cost, and his voice eventually won through. Such engines were starting to gain favour then thanks to the work of companies like Porsche and Saab.

Both these companies had proved that high power outputs and good torque figures were possible from an engine of only modest capacity. Both the Saab Turbo and the Porsche 924 Turbo were fast and civilised cars, although both suffered from that bugbear of all early and some more recent turbo cars, turbo lag.

In typical Lotus fashion (they've always been better at engineering than they have at aesthetics), the turbo transformation was extremely clever. The design of the car involved a massive revision of the S2 specification. To make it look more aggressive and increase the downforce, Giugiaro was asked to add some addenda to the Esprit body, and replied by designing wraparound bumpers, large front and rear spoilers and deep skirts under the door sills. The changes to the engine were far more extensive. A longer-stroke crankshaft increased its capacity from 1973 cc to 2174 cc and a Garrett AiResearch T3 blower rammed pressurised air into the two twin-barrel Dellorto carburettors. The compression ratio was lowered (a necessary adjunct to turbocharging) and the engine was strengthened to take the greater internal pressures. The power went up by 35 per cent, to 210 bhp at 6000–6500 rpm, and torque rose by 43 per cent, to 200 lb ft at 4000–4500 rpm. The clutch diameter was increased by an inch (2.4 cm), although the gearbox and final drive remained unchanged.

The chassis and suspension were also extensively altered. The chassis, in fact, was new with Lotus-designed and built upper wishbone/lower transverse link front suspension (replacing the Opel system) attached to a new front box section. At the rear, where there had always been a handling problem on the S1 and S2, short top suspension links were added to take the loads imposed on the driveshafts. The trouble with the old system had been that to a large extent the engine mounts' compliance had determined the handling. If good road-holding was to be maintained the result was excessive engine noise and vibration. The new chassis also had 50 per cent better torsional rigidity than that of the S1/S2, which also helped to explain the better handling composure of the Turbo when compared with earlier models. Bigger 60-aspect ratio tyres were fitted front and rear, the interior was leather-trimmed, (although this later became optional), air conditioning was standard and a better steering wheel was fitted. Top speed was 152 mph (245 kph) compared with the S2's 135 mph (218 kph), with 0-60 mph in 5.5 seconds (7.5 seconds for the S2). In April 1981 the mechanically identical but less luxuriously equipped 'normal' Esprit Turbo came out to replace the colourfully adorned Essex machine. At less than £17,000 – compared with £21,000 for the Essex – it was far more sensibly priced.

Numerous road tests soon verified that the Turbo was one of Europe's most competent supercars. Its beautifully engineered turbocharged engine gave silken yet strong performance, it had razor-sharp handling, prodigious roadholding and the brakes were superb. It still didn't have the ultimate status or sheer beauty of the Ferrari 308GTB, but as a sheer driver's car it probably beat the Italian stallion.

The Esprit Turbo technology also helped to procreate a better normally-aspirated Esprit. Although the Series 2.2 – launched not long after the Turbo, in April 1980, to replace the Series Two – was nothing to write fan letters to Hethel about (it used the non-turbo 2.2-litre engine in the existing – and flawed – S2 chassis), its replacement, the Series 3, launched in early 1981, was an altogether superior machine. At last Lotus had given the car the strong chassis and suspension of the Turbo. The exterior was also neater than the S2.2, with no obtrusive matt black paint, and the quality control was noticeably better. Lotus's standards have improved in leaps and bounds since 1980, and to compare an S3 or Turbo with an S1 is like comparing a plastic model built by a child with one built by an expert, differences which are also very apparent when the cars are taken on the road.

Lotus thus achieved their goal and became makers of expensive luxury sports cars. That reputation is due, more than anything else, to the Esprit Turbo. With that model, Lotus grew up.

RIGHT *The Turbo Esprit never looks spectacular when put through its paces on the track, staying very stable at all speeds* **BELOW** *Esprit interiors have grown steadily more luxurious, particularly on the Turbo* **BELOW RIGHT** *An '84 Turbo Esprit*

EVOLUTION

Introduced in 1975 at the Paris and Earls Court Motor Shows, the Esprit was a mid-engined two-seater with an aerodynamic glassfibre bodyshell on a steel backbone chassis. It was fitted with the 2-litre 16-valve Lotus 907 engine which developed 140 bhp and 140 lb ft of torque. Braking was by discs all round and suspension was all-independent

1978 Limited edition Esprit S2 was launched to celebrate the team Lotus World Championship title. 100 were built for each of the company's three markets, and the cars were available only in black with gold coaching and insignia.

1980 Essex Lotus Turbo Esprit launched at the Royal Albert Hall, London. The first 100 were built in Team Essex racing livery. Engine size was increased to 2.2 litres, which in normally aspirated form produced 160 bhp and 160 lb ft of torque and in turbo form delivered 210 bhp and 200 lb ft. Top speed of the Turbo Esprit was 152 mph (245 kph), with 0-60 mph in 5.5 seconds. The bodyshell was competition-modified to improve the aerodynamics, with scoops under the nose and on the sills (the latter to feed air to the engine) and aerofoils on the roof and tail. The chassis was galvanised and suspension modified, and bigger tyres were fitted.

1981 Launch of 'normal' Turbo Esprit and Esprit Series 3, the latter incorporating the chassis and suspension modifications of the Turbo model

1983 Esprit Turbo was given a larger boot and offered with the option of a removable glass roof

1985 Suspension modifications to Esprit range, including ventilated discs fitted at the front, larger rear disc calipers, and front anti-roll bar separated from front suspension

1987 Major restyling of body undertaken giving softer lines. Interior trim improved and performance increased

Lagonda 4

GPD 939

½ Litre

Lagondas were splendid-looking and powerful cars, but money problems were never far away. Then came a glorious win at Le Mans . . .

EVERYBODY KNOWS about the Jaguars at Le Mans in the 1950s. Quite a lot of people remember the Bentleys at Le Mans, a quarter of a century earlier. Ask a man in the street if there were any British successes in between, and it is most unlikely that he would recall any; was that not the point about the Jaguars making a come-back for Britain – in the wake of the Bentleys? What a shame that so few folk can remember – indeed, that so few ever knew – that the most significant sports-car race in the calendar was won in 1935 by another British car, a 4½-litre Lagonda.

It cannot have helped matters that Lagonda were pronounced bankrupt the day after the race. That sort of thing is inclined to make people grow suddenly quiet, just when they might be tempted to throw a party and tell the world why. Alas, just as doing rather well in competition was something of a habit for the big Lagonda, so was doing rather badly in business habitual for the company.

It had been trying to do well for quite a long time, ever since founder Wilbur Gunn started making motorcycles in Staines in 1900. Tricars followed soon after, and a small car in 1907. There followed some biggish cars (very popular in Russia), but it was not until after Gunn's time (he died in 1920) that designer Arthur Davidson hit upon a type of car that was to fix the essential characteristics of the marque. By 1927 it had settled into production as the Lagonda 2-litre, a stylish and well-balanced sporting tourer with an otherwise clever four-cylinder engine spoiled by ghastly porting, and a gearbox which could not be included among the world's best. By 1929, the Speed Model was being offered in low-chassis form (a strictly relative expression), and it had a lot to commend it.

It was not terribly fast, and definitely not very accelerative (construction was very substantial), but it held the road well, steered and handled well, stopped very well, and was nicely built. What was more, it was a good deal cheaper than anything of comparable qualities that was notably faster (the 3-litre Bentley was the obvious comparison), and it was extremely handsome.

All the reckless proliferation of models which followed during the next five years (with the exception of the little 1.1-litre Rapier) reflected attempts to make the Lagonda faster, easier to drive, easier to sell, or cheaper to make. The 90 mph (145 kph)

LEFT *A 1937 Lagonda LG45 Rapide of 1937, one of only 25 built – 24 of which still exist – and now extremely valuable*

99

supercharged version was not the answer, though it was a very good performer. Really the best thing that happened was the switch to six-cylinder engines, some of them proprietary and some (originating in the 2.4-litre 16/65 of 1928) made by Lagonda themselves.

By the time that the 16/65 had grown into the 3-litre, it was clear that the chassis could handle a lot more power, though sadly what usually happened with each new model was that it acquired a lot more weight. However, a syndicate of amateur racing drivers approached the Lagonda boss, Brigadier-General Metcalfe, early in 1933 with a proposition for a 4½-litre engine in a 3-litre chassis for them to race. The draft contract produced by the General contained provisions for the company going into receivership (evidence of the financial difficulties which were commonly blamed on the vast range of different models being concurrently offered) and the deal eventually fell through – but only after most of the work had been done.

Quite fortuitously, Invicta had just collapsed, which meant that supplies of the 4½-litre Meadows engine they used were immediately available.

The Invicta 4½ had been made in two forms, the high chassis and the low chassis and equipped with the Meadows engine, the cars had proved popular and successful on the race track. Unfortunately a well-publicized accident at Brooklands undermined faith in the model; hence, ultimately, the availability of engines to Lagonda.

Compared with previous Lagondas, that 4½-litre car – it was designated M45 – was quite a performer. To be fair, compared with most things then on the roads it was quite a performer: a handful were a shade faster (it would do about 95 mph/153 kph, depending

EVOLUTION

Introduced in 1933, the M45 Lagonda was fitted with the 4493 cc six-cylinder Meadows engine, a unit which developed 108 bhp and 215 lb ft of torque. The car was capable of about 95 mph (153 kph) and the first models were fitted with Lagonda's own four-speed gearbox with synchromesh on third; the Meadows unit was thereafter adopted

1934 The M45R Rapide was announced, with a shorter wheelbase and Girling brakes. The engine was modified and fitted with a stiffer alloy crankcase, lightened valve-gear, higher compression ratio and a freewheel behind the gearbox

1935 The Lagonda company was in desperate financial straits. After winning Le Mans with a 4½-litre car all other models were dropped from the range

1936 The LG45 was announced, a slightly detuned Rapide clothed in new streamlined bodies designed by Frank Feeley. It also featured synchromesh on third and top gears, hydraulic dampers, smaller wheels and automatic chassis lubrication. W.O. Bentley's design improvements to the engine included an improved crossflow inlet manifold cast into the cylinder head and a lightened flywheel

1937 The LG45 Rapide was announced, an open four-seater with helmet wings, external exhaust pipes and rounded tail. Maximum speed was 108 mph (174 kph)

1938 The LG6 Lagonda V12 was announced and exhibited at Earls Court. its engine, designed by W.O. Bentley, developed 156 bhp and could rev to 5500 rpm, but it developed less torque than the Meadows sixes. Maximum speed was 108 mph

1940 Production of the cars was halted by the war

ABOVE *Although overshadowed in the popular mind by Bentley's exploits at Le Mans, Lagonda enjoyed their fair share of success too, winning the 24 Hours in 1935 with Hindmarsh and Fontes at the wheel*

on how much drag the body imposed), not many handled better and scarcely any stopped better. In short, the M45 was an uncommonly practical fast car, having the sort of performance that could actually be used instead of just being admired on paper.

Much of the credit belonged to that Meadows engine. A pushrod in-line 4493 cc six with the correct number of main bearings (four, of course) and, despite its iron head and block, lighter than a 3.8 Jaguar XK engine – if you will pardon the comparison – it was replete with what used to be called 'back-up torque' because as the rev-counter needle fell back the torque went up. Peaking at 215 lb ft and only 1500 rpm, it could give at least 200 lb ft all the way from 2300 rpm down to tickover. Lagonda red-lined the

tachometer at 3800 (Invicta had set it as 3500), but power deteriorated beyond 3200 rpm anyway. What that power amounted to was anybody's guess, and when Lagonda were persuaded out of their usual reticence they talked of 108 bhp.

Not that it really mattered. All that did matter was that steamy torque: the M45 could, with due attention to the ignition lever, be treated as a top-gear car. Use all four in the box, though, and it would fairly romp away, reaching 33 mph (53 kph) in bottom gear, and 50 mph (80 kph) in 10 seconds; for a car weighing at least 3600 lb (1633 kg) that was then jolly good going. At first Lagonda used their own gearbox, expensively revised to incorporate a double-helical constant-mesh 'silent' third in recog-

nition of the spreading contagion of synchromesh elsewhere. Later they adopted the Meadows box.

As it first appeared, the M45 attracted warm praise and (once a Clayton-Dewandre brake servo had been added) lots of customers, many of them fairly flashy individuals in the public eye. At a time when xenophobia made foreign cars as unacceptable as they were incomprehensible, the Lagonda had little opposition: the new 3½-litre Rolls-Bentley was slightly slower off the mark, even if slightly faster at the top end and a bit more nimble, and although it was much more refined it was *very* much more costly.

On 1 September 1934 the two rivals met in open combat, racing at the Newtownards circuit in Ireland for the Tourist Trophy. The Bentley was the extremely special ultra-light 3½ of Eddie Hall; the Lagonda was prepared by the meticulous Arthur Fox of Fox Nicholl, a Tolworth firm who had been notable Lagonda entrants in the days of the 2-litre and had afterwards done wonders with Roesch Talbots. Stripped bodies were the order of the day (no lights or any such nonsense) but the three team Lagondas enjoyed many mechanical changes. Practically all of these – the stiffer alloy crankcase, bigger crankpins, lightened valve gear, and so on – could be justified, in that they shortly

LEFT *Stripped 4½ Litres formed very effective racing models – this is one of the 1934 works team*
BELOW *A 4½ in more conventional guise with elegant bodywork, yet still a fast car*

afterwards were adopted in production.

Not that many customers could drive like the Hon. Brian Lewis (later Lord Essenden), who was fastest of the Lagonda team. Halfway through the race (run to a complex handicap) he came wheel-to-wheel with Hall, and the two fastest cars in the race began a ding-dong struggle which was the highlight of the day. Seldom more than a length apart, swapping the lead frequently, using absolutely all the road and in places some of the pavement and shopfronts too (those were the days of real roadracing on real roads), they fought thus for six laps – more than an hour, on that lengthy circuit. The Lagonda's tyres were worn smooth, but that did not matter until the rains came, just two laps before the end, and Lewis had to be called in for their replacement. The second place for which he had been fighting went to Hall, but the worth of the Lagonda had been publicly demonstrated.

A week later, Lagonda announced the M45R, the Rapide. This new flagship embodied most of the special features of the TT cars, including the new Girling brakes and the shortened wheelbase, 6 inches

the bodies which sometimes graced and almost invariably burdened that most amenable chassis with its handsome radiator. Fortunately the basic proportions were good, so most bodies looked attractive and several were real stunners: 1934 was a good year. It was quite amazing how General Metcalfe had kept the firm going through the long and bitter years of the depression, when so many rivals had collapsed. Alas, he himself was doomed by an internal cancer, so 1935 was to be a shocker.

Mr Hore-Belisha made it worse on 18 March, introducing driving tests, pedestrian crossings and the 30 mph (48 kph) speed limit. This last temporarily killed the sports-car market stone dead, taking Lagonda fortunes with it. Things had been bad enough already; now the factory was clogged by unsold cars (especially Rapiers) and just before Easter the bank appointed a Receiver. He sold everything possible, reduced the staff to skeleton proportions, and maintained sales by assembling existing parts.

Meanwhile, strange things were happening elsewhere. A Lincoln's Inn solicitor aged 29, one Alan P. Good, was gathering a consortium to buy the company, and approaching some very notable people. Fox Nicholl, having bought the car that Arthur Fox knew to be the best one, put in an entry for Le Mans, naming as drivers John Hindmarsh and Luis Fontes. Hindmarsh was a serving RAF officer, soon to be killed in the crash of a prototype Hawker Hurricane; he

BELOW AND BELOW RIGHT *Two examples of the 1938 Lagonda V12. The engine is regarded by some as W. O. Bentley's finest, but others were less impressed*

(153 mm) less than the 129 of the M45. The steering was even higher geared, going from lock to lock in just 1½ turns as against 1¾ for the M45. There was a freewheel (then in vogue) behind the Meadows gearbox, and Lagonda (who were now assembling the engine) claimed 135 bhp – a fairly gross exaggeration, not atypical of the times. More to the point, they claimed £1000 for the Rapide chassis with an open tourer body.

Lagonda built a lot of their own bodies, and built them very well: they had some of the finest panel-beaters working for them at Staines. Many a customer would stipulate something special; many others went to the independent coachbuilders, and many were

had often driven for Fox Nicholl in the Talbot days. Fontes, a very studious-looking Englishman of Spanish extraction, was only 21 and had seemingly come from nowhere to be the sensation of British motor racing in 1935 – and then to retire from it, continuing his flying until killed in the RAF during the war. Another driver of much longer standing, erstwhile Bentley Boy and burgeoning entomologist Dr J.D. Benjafield, got hold of another Lagonda and Fox entered him too.

The big names of racing all had impressive entries in for the big race of the year. Type 50 Bugatti vied with 2.3 Alfa Romeo, Delahaye with 7-litre Duesenberg…. There was a record entry of 58 cars, and the

Benjafield/Gunter Lagonda was only promoted from the reserves at the last minute. The weather was foul, the rain almost endless and the skids monotonously frequent; and through it all the Lagondas soldiered on, sticking firmly to their schedule and ignoring the usual frenzied sprint which often decimated the field in the first hour. Oddly, there were few retirements this time, yet after two hours Hindmarsh was up in second place and Benjy, with a slower car, was sixth. Then the pit stops came, but not for the Lagondas: they could go for 350 miles on a 28-gallon tank, even when lapping at about 81 mph (130 kph)

Before Hindmarsh was due in, he came

in. Momentarily trapped in another car's accident, his Lagonda had been knocked about a bit. Loss of a headlamp and damaged steering were immediately apparent; other symptoms emerged much later, but the car went on with little regard for the ebb and flow of Alfas rushing past and falling back. By noon on Sunday the Lagondas were first and third, but then Benjy's car – poised to displace an Alfa from second place – lost all its gears except top, and had to race the last four hours like that, falling back to 13th place. Fontes brought the faster Lagonda, low on oil but otherwise healthy, in to win after about 1869 miles at 77.86 mph (125.53 kph) – slower than 1931 and 1933, but those years it had been dry.

It was really a beautiful performance; but the firm was in the hands of the Receiver and could make nothing of it. Lagonda had no money with which to do anything; but Good knew where to find some, and how to woo it. Those notables he had been talking to were none other than Dick Watney (who had just left Rootes) and W.O. Bentley! Time had just forced open the iron grip of Rolls-Royce on W.O., and as soon as the Le Mans results were announced he agreed to serve

Good as chief designer for Lagonda. That name, and the race result, were together enough to open numerous purses, and in a matter of days Good was in charge.

The factory was in a dreadful state of disrepair, but plans were made to make things better, all subservient to the main object of making Lagonda the best car in the world. Frank Feeley was promoted to body designer and was destined to produce some of the most beautiful cars ever seen. Good decided that a one-model policy should be pursued, and everything but the 4½ was stopped – even the Rapier, production of which was hived off to a separate company.

Bentley's object was refinement, and he got busy right away. The new model, announced in September for the 1936 season, was the LG45, mechanically a slightly detuned Rapide with lots of detail alterations. Heavily silenced inside and outside, it now had synchromesh on third and top gears, hydraulic dampers in lieu of the friction type, smaller wheels, softer tyres and slower steering, more weight and lower gearing. The centralised chassis lubrication

acceleration. Bentley had worked the Meadows engine through three sets of modifications, all aimed at smoother running and better top-end power, made possible by the more robust Rapide bottom half which in 1936 had allowed him to raise the red-line rpm to 4000. Henry Meadows sanctioned the changes, so the engines were known as Sanction 1, 2 and 3 – the last of them with a new head, the design of which was farmed out to Harry Weslake who had gas-flowed the Le Mans Speed Six Bentley seven years earlier. As often with Weslake's work, it functioned tolerably well but was grotesque in its solecisms, such as holding-down studs passing through the inlet ports. Still, this was the engine which, with higher compression

Views of an immaculate 1937 LG45 Rapide which has covered just 60,000 miles from new with but two owners. The elegant body was designed by Frank Feeley and the Meadows straight-six engine improved by W.O. Bentley, with a more efficient crossflow inlet manifold cast into the cylinder head, and a lighter flywheel

that had been a feature of Lagondas since the days of the 2-litre was now automatic; what with the Luvax booster system for the dampers and the Smith's built-in hydraulic jacks, the chassis carried enough capillary pipes to keep a Citroën healthy! Frank Feeley drew much smoother, more curvaceous yet more sober bodies, featuring twin wing-mounted spare wheel covers, one of which was a dummy housing the toolkit.

Where he really excelled himself was with the LG45 Rapide. Planned for 1937, this was a wonderfully glamorous open four-seater with helmet wings, external exhaust pipes, a rounded tapering tail and a fabric hood at once practical and smart. The car went as well as it looked: 0–50 mph took 9.4 seconds, and the top speed was over 108 mph (174 kph).

Even the standard LG45 could now sometimes see 100 mph (163 kph), though it could not match the old M45 for bottom-end

ratio, powered the LG45R, though not with the 150 bhp that was claimed.

One other thing which that Rapide did not have was the new gearbox. Faced with synchromesh on the top three gears in many rivals, and on all four in the Alvis, Bentley created a new box with synchromesh for the top three, and with a central gearlever – something that was becoming acceptable in cars of this class, as was the central brake pedal where the M45 had the classical (and still desirable) central accelerator. In the Rapide – the one model in which the noise of the new box would have passed un-

ABOVE *The LG45 cockpit was a well proportioned affair with a dashboard dominated by large, clear dials and easily identified switches*

noticed – there was no room for the central lever. Anyway, drivers of sports cars were presumed able to change gear unaided!

By the eve of the Motor Show in the autumn of 1936, it became evident that the new gearbox had actually been intended for something else, and that all Bentley's uprating and updating of the old Meadows engine was merely a stopgap pending the production of an entirely new engine for a substantially new Lagonda. In fact the Sanction 3 Meadows would also be fitted in the new chassis (which was a magnificent job, with independent front suspension) and the car so composed would be known as the LG6, with bodies ever more lovely as Feeley's pencil translated Watney's demands. But the car for which the chassis was conceived, with bodies practically identical, would have a new Bentley-designed engine intended to raise performance and refinement together to unprecedented heights. That was the

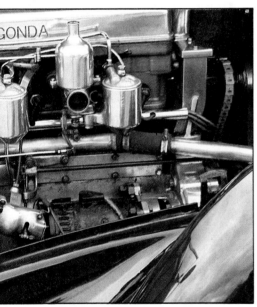

Lagonda V12, and that (albeit sadly curtailed by the war) was another story...

The gist of it was that the V12 4½ litre, upon which Bentley had been working since he started at Staines, had a non-working engine (with wooden sump!) at the 1936 Show, and was barely ready for the market when it reappeared at Earls Court in 1938. In its design, W.O. had been more wooden than that sump: apart from a clever crankshaft with duralumin conrods running directly on its nitrided crankpins, the V12 was an old-fashioned engine.

It was heavy, and stripping it was a fearful task. The iron block stopped short at main-bearing level; the iron heads had their in-line valves (beneath single stratospheric camshafts) arranged with exhausts juxta-posed, leading to overheating and cracking. The ports were promising, but the breathing was ruined by labyrinthine hot-spot arrangements and by Bentley's refusal to have more

than two carburettors.

So the V12 developed less torque than any of the sixes – but because it could run up to 5500 rpm, it developed more power, some 156 bhp. Thus the car, heavily bodied on any of three different-length chassis, felt refined and cruised fast, but needed more driver-input – not only at the gearlever but also the steering, now with 3¾ turns from lock to lock. Still, it was fast: a demonstrator put over 101 miles (163 km) into an hour (including a puncture) at Brooklands, with the final lap at 108 mph (174 kph).

Two very special V12s were hurriedly

ABOVE The rear end styling of the LG45 is one of the car's most distinctive features with a pointed opening tail plus an exhaust issuing from the inner wing

readied for the 1939 Le Mans race. With proper carburation they had over 205 bhp, and more torque than any six; and they were very much lightened. W.O. set them to run strictly at a speed 1 mph (1.6 kph) higher than the previous winner's average, and that was how they finished – third and fourth, cracked heads and other troubles notwith-standing (nor admitted!). Stripped for Brooklands later, one of them lapped at 128 mph (206 kph) in the last meeting be-fore war broke out.

That war stopped a promising career. Not only was the 1939 Le Mans entry merely a rehearsal for 1940, but also Lagonda built a prototype for a really fast four-seat stream-liner which, with 'Le Mans' engine and re-vised Lockheed brakes, would have outper-formed the prototype Rolls-Bentley stream-liner that it so brazenly resembled. That would have been a nicer war, had we been given the choice.

MG T Ser

The MG Ts were the epitome of the traditional open British sports car, a now classic series that lasted for nearly 20 years

THE T-SERIES MGs are for many people the most classic examples of that famous marque; to some, indeed, a T-type MG *is* the classic sports car, period, which makes it all the more strange that they originated after a change of management that put Cecil Kimber, MG's founder, in a relatively subservient position. In fact he had little to do with their design, which was dictated from outside the Abingdon factory.

Although the highly-developed overhead-cam MGs favoured by Cecil Kimber had proved immensely successful in competitions throughout the world by the mid-1930s, those successes had brought no dramatic improvement in the sales of ordinary sports models. This did not go unnoticed by Lord Nuffield, the man behind the MG Car Company, who was, in any case, becoming tired of Kimber's preoccupation with motor racing. In the summer of 1935, as part of a wider reorganization of the Nuffield empire, he sold the MG Car Company to Morris Motors Ltd of Cowley, and appointed his right-hand man, Leonard Lord, to be managing director with authority over the unfortunate Kimber, who now found himself merely the director and general manager of the MG factory.

Leonard Lord lost no time in applying the sort of methods that were later to put him at the head of the mighty British Motor Corporation. He closed down MG's racing department in mid-season and discontinued all further work on the new 750 cc R-type, a car that had been hailed as a brilliantly advanced design. He also closed down MG's design department, leaving only two people there as liason men; the remainder either transferred to Cowley or left to find new jobs elsewhere. As a temporary measure for the forthcoming Motor Show the P-type Midget was given a larger engine and the N-type Magnette a new body, but the rest of the models were dropped.

It was made clear to all concerned that Kimber's policy – to design high-performance competition cars on which would be based future production sports models, using virtually the same components – was no longer acceptable. Future MGs would be designed by Morris Motors at Cowley, with the emphasis on low-cost production methods, making the fullest possible use of the Nuffield corporate parts bin. If this meant they were unsuitable for competition work, it mattered not a jot to either Nuffield or Lord.

The first of the new-generation MGs was announced in 1936, the SA 2-litre saloon, which had a Wolseley Super Six engine. A few months later the short-lived PB, last of the overhead-cam Midgets, was replaced by the MG TA, whose pushrod-overhead-valve engine was basically that of the contemporary Wolseley Ten.

The TA two-seater, although still called a Midget, was appreciably larger than its predecessors. With a wheelbase of 7 ft 10 in (236 cm) and track of 3 ft 9 in (114 cm) it was actually more like a Magnette in chassis dimensions and also in engine capacity, the latter having gone up from 939 cc to no less than 1292 cc. It was indicative of Kimber's now limited influence on design that hydraulic brakes, which he had always disliked and distrusted, were a feature of both the SA and TA models. The chassis frame still bore a close resemblance to those of previous MGs, having channel-section side-members that passed under the rear axle and swept up over the front one, tubular cross-members and leaf springs all round. As before, there was no eye to the trailing edges of the main leaves, which passed through split bronze bushes carried in the ends of the cross-members.

The chassis frame was boxed in for greater rigidity around the engine and gearbox, and its larger dimensions allowed for a roomier body with more space for the occupants and quite a lot more for their luggage. The TA was inevitably heavier than previous Midgets but the new engine gave a respectable 52.4 bhp at 5000 rpm compared with the PB's 43.3 bhp at 5500 rpm, and road tests soon showed that despite the increased space and comfort the grown-up Midget performed quite well. At £222, the same price as before, it offered good value, and during the production life of the TA its sales easily outstripped those of the PA and PB together. Some cars were offered with Airline Coupé bodywork, a 'streamlined' alternative built by Carbodies of Coventry and previously sold on the PA/PB chassis, but at £295 this was rather too expensive for most folk. More popular was the Tickford drophead coupé, a handsome if rather heavy little car costing £269 10s.

Most magazines rated the acceleration of the two-seater as good, with a 0-50 mph (80 kph) acceleration time of about 15 seconds and a standing quarter-mile in about 22 seconds, and most of them recorded a one-way maximum speed of almost 80 mph (129 kph). The testers were equally content with no more than 28 mpg, but a new 15-gallon tank provided an adequate range. Three gallons were held in reserve, with a two-way tap on the dash.

As indicated earlier, the TA was certainly not designed as a competition car, but the whole history of Abingdon demanded that the new MG should make some kind of

LEFT In every way a classic British sports car, this is a 1939 MG TA, originally priced at £222. The 1292 cc engine produced 52.4 bhp at 5000 rpm, and gave a top speed of almost 80 mph (129 kph)

showing in motor sport. Its predecessors had always performed well in that peculiarly British happening, the sporting trial, which was sufficiently widely supported to attract useful publicity. So the works built six special TAs for the Cream Cracker and Three Musketeer trials-team drivers, with lightened bodies, lower first and second gears and high-compression engines. In this form they won many awards, the Cream Crackers taking the MCC's Team Championship Trophy for the 1937 season. The Three Musketeer TAs were also entered for a 12-hour sports-car race at Donington, where they carried off the team prize.

For the 1938 season the two teams had new cars – TA Midgets once again, but extensively modified to meet a growing challenge from other teams. The Musketeers used Marshall superchargers to provide extra performance and gained many more awards. The Cream Cracker cars were at first fitted with 1548 cc unblown engines from another pushrod-overhead-valve MG of the period, the VA, but these were disappoint-

ing. Opened out to 1708 cc, however, they went well and again won the MCC Championship in 1938.

In the market place the TA Midget went through the same stages that every new MG has faced through the years, being at first regarded with deep suspicion by the diehard enthusiasts, then accepted almost grudgingly, and finally treated with ever-increasing respect. MG sales had been very poor in the year of the Nuffield takeover but they improved considerably in 1936 and hit a new record in 1937. In 1938 the Munich crisis caused another fall, but it was interesting to see how MG's export sales had started to grow, even in those pre-war days.

In 1939, completely unannounced, there arrived a new T-type which went into production only a few months before war broke out. The TA engine had been something of an oddball with its enormously long (102 mm) stroke, and cork-lined clutch running in oil. The unit which became available in the spring of 1939 had a peak power output only 2 bhp higher – 54.4 at 5200 rpm – but it was a far better piece of machinery, destined to become one of the classic engines of all time and still to be found under the bonnet of popular cars in the mid-1950s.

The ancestry of this new XPAG engine was Morris rather than Wolseley, for it was essentially the M-10 unit, but when given a bore of 66.5 mm to its stroke of 90 mm, it

BELOW *An immaculately restored TC with some weather equipment in place. The screen offered surprisingly good protection and the hood would seldom be raised*

ABOVE *The driver's view from a 1947 MG TC fitted with period aeroscreen which came into play when the fold-flat screen was lowered onto the scuttle.*

became an 11 hp instead of a 10 hp motor under the old RAC formula, which meant that a higher Road Fund tax was payable. As the amount payable per horsepower had also gone up that year, this was perhaps why Nuffield omitted to tell the motoring world that the 1292 cc TA Midget had been replaced by the 1250 cc TB in May 1939. None of the motor magazines did a comprehensive road test of the TB, which was almost indistinguishable from the TA in any case apart from the new engine and a dry clutch. Total TA production came to 3003, more than that of all previous MG models except the original M-type Midget, and the TB added a further 379 before car-building ceased with the outbreak of war.

In October 1945, just five weeks after the official ending of World War II, the MG Car Company announced their first – indeed, for some time their only – post-war model, the TC Midget. If Cecil Kimber had rather mixed feelings about the first of the T-types in 1936, it is even more ironic to remember that he probably never laid eyes on the TC, the most widely renowned and respected MG of all time. Kimber had been dismissed from his own company in November 1941 by Miles Thomas, a Nuffield director even more ambitious than Leonard Lord, and was killed in a railway accident eight months before the TC was announced in 1945.

It is difficult now to realize how desperately new cars were needed after six years of war. The only way that MG could even attempt to meet the demand was to do as all the other manufacturers were doing: get into production as soon as possible with an

essentially pre-war design. It might have been thought, too, that an open two-seater sports car was not the ideal choice for a one-model programme in the midst of post-war austerity, when petrol was of low octane rating, strictly rationed, and most of the magazines believed that the popular choice would be a no-frills economy four-seater saloon. However, MG's own records showed that only four of their pre-war models had topped a production rate of 1000 cars a year, and all of them were two-seater Midgets. On that basis the decision was reached to take the TB Midget, simplify the chassis slightly by fitting conventionally shackled leaf springs and make the body a little wider across the cockpit. There were new instruments, new shock absorbers, the wiring layout was improved and a single 12-volt battery was installed under the bonnet instead of the previous fitting of two 6-volt units at the rear of the car. In all other respects the post-war TC was virtually the pre-war TA/TB.

The Airline Coupé had disappeared with the TA and the Tickford drophead had followed it into limbo when the TB was discontinued, and thus the only body style for the TC Midget was the open two-seater. It cost, when announced, £375 plus another £105

ABOVE *Essentially a TA fitted with a 1250 cc Morris-based engine, this is a 1939 MG TB, only a few of which were built before the outbreak of war*

of purchase tax in the UK, but by the summer of 1946 the basic price had crept up to £412 10s.

The performance of the new TC became something of a *cause célèbre* when the first road test appeared in the January 1947 issue of *Motor Sport*, for the journal announced that the TC's 0-60 mph (97 kph) acceleration had occupied a leisurely 27.25 seconds, the standing quarter-mile had been timed at 23.45 seconds and the highest attainable speed was a one-way 65.75 mph (106 kph): the two-way mean maximum, it said, was a mere 63.5 mph (102 kph). Not surprisingly, the Nuffield publicity chief of that time, one Reg Bishop, invited the magazine's editor to explain how he had arrived at such extraordinary figures. Bishop's invitation was declined, and in retaliation he withdrew all Nuffield advertisements from the magazine in what other journalists dubbed the Bishop Ban. When the weekly magazines tested the TC later in the year, *Motor* reached 60 mph in 21.1 seconds, recorded a four-way average of 72.9 mph (117 kph) with the screen up, and their best one-way speed was 77.6 mph (125 kph). *Autocar* put the maximum at 75 mph (121 kph) and their 0-60 mph figure was 22.7 seconds. These figures, of course, were achieved on the low-octane Pool petrol of the post-war era. Overseas magazines published better performance figures, having access to fuel of better quality.

Such performance figures should perhaps not be regarded in the same way as modern figures. The art of road testing as we understand it today was still in its infancy and the testers did not have access to the equipment that is available nowadays. Nevertheless those low figures published by *Motor Sport* were quite widely cited.

The success story of the MG TC has often been told, but even in its native land the car was already an anachronism in the late 1940s, and very much more so overseas, where, in some countries, the production and development of modern cars had continued until 1942 or even later. Nevertheless in 1947 more TCs were sold overseas than in Britain, although the car still had a separate chassis frame when the majority of makers had gone to monocoque construction, and non-independent leaf springs when most had independent front suspension of one type or another. It was also fitted with an exposed radiator with an unpressurized cooling system, separate mudguards and headlamps, a massive exposed fuel tank at the rear and large-diameter wire-spoked wheels. It could not be bought with a radio or heater, there were no bumpers and, no matter where it was sold, every car was built with right-hand steering.

It was the American writer, Warren Weith, who expressed it better than anyone else when he referred to the TC simply as 'A way of life. A wildly different car that you jazzed around in on weekdays and raced on weekends…A moving spot of color on a still-drab post-war landscape.' Contrary to popular belief the vast majority of exported TCs were not sold in the USA, for the Americans remained conservative as always in their buying habits, and it was only a select minority that tasted the delights of the car when first it appeared. Of 10,000 cars built, only 2001 went to the USA, 4591 to other overseas markets and 3408 remained in Britain. And yet, although so few Americans actually bought the TC when it was new, the impact that it made upon them was something that persisted for many years.

The TC was raced with enthusiasm by the likes of Briggs Cunningham, John Fitch, and Phil Hill, the latter the first American to win the World Championship. It was also raced in Australia, Africa, Ireland, Switzerland, Singapore, Spain and, among many other places, in France, where a rebodied car ran twice in the Le Mans 24 Hours and one was entered in the French GP of 1949, when it was held as a sports car event.

Outselling previous MG models three to one, the TC Midget sowed the seeds of its own destruction, for in many countries where sports cars had previously been almost unknown, local salesman now demanded a new MG sports car that would be a little more comfortable and roomy. Abingdon took the chassis of the contemporary Y-type saloon, with its independent front suspension and pressed-steel disc wheels, cut five inches (13 cm) out of the wheelbase and fitted a TC body. This was the prototype TD Midget, which in production form had the same wheelbase as the TC, a front track of 3 ft 11½ in (121 cm) and a rear track of 4 ft 2 in (127 cm). The box-section chassis passed over the rear axle and the Y-type independent front suspension was retained, together with that model's rack-and-pinion steering. The wheels were a mere 15 in (38 cm) in diameter, more powerful two-leading-shoe front brakes were fitted and hypoid-bevel rear axle lowered the transmission line.

With more generous mudguards, a wider and more rounded body and bumpers front and rear, the new TD looked surprisingly different from the lean and lithe TC. Once again there were loud protests from many enthusiasts, but it was a more practical car than its illustrious predecessor because it offered at least the same performance with very much more comfort, a substantial increase in weight having been countered by lower overall gearing. Because of this their acceleration figures were virtually identical, but the TD was a thirstier car. On the other hand, most magazines recorded a higher maximum speed for the new model. Priced at a basic £445 on the home market, the TD was for a long time virtually unobtainable in the UK, no less than 32 cars going overseas for every single TD sold at home. This was partly because unlike the TC the TD was

RIGHT *Views of a 1952 MG TD, fitted with the 54.4 bhp 1250 cc engine. Apart from the restyled body, the TD differed from the TC in having independent front suspension, by coils, wishbones and lever-arm damper units*

EVOLUTION

MG TA introduced in 1936, replacing the P-series Midgets. It featured a 1292 cc overhead-valve engine rather than the 939 cc overhead-cam unit of the PB and hydraulic brakes. It sold for £222 and was available as an Airline coupé and drophead coupé as well the normal two-seater open sports body. 3003 TAs were built

1939 MG TB introduced. It was essentially the same as the TA except for its Morris-based 1250 cc engine and a dry clutch. TB production totalled 379

1945 MG TC introduced. The 1250 engine was retained. Its body was slightly wider than that of the TB and it now had 12-volt electrics. 10,000 TCs were built and two-thirds of them were exported

1949 MG TD introduced. It was loosely based on a shortened MG Y-type saloon with the Y-type's independent front suspension. It was powered by the 1250 cc engine. The TD was the first MG Midget that could be built with left-hand drive and consequently the vast majority of the 29,664 TDs built were exported

1953 MG TF introduced. It was basically a face-lifted version of the TD with more rakish bodywork

1954 The 1466 cc engine was made available in the TF from July. 6200 1250 cc TFs were built, along with 3400 of the 1500 version

1955 MG T series discontinued in favour of the MGA

designed so that it could easily be built with left-hand drive, and in the end it outsold the TC three to one.

Total TD production was 29,664 cars, including the mildly-tuned TD Mark II which was really a homologation special with re-worked cylinder head, larger valves and stronger springs. It also had a 9.2:1 compression ratio, larger carburettors and twin fuel pumps. Three of these works-prepared cars ran in selected races, scoring a class first, second and third in the 1950 Tourist Trophy at Dundrod.

But these were rapidly changing times. As the exciting new Jaguar XK120 two-seater was followed by other more modern sports cars in the early 1950s, the TD was increasingly criticized for its old-fashioned shape, and sales began to fall sharply, especially overseas. Abingdon designed a new two-seater based on the rebodied TD that George Phillips had driven at Le Mans in 1951, and a prototype was completed late in 1952. Earlier that year the Nuffield Group had merged with Austin under Sir Leonard

LEFT A stylish 1250 cc 1952 MG TD
INSET AND ABOVE Two examples of the
MG TF, held by many to be the most
attractive of them all

Lord, as he now was, to form the British Motor Corporation, and as he had also arranged to build a new two-seater designed by Donald Healey, the Abingdon project was turned down.

Thus the MG TF was made, a rather hurried facelift of the TD for the 1953 Motor Show, using a lower-compression version of the TD Mark II engine. The scuttle was lowered and the bonnet (now with fixed side-panels) dropped to a sloping imitation radiator with dummy filler-cap. The head-lamps were partly faired into the front wings, the tail was sharply raked and the dash was redesigned. Bucket seats were fitted and wire-spoked wheels were an option because the hubs had also been redesigned.

In its day the TF was not a commercial success, even when fitted with the 1466 cc engine that was available from July 1954 to counter the challenge of Triumph's much faster 2-litre sports car. When it was discontinued in 1955, to make way for the new MGA model, only 6200 of the 1250 cc TFs and 3400 of the 1500 cc cars had been built.

Nowadays, of course, the situation has changed completely. It is the TF which has become revered as the last of the 'square-rigged' MGs, commanding the highest prices among T-series models and, more recently, the subject of recreations using modern mechanical components.

ASTON M

Aston's need for a more competitive power unit spelt a change from straight-six to V8 layout. The result was a fine engine, although development was not problem-free

AS THE 1960S WORE ON, the Aston Martin management of the David Brown era increasingly realised the company would lose its position as a pre-eminent builder of high-performance GT cars – 'supercars' in 1980s jargon – unless it could offer more power. Its rivals, most of all Ferrari and Maserati, had steadily increased their power on offer and it was clear that for all its virtues, the Aston double overhead camshaft 3.7-litre 'six' was soon going to look pretty weak by comparison with 4.4 litres of V12 in

the Ferrari Daytona, for instance.

Accordingly Tadek Marek, the gifted Polish engineer who had designed the in-line six, turned his thoughts to an engine with greater capacity and therefore with more cylinders. If Marek ever thought of following Ferrari down the V12 road, no evidence of it has survived; the appeal of the V8 was as obvious as it had been to Maserati's Alfieri, it was compact, naturally stiff and quite smooth enough to give the kind of refinement Aston needed. As if that were not

ARTIN V8

encouragement enough, it was the era when America's V8 'musclecars' were showing remarkable performance even with relatively crude-looking OHV power units.

There was no question of Aston's V8 being crude-looking or overhead-valve. The only question was whether a single overhead camshaft per bank would suffice – which would keep down the cost but also save space immediately beneath the bonnet. The alternative was a proper twin-cam layout which would make the engine far bulkier but which promised greater potential power output plus the sales appeal of four cam-covers in Aston's prestige-conscious market.

Marek's initial approach was to use as much of the straight-six engine as he could. The object was clearly to use the tried and trusted cylinder head layout which, to begin

with, was carried across intact – a move made possible by retaining the 3.78 in (96 mm) bore. Thus the earliest V8 consisted in effect of two four-cylinder adaptations of the straight-six top end bolted to a 90 degree V8 crankcase and two-plane crankshaft. The stroke was 3.27 in (83 mm), giving a swept volume of 4.8 litres.

Sadly, things are never that simple. Even on the drawing board, the convenience of this adaptation was sacrificed when it was found that the original V-angle between the inlet and exhaust valves would have to be narrowed from 80 to 64 degrees to avoid the

The looks of the 1986 Aston Martin V8 Vantage belie its age, while its engine is still one of the finest produced by any manufacturer in the world.

inlet camshaft covers sticking up too far. That however was a minor inconvenience compared with the problems uncovered by an essay into Le Mans racing, powering the 1967 Lola team cars. The results of this exercise – for which the original design was bored-out to give the required 5-litre capacity – showed that too much reliance had been placed on the V8's natural rigidity, and that a combination of high stress and overheating had distorted the block to the point where the main bearings were buckled and the 'wet' liners had lost their sealing.

This was a major embarrassment because work was already well in hand on the new car to be powered by the V8. This was the work of Bill Towns, whose original concept was first to style a four-door car – which would be the new Lagonda that David Brown dearly wanted to introduce – from which the new two-door Aston would be derived by shortening the body. The result was that the car emerged very wide: a full six feet (183 cm), six inches (15 cm) wider than the DB6 it was intended to replace. That in turn meant it was heavier, to the extent where an extra two hundredweight (101 kg) seemed almost reasonable considering its visible bulk. At least the extra sprung weight suggested an improved ride, while decent handling was ensured by the adoption of de Dion rear suspension instead of a live axle, plus the wider wheelbase and fatter tyres. Meanwhile, though, economic problems had called a halt to the Lagonda end of the project, leaving the Aston Martin DBS looking uncomfortably bulky when it was launched in 1967.

After the long line of Touring-styled Aston Martins, culminating in the DB6, the lines of the newcomer were something of a change. The new car was much more modern in appearance although the wire wheels were something of a throwback. Altogether it was an eyecatching car although at that point it could hardly be called 'pretty.'

At that stage, thanks to the problems of the V8, the DBS was powered (underpowered, it quickly became evident) by the straight-six engine. Urgent work was already in hand to redesign the V8 crankcase to make it far stiffer, and to root the cylinder head studs deep down in the casing more effectively to absorb the head-lifting stresses of combustion. The main bearing caps were made even stiffer, and the bore and stroke were adjusted to 3.94 in (100 mm) and 3.35 in (85 mm) respectively so that the capacity went up to 5340 cc. The engine was eventually ready for production in 1969; the official launch of the DBS V8 took place in September of that year, the car at once distinguishable by its high-class 'power bulge' in the bonnet, needed to clear the V8 cam covers.

There were other changes too. The wire wheels beloved of Aston Martin traditionalists (with an ample supply of spare time, soapy water and old toothbrushes) stood no chance of withstanding V8 torque and gave way to modern alloy rims, shod with the new-fangled 70-series radial-ply tyres. The

ABOVE *When the V8 first appeared in late 1969, it still carried David Brown's initials in its name. Early cars also had twin headlamps and fuel injection*

rather horrid Borg-Warner automatic transmission was supplanted by the much nicer Chrysler TorqueFlite (you could still specify the five-speed ZF manual gearbox and twin-plate clutch if you were hardy enough). The brakes were uprated to match the higher performance and power steering became standard, rather than a delete-option for the muscular.

A few months before, the overall picture had been put more clearly into perspective with a short ceremony at the Piccadilly showrooms in which a one-off Lagonda – complete with V8 engine – was unveiled. This car, specially built for Sir David Brown, looked almost remarkably better than the shortened two-door: sufficiently so for the assembled journalists to burst into spontaneous applause (which doesn't often happen). Finished in resplendent royal purple, this car showed what a difference the extra foot of wheelbase and body length made to the overall proportions – but it was five years before another four-door car emerged.

One of the annoying things about the launch of the DBS V8 was that no power output was quoted, the factory apeing the Rolls-Royce attitude that it was 'sufficient'. Stories quickly circulated among engineers and writers that the real reason was the inability of the 5.3-litre V8 to match the power output of the 4-litre, 3-carburettor 'Vantage' straight-six, which turned out a claimed 325 bhp. Others looked at that claimed specific power output of 81 bhp per litre and compared it with (for instance) the quoted 255 bhp of the 4-litre Maserati straight-six of very similar layout. Could it possibly be that to have quoted an honest output for the V8 would have pointed an accusing finger at the brochures of its ancestor?

It was manifestly clear that the V8 was, in fact, much more powerful than the Vantage 'six'. Comparing the *Autocar* figures for the original six-cylinder DBS of 1968, and the

V8-engined car of 1970, the latter has an advantage of no less than 21 mph (34 kph) in maximum speed, suggesting by rule-of-thumb that it had the benefit of at least an extra 85 bhp and probably more. Just as important, the V8 offered a huge torque advantage over the six, inevitably in view of its 35 percent greater capacity. That made itself felt in the lowering of the 0–60 mph time from 8.6 to exactly 6 seconds.

However, all was not entirely well with the DBS V8. There were drawbacks like the use of four small headlamps, which resulted in a dipped beam that would have disgraced a car with half the performance; the cooling system was under-specified for continuous high-speed motorway cruising or for mid-city jam-crawling; but most of the criticisms centred around the Bosch mechanical fuel-injection system which Aston Martin had adapted for the V8. To put it mildly, the results were less than successful and early V8s were plagued by difficult starting and erratic idling, and by poor drive-away characteristics when they were part-warm. It was also found that the injection system was a hindrance rather than a help when it came to developing the engine to meet the USA Federal exhaust emission regulations.

Things had begun to improve, at least on the engineering front, by 1972. The original, rather fussy nose styling and four small headlamps gave way to a new, smoother (though three inches longer) nose which has remained standard ever since, together with the two big headlamps which give excellent light output on main *and* dipped beam when fitted with H4 halogen bulbs. At that stage too, the original conventional contact-breaker ignition had given way to a Lucas Opus breakerless system, and the final drive ratios were raised from 3.54 to 3.31 for the manual-gearbox cars, and from 3.07 to 2.88 for the automatics.

It would be wrong to blame the 1973 energy crisis (the outcome of the October War) for Aston Martin's troubles of the time. The preceding years had already seen the collapse of its American markets, and an over-stocking situation even in Britain which led to an across-the-board slashing of £1000 from every model in the range (surely to the fury of anyone who had just bought one!). Early in 1972 David Brown could no longer afford to subsidise Aston Martin out of the

ABOVE AND RIGHT *One of the first Vantages, with its blanked-off grille. Its marked body roll couldn't disguise its tremendous grip. Later cars suffered from reduced roll and yet handled even better*

profits of his other major industrial interests, and the company passed into the control of William Willson's Company Developments Ltd.

This phase of Aston's history lasted but three years, though in that time the troublesome fuel injection was done away with and the cars returned to four Weber DCOE carburettors – which remained standard for the next 13 years. The switch overcame the persistent problems encountered with injection, and to that extent simplified certification for emission regulations. It must be observed though that many of the major car manufacturers at exactly this time were switching *from* carburettors *to* fuel injection for the sake of lower emissions! The essential difference was that few of them were working on 5.3-litre twin-cam V8s – nor were they tied down to Aston Martin's frugal development budget. One of the most crucial aspects of the change was that four Weber carburettors were significantly cheaper than one highly specialised eight-cylinder fuel injection system. Amid all these engineering changes there comes a small but psychologically important move: the old badges were thrown away and the former DBS V8 became quite simply the Aston Martin V8, or even AM V8 for short.

The carburettor-equipped cars were certainly less powerful than the fuel-injected ones. The customer was not to know this, at least not officially, since quoted output figures remained taboo; but it was clearly reflected in road tests results which mostly showed the maximum speed down by 5 mph or more – which our previously-mentioned rule of thumb equates to a deficit of perhaps 20 bhp. That however was the least of Aston's troubles as the energy crisis spread its pall of gloom over the motor industry (especially the specialised high-performance end of it) and it was just at this time that Maserati went to the wall and Lamborghini encountered major problems. In 1975 the company officially ceased trading for a time, until Alan Curtis and two American partners came to the rescue just before it was too late: Rolls-Royce and others had already recruited many of Newport Pagnell's skilled panel-beaters, the core of the workforce.

However, the attachment of many of the workers to Aston Martin and the loyalty of the Newport Pagnell community to the firm meant that many key workers soon returned to the company from the alternative jobs they had taken at the time of the closure. With Alan Curtis at the helm, Aston Martin was soon tentatively back on its feet.

While master-minding the design and initial development of the new Lagonda, Curtis (who became Managing Director in 1977) also came to grips with the problems of quality control, and applied new impetus to the V8 range, following three distinct avenues of advance. The first was to develop the basic engine sufficiently to recoup the performance lost in the change from injection to carburettors; the second, a much more extensive programme of engine and chassis changes, to create a genuinely high-performance model (the V8 Vantage); the third, to recreate after a gap of several years a convertible variant (the Volante).

The first development involved the adoption of a new camshaft profile giving more uniform valve acceleration and thus reducing the necessary clearances and making for quieter operation. This was combined with an additional five degrees of valve overlap. Although this must have raised the peak power speed, the overall result was a quieter and altogether more refined power unit with useful extra punch. By 1978 it had been combined with a batch of 'Stage 1' improvements to the body and its equipment to produce a significantly better car.

Neither the Vantage nor the Volante names were new, since the former had long been applied to the up-rated 'special equipment' versions of the DB series from the DB2 onwards, while the DB5/DB6 convertibles had been Volantes. Curtis' notion was to make both V8 developments models in their own right. The Vantage obtained substantial extra power mainly through improved breathing: new camshaft profiles, bigger valves with more overlap, and bigger-choked Weber carburettors (48 mm instead of 42 mm!) to match. This is 30 percent more choke area, and rightly reflects the Vantage's power advantage. Again there were no official output figures, but in later years the gaff was blown by a German law requiring figures to be published there: no fluency was needed to understand 306 bhp (DIN) for the Stage 1 standard car, and 360 bhp (DIN) for the Vantage.

The greater power was matched by chas-

sis changes that included stiffer springs and wider rear track, re-rated Koni dampers, 255/60 section tyres and deep 'beard' spoiler as well as a boot-lid lip at the rear. The author's road test for *Autocar* in 1977 was brought to a halt by a rear brake pipe fracture at Volkswagen's Ehra Lessien test track, but an indicated and still-accelerating 167 mph (269 kph) at nearly 6500 rpm had already been seen on the autobahn on the way out, even if it could not qualify as a genuine two-way mean maximum. The 0–60 mph time of 5.4 seconds was just as impressive considering the car's weight.

As for the Volante, a soft-top adaptation should have been simple in view of Aston Martin's immensely strong chassis of welded sheet-steel sections. In the event, the removal of the roof nevertheless caused some scuttle shake problems until local stiffening was added to the chassis to tie the windscreen footings more positively to the centre bulkhead and tunnel area. The hood, of course, was power-operated and was installed in such a way that its stowage robbed the car of boot space rather than back seat room (whatever accusations may have been levelled at it, nobody has ever accused the V8 of not being a tolerable four-seater). Mechanically the Volante was identical to the standard V8 – the extra Vantage torque might have posed more problems for body stiffness, and in any case the convertible was not truly a high-performance car if only because it suffered badly from wind noise at anything approaching 100 mph (161 kph).

There have been two further stages of mechanical development in the standard V8. The first was announced in 1980 and took the form of a higher-compression engine (to 9.3:1 from the standard 9.0:1) with reworked cylinder heads and valve gear. The valve overlap was reduced, as was the port area, while the valve area itself was increased. The object was to match the whole flow system to the same rate of gas flow, and the logical result (no figures, yet again!) was a useful lift in torque output for little if any loss of power – accompanied by extremely worthwhile gains of 10 percent or more in the official fuel economy test results.

The final major development in the V8 saga – thus far – took place yet again under new management, for early in 1981 the Curtis-led consortium sold out to two British companies, Pace Petroleum and C.H. Industrials. Pace's Chief Executive, Victor Gaunt-

A 1971 example of the DBS V8 with its fuel-injected engine FAR LEFT, and its traditional-looking interior, LEFT. Note the large steering wheel, the upright handbrake lever and the large array of warning lights and instruments. The Aston is a big car to drive and the clutch and gearchange require a firm hand which can become quite wearing in traffic, hence the popularity of the auto 'box'

EVOLUTION

The Aston Martin DBS V8 was introduced in September 1969 with a 5.3-litre four-cam V8 and a choice of Chrysler TorqueFlite three-speed automatic or ZF five-speed manual transmission

1972 The front of the car was restyled and lengthened and the lights were improved. Electronic ignition was fitted and the final drive ratio increased

1973 Fuel injection was dispensed with due to emissions problems and Weber carburettors fitted. Power output declined by around 20 bhp

1977 The more powerful V8 Vantage version was introduced along with the Volante convertible

1980 The standard V8 engine was given a higher compression ratio and larger valve area

1983 The Vantage's wheel arches were flared to accomodate wider wheels and Pirelli P7 tyres

1985 A Zagato version of the Vantage was proposed

1986 Fuel injection returned to the V8s, except for the Vantage which remained with Weber carburettors. The Vantage Zagato was introduced at the Geneva Show

1989 V8 celebrates 20 years of production

A late version of the elegant Volante Cabriolet whose looks are as striking as those of the coupé. Although the car's interior has been improved by the inclusion of a walnut dashboard, the layout is still 'Classic Aston'

1984 – ensured there would be no such snags as plagued the 1970s system. In a notable shift of policy, Aston Martin announced that power output was 305 bhp ('identical to the previous carburettor unit') while torque was quoted as 320 lb ft. Official test fuel economy was improved by 11 per-cent; and to ice the cake, so to speak, the system's compactness meant the bonnet-bulge could be removed to leave the panel flat, as it was in the original DBS.

This development did not apply to the Vantage, however, which continued to use its four huge Weber carburettors; this mod-el's most recent visible changes (at the time of writing) were made in 1983 when its wheel arches were flared to accommodate even wider wheels – 8 in rims carrying Pirelli P7 tyres.

A further note in the V8 story was sound-ed early in 1985 when Aston Martin announced that the Vantage would serve as the basis for a new Zagato-styled model which would be lighter, have lower aerody-namic drag and an engine modified with higher-lift camshafts and even bigger car-burettors to produce 432 bhp – such accura-cy suggesting it may already have been seen on the test-bed – to give a maximum speed of 188 mph (302 kph). While not strictly a continuation of the V8 line, the Zagato will therefore depend on its well-proven under-pinnings. Meanwhile, as the painstaking fuel injection programme proves, the V8 story itself is far from written and the car is likely to continue in production, with further im-provements, at least until 1990.

lett, has since taken a major and direct interest in Aston Martin's progress. Early in 1986, this included a return to fuel injection.

The new injection was the advanced elec-tronic system developed by Weber, whose Aston Martin associations have of course been long, close and continuous. Extensive development work – injection-equipped Astons were running around Bologna in

Germany

Throughout its history the German automobile industry has been marked by peaks and troughs associated with the ravages of conflict – and yet out of that conflict came inspiration for some of the greatest cars of all time.

The Volkswagen Beetle, (the people's car) for instance, was the direct result of Hitler's desire to put the whole of his nation on wheels, and as part of his grand scheme, he had a network of fine roads built, upon which the cars could run.

The VW's success continued and in the post-war period it became the world's best selling automobile – and from it

Professor Ferdinand Porsche, the designer of the VW's rear engine, produced the amazing Porsche marque. In pre-war Germany, the BMW 328 set new and revolutionary standards of performance and styling that influenced a generation of post-war machines. However, not many other cars have matched the grandeur and power of the Mercedes and the Maybach. Latterly, with characteristic skill, the German car industry has re-asserted itself at the forefront of technical progress, with flagship cars such as the turbo-charged, four-wheel-drive Audi Quattro, and the 'supercar' racing prowess of the BMW M1.

The 911 is now twenty years old and has developed from an adequate 130 bhp sports coupé to a true supercar in the form of the 3.3-litre 160 mph Porsche Turbo and one of the world's fastest convertibles

IT IS DOUBTFUL if anyone realised, when the Porsche 911 first appeared in 1963, just how long the car would remain in production and how many versions it would spawn. Even now, in 1984 we are not sure: all we know is that the design has just been updated yet again, and given its biggest-yet engine.

The reasoning behind the 911 was simple. By the early 1960s the bulbously-styled twitchy-handling Porsche 356 was becoming outdated. Its Volkswagen origins were too obvious, and extra power had done nothing to make it an easier car for anyone but an expert to drive. Certainly there was no way it could be given more power without making it near-lethal and Porsche had ambitions to move up a league in the sports car world.

Thus the 911 was not a 356 replacement, but rather a more up-market design which learned a great deal from the older car's shortcomings.

The only way to move up the sports-car market is to add more power and Porsche did this by designing one of the classic engines of all time, an air-cooled flat-six made entirely of light alloys, aluminium and magnesium. Originally, the engine was of 2-litre capacity, equipped with Weber carburettors and delivering 130 bhp; but one of its most notable attributes was the way it could be 'stretched' to achieve greater swept volume and (in the end) over twice as much power.

To go with the new engine, Porsche styled an equally classic body, a smooth coupé whose lines excited universal admiration. Under this attractive new skin the engineers remained faithful to the mechanical layout they knew well, placing the engine at the rear of the car, aft of the back axle which formed part of a transaxle in unit with the all-indirect gearbox. If today, that seems an unwise thing to have

done, you must remember that in the early 1960s rear-engined cars were all the rage. The VW Beetle was at the height of its success, while Fiat, Hillman, Renault and Simca all had new rear-engined designs which were destined for large-scale production.

At the time, Porsche's engineers obviously thought they had done enough to overcome the wayward handling of the old 356 by changing the rear suspension from swing-axles (borrowed from the VW Beetle, of course) to semi-trailing arms. That did overcome the awful camber-change problem of the old suspension and the dreaded jacking-up effect which left so many inexpert drivers facing the way they had come without knowing exactly how or why. In other respects, the rear-engined layout still seemed a good one. It gave good weight distribution for traction on slippery surfaces, and for effective braking; and it kept the engine well away from the cabin, and reasonably accessible for service. The real disadvantages of a tail-heavy weight distribution where the handling was concerned, only became evident later. Even then, Porsche engineers argued with some force that they had made the engine as light as possible, while its flat-six layout kept the centre of gravity low; but it wasn't enough.

In 1963, all that was for the future. The only hiccup of the 911 launch came right at the beginning: Porsche was going to call the car 901, until somebody pointed out that Peugeot had already registered all the three-figure numbers with an 0 in the middle. The 1 was then substitute

LEFT *The 911 Cabriolet now numbers itself among the world's fastest open cars. This example bears one of the private number plates of Porsche Cars GB's press fleet*

There was also, to prevent the 356 enthusiasts from complaining too much, a tamer, 90 bhp, 1.66-litre four-cylinder Porsche 912 with the same body. That *was* a direct replacement for the 356, but it didn't last long: it was soon replaced by the ugly, but cheaper to make, 914 which reverted to the tradition of a Volkswagen basis.

In 1963 the 911 set out on its long and illustrious career, and Porsche entered it in as many sporting events as possible to build up its reputation. In particular, with its excellent braking and traction it became a formidable rally car – in the hands of experts who saw its tail-happiness as a virtue, if anything. The early road tests were also full of praise, though careful phrases about the 911 being 'more of an expert's car…' often worked into the text.

Although the 911 first made its mark as a rally car, remaining competitive in its various forms right up to the end of the Seventies, it also quickly made its mark in circuit racing not only as a sprint car and as a long distance machine, but also as a saloon car which, by some quirk of the regulations, it qualified as!

In 1969, the 911 was redesigned to the extent where it might almost have justified another type number. It emerged with a wheelbase 2.3 inches longer than before, with wider front and rear track, and with the front suspension completely reworked into a MacPherson strut layout instead of double-wishbone. The steering and handling were certainly improved as a result, and the way was clear at last for a steady increase in

power. Sales of this revamp were helped just as much by the fact that the 911's competition success was at a peak. It won the Monte Carlo Rally three times on the trot in 1968/69/70, in the hands of Vic Elford and then Björn Waldegård: it says much for the long life and steady development of the design that it won *again* in 1978 – and was only narrowly beaten in 1981!

The development of the 911 proceeded through a number of careful stages. First came the introduction of Bosch fuel injection, which gave rise to the 911E (for *Einspritz* – injection). Porsche's policy was to offer a basic model, still carburettor-

equipped and usually known as the 911T, with the 911E above it offering a modest power boost, and then a 911S, also fuel-injected but tuned for much greater power. In 1969 the T, E and S models offered 110, 140 and 170 bhp respectively: and far more output would have been available had not the company, as part of its 'Mark 2' development, decided to drop the compression ratio of the 2-litre engine so that all models could be run on 2-star fuel.

The next stage of development came when the engine was given its first capacity stretch. The flat-six was 'over-square' anyway, with a bore of 80 mm for a stroke of

The 911 made its debut at the Frankfurt Show in 1964 (LEFT) but by 1974 had developed into the more purposeful-looking 210 bhp Carrera (ABOVE). The interior of the original car (RIGHT) remained essentially the same for many years as the cabin of the later Sportmatic (BELOW) shows

cial' to enable the 911 to compete in production car events. Yet in 1974 the whole range switched to the bigger engine, its capacity once again increased by enlarging the cylinder bore (from 84 to 90 mm). The reaction to the 2.4 litres had been good enough to convince Porsche it was on the right track with the high-torque, greater-flexibility approach. The new Bosch K-Jetronic fuel injection was adopted across the board – 1974 was the year the 911 said goodbye to carburettors with very little regret – and the long-established T/E/S model lineup was scrapped. In its place there was a basic 911 with 150 bhp, a 911S with 175 bhp (still on a compression ratio of only 8.5 : 1, still running on 2-star fuel) – and an exotic and expensive RS Carrera with 210 bhp. Tests had already shown this last model to be one

EVOLUTION

1966 Carrera competition model introduced with twin-cam version of the 1991 cc six producing 210 bhp, and glassfibre body.

1968 Semi automatic transmission available.

1969 Wheelbase and track increased significantly and front suspension changed from wishbones and torsion bars to McPhersons struts.

1970 Fuel injection introduced to form the 911E (*Einspritz*) and displacement increased to 2195 cc. 911T produced as the basic carburettor version producing 110 bhp. Above it came the 911E (140 bhp) and above that the 911S with 170 bhp.

1972 Engine displacement again increased, to 2343 cc and the 911S now produced 190 bhp with a top speed of 143 mph (230 kph).

1973 Carrera RS introduced with 2.7-litre version of the six cylinder engine producing 210 bhp.

1974 T/E/S line up discontinued in favour of basic 911 (150 bhp), 911S (175 bhp) and RS Carrera (210 bhp).

1975 Turbo introduced with displacement increased to 3 litres and power to 260 bhp.

1978 Five-speed gearbox becomes standard equipment. Turbo engine displacement rises to 3.33 litres and power to 300 bhp.

1982 Carrera becomes the standard 911 with 3164 cc displacement and 231 bhp.

1983 Carrera Cabriolet introduced at Geneva Show.

1988 25 years after announcement of model, range comprises 'standard' 911s, plus four-wheel drive and 'flat-nosed' variants. No sign of production ending.

only 66 mm, and this showed in its free-revving nature. Nevertheless there was still room to take the bore out to 84 mm without much trouble, giving a capacity of 2.2 litres, and this was done for the 1970 models. As a result, the power outputs of the three versions went up to 125, 155 and 180 bhp respectively. For the first time in production, lower-profile tyres were also adopted, the 911E and S coming with 185/70-15 covers.

The engine changes made the unit even higher-revving than before in character, and in retrospect the 2.2-litre cars were probably the least pleasant of the whole 911 series, except perhaps for those drivers who took a

positive delight in shifting gears and listening to a high-pitched roar. Others must have been heartily relieved that the 2.2-litre models only lasted a couple of years before they gave way to the 2.4 litres.

In a sense, Porsche was cheating to call the new version the 911 2.4, because the greater capacity – achieved by stretching the stroke to 70.4 mm while leaving the bore alone – was actually only 2341 cc. What was more interesting was that Porsche had somewhat changed tack with the new unit. True, the power output of each version (still T, W and S) was up: but only to 130, 165 and 190 bhp respectively. What Porsche had done was to concentrate on improving the torque, making the car more flexible and generally easier to drive. Far from making the 911 slower against the stopwatch, the changes eased the problems of getting the car off the standing-start line so that Porsche moved closer to the 'supercar' league: the author recorded a 0–60 mph time of 6.4 sec in a 911E 2.4 road test. That time made it quicker than a Jaguar E-type V12 or a Lamborghini Miura, for instance, though the Porsche was still some way short of supercar top speeds at 'only' 139 mph (224 kph).

However, the 2.4-litre models in their turn lasted only a couple of years before being replaced by the 2.7-litre versions. This time the trail had been blazed, in 1972, by the appearance of the Carrera which was originally supposed to be a 'homologation spe-

of the fastest-accelerating of all production cars, with a 0–60 mph (96 kph) time of about 5.5 sec and a maximum of approximately 150 mph (241 kph). Nor was the RSC ridiculously expensive, for what it was, considering it still had the lightweight body panels of the prototypes: early in 1974 it listed at £8580 in Britain, compared with £6993 for the 'ordinary' 911S 2.7 version.

Porsche buyers discovered to their pleasure that the 2.7s were an all-round improvement. While giving much the same performance as the 2.4s, they were around 15 per cent more economical, while their higher gearing also tended to give the engine an easier time. Porsche must have decided that the trend was too good to give up, because the next move was to add a turbocharger – something which, while it adds considerably to the power of an engine, does even more for the torque.

Actually, the Porsche Turbo carried the designation 930 rather than 911, but that didn't stop almost everybody referring to the new version as the 911 Turbo. The body shape was the same, so was the mechanical layout and so, in essence, was the engine. In detail it differed, partly in having the lower compression ratio needed to prevent knocking under turbocharger boost, but also in having the cylinder bore opened out (yet again) to 95 mm, to give a capacity of just under 3-litres.

If the 911 had been hovering on the border of supercar performance for a long time, the Turbo moved directly into the big league. The trouble was that on paper, the effect was less than obvious. The noticeable turbocharger 'lag' and the grip of the very wide tyres meant that the 3-litre Turbo was difficult to get quickly off the standing-start line: indeed, the 2.7-litre RSC was certainly quicker, and didn't sacrifice much in maximum speed either. But once the Turbo was actually on the move, the engine running fast enough to keep the turbocharger wound up, the Turbo was an electrifying car to drive. It proved beyond all doubt that the really important thing was not so much the ability to blast off the line, as to have the torque to burst quickly from 60 to 90 mph (100 kph to 145 kph) and beyond. Here the Turbo was almost in a class of its own. Such was the spread of its torque curve that Porsche fitted the Turbo with a four-speed gearbox rather than the five speed which had become standard in the normally-aspirated cars.

The Turbo was only one avenue of Porsche development. It came quickly on to the production scene: following its first showing at the Paris Salon in 1974, it was launched in Britain in the spring of 1975 at a price of nearly £15,000. That price, so very much higher than the standard 911 range, showed the need for continued development of the latter. In a way, the Turbo was doing its bit

Whether in a single-tone finish or in the colours of their racing-team sponsors of the late 1970s, the Porsche Turbo has never failed to turn heads with its brutal look

towards the extension of the 911 range as a whole. Not only did it attract renewed attention just when interest might otherwise have been running out: it also proved the full 3-litre engine which, sure enough, found its way into the rest of the 911 range (in normally-aspirated form) for the 1977 model year. The extent to which Porsche valued that fat torque curve could be judged from the fact that the 3-litre 911SC produced just 185 bhp – slightly less than the 1972 2.4-litre 911S! That didn't alter the fact that the 3-litre car was just as quick, easier by far to drive, and still more economical.

For the following model year, 1978, Turbo owners got back their capacity advantage. The Turbo engine was stretched in both bore and stroke (to 97 mm × 74.4 mm) to achieve a swept volume of 3.33 litres. Power rose to 300 bhp, and torque more than accordingly: whatever the remaining problems of turbo lag (and they had in any case been reduced by three years of detail engineering development) the Turbo – now with the official designation 933 – became one of the quickest true production cars in the world. It came close to the magic 5 sec to 60 mph, and its maximum speed was comfortably over 160 mph (258 kph).

Interestingly, however, in modern-day Porsche racing which has proliferated in the UK, the Turbo 911 seldom gets the better of the lighter and more agile normally aspirated cars, in particular the RS Carrera. On the long straights the Turbo may have the edge, but under braking and between tight corners the RS is usually the faster.

Whatever its reputation as a builder of high-performance sports cars, Porsche has always been keen to show a responsible attitude towards the real world of motoring and pressures such as the energy crisis – even though one might assume most Porsche buyers are well insulated against its effects. The 911 was, for instance, one of the first cars to carry several years' warranty against body corrosion; and in 1982 we saw the 911 range given engines of higher efficiency, gaining in fuel economy as a result but also enjoying a performance bonus. By now, the power output of the 911 was up to 204 bhp in European form, a long way from that original 130 bhp. Yet there was still more to come. At a time when people were asking whether the 911 had not finally run its development course, Porsche put together yet another engine variant. This time the Stuttgart engineers combined the standard 95 mm bore with the Turbo's longer 74.4 mm stroke, to give a capacity of 3,164 cc. Now the Carrera name was made standard, and with good reason, since the 'basic' 911 design had 231 bhp available – in other words, appreciably more than the original 'exotic' Carrera of the 1970s. That, for the moment, is as far as Porsche 911 engine development has gone – though in the light of so many previous happenings, it would be a brave man who predicted it would be the *last*.

Compared with the ultra-complicated 911 engine story, body developments have been

simpler by far. That classic shape has a habit of remaining obvious even when considerable attempts have been made to spoil it. In this context, the word spoil has a double meaning. The most obvious trend of 911 body development has been the sprouting of spoilers at both ends of the car. At the front, a moderate beard-type spoiler is all that is needed, but the 911 rear has, since the mid-1970s, sprouted a bigger and bigger rear wing immediately below the rear window. The spoilers are not there for mere appearance. They are badly needed for the downforce they create, because the 911's basic shape and rearward weight distribution do nothing at all for high-speed stability or cornering power. That is why the rear wing has grown progressively bigger as more power has been added. That in turn explains why the 911's maximum speed has always been ultimately disappointing in the

sense that even the 3.3-litre Turbo falls some way short of 170 mph (274 kph). The penalty of downforce is extra drag, and there is no doubt that the standard 911's drag coefficient is a very long way short of the figures boasted by the current generation of European front-driven cars. Ultimately, then, that 160 mph (260 kph) 'wall' is the result of the rear-engined layout and the original body shape: you could take off the rear wing and go a lot faster, if you could stay on the road.

By most definitions, a sports car is an open car. Porsche's answer to this marketing requirement came very early in the model's life, in the form of the Targa – a much-imitated body shape in which a permanent roll-over hoop could be bridged to the windscreen header rail by a rigid roof panel, or covered by a soft-top. The Targa kept the open-car enthusiasts quiet for more than 15

ABOVE LEFT *The dashboard of the 1984 Carrera Cabriolet which still bears more than a resemblance to those of yore*
ABOVE *The Carrera engine which delivers its 231 bhp from behind the rear wheels and gives the car excellent traction out of bends but which can also upset the handling getting through them*
BELOW *The full convertible '84 Cabriolet*
ABOVE RIGHT *The 3-litre 911SC of 1977*

years; but the early 1980s saw a new European enthusiasm for proper open cars – a fashion sparked off by the VW Golf GLi – and in 1982 Porsche showed a 911 Cabriolet at the Geneva Show. The version was in production for the 1983 model year, and now forms a part of the regular line-up.

It may be part of the sports-car image which has meant the 911 never appeared either with full automatic transmission, nor with power-assisted steering. True, with a rear engine and little load on the front wheels, power assistance would hardly be necessary. Even with the very wide tyres fitted to current 911s (the front tyres are now 205/55-16s, while those at the rear are 225/50-16) the low-speed steering loads are not unduly high. As for automatic transmission, Porsche has for a very long time trodden a diplomatic middle-way with the Sportomatic, a transmission which combines a conventional 'manual' gearbox, an automatic clutch operated by a switch in the gear lever knob, and a torque converter to soften out the changes and allow clutchless stopping and starting. Because the torque converter is also a torque multiplier, fewer gears are needed. Early Sportomatic 911s had four speeds; the 3-litre models had three-speed boxes. In any case, the Sportomatic has died with the introduction of the 3.2-litre Carrera, Porsche's philosophy being that today's 911 buyers are more than ever out-and-out enthusiasts who want a manual shift: there are fully-automatic versions of the 924, 944 and 928 for customers who are less keen on doing it themselves.

It remains extremely hard to explain the 911's appeal – its downright refusal to die even though ten years ago, the end of 911 production was a firm date in the Porsche management plan. By comparison with many supercars the 911 is extremely practical: it is easy to see out of, it has leg and headroom for really big drivers, the ground clearance to be taken over rough roads without worry, and a deserved reputation for reliability and lack of temperament: Porsche service schedules are as wide-spaced as Volkswagen's. Yet by modern standards the 911 has plenty of drawbacks. Its cabin is narrow and poorly ventilated, its control layout is awkward, its ride by no means good – and there is the whole question of stability and handling. The 911 is, as so many people have said, an expert's car. It has always had a trick of going faster then the driver thinks. It responds best to the driver who thinks ahead, and especially to the one who, in the old racing mould, is 'slow in, fast out'. The 911 bites hardest when you make the mistake of going into a corner too fast and trying to shed the speed half-way round. Do that, and you can find yourself facing the other way almost as quickly as you might have done in the old 356.

Perhaps that *is* part of the 911's appeal: that everybody who buys one is prided to think of himself as an expert. And it is true that until the moment when you discover that by 911 standards you are not, there is great pleasure in the sheer response of the steering and the engine. Other cars can give you the same pleasure: but they demand sacrifices in other directions beside which the 911 appears the height of civilisation.

Porsche has made rather more than 200,000 911s since 1964. Production continues at the rate of about 80 per day – and nobody, any longer, seems prepared even to guess when it will stop.

BMW 328

Its performance was nothing less than breathtaking, yet the pre-war 328 was solidly built and untemperamental. Its 2-litre, six-cylinder engine was a German classic

THERE ARE MANY knowledgeable enthusiasts who would say that if one had to choose one single pre-war car as the most significant in the early development of the modern high-performance sports car, it would have to be the BMW Type 328. Half a century ago, when most German sports cars were uninspired and lacking in performance, the Type 328 made its first appearance at a Nürburgring race meeting, winning its category so convincingly that everybody was highly impressed, and before that first season of competi-

tions ended it was clear that the new model stood head-and-shoulders above the rest.

The 328 was light in weight and good to look at, with lines so far ahead of their time that the car still looked modern a decade later. Its rigid tubular chassis and independent front suspension, allied to rack-and-pinion steering, provided a standard of roadholding and handling that was revolutionary in the middle 1930s, while the six-cylinder engine with its highly unusual valve-gear gave an exceptional power output and a maximum speed of around 100 mph (161 kph).

Until the advent of the Type 328, Bayerische Motoren-Werke had not been greatly admired for their cars. The company had started during World War I as builders of aero engines, and in the early 1920s had earned a fine reputation for their motorcycles, but no cars were produced until in 1928/9 they took over the Dixi factory at Eisenach, where a modified version of the humble Austin Seven was built under licence. For some time the German army had

to do their manoeuvres in these unlikely vehicles, because the Treaty of Versailles forbade their using heavy machinery. There was also a sporting version of the Dixi, not unlike the Austin Seven Ulster model but known as the Wartburg, reviving a name that the Eisenach company had first used at the turn of the century. BMW's experience of the competition world, gained with their motorcycles, helped the little Dixi sports models to win the team prize in the 1929 Austrian Alpine Trial.

In 1932 the BMW company began to move away from their Austin associations with the introduction of the AM-1 or 3/20 model. Its 782 cc engine was related to the Seven unit but had overhead valves, and the chassis was changed completely, being now a central backbone with independent suspension all round by swing axles. This arrangement was not entirely successful, and for the Type 303 of 1933 they reverted to semi-elliptic springs carrying a live axle at the rear. But the chassis frame was now tubular, and there were lower wishbones

The beautifully balanced lines of an immaculately restored BMW 328; its dashboard was extremely informative

instead of swing axles at the front, with a transverse leaf spring.

More significant in BMW's future history was the fact that the Type 303 also had a six-cylinder engine. It was really just the 3/20 engine with two extra cylinders, making the capacity 1173 cc, but this 30 bhp power unit was ideal for Hitler's new autobahns where German drivers were able to maintain a cruising speed of 100 kph (62 mph) for long distances. The Type 303 was also the first BMW with a divided front grille, nicknamed *Nieren* by the Germans (it means 'kidneys') which the shape was thought to resemble!

It was in 1933 that Fritz Fiedler of Horch joined BMW, where he devoted his considerable abilities to developing the six-cylinder cars. His first effort was the Type 315, in which the engine was enlarged to 1490 cc and power went up to 34 bhp, raising the maximum speed to 68 mph (110 kph). An indication of things to come was BMW's entry in the 1934 Monte Carlo Rally with a team of neat, sports two-seaters with three-carburettor, high-compression versions of the Type 315 engine which produced 40 bhp. The type 315/1, as this first true BMW sports model was called, was sold with a guaranteed top speed of 75 mph (120 kph) and made quite an impact on the European sporting scene that year, winning the team prize in the Austrian Alpine Trial. In 1935 the Type 315/1 was joined by the near-identical Type 319/1, which had a 1911 cc, 55 bhp engine and was capable of 81 mph (130 kph). Like the 315/1, the 319/1 had disc wheels, but in this case they were of centrelock type.

The Type 319/1 added to the successes of its predecessor in rallies and speed events, attracting the attention of the Aldington brothers at Isleworth. They bought some of the engines to install in their 'chain-gang' Frazer Nashes, and then asked permission to market the sports BMWs in England. These cars were built in Germany specially for the British market, and had right-hand drive, while others were also supplied in chassis form only to be bodied in England and were fitted with wire wheels to suit British preferences.

At the Berlin Motor Show in February 1936 it seemed that Fielder and his assistant, Rudolf Schleicher, were moving away from sporting cars, for the new Type 326 had a box-section chassis with completely new suspension and hydraulic brakes. With a 1 mm bore increase the six-cylinder engine was enlarged to 1971 cc and had a power output of 50 bhp at 4500 rpm to propel this five-seater saloon. Certainly no sports car, it was still the best-selling BMW of its day.

However, when the popular Eifel races were held at the Nürburgring on 14 June 1936, the well-known BMW motorcyclist, Ernst Henne, appeared in a very smart new two-seater powered by the 1971 cc engine, which now had a new type of cylinder head. In this, the first BMW Type 328, Henne ran away with the 2-litre sports car class at an average speed of just over 62 mph (100 kph), finishing more than three minutes ahead of the runner-up.

What Fiedler had done was to design new valve gear for the now familiar six-cylinder BMW engine, achieving a massive power increase to 80 bhp at 5000 rpm. The chain-driven camshaft still occupied the same position, low down on the nearside of the engine, from which it had previously operated in-line valves through pushrods and rockers. Now there were hemispherical combustion chambers in the new alloy head, with inclined valves. The inlets were opened by pushrods and rockers as before, but the exhaust valves now had two sets of pushrods and rockers, one set of pushrods being placed horizontally so that the valves could be located on the other side of the combustion chambers. This arrangement worked well despite its apparent complexity, and provided most of the advantages of overhead camshafts without the need to redesign the whole engine; indeed, with its twin rocker-boxes the Type 328 engine looked very much like a double-overhead-cam unit.

As the inlet ports were paired, and passed

LEFT *Like the example on the previous page, this 328 was built in right-hand-drive form for the British market, and sold through Frazer Nash of Kingston upon Thames, Surrey, originally for £695*
RIGHT *A BMW 328 on the open road – an environment in which it is still a surprisingly quick and agile performer*

ABOVE *The 2-litre overhead-valve straight-six produced 80 bhp at 5000 rpm offering performance which matched the car's superb and highly influential looks*

vertically downwards to the combustion chambers, it was convenient to provide the engine with three downdraught Solex carburettors above the cylinder head, although this made the engine rather a lofty affair and a tight fit under the bonnet. Another minor disadvantage was the placing of the sparking plugs symmetrically at the centre of the combustion chambers, making them fairly inaccessible and calling for the use of a special plug spanner.

The crankshaft, running in lead-bronze bearings, had a vibration damper at its forward end and a pulley driving the dynamo and water-pump by vee-belt. A mechanical fuel pump on the nearside was driven from the rear end of the camshaft, which also drove the distributor from a skew gear at its centre, via a long vertical spindle. A single-plate clutch took the drive to a four-speed gearbox, and thence by open propeller shaft to the spiral-bevel rear axle. An oil-cooler was provided, mounted just ahead of the radiator in two parts to match the two halves of the 'kidney' front grille, and there was a full undertray beneath the car.

The side-members of the chassis were not simple tubes, having been fabricated from sheet steel so that their diameter varied in accordance with the load at each point. A welded box structure carried the transverse leaf spring, lower wishbones and telescopic dampers of the front suspension assembly, with its rack-and-pinion steering, and the

live rear axle was mounted on long semi-elliptic leaf springs. The hydraulic brakes had 11 in (28 cm) drums, and the perforated pressed-steel disc wheels were fitted to peg-drive hubs, with central locking nuts.

At a time when most sports cars still had separate mudguards and headlamps, the Type 328 BMW paved the way for the transition to all-enveloping bodywork: the mudguards merged into the body, with no more than vestigial running-boards, and the headlamps were let into a cowling that united the mudguards with the front grille, while the spare wheel was partially sunk into the shapely tail, where the hood, sidescreens and luggage were stowed out of sight. There was no boot-lid, access to the luggage compartment being made by folding the seat squab forward. The leather bonnet straps – paired and fitted with sprung fasteners – were standard equipment, and the vee-shaped windscreen was split in the middle so that it could be folded down on the scuttle. Even now, half a century later, the Type 328 is so close to modern ideas in body shape that it is difficult to imagine the impact it made when it first appeared, looking almost futuristic among its contemporaries.

There was a three-spoke steering wheel, and instruments included a speedometer, tachometer, oil and water temperature gauges and an oil pressure gauge. The electrical system was 6-volt. The semi-bucket seats were made of leather, and there was a

LEFT *In no way flamboyant in style, the 328 was both smooth and aerodynamic*
BELOW *With the windscreen up, the car's top speed was 100 mph (161 kph); when lowered, it rose to 103 mph (166 kph)*
RIGHT *The smooth rear-wing contours were both functional and attractive*
BELOW *A 328 at the Beaulieu museum*

'one-shot' chassis lubrication system actuated by a separate pedal. One of the weaker points of the Type 328 was the gear-change, for there was synchromesh only on third and top, whilst instead of a proper remote-control there was a rather long gear-lever.

As a sports car it was just a nice, handy size, its overall length being 12 ft 9½ in (390 cm). The wheelbase was 7 ft 10½ in (240 cm) front track 3 ft 9½ in (116 cm) rear track 4 ft (122 cm) exactly. Surprisingly, the ground clearance was almost 8 in (20 cm), which made the Type 328 quite at home on rough surfaces in rallies or trials. As most of the bodywork (apart from the mudguards) was aluminium, the all-up weight was a modest 1830 lb (830 kg), a good figure for a 2-litre car.

Only two cars were built in 1936, and as these were intended to publicise the model in competitions they had lightweight, doorless bodies and one-piece windscreens. Not until February 1937 was the Type 328 available to the public, and these cars, of course, were fully equipped for road use. Soon after, one of the lightweight cars was sent to England, where the sports editor of *Autocar*, S.C.H. Davis, drove it at Brooklands under RAC observation on 15 April, covering 102.2 miles (164 km) in the hour. Running on Discol pump fuel, the BMW maintained a steady 4600 to 4900 rpm and carried a spare wheel, full toolkit and hood in the tail.

The publicity value of such an exercise was considerable for S.C.H. Davis, a famous figure known universally as 'Sammy'. He was also an author, journalist, rally and race driver; a former Bentley boy and winner of Le Mans. At a time when most road cars managed little more than 40 mph, 100 mph was little short of incredible to most people.

Although a standard production Type 328 could scarcely be expected to put more than 100 miles into the hour, it needed little attention to achieve 100 mph, and up to

120 mph (193 kph) was possible with more extensive tuning. To take full advantage of this sort of performance – which was truly amazing for an unsupercharged 2-litre carrying full equipment – the factory made available a wide range of special equipment, including better brakes and dampers, tougher transmission and suspension parts.

Four cars ran at Le Mans in 1937, three of them factory-entered, but one of them, driven by Pat Fairfield, was unfortunately involved in a multiple crash in which he lost his life. Another of the BMWs was badly damaged in the same accident (caused by an inexperienced driver), and the remaining two retired. Four cars were again entered for the RAC Tourist Trophy Race, held that year at Donington for the first time. Dobbs broke a half-shaft as the flag fell, but Fane, always one of the fastest BMW drivers, led the race until he dropped a valve, leaving

Bira to finish third overall at 68.7 mph (111 kph), with H.J. Aldington in sixth place overall. Bira won the 2-litre class.

Fane was prominent again in the Mille Miglia of 1938, driving the 1000 miles (1609 km) singlehanded in a time of 13 hr 38 min 11 sec to win the unsupercharged 2-litre International class at an average of 74 mph (119 kph), finishing seventh overall. His team-mates came second, third and fourth in the class behind him, Prince Schaumburg-Lippe and Count Lurani being ninth overall, Richter and Werneck 10th and Van der Muhle and Holzclub 11th. The following month saw the Type 328 score another 1–2–3 victory at the Avusrennen in Germany. Soon afterwards the first Antwerp Grand Prix was held in Belgium. Being staged as a sports car event, it too attracted a full entry of BMWs. In this exciting 10-mile (16 km), round-the-houses race the Type 328 achieved a class 1–2–3 once again, this

RIGHT & BELOW *Views of the Frazer Nash BMW Grand Prix Two-Seater, a car of which* The Autocar *said: 'Very nearly unique, it is certainly a most unusual motor car, and sold ready for serious sports car competition work…'.*

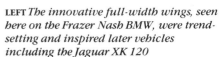

LEFT *The innovative full-width wings, seen here on the Frazer Nash BMW, were trend-setting and inspired later vehicles including the Jaguar XK 120*

second on Index of Performance. Naturally they also won the 2-litre class ahead of Rose and Heinemann (who were seventh overall) and Briem and Scholtz (who were eighth overall), their race average breaking the class record by an easy margin. For the remainder of the season the Type 328 BMWs continued their winning ways to the extent that in Germany, at least, it was rare for anything *but* a Type 328 to be entered for the 2-litre class.

The 1938 Mille Miglia had been the occasion of a disastrous accident when a competing car ran into the crowd, killing nine spectators, and for this reason Mussolini declared that the race was not to be run again. However, the organizers managed to arrange for it to be held – officially as the Coppa Brescia – over a 100-mile (161 km) closed circuit instead of the traditional 1000 miles (1609 km) of open road, the race distance totalling 923 miles (1485 km). Astonishingly, it was held more than seven months after World War II began, on 28 April 1940, for Italy was still a neutral country at that time.

BMW made careful preparations for the race, entering five cars which were extensively lightened and fitted with highly-tuned engines giving 135 bhp at 5500 rpm on a 9.6:1 compression ratio. Three were roadsters, one a coupé built under Fiedler's supervision in Germany, and another coupé was built for BMW by Touring of Milan.

The two closed cars proved capable of more than 130 mph (209 kph), and in the Touring coupé, Huschke von Hanstein (later to become Porsche's racing manager) and Bäumer succeeded in averaging 103.6 mph (167 kph) for the entire race – slightly better than the fastest lap of the pre-race favourite, the Alfa Romeo coupé of Farina and Biondetti! Brudes and Roese came third in one of the open Type 328 cars, and only one of the team, the Lurani/Cortese coupé, had to drop out, having carburettor trouble.

BMW built a total of 461 Type 328 models, including chassis supplied to specialist coachbuilders, but after the war the Eisenach factory was nationalized, and it was not until 1952 that the company were able to build cars again at Munich. A few cars were assembled from parts by the Aldingtons in England, and the classic six-cylinder engine was turned into the Bristol for the post-war cars built by the Bristol Aeroplane Company from 1947. It powered the AFM, the Veritas, the Monopol, Cooper, Frazer Nash, AC Ace, Arnolt and a myriad other high-performance cars in different parts of the world. As the *Autocar* testers said in 1937, 'it has the mark of a racing unit', and gave the impression that it was supercharged, so freely did it increase its revs.

time with Ralph Rouse in the lead at an average of 76.05 mph (122 kph), ahead of Briem and Heinemann, while Prince Schaumburg-Lippe finished fifth in the 2-litre class.

Rouse did it again in the Grand Prix des Frontières at Chimay, winning the 2-litre class ahead of Gubelin's BMW at an average of 72.89 mph, but at Le Mans the team were again out of luck. However, they made up for it in the 24-hour race on the Belgian Spa/Francorchamps road circuit, where Schaumburg-Lippe and Rose shared a Type 328 to win the 2-litre class, followed by Heinemann, Briem and Scholtz – a performance which also gained them the team prize.

In winning the 2-litre class of the French Alpine Rally, Van der Muhle was one of only two competitors to finish the event without losing a single mark. Inevitably, the sports car races accompanying the 1938 German Grand Prix at the Nürburgring saw the Type 328 achieve its usual dominance in the 2-litre class, Greifzu winning from Von Hanstein and Heinemann. It was with understandable confidence that BMW entered four works cars for the RAC Tourist Trophy Race, nominating Dick Seaman (who had won the German Grand Prix for Mercedes-Benz), Prince Bira, Fane and Aldington. There were also two private entrants, the Hon. Peter Aitken and David Murray. But at Donington, as at Le Mans, the BMWs were out of luck, all of the cars giving trouble.

For their third attempt at Le Mans, in 1939, BMW entered three cars, one of which had a most attractive coupé body. It was certainly a case of 'third time lucky'. Prince Schaumburg-Lippe and Wenscher drove the coupé at a tremendous pace to finish fifth overall, averaging a splendid 82.5 mph (133 kph) for the 24 hours and finishing

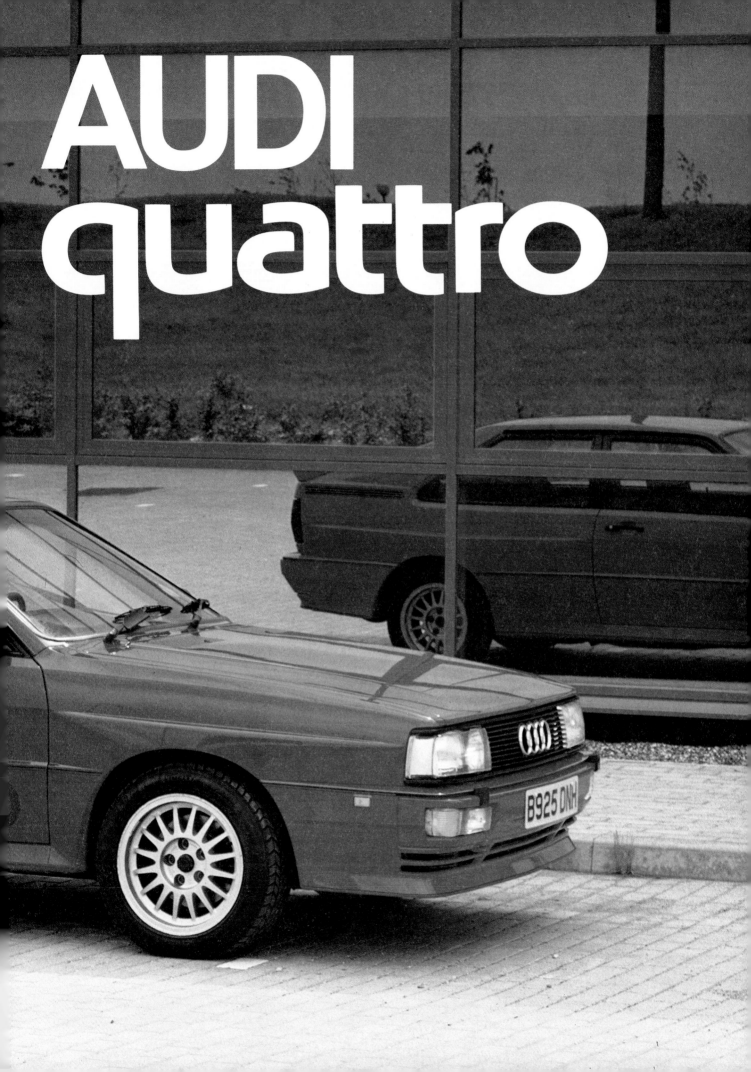

AUDI
quattro

quattro

Audi designer Ferdinand Piech promises that four-wheel drive will become as common as four-wheel brakes. The great quattro has already started the ever growing trend

IT WAS IN MARCH 1980 that Audi revealed their interpretation of a high-performance four-wheel-drive coupé. There, at the Geneva Show ready for the press to drive and the public to view, was a new four-wheel-drive design clothed in two-door bodywork that would serve as the basis for a multiple winner of the World Rally Championship during the 1980s.

More significantly, the quattro (the lower-case q was registered as the company's official trademark in 1984) would make every other motor manufacturer look at four-wheel-drive in a new light. Many of them followed the all-wheel-drive route (albeit using different technical solutions of varying merit), with more new four-wheel-drive cars to be announced in the late '80s.

Audi had studied what had gone before in this field and made unprecedented use of existing parts and previous military four-wheel-drive knowledge, slashing development time and production costs with unmatched ingenuity.

In effect the company's engineers reinvented four-wheel-drive for two primary purposes. The first was to overcome the limited ability of powerful front- or rear-drive cars to cope with the new high-output generation of turbo motors. Secondly, hav-ing shown that speed and safety could be incorporated in one practical package, they then had to demonstrate its advantages in the most public manner possible. They chose world championship rallying, and caused the rule book to be rewritten in the process... .

Audi did not, however, invent the first high-performance four-wheel-drive coupé. The prophetic voice had come from Jensen in Britain's Midlands, who between 1966 and '71 made 318 Ferguson Formula (FF) Interceptor V8 coupés, superb machines which only failed to have greater influence on the industry and car-buying public because of their very high price.

During the 1970s, Audi's chief chassis engineer Jorg Bensinger had the occasional task of explaining to outsiders, such as journalists, the advantages and disadvantages of front- and rear-drive systems. He made up a chart which compared the strengths and weaknesses of the popular engine/transmission and drive layouts. It contrasted systems such as Audi's front drive, front engine and gearbox with Porsche's rear-engined 911. Also shown were then conventional cars such as the Ford Escort, with front engine and live-axle rear-drive.

This chart made it obvious that when it came to handling over 200 bhp at the driven wheels, two-wheel-drive systems had severe drawbacks. Former Porsche, BMW and Mercedes employee Bensinger came to the conclusion that the worst snags in such cars were poor traction under full power, constant danger of skidding in bad weather, wildly varied cornering performance when power was abruptly removed or applied in mid-corner, and very rapid tyre wear on all really powerful cars.

All-wheel-drive was the obvious theoretical answer, but when Bensinger was making such comparisons Audi showed no sign of having the resources for such a radical solution.

However, in the '70s Audi began to blossom under VW's ownership, and the key ingredients of what would become the quattro started to appear.

For example there was the unique in-line five-cylinder engine, also part of every quattro until the four-cylinder 80q was introduced in Germany last year. That tough engine, with its steel crankshaft, iron block, alloy cylinder head and single-overhead-cam first appeared in the rebodied Audi 100 saloon of 1976. That was a front-wheel-drive saloon with the engine mounted way ahead of the front axle, a layout that was to become an Audi tradition.

Even in 1972 Audi listed an 80 saloon of similar design (but with a four-cylinder engine) and it was this model that literally provided the foundation for the first quattro coupé, for its stretched floorpan was incorporated under both the front-drive Audi Coupé of 1980 and the Geneva Show quattro prototype. The two-wheel-drive coupé was actually announced after the quattro, but VAG in the UK introduced them simultaneously in England in the spring of 1981.

The reason why this first quattro was a turbocharged five-cylinder can be traced to September 1979's top model Audi 200 saloon, a derivative of the 100. This car, capable of over 130 mph (210 kph), was the most powerful front-wheel-drive saloon in the world when it was announced, less than a year before the quattro, for its non-intercooled version of the 2144 cc (79.5 mm × 86.4 mm) five produced 170 bhp. This engine was thus a considerable help in providing a reliable 200 bhp for the following quattro coupé, which featured an intercooler as standard.

Other key items in the transmission and suspension were production parts from

PREVIOUS PAGE *A 1985 Audi quattro*
TOP LEFT *Stig Blomqvist on his way to winning the 1983 RAC Rally*
LEFT *Hannu Mikkola and Arne Hertz during the 1984 RAC Rally*
BELOW *The RAC again, this time in 1982 with Michelle Mouton and Fabrizia Pons. With superb traction and acceleration in the slippery forest conditions, the quattro became a dominant force*

other models, but where did Audi find the resources to incorporate four-wheel-drive?

Jorg Bensinger recalled the significance of a drab military vehicle called the Iltis that Audi had developed and manufactured for Audi's VW parents to sell for German army use: 'I think it was in 1976 that I realised what was possible with four-wheel-drive for us. We tested the Iltis on the road, and then during the following winter we tested it in Scandinavia. It only had the four-cylinder 1.6-litre engine, no more than 75 bhp, and it was very tall with a short wheelbase. I didn't expect much handling from a machine with the centre of gravity so high in the air, but I was really pleased with its performance on the ice and snow: I became convinced that this could be the future for road cars too.'

Initially Herr Bensinger's inclination was to convert something like the 100 saloon, but Ferdinand Piech, Audi's board member with responsibility for all research and development, had very different ideas. Herr Piech, a significant figure in Porsche's his-

tory and particularly in the development of the 911 road car and 917 flat-12 racer, thought about Bensinger's proposal overnight. Thereafter he became *the* top level quattro loyalist within the Audi company, taking ultimate responsibility for the engineering (but not the detailed execution of the design) both in competition and road car development. It was Dr. Piech who decreed that competition was the only credible way to demonstrate the quattro system's advantages and reliability, and Dr. Piech who realised the advantages of applying the system to a sporting car rather than an everyday saloon. Thus the company could go into production gradually, introducing the system into cheaper and more mass-produced cars if all went well.

Bensinger actually went ahead and issued instructions for the first prototype to be built before official approval was given, and thus had already had some running experience of that A1-coded quattro 80 with the simple Iltis drivetrain (no centre differential was

ABOVE *The quattro in full flight during the 1984 San Remo Rally*
ABOVE RIGHT *The quattro of Mikkola and Hertz in the '83 Safari*
RIGHT *Walter Roehrl's quattro receives attention during the '85 Monte Carlo*

installed) when the instruction to proceed with a full-scale programme was issued in September 1977.

Naturally there were development dramas, but usually only when testing to the limit – for example there was a fire in the Sahara desert with a 286 bhp prototype, an engine which nevertheless confirmed its basic bottom-end strength.

Former Mercedes competition and road-car engineer Hans Nedvidek was given the task of designing a suitable transmission system which would also be as light as possible. It was not an easy task, for most modern four-wheel-drive systems not only have front and rear differentials, but also a central one that civilises road behaviour by harmonising front and rear wheel speeds after interconnection, and of course this takes up much valuable space. Such differentials are frequently housed in a separate transfer case and need additional propshafts front and rear, and that case will often house extra gears to split the power front and rear.

Typical modern systems split roughly a third of the power to the front wheels and two-thirds aft, whereas competition Ferguson systems vary the front/rear power splits between 25/75 for tarmac to a 50/50 balance for the most slippery surfaces. Nedvidek and his team decided on a straight forward 50/50 split, achieved with bevel gearing, but the cleverest feature was to incorporate a hollow shaft within the largely standard Audi 100/200 five-speed gearbox.

Within a length of just over 10 inches (25 cm), Audi included a shaft within a shaft, feeding power from the central differential to the forward diff. Power to the rear was taken simply by propshaft from the rear of the gearbox. Audi were exceptionally fortunate that their standard front-drive layout was a simple longitudinal one, for it made the conversion comparatively easy once they had come up with the hollow transmission

LEFT *Roehrl again, this time winning the 1984 Ulster Rally*
FAR LEFT *A 1985 short-wheelbase quattro Sport which produced 305 bhp at 6500 rpm*

ABOVE *Detail of the quattro's turbocharged in-line five-cylinder engine which produces 200 bhp at 5500 rpm in the form shown, plus plenty of torque*

idea for the lower gearbox shaft, which still wore its gear-ratio clusters externally.

As can be imagined, the precision machining needed to achieve the reliable shaft within a shaft was an expensive process, but the weight-saving value could not be ignored. Even today, Audi engineers have some difficulty in convincing the outside world just how expensive that sort of work was in the low-production early days; the quattro's cost was further boosted by the fact that each floorpan had to be individually converted to accomodate the additional rear drive at Baur in Stuttgart. Since then the quattro system has remained fundamentally unchanged, the only significant detail changes concerning the locking centre and rear differentials. These were originally cable-operated from a central transmission tunnel lever set, but vacuum assistance and push-pull knobs and then rotary switchgear, have replaced the original layout, which transmitted too much road noise.

The suspension and braking typified Audi's parts-bin ingenuity, for virtually all the components had served in other models. In fact the rear suspension was simply the MacPherson strut/wide-base wishbone system found at the front of many Audis, reversed and with the steering arms replaced by solid transverse links. The struts were taken from the Audi 80/100 series and the driveshafts also came from other models.

Disc brakes were fitted all round, ventilated at the front, and the system was hydraulically powered, like the rack and pinion steering, by a new engine-driven pump. The latter is one of the nicest variable-assistance power steering systems on the market, and its precision and worth can be gauged from the fact that the rally team continued to use it with their 500 bhp cars.

That first quattro coupé used the usual 2144 cc of the largest Audi five-cylinder in association with a KKK-K26 turbocharger which had a boost pressure maximum of just over 12 psi. Compression within the two-valve per cylinder combustion chambers was the then high figure of 7:1, made possible by an intercooler, transistorised Bosch ignition and the carefully monitored K-Jetronic fuel injection.

The first steel-bodied quattro was no flyweight. The official figure was just over 2800 lb (1270 kg), yet with 200 bhp at 5500 rpm, plus 210.5 lb ft of torque, the distinctive quattro coupé would exceed 135 mph (217 kph), despite its poor aerodynamic qualities when compared to the later Audi 100. According to *Autocar* it could reach 60 mph (97 kph) in 7.1 seconds, and average fuel consumption was 19–21 mpg.

Deliveries of the first quattro commenced in September 1980, but it was March 1981 before they began to arrive in Britain, still in left-hand drive and priced at £14,500 (right-hand-drive models arrived in

1982). In 1980 Audi made less than 300 quattros, but by 1983 they were talking in thousands, for the plan to make four-wheel-drive available downmarket had resulted in the 136 bhp Audi 80 saloon. To get the price well below the equivalent of £10,000 in Germany, the four-door quattro used a straight-forward fuel-injected 2.1-litre five, and after it was shown to the press, in December 1982, sales reached over 5000 in the first year on the German market. With a 136 bhp engine in a body only 200 lb (91 kg) lighter than the original turbo coupé, the 80q's performance was much less exciting, but with a top speed of nearly 120 mph and a 0–60 mph time of under 10 seconds, it competed very well against BMW's 3-series.

The 80q arrived in Britain in the summer

EVOLUTION

Introduced in 1980, the four-wheel-drive Audi quattro coupé was a two-door five-seater based on the modified floorpan of the Audi 80 saloon. The transmission consisted of permanently engaged four-wheel-drive with dual-cable operation for the centre and rear differential locks. The quattro was powered by a 2144 cc five-cylinder engine with Bosch K-Jetronic fuel injection and a KKK-K26 turbocharger, with a 12.09 psi wastegate maximum. It produced 200 bhp at 5500 rpm and 210 lb ft of torque at 3500 rpm, and the car was capable of 135 mph (217 kph) and 0–60 mph in 7.3 seconds. The suspension was all independent, with MacPherson struts front and rear

1981 Group 4 quattro coupé announced, for homologation purposes. The engine was available in a variety of tunings, producing up to 320 bhp and 304 lb ft of torque. Its transmission featured a limited-slip differential at the rear, a solid-shaft centre differential and a competition clutch. The bodyshell was much strengthened with an internal roll cage, the rear spoiler was enlarged and wheel arches flared to accommodate wider wheels – which could be specified with 10 in rims. Depending on the gearbox ratios, maximum speed ranged between 108 mph (173 kph) and 158 mph (254 kph), with 0–60 mph times as low as 4.9 seconds. The Group 4 car was up to 200 lb (90 kg) lighter than the standard coupé, depending on modifications.

1983 Audi quattro A1 announced, its engine available in 2145 cc or (with larger bore) 2178 cc forms. Turbo boost maximum was 27 psi, giving the engine a turbo-multiplied capacity of 3048 cc. Maximum power output was 340 bhp at 6000 rpm and 305 lb ft at 3600 rpm. The bodywork was extensively modified to be both lighter and stronger, and a variety of suspension options were available. A typical example had a maximum speed of 115 mph (185 kph) and a 0–60 mph in 4.5 seconds, delivering 5–6 mpg. The price was around £75,000. Also announced that year was the Group B quattro A2, its engine further modified to produce up to 400 bhp at 7000 rpm and 362 lb ft of torque. It had no centre differential and its weight was reduced to between 2200 lb (100 kg) and 2420 lb (1100 kg), the latter version for forest use. In September appeared the Audi quattro Sport, a short-wheelbase model with a 300 bhp/243 lb ft engine, and its transmission included a pneumatic two-stage control to engage either the centre differential lock or the centre plus rear differential locks.

1984 The coupé was fitted with an LCD illuminated dashboard and the wheel arches were flared to accommodate wider wheels.

1989 Production of classic quattro ends after nine years. Quattro option remains across board on entire Audi range

CENTRE *Rear detail of a 1985 spec quattro with its modest identification*
LEFT *The interior of the quattro was fairly basic and not a strong point*

of '83, right-hand drive and priced at over £11,000, and that year the signs of the quattro's explosive growth became clear, both up and down market.

At the Frankfurt Show Audi displayed a short-wheelbase Sport version of the quattro coupé, designed to defend their honour from 1984 onwards against a new breed of four-wheel-drive rally supercars specially built to depose the quattro. It had won its first rally world title in 1982, when Hannu Mikkola had become champion driver in a 360 bhp quattro.

The Sport quattro's wheelbase was shortened by more than 13.5 in (34.3 cm) and the wheel-arches fitted with bulging light-weight panels. It was powered by a four-valve per cylinder (20-valve) version of the faithful five, topped with a double-overhead-cam cylinder head. In road trim this provided 300 bhp and a maximum speed of over 150 mph (241 kph) for a purchase price of over £50,000. Production was not expected to go much beyond the necessary 220 units for homologation, and all were left-hand drive.

Down-market, the 80 was offered from September 1983 with a 2-litre five, priced at less than £7000 in Germany (and never imported to Britain). This was the slowest quattro made, capable of 114 mph (183 kph) and 0–62 mph in 10.3 seconds, but with the compensation of nearly 40 mpg at a constant 56 mph (90 kph).

The company have continued their policy of offering an alternative quattro version for each mainline Audi, and although not all have been exported, here is a full list of the quattros currently offered in Germany; the 200 bhp/2.1-litre 200 turbo saloon, the 138 bhp/2.2-litre 100 saloon, the 136 bhp/2.2-litre 90 saloon, the 90 bhp/1.8-litre, carburated 80, and the 112 bhp/1.8-litre 80 saloon (the 80s are the only four-cylinder quattros), plus the Avant sporting estate bodies upon 100 and 200 saloon running gear. The Avants have a quattro equivalent for both turbo and non-turbo five-cylinder engines.

Quite a quattro list! Now add in the fact that, struggling or not, Audi gained a record number of World Championship rally victories in 1984, to take both the world marque and driver titles.

Having paved the way for a new generation of four-wheel-drive rally cars, the quattro eventually found itself left behind in the race for more speed and grip. Basically the engine is too heavy and too far forward to complete with the lighter, more compact machines such as the Lancia Delta which took over where the quattro left off.

The quattro is also assured of a place in motoring history as the car that influenced a wave of similar high-performance cars all over the world, including prestigious performers from Porsche, BMW, Lancia-Ferrari and (possibly) Mercedes. Audi have proved that four-wheel-drive can be combined with performance and economy, and the development story is still unfolding. Perhaps one day 4WD will be universal.

The all-time best-selling car has captured the hearts of millions with its rugged charm. Despite dated design, it is still manufactured forty years on

THREE PERSONALITIES are responsible for the Volkswagen Beetle being the most popular car in the history of the automobile. They are Adolf Hitler, who conceived the idea of a car cheap enough for the German working man to afford, Ferdinand Porsche, who created the distinctive air-cooled rear engined design while in the post-war years Heinz Nordhoff turned the Hitlerian dream into a reality. To date over 20 million Beetles have been built and production continues in Mexico and Brazil.

The starting point of the Beetle project was 30 January in 1933 which was when Adolf Hitler became German chancellor. Determined that Germany should once again become a world power, he was also intent on building a web of special roads, designed for the needs of the motor car. But this was only the first part of Hitler's grand automotive plan. The all important second stage was for the government to initiate the production of a Volkswagen or People's car. These ideas had been exercising Hitler's thoughts ever since he had been imprisoned in Landsberg Castle, near Munich in 1924 after his unsuccessful attempt to overthrow the German Government with his National Socialist, or Nazi party. Already a committed anti-semite, Hitler was attracted to the writing of Henry Ford, who was not only of the same persuasion but had also put the world on wheels with his famous Model T. While in prison Hitler read Ford's ghosted autobiography *My Life and Work*. It was early in 1924 that Hitler received a visit from a young Munich lawyer named Hans Frank. Hitler confided that he had conceived a plan for mopping up the nation's unemployed; they would be set to work building a network of motor roads.

This idea was clearly inspired by the Italian *autostrada* which Mussolini had recently initiated, but this was not all. A Hitler-lead government would then mass produce a car that would be within the reach of the man in the street; once Hitler had come to power he wasted little time in pursuing these objectives. The *autobahnen* programme was announced in February 1933, only weeks after he had taken office, and work on the first section, between Frankfurt and Mannheim, began eight months later, in September. By 1943 there would be over 2300 miles of motorway in Germany and they were by far and away Europe's finest roads. With the

RIGHT *This is a 1953 Volkswagen Beetle which was built for the export market*

VOLKSWAGEN

BEETLE

autobahnen programme well under way, Hitler turned his attention to the Volkswagen project. He was already acquainted with one of Germany's most famous car designers, Ferdinand Porsche, and in the autumn of 1933 he met with him at Berlin's Hotel Kaiserhof to discuss the project.

Porsche, like Hitler, was not German but had been born in the small town of Maffersdorf in the old Austro-Hungarian empire. In 1905 he had joined Austro-Daimler and did not leave until 1923. He left to take one of the prime jobs in the German motor industry: that of technical director of Daimler-Benz. But in 1929 he was on the move again and returned to Austria and the Steyr company. Unfortunately, the Depression had hit Steyr and in 1930 Porsche found himself without a job, deciding, rather than work for others, to set up in business in Stuttgart to offer a design facility for motor manufacturers. The firm, established at the end of 1930, was staffed exclusively by Austrian engineers whom Porsche had met during his working life.

Ferdinand Porsche was therefore the ideal person to take on the Volkswagen project though when he heard that the car was to have a selling price of less than RM (Reichsmarks) 1000 (£86), have a top speed of 100 kph (62 mph) and a fuel consumption of seven litres of petrol per 100 km (around 42 mpg), he nearly turned the project down. Hitler was also insistent that the car have an air-cooled engine. Fortunately these specifications came fairly close to two designs that Porsche's design bureau had already created. The first, designated Type 12 in the Porsche register, had a rear mounted water-cooled five-cylinder radial engine with backbone chassis and all independent suspension. Although Zündapp, who were motor cycle manufacturers, expressed interest in the idea, they did not pursue it and the similar Type 33 produced for NSU suffered much the same fate. This model boasted a rear mounted air-cooled four-cylinder boxer (horizontally-opposed) engine and Porsche's patented torsion bar suspension.

It was this later experimental car that formed the basis of the Volkswagen that was alloted the designation Type 60 in the Porsche design register in 1934. However, on the grounds of cost the four-cylinder boxer

TOP LEFT *The 1932 Zündapp, predecessor to the Beetle*
ABOVE CENTRE *This 1936 VW30 was purely experimental*
LEFT *The first production topless VW appeared in 1949 and set the scene for a whole cult of open-topped Beetles which persists right up to the present day. Latterly the open cars were made by Karmann who developed a remarkably efficient and attractive hood system for the car*

ABOVE *This military amphibian has an enclosed Beetle chassis with a crank driven propeller and is just one of the numerous versions of the Beetle that were made over the years*

motor was dispensed with. Instead a series of experimental engines was built. There was a vertical four, which alas, broke its crankshaft and then a variety of twins with sleeve and overhead valves. While the design team were wrestling with the problem of trying to produce a cheap, relatively quiet power unit, Franz Xavier Reimspiess, a new Austrian recruit, came up with a four-cylinder boxer motor of such simplicity that, when costed, it was found to be cheaper than the twins then under development. This over-square four is substantially the same design which is still in production today though, of course, it has been considerably refined over the years. In addition to making this immeasurable contribution to the Volkswagen, Reimspiess was also responsible for the world famous VW badge.

With the all important matter of the engine resolved, work could now proceed on testing the prototypes. Two had been built in the double garage of Porsche's Stuttgart home in 1935 and a further three were made in 1936. These cars were then handed over to the German Automobile Manufacturers' Association for a rigorous 30,000 kilometre test programme. The most serious problem encountered was the continual breaking of the cast iron crankshafts and they were replaced by conventional forgings. Minor problems were also experienced with the front suspension and cable

brakes and practically every car broke its gear lever.

The Manufacturers' Association issued a 100 page report in January 1937 as a result of these trials. It was generally in favour of the project but felt that the RM 990 selling price could not be realised. Nevertheless the Association offered to take the Volkswagen over but Hitler had other ideas. From May 1937, the VW became a state-funded project and the responsibility of the German Labour Front which replaced the abolished trade unions. This resulted in an immediate cash injection of RM 50,000 (£42,918) and Daimler-Benz was commissioned to produced a further batch of 30 cars. Hitler, speaking of the Volkswagen's appearance, said on one occasion: 'it should look like a beetle, you've only got to look to nature to find out what streamlining is'. This new series of experimental cars certainly did look beetle-like, accentuated by the fact that they still lacked a rear window. There followed yet another series of exhaustive tests with the drivers recruited from the SS and

the cars based at their barracks at Kornwestheim.

There was just one more series of experimental cars to be produced. At long last a divided rear window was introduced and the number and frequency of the louvres in the engine bay lid were reduced as the output of the engine's cooling fan was boosted. In addition, running boards were introduced and a one piece bonnet replaced the divided versions that had hitherto sufficed. The capacity of the engine was upped 1 cc to 985 cc and the remaining mechanical features, the backbone chassis and all independent suspension by transverse torsion bars, were confirmed. Here, in 1938, was a Beetle that would have been instantly recognisable today.

With the car's design at last resolved, the German government had to find somewhere to build it. They chose a green field site in the north about 50 miles east of Hanover, near the village of Fallersleben on the banks of the Mittelland Canal which joins the River Rhine to the Elbe. This followed a visit by Porsche and a small team to America and the motor city of Detroit in 1936 and 1937.

Work on the factory began in 1938 and in May of that year Adolf Hitler ceremonially laid the foundation stone. It was then that he announced that the car would henceforth be known as the KdF-Wagen (Strength through Joy car) which was the name of the Labour

Front's leisure section. Then, in August, Front chief Robert Ley announced that the KdF-Wagen could only be bought by a unique hire purchase arrangement whereby prospective buyers would be issued with a savings book and savers would be commited to a minimum payment of RM5 (58p) per week. However, unlike the more usual hire purchase arrangement, the car would be delivered on the completion of payments rather than at the outset. Price of the two-door saloon was set at RM 990 (£85) while a version with a roll-back sun roof was RM 60 (£5.15) more. There was just one colour available: blue grey.

In 1937 Ferdinand Porsche, with his traditional love of fast cars, decided to approach Labour Front officals with a view to producing a sports version of the KdF-Wagen. But the idea was turned down as it was felt that a utilitarian vehicle such as this should not have a glamorous image. So Porsche pushed ahead with his own design and came up with a streamlined coupé with a mid-mounted water-cooled V10 engine. The authorities then had a change of heart and Porsche was given the green light to build three special Volkswagens, which were alloted the designation Type 64 in the Porsche design register, as it was intended to enter them for a race from Berlin to Rome, scheduled to take place in September 1939. Although the outbreak of war put paid to the project, the streamlined cars were built and represented the first stirrings of the Porsche marque that emerged with the 356 in 1948.

The first stage of the KdF-Wagen factory was completed by the spring of 1939. It was to be capable of producing 150,000 cars in its first full manufacturing year. Further ex-

pansion would result in the plant being able to produce 1.5 million cars in 1942 which would have challenged the American automotive giants. But, of course, it was not to be. On 1 September 1939 Hitler invaded Poland and World War II began. As all the tooling had been delivered, a pilot run of KdF-Wagens was produced from 1941 though only 630 examples were built during hostilities. Made in rather larger numbers was the Kubelwagen, the military version of the Volkswagen, which entered production in 1940 and by the end of the war 50,435 had been manufactured. By contrast, the Americans built over half a million Jeeps.

When the war came to an end in 1945, the KdF-Wagen plant fell within the British military zone. In July 1945 the Royal Electrical and Mechanical Engineers moved in to the works and the following month Major Ivan Hirst took charge of the factory.

One of the first things that the British did was to give the settlement that had grown up around the Volkswagen factory a name. The Nazis had called it KdF Stadt (town of Strength through Joy) but the community was renamed Wolfsburg after the nearby 14th century castle. Incredibly, for a short time, Kubelwagen bodies continued to ar-

A 1947 Beetle, LEFT. The engine, FAR LEFT, is essentially unchanged to this day, this unit being of 1131 cc. BELOW CENTRE is the austere 'people's' accommodation while the weird creation BELOW is a Porsche-developed Type 60 streamlined coupé of 1939. Three were prepared for the 1939 Berlin-Rome-Berlin marathon with 32 bhp engines giving a top speed of 80 mph (130 kph)

rive at the plant so for the rest of 1945 these were assembled from spare parts and by the end of the year 522 examples had been produced; 58 saloons were also built in the same year.

As Wolfsburg fell within the British military zone, inevitably it received a visit from the Society of Motor Manufacturers and Traders who were investigating the activities of the German motor industry during the war. They were clearly impressed by what they saw. 'It can be said that the Volkswagen is most advanced and interesting for quantity production . . . both the car and factory in which it is produced are wonderful achievements in their respective spheres.' The car's importance was reflected in it becoming the subject of a second report, published in 1946. Conducted by Rootes, it consisted of a road test between a Volkswagen and a Mark III Hillman Minx. The British car proved to be a good 6 mph (10 kph) faster, with a top speed of 61.5 mph (100 kph) for the Beetle could only manage 56.3 mph (90 kph). In addition it incorporated a war-time report, undertaken by Humber, on a Kubelwagen that had been captured in North Africa, following General Montgomery's triumphal victory at El Alamein. The Kubel was dismantled and 100 lb (46 kg) of sand removed in the process. The subsequent report completely failed to appreciate the ingenuity of the Porsche design and one paragraph, in particular, has echoed down the years. It reads: 'We do not consider that the design represents any special brilliance, apart from certain of the detail points, and it is sug-

gested that it is not to be regarded as an example of first class modern design to be copied by the British industry'. Inevitably history has had the last word for Humber and Rootes have disappeared and the Volkswagen has gone on to become the most popular car in the history of the automobile.

Morris Motors too had the chance to acquire the Volkswagen project and a discussion on the matter is detailed in a set of company minutes. Under 'Any Other Business' the subject was discussed briefly but then unanimously rejected as being a project of little merit.

The other difficulty facing Volkswagen was the ever present danger that it might be taken as reparations by the victorious allies. The French government were all for moving the entire facility, *en masse*, to France although the French motor industry was united in opposition to this project. Then, in February 1948, Henry Ford II took a look at the Wolfsburg facility. There were thoughts about buying Volkswagen and Ford even drove a Beetle but complications about the firm's ownership and the air-cooled rear engined vehicle flew in the face of practically every law in the American automotive design canon.

Transport was a major problem in postwar Germany, and Hirst was fortunate to receive a request for 10,000 cars from the British army; there being also a valuable order from the German Post Office. Amazingly out of the chaos (the factory had been heavily bombed in 1944) cars began to appear; no fewer than 7677 were made in

1946. With great difficulty output was maintained for the next two years, then, in January 1948, Heinz Nordhoff took over as General Manager. A former Opel executive, he had run that company's Brandenberg lorry plant, which was Europe's largest, and he immediately set about turning the Beetle into a world beater. In July 1949 he introduced a greatly improved export model and in 1947 Ben Pon, a Dutch motor trader, signed up as Volkswagen's first overseas agent. The cars sold well enough in his native Holland and at Nordhoff's behest he took one across the Atlantic to America in January 1949 with a hope of awakening interest in the car there. But Pon had little luck as did Nordhoff himself who arrived, not with a car, but photographs. Convinced of the potential of the American market, in 1955 Volkswagen of America was established and that year the Beetle became the continent's best selling import. Sales peaked in 1968 when 423,008 cars were sold; by contrast, only 601 Beetles had been registered there in 1950.

The Volkswagen was becoming a world car, following in the wheel tracks of its famous Model T forebear. Manufacturing plants were established in South Africa in 1951, Brazil two years later, Australia in 1957 and Mexico in 1964.

Meanwhile the VW was being progressively refined. During the war, the car's capacity had been increased from its original 985 to 1131 cc to bring it in line with the Kubelwagen's specifications. In 1954 the car's capacity was upped to 1192 cc and

EVOLUTION

Introduced in 1945, the Beetle was first available as the VW 1200, equipped with an engine of 985 cc capacity and a four-speed manual gearbox. It offered comfortable accommodation for four in a compact body combined with frugal fuel consumption

1949 The export model was introduced, sporting high-polish finish, chrome decorative strips and a bonnet lock operated from inside

1950 Draft-free ventilation was achieved via recesses in the side windows; sunroof production commenced

1951 Side ventilation flaps were fitted

1952 Tyre size was changed to 5.60 × 15 in and quarter lights were also added further to improve ventilation. The bumpers were modified and two brake lights were incorporated into the rear light/reflector units

1953 The small, two-part rear window was replaced by one larger single one

1955 New rear light clusters were installed higher on the rear wings while the exhaust system received two outlet pipes. PVC was first used for the sunroof

1957 The rear window was further enlarged and the windscreen glass area was also increased. A new shape of engine compartment lid was first seen

1958 A larger outside mirror was fitted

1959 Pushbutton fixed door handles were introduced

1960 The Beetle was equipped with a windscreen washer unit, asymmetric dipped beams and turn signals

1961 Dual chamber rear lights replaced the previous units

1963 The front turn signals were modified, a steel sunroof was made available and the licence plate lamp received a wider housing

1964 saw enlargement of the window area while the windscreen wiper rest position was moved to the left and the engine compartment lid was fitted with a pushbutton catch

1965 The VW 1300 first saw the light of day and perforated disc wheels with flat covers were introduced

1966 The VW 1500 was launched, with a wider rear track, modified rear lid and licence plate light, thinner decorative strips and new door locks

1967 saw better fresh air ventilation introduced on the Beetle and three-point safety belt anchorages for all seats. Plastic control buttons, heavy-duty bumpers and an outside fuel filler neck on the right-hand side also featured

1969 Road wheels were changed

1970 The through-flow system of ventilation was adopted and an additional 1302 saloon was introduced featuring a larger boot and increased engine power of 50 bhp. The suspension was completely revised with MacPherson struts replacing the front torsion bar system and semi-trailing arms the rear swing axles

1971 The ventilation was even further refined while the engine lid received more air slats

1972 The VW 1303 was launched offering a 'panorama' windscreen and larger rear lights

1974 The turn signals were integrated in the bumpers

1975 The VW 1200 had its bumpers painted black and black mudwing beading was fitted. The VW 1200L was given chrome bumpers with rubber bump strips, chromed wheel covers, reversing lights and forced air ventilation

1977 saw a VW 1200L version from Mexico, featuring chromed bumpers and wheel covers, reversing lights, upgraded equipment with padded dashboard, adjustable front head restraints, three-point inertia reel safety belts, lap belts in the rear, a heated rear window and radial tyres.

---

although this had little effect on the Beetle's 62 mph (100 kph) top speed, acceleration perked up somewhat. However, it was not until the 1966 model year that capacity again increased, to 1285 cc, for an additional 1300 model while a 1500 model arrived for 1967.

Volkswagen sales were by this time soaring. The 100,000th car had been built in 1950 with the millionth example produced in 1955. Output continued to rise and in 1965 Wolfsburg had its first million Beetle year and between 1968 and 1971 the feat was again repeated. Alas, Heinz Nordhoff died in 1968 and the mighty Volkswagen factory stopped work for one minute in silent tribute to the man who had built Volkswagen up to be not only Germany's largest car company but also one of Europe's.

The Beetle's refinement continued for 1971 with the arrival of the 1302 with a new 1600 cc engine. This car marked the first departure from Porsche's original specification with MacPherson struts replacing the intrusive transverse torsion bars to increase luggage accommodation while semi trailing arms took the place of the rear swing axle. These changes were made to improve sales on the all important American market. It was replaced for 1973 by the 1303 with its new distinctive curved windscreen but this did not prove a success. In February 1972 the Beetle finally overtook the record of 15,007,033 Model T Fords produced to become the best selling car in the history of the automobile. (Ford subsequently revised its T output figure to 16.5 million but Volkswagen overtook that in 1973). But VW was in danger of repeating the very same mistake that Henry Ford had made when he kept the T in production for too long. The Beetle was getting long in the tooth and attempts to

replace it by a 1500 car in 1961, the 411/12 of 1968 and the front wheel drive K70 in 1970 proved unsuccessful. Then, in 1974, the impossible happened and Volkswagen recorded a loss, the first in its history. In May of that year the German motoring press were treated to a preview of the car that Volkswagen and the country were waiting

LEFT *Karmann's stylish Beetle Cabriolet is a desirable car which is beginning to fetch extraordinarily high prices. The first Karmann Cabriolet was built in 1949 and production continued to 1980 and inspired the Golf Cabriolet*
BELOW *This VW 1303 is seen tackling the rigorous Land's End Trial of 1984*

for, the front-wheel-drive Giugiaro styled Golf which had nothing in common with the Beetle apart from its wheelbase. At last a replacement had been found. The last Wolfsburg-built Beetle left the factory in July 1974 though production continued at the firm's Emden factory and was maintained until 1978. This was not quite the end of the Beetle in Germany for the Karmann-built cabriolet, introduced back in 1949, continued until 1980. The European market was serviced with spare parts from Volkswagen's Mexico plant though deliveries ceased in 1985.

To date over 20 million Beetles have been produced, an astounding success story for a 40 year old plus creation that still looks and sounds like no other.

MAYBACH

A luxury car with a prototype airship engine, the sophisticated Maybach Zeppelin was a fabulous yet over-priced machine offering the sophistication of eight gears

NOT MORE THAN three hundred Maybach Zeppelins were made in total over a ten year period of manufacture, less than twelve of these selling in the Zeppelin's homeland during 1938. Not one of the three hundred had a factory-built body and the two which were equipped with Saoutchik coachwork proved to be impossible to sell – due, no doubt to their somewhat controversial looks and hopeful price. These two examples had to be re-bodied to please customers with more conservative tastes who were nonetheless keen to pay top money for a reputedly superb motor car.

The Maybach Zeppelin was indeed a superb car; it was neither as exciting as a Duesenberg nor as prestigious as a Rolls-Royce Silver Ghost, but the V12-engined machine from Friedrichshafen claimed to be the most perfect car ever designed in Germany.

Wilhelm Maybach was not only Gottlieb Daimler's first chief designer, but he was also the man responsible for *the* Mercédès of 1900 and 1901. Wilhelm Maybach's son, Karl, started a business of his own in 1912, dealing in the manufacture of aero-engines. His factory was situated just opposite the Zeppelin works in Friedrichshafen on Lake Constance. This enterprise was well received by Count Zeppelin, who had for long been on the look-out for a suitable engine to propel his airships; Maybach proved able to supply such a device and soon became Zeppelin's steady supplier, aero-engines remaining the mainstay of his business thereafter.

Maybach later supplied a great number of straight-six and V12 units to the German naval industry, however, as well as to Krauss-Maffei and others producing armoured vehicles and military trucks for the Wehrmacht. Some 140,000 engines (fuel-injected ones among them) left the Friedrichshafen works up until 1944, and demand for aero, naval and military machinery was so great that the production of motor cars had to take second place. Only 2300 cars were built by Maybach over twenty years, a mere 300 of these being powered by the distinguished V12 engine.

When Maybach presented his first twelve-cylinder car in 1929, he proudly made it known that it was his extensive experience of aero-engines which had inspired the V12 and which had enabled him to design so many progressive features into his new motor car. A statement made by a Maybach factory spokesman at the time reflected that 'Among the cars that fulfil the primary needs of top speed, maximum comfort and utmost safety, the Maybach twelve-cylinder is indisputably regarded as the leader. The name

TOP & FAR RIGHT *The grand lines of a Maybach Zeppelin Cabriolet Sport. This is a short-wheelbase version bodied by Spohn and first shown at the Berlin Salon of 1938. The plush interior* **RIGHT** *marks its claim to being Germany's most perfect car*

ZEPPELIN

Zeppelin indicates that the Maybach twelve-cylinder engine which propelled the Graf Zeppelin airship was a prototype of the engine which we use in this car'.

The first cars of this new line (the six-cylinder vehicles remained in production simultaneously) were simply designated DS7, this standing for 'double-six, 7-litre', When the displacement of the engine was enlarged from 6962 to 7922 cc in 1931, the designation was suitably amended to DS8 and the name Zeppelin became the machine's official *nom-de-guerre*.

With a bore and stroke of 86 mm × 100 mm, the DS7 produced 150 bhp at a lowly 2800 rpm. With the bore enlarged to 92 mm, but the stroke retained, the DS8 version boasted a mighty 200 bhp at 3000 rpm. A single camshaft positioned in between the 60-degree inclined banks operated the valves by levers and tappets, the eight-bearing crankshaft was equipped with a vibration damper and the light alloy pistons were of the then-popular Nelson-Bohnelite type. Fuel supply to the engine was by two twin-choke Solex carburettors and the 12-volt battery-and-coil ignition system claimed impressively to have fully automatic timing adjustment.

Maybach cars were renowned for having sophisticated transmissions, although some models never actually had a gearbox at all, so flexible were the engines. Other models featured an eight-speed semi or fully automatic transmission with or without overdrive and pre-selector facility. The first Maybach twelve had a three-speed manual gearbox with *Schnellgang* (overdrive) operated from the centre of the steering wheel. For the Zeppelin, however, Maybach developed an all-synchromesh four-speed gearbox which could – again, by little levers at the steering wheel – be pre-selected without using the clutch pedal; all that was necessary was to lift the foot off the throttle, switch a lever, and then reapply the throttle, There was a clutch pedal, of course, and a traditional gear lever which offered a very low gear for steep hills and reverse; this so-called '1A' position could also be used in all four forward gears and was also switched in from the steering wheel, so the Zeppelin's chauffeur had the wide choice of eight forward and two reverse gears in total. Certain Lagonda models of the early 1930s also employed this remarkable transmission unit.

RIGHT *Imposing detail from the 1938 Maybach Zeppelin Cabriolet Sport. The cars were very expensive but superbly engineered and every one of the 300 made found a ready home*
FAR RIGHT *This convertible Zeppelin was made in 1931 and represents just one of the large variety of body styles that clothed these sophisticated chassis*

The U-section pressed-steel chassis of the Zeppelin had a wheelbase of 146 in (370 cm) and weighed 36 cwt – 1.8 tons. Front and rear axles were of the rigid type, held in place by conventional semi-elliptic leaf springs. These springs did not rely on inter-leaf friction for damping, but were supplemented by double-acting dampers. Application of the four-wheel brakes was assisted by vacuum servo (manufactured by Bosch-Dewandre) and a clever equalising device gave increasing brake efficiency with rising road speed. A minus-point, however, was that a Maybach Zeppelin on tow could not be braked!

The Zeppelin was equipped with central chassis lubrication, as were so many luxury cars of the 1930s, and this required very little attention – just a press of a pedal at every

ABOVE *A less than sightly attempt at streamlining by the coachbuilding firm of Spohn on a 1933 DS8 chassis. The reverse rake radiator was just one of the car's novel features*

100 kilometres (62 miles). For the same distance, 27 litres (6 gallons) of fuel would meet the needs of the thirsty engine, providing 10 miles of progress for a gallon of petrol. Tank capacity was fortunately generous, at 30 gallons, so some reasonable long-distance travelling could be achieved between re-fuelling stops.

Other extra features that the Zeppelin offered were a built-in hydraulic jack for each wheel and an auxiliary tyre pump for

the 7.0/7.5 × 20 (truck-type) tyres – perhaps the most fragile aspect of the whole car, since a speed of 110–115 mph (177–185 kph) could be achieved. The roadholding, however, was no match for this pace (although the brakes were) so 80 mph (129 kph) was perhaps a more realistic maximum safe speed.

Although the Maybach works were located so close to the Zeppelin factory and Zeppelin were very experienced in light alloy construction, that company never actually did any coachbuilding for Maybach. The Maybach concern was not equipped to produce bodywork for its chassis, so some of the better-known German coachbuilders supplied luxury bodies to the customers' specifications; Spohn of Ravensburg, for instance (only 40 miles from Friedrichshafen)

TOP LEFT & RIGHT *Details of the one-off Spohn-bodied Cabriolet Sport. Attention to finish was all important to Maybach as the neat routing of the ignition leads on the engine testifies*
LEFT *A 1934 Zeppelin convertible saloon with coachwork by Graber; it weighed 2.5 tons but still managed 100 mph (161 kph)*

were Maybach's preferred coachbuilder and some 80 per cent of all Maybach cars were bodied by them, some being clothed in impressive, though often ugly, streamlined bodies.

The first two Zeppelins built were sent off to Paris to be attended to by the renowned stylist Saoutchik and the result was a highly extravagant vehicle, which caused quite a stir at the 1931 Paris Motor show. Surprisingly enough, these two examples

were not sold, so they were taken to New York by Maybach's American representative with a view to a sale. The outcome of this move was further disappointment, however; it seemed that the cars were too expensive by far when compared with other twelve-cylinder luxury cars. Both cars were sent back to Friedrichshafen, dismantled and given Spohn bodywork some time later; they cost the Maybach concern a lot of money, all in all!

The basic price of a chassis was 27,000 Reichsmarks in the early '30s, a Spohn or Erdmann & Rossi-built body costing a further 10,000–15,000 RM. A well equipped Zeppelin ready for the road would fetch about 40,000 RM (£2000) – a sum which in 1933 could also buy a Mercedes 540K and two Ford V8 saloons!

One or two Zeppelins were later clothed

These are further views of the Graber-bodied convertible saloon; a little more austere in both external appearance and interior appointment than the sleeker Sport variant but a luxury limousine nonetheless. The V12 engine is a great height-saver but a tall bonnet was kept anyway, partly for looks and partly to accommodate the large radiator

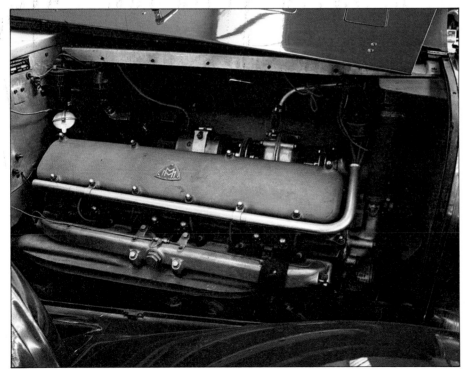

in Saoutchik bodywork and sold to wealthy French clients, while Spohn, Gläser, Erdmann & Rossi, Dörr & Schreck were building some quite wonderful cabriolets, sedancas (known as Transformation Cabriolets in Germany) and saloons for clients in Germany, Switzerland and even South America.

A close friend of Karl Maybach, Carlos Zingg of Venezuela, who was the German Consul and a successful businessman, acted as Maybach representative between El Paso and Buenos Aires and sold at least 20 cars down there. As with Porsche and BMW today, Maybachs were sold mainly abroad; only 800 of the 2300 cars produced at Friedrichshafen found private homes, the majority serving as staff cars during the war. Most of the Maybachs left over after the war were bought by American collectors of classic cars, between 1945 and 1948, and few of them have ever returned to Europe. There are about 120 known 'survivors', 30 V12s.

Karl Maybach died on 7 February 1960, aged 80. The production of his cars was not continued after World War II, although some restoration jobs were carried out by the factory for owners who had been special customers. In 1966, the Maybach Motorenbau GmbH was taken over by Daimler-Benz, two generations after the first attempts of Wilhelm Maybach and Gottlieb Daimler to power a vehicle with an internal combustion engine.

Proud Maybach owners should always remember the words spoken of Karl Maybach by Count Zeppelin, 'Hold on to what Maybach supplies you – he won't bring you anything bad.'

Mercedes-Benz 540K

THE SUPERCHARGED MERCEDES-BENZ models of the 1930s reached their ultimate expression with the 540K of 1936, but to discover the origins of this extraordinary model we must first retrace our steps to find out just how the supercharged Mercedes came to fruition.

Daimler, along with Benz, had effectively created the motor industry in Germany in 1886 with Gottlieb Daimler's great contribution being the creation of the high-speed internal combustion engine. Indeed he envisaged it powering transport on land, sea and air, a commitment to be represented in the make's famous tri-star motif. Daimler, alas, died in 1900 and his son Paul took over the design of the firm's cars. But the car that really raised Daimler's products head and shoulders above the competition was the Mercedes, introduced in that same fateful year of 1900. With its channel-section chassis, honeycombe radiator and 5.9-litre four-cylinder engine with mechanically operated, rather than atmospheric, inlet valves the model showed the way forward. Named Mercedes after the daughter of Daimler director Emil Jellinek, not only did the firm soon call its cars by this title but that car established a sporting tradition for the marque which continues to this day.

The firm also expanded into Grand Prix racing. A Mercedes scored a victory in the celebrated French Grand Prix of 1908 and scored a magnificent 1–2–3 triumph in the 1914 event, held just prior to the outbreak of World War I. The four-cylinder overhead-camshaft engines of these cars echoed the design of the aero engines which the Stuttgart company had built since 1909. Yet another variation on engine design also came in 1909 when the firm acquired a licence to produce sleeve-valve engines to the designs of American Charles Yale Knight.

With the coming of World War I, Daimler not only stepped up aero-engine production but also, at the end of 1915, began to manufacture complete aircraft. It was this aviation work that provided the spur for the firm's experiments in supercharging which would have permitted planes to operate at higher altitudes than hitherto. This work started in 1918 and began with Roots superchargers being tried with aero engines and with diesels built by Daimler for use in submarines. Although Germany's defeat in 1918 put an end to all these activities there were still, of course, Mercedes cars.

At the end of 1918 Paul Daimler began experimenting with a Roots supercharged sleeve-valve 16/50 model, this 4048 cc car being a development of the 16/46 of 1909. Unfortunately its engine did not respond to supercharging; there were lubrication problems and the work was discontinued on this model. But in the summer of 1919 Paul

Along with the British SS100, the supercharged Mercedes-Benz 540K represented the absolute pinnacle of pre-war open sports car styling

Daimler tried again; this time he used a smaller 10/30 sleeve-valve unit, which dated from 1912. A tiny Roots blower, capable of spinning at 10,000 rpm, was mounted underneath the engine's carburettor and driven, with suitable changes to gearing, from the unit's dynamo drive. A multi-disc clutch was incorporated in the drive mechanism so that the supercharger only engaged when the accelerator was fully depressed. This meant that for most of the time the blower was not working and so did not impose any drag on the engine to the detriment of its power and fuel consumption. The supercharger pressurised the carburettor, which was accordingly placed between it and the engine's inlet tract. Although this layout was popular at the time, other manufacturers were soon placing the carburettor on the inlet side of the supercharger but Mercedes remained wedded to its original system. Although refined over the years this layout was employed on all subsequent supercharged Mercedes and Mercedes-Benz road cars though, fortunately, the sleeve valve concept was soon dispensed with.

This followed experiments which had begun on 17 October 1919 with the suitably modified sleeve-valve 10/30 actually on the road. These were completed by the end of November but, like its larger brother, the 10/30 engine reacted adversely to forced induction with the area of the exhaust ports charring instead of lubricating. As a result the all-important sleeves seized and the drives fractured. Consequently the 10/23 was perpetuated in unsupercharged form and lasted until October 1921 when the Knight sleeve-valve licence expired.

The experiments told Daimler that if the

The immaculate 540K Cabriolet from the Blackhawk Collection in California. It was one of only six built with a disappearing top and 'clam shell' wings

firm wanted to supercharge its engines they would have to be of the conventional poppet-valve type. By this time work was well advanced on a 2.6-litre overhead-camshaft unit, designated the 10/40, which bore a close resemblance to the 1914 Grand Prix engine. The model was introduced late in 1921 but before it went into production in 1922 it became the 10/40/65. This rather clumsy designation referred to first, its taxable horsepower, next its approximate power output in unblown form and, finally, the output with the supercharger engaged. This engine followed the layout employed on the sleeve-valve units although the supercharger was driven off the front of the crankshaft, via a set of bevel gears, and the obligatory multi plate clutch was controlled from the accelerator pedal. The 10/40/65 has the distinction of being the first series production supercharged road car in the world. Later in 1922 came a smaller 1568 cc 6/25/40 version which was the first Daimler engine to have been specifically designed for a supercharger.

Germany was banned from participating in Grand Prix racing in the immediate post-war years so the Daimler company looked far afield to Sicily for a chance of competitive racing. There, in 1921, a veteran 28/95 gave a spirited performance to finish second to a Fiat in the Targa Florio. For the 1922 event a supercharged 28/95 was entered though with the Roots blower driven from the rear rather than the front of the engine. It won the event in this form, although a duo of 6/25/40-based racers fared less well, one retiring and the other finishing in 20th place.

These were, of course, out and out racing models but the 6/25/40 and 10/40/65 were road cars and remained available until 1924. There were other excursions into supercharging for the production models with the arrival of the touring six-cylinder overhead-camshaft 15/70/100 and the 24/100/140 cars, designed by Ferdinand Porsche, who had taken over from Paul Daimler as chief engineer in 1923. It was this latter model that paved the way for the illustrious 600K sports model of 1927 which was the first Mercedes-Benz, Daimler and Benz having merged in 1926, supercharged sports car. The K suffix, incidentally stood not for *kompressor* (supercharger) but *kurz,* which is German for short, and relates to the model's chassis length. For 1928 came the 7.1-litre six-cylinder overhead-camshaft SS while the short-chassis SSK was for many the personification of the Teutonic sports car of the 1920s; functional and fast with external exhaust pipes, chromed and flexible, and renowned for the scream of the supercharger suddenly heard to cut in as the revs rose. Most famous of all variants was the SSKL of

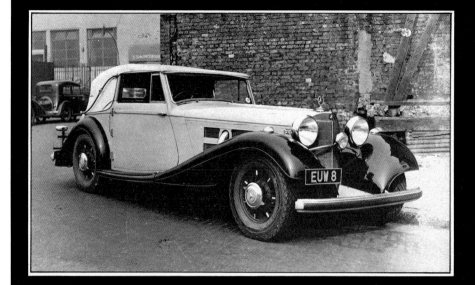

TOP INSET *The Mercedes Benz 540K as tested by* The Autocar *in 1937. At that time it was one of the most exotic and fastest road cars tested by the magazine's staff*

1931, the L referring to the car's weight; in German it stood for *leicht*. Caracciola won the 1931 Mille Miglia in one but that year Daimler-Benz decided to withdraw from racing in view of the arctic economic climate.

This did not mean the end of the supercharged models, however, for in 1930 had come the 7655 cc Grosser Mercedes-Benz; its eight-cylinder engine now featured pushrods rather than the more expensive single-overhead camshaft. It produced 145 bhp in unblown form with 200 bhp on offer when the supercharger engaged. The Grosser remained in production until 1939.

The Grosser was a traditional cart-sprung model but, in 1931, came the 170, which was to influence all the Mercedes-Benz models of the 1930s for it was offered with all-independent suspension. At the front was a pair of transverse leaf springs while swinging axles were featured at the rear. The low-built frame was deeply arched at the rear to provide plenty of movement for the exposed half-shafts while the suspension medium was two coil springs on either side of the chassis. This swing-axle layout was to endure on Mercedes-Benz models well into the post-war years. However, the cruder transverse leaf suspension was dispensed with in 1933 when the supercharged sports 380 made its debut. This significant model, from which was to spring the 540K, was of great significance because although it retained the swing-axle rear suspension, at the front was a new and revolutionary coil and wishbone independent suspension that was subsequently widely copied.

Like the Grosser, the 380 had an eight-cylinder pushrod engine of similar layout although substantially smaller at 3820 cc, the displacement being reflected in the model's title, which by then was the norm at Stuttgart. As it represents the starting point of what finally became the 540K it is of great relevance to our story. The imposing eight was mated to a four-speed gearbox in which third was direct drive while fourth was a top overdrive gear and ideally suited for the new *autobahnen* which began to appear in Germany from 1934 onwards.

The car was available with a 10 ft 6 in (320 cm) chassis while there was a 10 ft 3½ in (314 cm) version which was offered as the 380K. Practically all models were supercharged and a total of 151 examples was built. A few had their blowers mounted

TOP RIGHT AND LEFT *The imposing bodywork on the 540Ks was as heavy as it looked with some examples weighing in excess of two and a half tons, or 2500 kg. Nevertheless with the power available, the cars were still very fast and even some of the larger ones were capable of exceeding 100 mph on the new Autobahns of pre-war Germany*

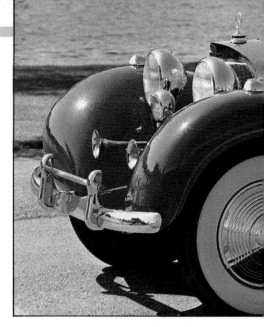

integrally with the engine crankcase and produced slightly more power than the 140 bhp at 3600 rpm, which was the norm on the short-chassis version. The longer car, by contrast, developed the same power but at 3400 rpm.

When the 380 was announced at the 1933 Berlin Motor Show, the German motoring magazine *Motor und Sport* commented that the all independent 380 represented the link between 'the very latest trends in automobile engineering and the *nec plus ultra* of the classic school' represented by the earlier SS. The 380 was offered with a range of seven body styles made at the Daimler-Benz factory at Sindelfingen, a manufacturing facility that had been built during World War I for the production of Daimler aircraft. There was a four-seater saloon and no less than four types of cabriolet on offer titled A, B, C and D. This range of body work was to endure, with modifications, with the 380's 500 and 540K successors. Cabriolet A was a two-seater with occasional accomodation

BELOW *A superb Mercedes-Benz 540K Cabriolet from 1936. Wire wheels were more common than the covered wheels shown on this white-walled American-owned car*

behind while B was a proper four-seater with a shorter bonnet than the A. The Cabriolet C was similar to the B with glass quarter lights. All these cars had two doors but the D had four and was a five-seater. In addition there was a handsome two-seater roadster and an open tourer with sidescreens. Incredibly all these versions were offered at the same price of RM19,500 (£1383) though it was possible to buy a 380 in chassis form for RM13,000 (£921).

Yet for all its impressive looks and mechanical specifications the 380 could not really be regarded as a sports car even though it had a top speed of 100 mph (161 kph). Even though the engine developed 90 bhp in unsupercharged form, and 120 bhp with the blower engaged, it was not really up to the job to propel a car that weighed close on two tons at anything like a respectable rate of acceleration. What was required was a larger capacity engine to pep-up performance. By 1934 Daimler-Benz were consequently experimenting with a more powerful version of the 380. This had a bore of 80 mm rather than 76 mm and there were experiments with underslung chassis. However, when the 500, the 380's replacement, emerged in 1934, the bore size had been increased to 86 mm and the stroke increased from 100 to 108 mm. At 3400 rpm the result was 100 bhp in unsupercharged

form and 160 bhp with the supercharger engaged. Compression ratio was 5.5:1 and capacity 5013 cc.

Although the 500 was offered, like its predecessor, in two chassis lengths, they differed in dimensions from the earlier model, the longer version having a 10 ft 9½ inch (329 cm) wheelbase while the 500K's was 9 ft 8½ in (296 cm). However, most 500s were built in long-chassis form with saloon bodywork with the two seaters

size of the straight-eight engine must have been irresistible to the Daimler-Benz engineers.

The result was the most sensational and, indeed, most popular of this range of supercharged speedsters; the 5401 cc, 540/540K range. Designated W29 by the works, prototypes were on the road in 1934, the model, however, did not reach production status until 1936. Experiments were undertaken in which the swing-axle rear suspension was replaced by a de Dion unit which echoed that which eventually appeared on the Mercedes-Benz W125 Grand Prix car of 1937. There was not, alas, sufficent time to perfect the system for the 540 so it retained the tried and proven swing axle layout. The principal difference was, of course, the robust nine-bearing engine which was stretched to 5401 cc by increasing the bore and stroke to 88 mm × 111 mm. With a 6.13:1 compression ratio, the engine developed 115 bhp without supercharger and 180 bhp when the driver's foot was hard down and the blower noisily engaged, pumping in more and more mixture to give the engine its extra surge. Badly adjusted or worn superchargers still produced just as much of the noise but very little of the power!

Although the chassis lengths of the 500 were perpetuated on the 500K, this time the suffix did not refer to the shorter of the two

wheelbases but the fact that the model was supercharged. For this car the coachwork options, which will subsequently be considered in greater detail, were subtly refined and are undoubtedly the finest of the 380/500/540 range. The chassis, however, was substantially the same as the 500's. The coil and wishbone independent front suspension, claimed Daimler-Benz, was 'totally unaffected by the conditions on any given road surface . . . Thus even on the most dilapidated roads the car will travel as smoothly and safely as on the level asphalt road surface of the motor road.' The servo-assisted Lockheed hydraulic brakes with finned drums were of the same type employed on Mercedes-Benz racing models.

The pushrod straight-eight boasted twin chrome-plated external flexible exhaust pipes and was rubber mounted at four points. The gearbox differed from the 380/500 cars as fourth, rather than third gear, was the direct drive. Synchromesh featured on the bottom three gears while top could be

ABOVE LEFT *The mighty exhaust protruding through the sides of the bodywork were key features of the 540K's styling emphasising the sheer power of the great car*

being offered in 500K guise. In addition to the existing body range, the styling of which was newly tailored for the different chassis lengths, there was a timely streamlined two-seater coupé marketed as the *Autobahn-Kurier* or Motorway Express. Like the 380, the 500 range was offered at the same price though by this time the price had risen to RM22,000 (£1617). But weight was up again to around two and a half tons (2540 kg) unladen and the temptation to expand the

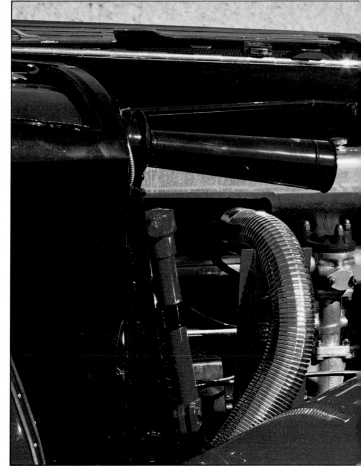

engaged without recourse to the clutch pedal 'since it is only necessary to move the gear lever into the required position, without any operation of the clutch'.

As mentioned earlier, the 540's coachwork was particularly impressive and perfectly complemented the model's 106 mph (171 kph) top speed. First came a five-seater saloon while Cabriolet A was essentially a two seater, although 'the space behind the two seats can be utilised… either for a third seat placed sideways, or for a children's bench, or for stowing away horizontally for two travelling cases'. Cabriolet B, by contrast, was somewhat roomier and a genuine four-seater. But the *crème de la crème* of the 540K styles was the Sport-Roadster, which Daimler-Benz rightfully claimed: 'has been distinguished in numerous international coachwork awards… its graceful lines, elegantly designed bonnet, drawn out mudguards and its divided V-shaped screen all impart to this car a distinctive sporting character.' Three people could be accomodated though the drivers seat 'is kept separate and is very easily adjustable'. There were two rear seats that could be dispensed with, 'the space utilised for stowing away luggage'. Next in the model line up was effectively a hardtop version of the roadster known as the Sport-Coupé. This contained rear folding seats and, unlike the open car, was provided with three 'exactly fitting suitcases'. The Convertible Coupé, on the other hand, had a detachable roof 'being easily exchanged in the summer, against a water proof hood of the folding type'. Last was an Open Tourer, capable of taking five and, like all the other body styles, was offered with two spare wheels which were offered, on all but the Sport-Roadster, mounted in recesses in the front wings. But on that illustrious model they would have destroyed the lovely body lines so they were relegated to the boot. Most models, with the exception of the Sport-Roadster and Open Tourer, were fitted with a radio aerial as standard equipment with the radio no doubt obtainable at extra cost.

There was also a low-production Cabriolet F variant, designed specifically for state occasions and able to seat seven people. The sides were reinforced with 4 mm armoured plate while the windows featured 1 inch (2.5 cm) thick bullet proof glass. Three were delivered for use by members of the German government.

In view of all these impressive specifications, the 540K Mercedes-Benz was the most popular supercharged model to be built by the Stuttgart company, a total of 409 being produced. In 1936, the first year of production, 97 were made while the best year ever was 1937 when 145 were manufactured. But, as the war clouds gathered, output dropped

to 95 in 1938 and 69 in the following year. Three more cars were built during the war years, the last 540K being delivered in July 1942.

The 540K was, of course, very much at home on the new German autobahns but how did it perform on the narrow, twisting roads of the British Isles? Fortunately *The Motor* magazine provided the answer because, in May 1937, it tested a 540K with Cabriolet B coachwork and found it perfectly tractable in London traffic and capable of an unfussy 10mph in third gear. But to test the 540K's full potential it was necessary to take the car to Brooklands track where it was possible to confirm the manufacturer's 106 mph (171 kph) top speed. This was conducted on the Railway Straight over a flying half mile with the windscreen and hood erected. At this speed the supercharger was very much in action and was activated by the driver treading hard on the accelerator. At the normal full-throttle position the pedal was checked by a strong spring but when the driver floored the accelerator, the blower would immediately engage. Its characteristic whine was less obvious on the 540K, however, than its predecessors because of the use of an air silencer. The servo-assisted brakes came in for favourable comment for the car, with its three occupants, turned the scales at no less than 6020 lb (2730 kg). The poor Brooklands concrete also showed up the worth of the all-independent suspension. Petrol consumption at around 10 miles per gallon was much the same as the 500 the magazine had tested previously. The car sold in Britain for £1890.

The impending war did not prevent Daimler-Benz conceiving a successor for the fabulous 540K. This appeared at the 1939 Berlin Motor Show as the 5800 cc 580K and was built with the 540K's short chassis, the only version produced since 1938. It had a 95 mm × 100 mm version of the long-running pushrod eight cylinder engine which developed, in supercharged form, 200 bhp at 3600 rpm. Work had begun on the project in 1937 and the model was given the W129 factory designation. Unfortunately the car never went into production although 12 examples were built, 10 in 1939 and the remaining two in the following year. These cars were not sold but retained by Daimler-Benz for experimental work. But one 580 engine (it was never an offical designation) escaped, having been fitted in a 540 chassis.

But with the demise of the 540K went the supercharged Mercedes-Benz performance cars. A feature of the make from 1922 until 1939, the cars remain a glorious testament to the competence and vitality of German automotive engineering in the inter-war years.

Needless to say 540Ks are now among the world's most valuable cars.

The Blackhawk Collection's 540K has spent all its life in North America, originally having been bought by the owners of Corning Glass. The engine is a 5.4-litre supercharged straight-eight which produced 180 bhp, sufficient to give the imposing machine a 100 mph+ top speed, America's speed limit notwithstanding

M1

The M1 has the elegance of line of a Giugiaro design yet retains BMW identity

BMW M1

The M1 did not quite make it on the race track but it was certainly one of the most spectacular road cars of the '70s

IN THE LATE 1970s BMW's Motorsport boss Jochen Neerpasch wanted a new racer – a car to replace the ageing be-winged CSL coupé and fly the BMW flag on the world's circuits well into the '80s. It would need to be good enough to take on the dominant Porsches in Group 4 and have the potential to compete in Group 5 (silhouette) racing. No BMW road car past or present would have had more power, prestige or appeal.

In short, BMW needed a senior league mid-engined supercar, and it needed 400 examples for homologation in Group 4 in a hurry. The result was the M1: almost the best car BMW never made. The story of BMW's dream car reads more like a nightmare in its early stages. Neerpasch made all the right moves but was dogged by bad luck from the

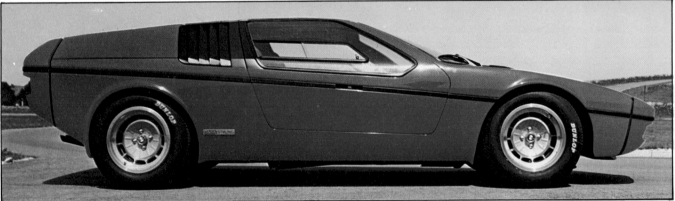

start. Because it would have disrupted the main-line production programme to have the M1 designed, developed and manufactured by BMW, Neerpasch looked to Italy for help. The major decisions were easy to make: body design was entrusted to Ital Design; chassis design, overall development and final assembly Modenese supercar specialists Lamborghini would look after. Power? BMW's own 3.5-litre straight six with a 24-valve head and close on 300 bhp had the right sort of credentials. Giugiaro gave BMW a shape as dramatic as anything from the Emillian planes, yet one their customers would be able to identify with. He even managed to incorporate some of the slicker styling details of the old Turbo showcar that fired everyone's imagination in the mid '70s. BMW and Lamborghini worked together on the M1's chassis and built half a dozen prototypes in the early months. Ing Dallara – Lamborghini's ace suspension man – was

active on the project from the start, offering guidance on the special properties of Pirelli's P7 tyres gained from experience with the P7-shod Countach S. That the M1 was shaping up well was a fact lost on neither party: its sheer speed was already a hot talking point in the bars around Sant 'Agata.

Any optimism this might have nurtured, however, was premature. The troubles gnawing away at Lamborghini's fragile financial infrastructure had suddenly opened up a gaping hole, and the £1.1 million loaned by the Italian government for component funding and assembly slipped down it before so much as a single M1 had been produced. It could hardly have been worse for the Germans. Already heavily committed to the project and under strict instructions from Munich not to invest Deutschmarks in Italy, Neerpasch had no alternative but to seek support elsewhere: the project was too advanced to abort. At least the component

suppliers Lamborghini had signed up were still willing to deliver. The welding of the tubular space frame chassis, however, was contracted out to an engineering outfit run by the brothers Marchesi while glassfibre specialists TIR supplied the panels. Ital Design agreed to mate bodies with chassis at their own premises. Final assembly was undertaken by Stuttgart coachbuilders Baur.

The M1 went on sale in February 1979 – a year later than originally intended – at a price of £26,500. The car's specification – conceived, remember, with an 850 bhp Group 5 version in mind – was as impressive as that of any contemporary exotic; its torsionally-strong square-section steel space frame was clothed entirely in unstressed panels. The longitudinally mid-mounted 3453cc 24-valve straight six (with a 93.4mm bore and 84mm stroke) developed 277 bhp (DIN) at 6500 rpm and 239 lb ft of torque at 5000 rpm. Electronic ignition provided a

cut-out at 7000 rpm and dry sump lubrication guarded against oil surge in hard cornering and braking. ZF made the transaxle with particularly tall fourth and fifth gear ratios, but this was tempered by a 4.22 final drive so that, in top, overall gearing was 23.4 mph/37.6 kph per 1000 rpm.

The M1 was 172 in (437 cm) long and 72 in (183 cm) wide with a 101 in (256 cm) wheelbase. Ready to roll it weighed 24 cwt. (2688 lb/1219 kg).

And that was certainly part of its problem. BMW realised at an early stage – long before the requisite 400 had been build for Group 4 qualification – that it would be a struggle to get the M1's weight down to the class minimum of 1005 kg (2211 lb), even with simpler, lighter interior trim and Perspex

BELOW LEFT AND BELOW *This is the BMW Turbo, an in-house styling-design of 1972. It sparked off the idea of a Bavarian 'supercar' and in many ways influenced the Ital-penned final product* **LEFT AND BOTTOM** *which was less well proportioned*

side and rear windows. The best BMW could manage was 1300 kg (2486 lb) but since the M1 was never seriously to challenge its great German rivals in its short Group 4 career this was ultimately of little consequence. Nor was it destined to turn a wheel as a Group 5 car; production lagged so far behind schedule, it simply missed its chance. In the end, Neerpasch elected to cut his losses. In league with the Formula One Constructors Association (FOCA), he enlisted the backing of Goodyear to put on the 'Procar' races: two years of the fastest and most spectacular single-make dicing ever seen.

Procar racing may have seemed an ignoble climax to Neerpasch's highsighted plans, but it made the M1 famous. Most of its drivers in the series were famous already. Procar was a sort of Race of Champions, matching 15 private owners – from top drawer campaigners like Hezemans or Quester to rising stars like Surer, Hottinger or Cheever – against the five fastest Friday afternoon qualifiers at each Grand Prix race to be run on the following day in strictly

identical M1s wearing identical Goodyear rubber. Over the two years, Procar featured some big names, by no means the least being those of Lauda and Piquet. In fact, the future Brazilian world champion drove the M1 to its best-ever World Sports Car Championship result: a fine third place overall with Hans Stuck at Nürburgring in 1980.

The Procar racers were essentially in Group 4 spec, with rose-jointed suspension, no brake servo but circuits with adjustable front-rear distribution, wider wheels and tyres, quicker steering, a deeper front air dam and, of course, a heavily modified engine. Power was hiked from 277 bhp (at 6500 rpm) to 470 bhp (at 9000 rpm), sufficient, according to the factory, to permit a 0–100 kph (62 mph) time of 4.5 seconds.

Not that the standard car was any slouch. Independent tests confirmed the factory's claim that it could crack 160 mph/(258 kph) flat out and, with plenty of traction off the line, hit 60 mph (96 kph) from a standstill in 5.4 seconds. With a 0–100 mph time of just over 13 seconds and 120 mph (193 kph) coming up in 20 seconds, the M1 ranked with the very quickest of contemporary supercars, and would be far from disgraced today. Moreover, the M1 delivered its mighty performance with an admirable lack of temperament or fuss. Its punch was granite hard but velvet-gloved, the engine pulling strongly and cleanly from as little as 1000 rpm, even in fifth. From 3500 rpm, the exhaust note would sharpen as the engine climbed on to its cams, then howl exultantly all the way to the 6900 ignition cut out. A 130 mph (210 kph) cruise on the autobahn could be held with the sense of effortless energy only the very swiftest of supercars possess. Getting there would see peak-rev change ups at 48, 71, 101 and 136 mph (77, 114, 163 and 219 kph) with a gearshift that was both quick and precise, though the rather abrupt action of the long-travel clutch required some mastering.

Dynamically, the M1 was a paragon of precision and predictability. Most of the traditional handling shortcomings of mid-engined cars – strong understeer in tight turns, snap oversteer on lift-off – simply didn't apply. The M1 turned in with great agility yet was endowed with superb balance, enabling even the less skilled driver to keep it neutral for far longer than he would have had any right to expect. Under power, the tail would come out but in a progressive and easily held (or corrected)

TOP *The BMW M1 was used in Group 4 sports car racing albeit with only modest success. The Team Denim car seems to be having less trouble than Goring's car,* BELOW

manner. In steady-state cornering on perfectly dry tarmac, the sheer bite of the squat, fat P7s was virtually impossible to overcome. There were some small vices – a mild tendency to follow cambers and white lines – but these were but small chinks in the BMW's heavy-duty armour. Certainly the M1's massive all-round ventilated discs (12 in/30 cm diameter) were beyond criticism, capable of hauling the car to rest from three-figure velocities time after time without the slightest signs of fading.

When *Motor* went to Germany in 1980 to drive the BMW they concluded that the M1 was 'a svelte road-going sports car in the finest supercar traditions, stunningly fast and yet with reserves of dynamic ability far in excess of its engine output.'

The M1 was a supreme driving machine, then, but did it make any sense as day-to-day transport? It did if you weren't too tall, for headroom was tight indeed: six footers were forced to adopt an awkward driving position. That accepted, the seats were well-

shaped and comfortable, the cabin wide and not at all claustrophic, despite the extensive use of black linings. A fine, supple ride with superb high-speed damping was more good news, though the suspension and tyres were far from quiet, thumping over ridges and rumbling over rough surfaces with barely disguised disapproval. Wind noise was reasonably well suppressed however, and if the engine made a lot of noise when worked hard, the quality of its vocalisations could hardly warrant anything but indulgence.

The M1's instruments might not have measured up to the high standards BMW demand in their saloon cars, but the display was undoubtedly good for an exotic combining a comprehensive array of dials (speedo, rev counter, oil pressure, oil temperature, coolant temperature and fuel level) with neat and business-like – if somewhat reflective – presentation. The rest of the interior was a comfortable but no-frills affair with appointments borrowed from other BMW models and the overall effect,

As well as making stunning road cars, the M1s have provided their fair share of entertainment on the circuits, not least when they ran in the Procar series at Grand Prix events. Indeed, with most of the GP stars piloting the M1s prior to their F1 races, the events turned into fiercely competitive and often rough races. Clay Regazzoni leads Alan Jones, Niki Lauda, Jacques Laffite, Hans Stuck and Nelson Piquet at Zandvoort BELOW RIGHT, *German GP stars Manfred Winkelhock,* LEFT, *and Hans Stuck,* RIGHT,

while failing to arouse any passion, at least prompting some respect for efficiency. The heating and ventilation, for example, not only worked but worked well providing enough fresh air to cool the most moistened brow while supplying warmth to the footwells at the same time. Interior stowage was virtually non-existent but, by exoticar standards, the boot was huge. The M1's fuel consumption was also surprising – *Motor* managed to return 15.4 mpg in high-speed autobahn travel while BMW claimed 27.7 mpg at a steady 75 mph (121 kph).

Although the track car was a measurably more fearsome beast than its roadgoing counterpart, its essential character was no different, cornering with a remarkably neutral balance and great stability. Anyone who witnessed the extrovert driving style of Hans Stuck could have been left in no doubt of that. In racing trim, the 24-valve engine exhibited astonishing flexibility, the sledge hammer punch starting at around 3500 rpm and being maintained until 7000 rpm when the real action was unleashed, hurling the car forward with unabated energy all the way to the 9200 rpm limit. That's no more than you would have expected with a power to weight ratio of 390 bhp per ton.

A total of 450 M1s was built, 397 of them roadgoing versions and 53 racers. The M1 never really had the impact on the track its specification suggested although when driven by Hans Stuck in the rain at Le Mans in 1980 it led the race briefly until the track dried and the BMW's moment of glory was past. Its very existence was a potent statement of BMW's yearning to succeed in the toughest arena of all: endurance motor racing. Conceived and developed as a pure racer, the M1 could easily have made it but for the many and seemingly interminable problems that dogged its passage into production and continued to hamper and delay target output. That it ended up as the basis for a sort of glorified R5 Challenge Cup was a waste for man and machine, even if it provided high-spirited entertainment for race goers in 1979 and '80. The Procar attrition rate was astonishing as seasoned Grand Prix drivers treated their expensive charges like disposable dodgem cars. The car deserved better. At least the road-going versions remain intact. Perhaps BMW Concessionaires were right in what they wrote in the sales catalogue 'BMW M1 drivers do not only know when to use superior performance intelligently and properly. They also know when not to do so. And this is genuine superiority. So while even the BMW M1 is naturally subject to physical laws, it is also and above all an expression of personal freedom. And experience shows that freedom is never abused by people who know its value.'

The Giugiaro shape has aged extremely well, the hallmark of a timeless design. The same, however, cannot be said of the interior which is disappointingly unattractive

The 1950's rear-engined 356 was fast, aerodynamic and reliable, and pointed the way for Porsche. Yet it was a pre-war design . . .

WHEN PROFESSOR Ferdinand Porsche was released in August 1947 from the French prison where he had been interned after the war, he returned to the family home in Gmund, Austria. He found that his son Ferry and his old design associates Karl Rabe and Erwin Komenda were installed in a small design office and workshop in the outbuildings of the family house. They had begun by designing and building agricultural machinery, including a new design of tractor, as motor cars were out of the question in the immediate post-war days, and their workshop also carried out repairs on war-time Volkswagen cars, especially the cross-country vehicle which Austrian farmers were finding very useful.

By 1947 Ferry Porsche and his two experienced designers had begun work on a car to carry the Porsche name, based on VW components, owing much to a one-off streamlined coupé that Porsche had built in 1939 on a Volkswagen base. That coupé had been intended to take part in the Berlin-Rome race, but the war had put a stop to that. The prototype Porsche built at Gmund was an open two-seater sports car for the simple reason that Porsche's facilities were limited and they were unable to make a coupé. This was the prototype 356, and when Professor Porsche returned home he was well-pleased to see the family name on this sleek little sports car.

Before the war the Porsche design office and workshop had been in Stuttgart, and it was imperative that they returned there so that work would begin on producing Porsches again. Unfortunately the American military were in possession of the Stuttgart premises and it took a long time to repossess them (until 1950 in fact). While negotiations were in progress a batch of 50 cars was built in Gmund, each one hand-made and with a hand-beaten aluminium coupé body. When series-production of the little coupés was instituted, the Reutter body plant next door to the Porsche premises was given the contract to produce the chassis/body unit in steel, while Porsche looked after all the mechanical components, most of which were of Volkswagen origin. Thus did the Porsche 356 go into production, in Zuffenhausen in north-west Stuttgart.

The coupé 356 had first been shown to the public at the Geneva Motor Show in the spring of 1949, and it had proved to be an instant success among the sporting fraternity, even though its capacity was only 1100 cc. By reason of its air-cooled rear-mounted engine it had a very smooth front and consequently very low drag, so that its modest power output enabled it to reach a maximum of 84 mph (135 kph). By the time production was under way in 1950 the engine had been enlarged to 1300 cc and delivered 44 bhp, giving the car a speed of over 90 mph (145 kph), which was very impressive for such a small car. Thanks to the rear-mounted engine and smooth body the car was remarkably quiet cruising at 90 mph (145 kph) and set new post-war standards of the sort that are normally associated with much larger cars.

Almost at once customers used their Porsches for rallies and speed hill-climbs, and the factory soon began a very rigorous competition programme of their own. Racing and rallying cars similar to those on sale was good publicity, and offered the chance to feed development work into the production line and set a standard of known competence. The factory retained four of the aluminium coupés as a basis for their

gain momentum over the years until it reached a standard that everyone else tried to emulate.

The Le Mans success was followed by a similar performance in the rugged Liège-Rome-Liège rally, when Von Guilleaume and Count von der Muhle won the 1500 cc class and finished third overall. This was the first appearance of another major production step forward, in the form of a 1500 cc version of the ubiquitious flat-four air-cooled Volkswagen engine.

Through the 1950s the Porsche factory made more and more of the mechanical components, gradually phasing out the VW connection. Engine development had been continuous since the prototype was built in Gmund, but graduaully Porsche began to produce the gearbox and final drive units, the shock-absorbers, suspension, brakes, steering, electrics and axles. It all went hand-in-hand with engine development aimed at more power and more performance, carried out in conjunction with the active racing and rallying programme. All these developments were passed into the production line, and whatever the engine, it was always available in two forms, 'normal' or 'super'. The 'normal' engine was the basic unit and naturally the 'super' was a tuned version giving as much as 25 per cent more power, and although intended for competition could easily be used for everyday purposes, for Porsche's idea of a competition engine was one that would last the Le Mans 24 Hours, the Nürburgring 1000 Kms or the Mille Miglia. Although the 356 could give a good account of itself in sprints or hillclimbs, it really came into its own in the more rugged endurance events.

Naturally the feed-back to the production cars ensured that reliability and longevity were the keynotes on which the Porsche reputation was built. During the formative years of the mid-1950's the firm gave an attractive enamel car-badge to owners who had covered 60,000 miles (96,000 km) without having the crankshaft and connecting rods looked at, and a gold watch to those who reached 100,000 miles (161,000 km) without attention. Porsche engineers expected their production engines to cover 100,000 miles (161,000 km) without being stripped down, and today this mileage is the normal expected figure for a Porsche 928.

works team, and these cars made the name Porsche synonymous with winning at a very early stage.

In 1951 the Porsche 356 really established itself on the sporting scene when one of the cars was driven in the Le Mans 24 Hours by the Frenchmen Veuillet and Mouche, the first entry of a German car in the French classic since the war. With its 1100 cc engine tuned to give 44 bhp and with all four wheels enclosed by 'spats' the little coupé was capable of 100 mph (161 kph), using a special high axle ratio. The car ran like a clock and won the 1100 cc category with ease, starting a Porsche reputation for reliability that was to

LEFT The 356 has dumpier lines than the later 911 and reveals elements of the Volkswagen ancestry. This Cabriolet is a late model car from 1963

By 1955 there had been so many development changes to the original design that the type number was changed from 356 to 356A. A change in bore and stroke increased the engine capacity to 1582 cc and the gearbox and transmission had little in common with the original VW, although outwardly the casing was similar. Swing-axle rear suspension was still used, just as the Porsche-designed trailing-arm front suspension was still like that of the VW, but it was built to Porsche standards of strength and geometry. The basic shape of the coupé was only changed in detail, and such things as bumpers, lights, windscreen and rear window were improved slowly as the years went by. The little coupé, or Beetle as it became known, was the mainstay of Porsche production and was the 'real Porsche' in many owners' eyes. Concurrent with the coupé a drophead version was offered and by the end of 1954 a third model arrived in the form of an open two-seater, not unlike the Gmund prototype. As it was 135 lb (61 kg) lighter than the coupé, the Speedster, as it was known, was very popular among the racing customers, but for normal motoring the coupé was still favoured. The drophead model, known in Germany as the Cabriolet, was fairly popular in Europe and America, especially in the sunny climes of Florida and California, and Porsche sales in the USA

were very strong almost from the beginning. The Cabriolet was also favoured by the German police for use on the autobahns, as there was not much about in the mid-'50s that could get away from a 1600 Super Porsche.

In the racing world it was clear that the basic Volkswagen pushrod-overhead-valve layout could not compete forever, and a new engine was evolved by the Porsche design team, headed by Dr. Ernst Fuhrmann. The flat-four layout and air-cooling were retained but the valves were operated by overhead camshafts driven by shafts and bevel gears from the crankshaft. While the pushrod engines reached their limit at a

little over 6000 rpm the new engine was designed to run at 7000 rpm, with the possibility of going to 8000 rpm if necessary. This project was given the Porsche design number 547, these numbers stemming from Professor Porsche's first design in his own drawing office in 1930, which he gave the number 7 in case his first customer should realize that nothing had gone before! The numbers were given to all projects, be they engines or gearboxes, complete cars or even tractors! The new overhead-cam engine was destined for production but was first of all used in competitions in the special two-seater sports-racer Type 550, known as the Spider. After proving itself in strenuous

FAR RIGHT *The 356-derived sports racers paved the way for a Porsche dominance of sports car racing that began in the Sixties and persists into the late Eighties*

events like the Mille Miglia and at Le Mans the Spider sports/racer was put into limited production. Its first racing appearance, apart from brief excursions in practice, was in the 1954 Mille Miglia, and the following year saw a production line of something like 100 built. There was more to follow, for the overall size of the 547 engine was not much more than that of the pushrod 1600 cc engine, so it was only a matter of time before a 356A body/chassis unit received the four-cam engine. There was a lot of racing activity in Europe for GT cars, and the 356A 1500 cc four-cam was ideal. Naturally the first ones went to customers who intended to race or rally, but soon the 356A/1500GS was in full production and was given the name Carrera (the Spanish word for 'race'), after the Carrera Panamericana, the road-race that ran the length of Mexico. Porsche had taken part in that race until it was abandoned after the

1954 event, and named the new GT after it in memory of their successes. Carreras really caught on with the public and the term Porsche Carrera began to be used as a term for outstanding performance.

That illustrious Carrera name would later be associated with specialised lightweight and racing versions of the 911, the RS and RSR of 1973 plus subsequent models made after that year. When the 911SC tag was dropped from the 911 range in 1986, the name Carrera was added across the board for all 911 models except the turbo.

The advent of the Porsche Carrera changed the whole sporting scene, but the normal pushrod engine was still the mainstay of production. By the time the four-cam engine was in full production it had been enlarged to 1600 cc (the international capacity class limit) and the roller-bearing crankshaft had been replaced by a plain bearing

ABOVE AND LEFT *One of the earliest 356s, from 1949, distinguishable by its split windscreen and very low bumper line* **RIGHT** *A modified 356 chased by a Ferrari 166MM at the exciting historic races at Laguna Seca in 1984*

183

one. The compression ratio was lower on the production engine to make it more flexible and suitable for traffic, but even so it gave an easy 100 bhp at a time when the pushrod engines were giving 70 bhp. That meant that the Carrera buyers had a fully equipped fast-touring car that would do 125 mph (201 kph). From the early days the Porsche factory in Stuttgart-Zuffenhausen had been within sight of an autobahn, and naturally the cars were designed with high cruising speeds in mind. Even the simple *Damen* or standard 356 could be cruised flat-out, the gearing being such that it was

to 2 litres. The overall size of the car was still unchanged from the basic 356 coupé, and in the 2-litre form the Carrera was a landmark in the development of high-performance cars. In production form it was indistinguishable from a normal coupé, the only indication of its potential being the word 'Carrera' on the tail. The 2-litre version was known as the Carrera 2, but its production run was short as Porsche were planning bigger and better things in the shape of the new flat-six engine for the 911 series.

The development of the normal 356 series was continued right through until

ABOVE *The works Spiders of 1954-5*
ABOVE RIGHT *The functional cockpit of the 356 Speedster*
RIGHT *A 1959 356 Sprint. The flared rear wheel arches are a later addition, as are the slightly low profile tyres*
FAR RIGHT *A 356A Cabriolet. The 356As were built from 1955 to 1959*

impossible to over-rev the engine, even down an incline in top gear. The Carrera was geared in the same way in standard form, though naturally special gears were available for serious competition work. By 1959 the competition version of the Carrera could reach nearly 115 mph (185 kph), impressive performance for a 1600 cc coupé.

While all this high-performance activity was going on the normal customer was not forgotten, and the 1600 cc pushrod models were continually developed, improvements to body details eventually leading to the 356B model and later C and SC models. The horsepower of the production pushrod engine was increased steadily until 90 bhp was available, that model being known, reasonably enough, as the Super 90. Production figures had soared during the late 1950s and the personal touch at the factory inevitably suffered, but the idea of a Porsche family was still generated and extended by Porsche clubs forming all over the world.

With the success of the Carrera it was inevitable that Porsche would look for further fields to conquer in competition, and the first step was to enlarge the four-cam engine

1965 and the 356 could boast disc brakes by the time the factory stopped production and changed over to the 911.

The 356 was finally phased out in 1965, by which time 76,303 cars had been built, not very many in Ford or Volkswagen terms but a very satisfactory number for a firm that had only started in 1948, making their first cars literally by hand. Production of the original 356 model, using Volkswagen components, had continued until 1955 with 7627 cars being built. Then came the 356A which was rapidly becoming much more of a Porsche; it was introduced in August 1955

and was in production for four years, during which time 21,045 cars were built. The 356B ran for the following four years and saw 30,963 cars built, and in 1963 the 356C saw the series through to the end with 16,668 cars built. Throughout its life the basic concept did not change. The cars were built on a steel platform chassis to which the coupé body was welded to become an integral monocoque, the various open versions being made from the same basic unit. The flat-four air-cooled engine was mounted behind the rear axle line while the gearbox was ahead of it. Front suspension was by

EMX 200B

origins of all of them can be traced back to the Berlin-Rome coupé of 1939.

It was the formative years of 1950 to 1960 that saw Ferry Porsche lead the firm towards the engineering giant it has become today. His father died in 1952 at the age of 77 years, his health having been weakened by the years of imprisonment, but he was able to appreciate that his son had inherited all his engineering talents and was well able to carry the family name towards greater things. Ferry Porsche recently celebrated his 75th birthday, and though the Porsche empire is now run by new management and is partly publicly owned, Herr Porsche is still very much in the picture.

The 356 Porsche is now something of a collector's car and some really well-preserved examples are still in daily use in many parts of the world, while pampered and protected ones are preserved everywhere. The 356 is undoubtedly a classic but above all else it is a tribute to the small band of people who started making the cars in Gmund and had the courage and strength of purpose to return to Stuttgart and build the foundations of the present empire: solid foundations built on integrity and enthusiasm for the product, two aspects that are as strong today as they were in the beginning.

OPPOSITE AND BELOW *The last of the line in the form of a 356C Cabriolet. The 356Cs were built from 1963 to 1965*
ABOVE *A true cutaway. This is the car used as an exhibit at the motor shows of 1963, clearly revealing its VW Beetle origins*

EVOLUTION
Prototype 356, an open two-seater sports, built in 1948

1949 The 356 was unveiled at the Geneva Motor Show, powered by an 1100 cc engine and capable of 84 mph (135 kph)

1950 Production commenced with the flat-four engine stretched to 1300 cc, producing 44 bhp and a top speed of 90 mph (145 kph)

1951 60 bhp 1488 cc engine introduced

1952 1500 Normal (N) introduced with plain rather than roller bearings. The 1500 Super (S) continued with roller bearings, producing 70 bhp. It was given larger brake drums and baulk-ring synchromesh to match the 105 mph (169 kph) performance

1954 356 Speedster introduced in 1300 and 1500 N and S form. Front anti-roll bar added

1955 Engine bored out to 1582 cc. 1600 N produced 60 bhp and 1600 S 75 bhp, giving a top speed of 100 mph (161 kph). 7627 cars were built before the 356A was introduced with revised body and chassis details including thicker torsion bars, more vertical dampers, thicker anti-roll bar and larger tyres. First 356 Carrera introduced with 1498 cc twin-cam engine and top speed of 125 mph (201 kph)

1957 Roller bearing crank discontinued

1958 Carreras given the 1600 engine. Speedster discontinued in favour of Convertible D.21,045 356As were built in all

1959 365B introduced at the Frankfurt Show with raised bumpers and headlights, bigger rear seats and better brakes

1960 356 Super 90 introduced with the plain-bearing 1582 cc engine and transverse leaf spring attachment to improve rear suspension

1962 356 Carrera 2 introduced with 130 bhp engine, top speed of 125 mph (201 kph) and disc brakes all round. 30,963 356Bs were built

1963 356c introduced in Coupé and Cabriolet form, both with the 1582 cc engine. 356SC introduced with 95 bhp

1965 Porsche 356 range discontinued. 356C production totalled 16,668 and in total 76,303 356s were built

trailing arms with the transverse torsion bars which Professor Porsche had first designed for the Auto Union racing car, and rear suspension was by swing-axles also sprung on torsion bars. The 356 was essentially a two-seater sports car but two small 'jump seats' behind the driver and passenger gave the car a much wider appeal than a pure two-seater. The petrol tank, spare wheel and luggage space were located in the front, under the sloping nose, and because there was no radiator the penetration of the front of the car was excellent, as was forward visibility. Throughout its 14-year life the 356 was made in Coupé, Cabriolet, Speedster, Roadster and Convertible versions, but the

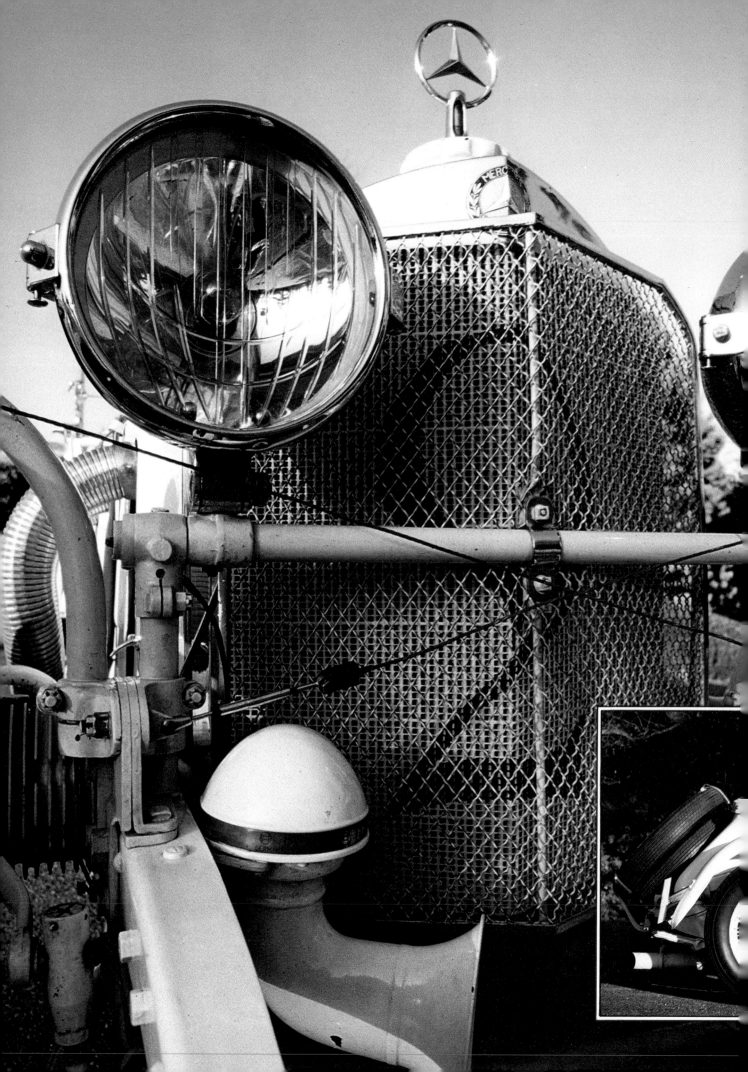

MERCEDES-BENZ S series

The S series cars of the '20s, with their Porsche-designed six-cylinder engines, were powerful, handsome and fast, and when supercharged well nigh unbeatable

WHEN STIRLING MOSS, navigated by Dennis Jenkinson in a Mercedes-Benz, won the 1955 Mille Miglia, it is fair to say that Italy was impressed and the rest of the world delighted. There had for too long been an assumption, bordering upon a superstition, that a foreign driver could never win this most Italian of races, that a foreign car could not do so either, and – although this was incidental and not at all xenophobic – that whoever led at Rome would not finally win at Brescia. By shattering all these illusions Moss did the race a considerable service, as everybody was keen to recognise; but their acclaim for him betrayed a sad dismissal of history. The race had been won before by a German, Rudolf Caracciola (the name was Italian, but removed by some hundreds of years from Italy), in a German car, a Mercedes-Benz SSKL, in 1931.

Maybe the celebrants of 1955 did not want their euphoria disturbed. After all, Moss did have a navigator to advise him of what lay ahead, and he had the support of a large army of Daimler-Benz mechanics, technicians and administrators who had made thorough preparations for the event through months of practice. Caracciola, by contrast, drove with a mechanic for company, and his support crew consisted of his wife and three men – one of whom had to drive over partially blocked roads from Siena to Bologna since the route demanded more refuelling points than the team had

men available. Times were hard....

They had been hard for all Germany since the end of the Great War in 1918. They were especially hard for motor manufacturers, who were numerous, over-ambitious and under-capitalised for reasons that had as much to do with the history of Germany as a loose aggregation of principalities in former centuries as with her history as industrial titan and failed warfarer in the twentieth. At the beginning of the 1920s there were 86 different firms in Germany producing at least 144 different cars. There was also a luxury tax of 15 per cent imposed on their products, yet import duties had been cut and so foreign cars could flood the market. What with poverty and inflation running riot as the victors stripped Germany of her wealth for reparations, one car factory would have sufficed to supply the whole market: accordingly, Benz & Cie and their erstwhile competitors the Daimler Motoren Gesellschaft entered into an association of common interest leading, after three years progressive collaboration, to their complete amalgamation as a new company, Daimler-Benz AG, at the end of June 1926.

Did they then attempt to market a car that would serve all the German people? Wisely, they did not. Both firms had traditionally cultivated high technology and high quality, and the new managing director Dr Hans Niebel (from Benz) insisted on the maintenance and furtherance of this tradition. Of

LEFT *Superb radiator detail from the ex-Malcolm Campbell 1928 SSK. The car has been fully restored and is still an impressive performer*

BELOW *A side view of the Campbell car showing its sheer size. For all its mass it had surprisingly agile handling on road circuits*

189

all Germany's surviving manufacturers, from Adler to Wittekind, theirs was the name least likely to perish. For steady business they had a more reliable stock-in-trade than any canny little cobbler of economy runabouts: they made lorries and public service vehicles that would remain economic necessities, however parlous the purchasing power of the private individual. Their cars, built for those individuals who still carried some weight, would be the heavy but flexible 16/50 Benz and the supercharged Mercedes.

Supercharging was something with which Daimler had been experimenting as early as 1915 for aero engines, at a time when the importance of high-altitude operation for military aircraft was becoming apparent. It would not appear in Grand Prix racing until Fiat introduced it in 1924, but as early as 1921 Daimler had added it to their catalogued 28/95, a 7¼-litre fast tourer that had been announced in 1914 and was put into production after the Armistice. In 1922 supercharging featured in their purpose-built competition cars too, still with the same arrangement which they were doggedly to persist with in some of their production cars until 1939. That is, the supercharger was for occasional use only, and was not continuously in engagement.

The compressor chosen was of the Roots type, driven from the the engine through a multi-disc clutch which was forced into engagement when the driver, having already reached the full-throttle position of the

accelerator pedal, pressed further and harder. When that happened, a flap valve diverted air from the long intake pipe feeding the carburettors and fed it to the blower, which returned it to the original route further downstream, just ahead of the carburettors themselves, simultaneously pressurising the fuel feed to maintain its flow. When the driver eased his foot the supercharger was immediately bypassed again and the engine reverted to atmospheric induction, which was why the carburettors had to be downstream from the compressor, and why the acoustics of the system produced such an eerie and sometimes frightening high-pitched scream when the blower was working.

The system was evolved under the guidance of Paul Daimler, chief engineer of the firm and son of pioneer Gottlieb who had actually toyed with the idea of forced induction for his engine back in 1885. In 1922 Paul left, and his place was taken by a fellow from Austro-Daimler called Ferdinand Porsche. To make his mark, he promptly produced some new engine designs including a big six-cylinder 6-litre supercharged touring device which was known as the 24/100/140 hp model. This triple rating displayed the German fiscal rating, the power unblown and the power with the blower engaged, and was to be applied to a long series of supercharged machines – so was the style of the engine, constructed in very different fashion from the aviation-inspired engines of Paul Daimler.

Porsche gave it, for the first time in the firm's experience, a one-piece crankcase and cylinder block cast in light alloy. The cylinder liners were cast iron, which was reasonable enough; so was the cylinder head, which was unfortunate – as indeed was the very fact of its being separate when

RIGHT One of Rudolf Caracciola's greatest drives was in the 1929 Monaco GP when he took the massive SSK to third place ahead of many more nimble cars

ABOVE *Manfred von Brauchitsch winning at Avus at an average 120.7 mph in an SSKL with specially designed streamlined coachwork by Baron von Faschenfeld*

BELOW AND BOTTOM *A 1929 38 250 SS originally built for Lord Cholmondeley. The instrumentation was comprehensive*

the best rival engines still enjoyed integral heads with no gaskets interposing their potential treachery. It was the only flaw in an otherwise impressive design, which numbered an overhead camshaft (driven by silent helical gears), an integral cooling fan, generous coolant passages, a vast sump and a properly robust four-bearing crankshaft (better than seven) among its virtues. The engine was very good-looking for its time, and was carried with its gearbox in triple bearers between the channel-section longerons of the chassis.

It was a big engine, but it was a very big chassis: the wheelbase, nearly 12 ft 4 in (376 cm) long, was appropriate to the six- and seven-seat bodies intended to be carried. Yet the temptation was there to run the car in competitions, and in 1926 a short-chassis version known as the K model (*kurz* – short) appeared, with a wheelbase of 11 ft 2 in (340 cm). It was still known as the 24/100/140, but in fact the true power figures were more like 110 and 160 bhp, for the engine had been enlarged to 6240 cc, with bore and stroke of 94 mm and 150 mm and a modest rev limit of 2800 rpm. In Britain, where the taxation system was different and where exaggeration of power figures was common, it was known as the 33/180, following the 33/140 of the long-chassis car; in Europe it figured in a number of races, though without any really noteworthy successes. In 1926 this was the world's fastest production tourer, but although it could go hammering on for hours at high speeds on the ill-maintained roads of the day it was far from being the best-handling or braked.

These deficiencies were very quickly cured. The chassis was lowered drastically: it would have been a shame to lose the superbly designed Daimler front axle, a lovely curved forging that put everything from brake-shafts to kingpins and spring-pads in what looked like just the right places; but behind it the side-rails were sloped down, with a sharper rise again over the rear axle which was now carried on underslung springs. The wheelbase was the same as in the K model before, but the engine had been enlarged internally, bores larger by 4 mm bringing the displacement to the memorable figure of 6789 cc. With stronger supercharging than before, and now with two carburettors instead of one, this engine really did produce 180 bhp; the British agents called it the 36/220, but in Germany the car was known as the 26/120/180, or

simply as the S model.

It was also known as a car blessed with far better behaviour than might have been anticipated from its sheer mass. Its straight-line performance was beyond dispute: in top gear it could do anything from walking speed up to as much as 110 mph (177 kph), the figure it set as a German sports-car record soon after its introduction. What really amazed people was its evidently superb roadholding, and those who actually drove it were equally enraptured by its steering. Obviously the geometry of the latter was inherently very good and was not corrupted by the motions of the suspension; less obviously the lowering of the chassis and the rear springs had produced just the

right suspension geometry, probably by lowering the rear roll centre (by adopting underslung springs) to compensate for the rear springbase being much wider than at the front. Balance was surely the secret of it all: that huge cylinder block being largely hollow and almost entirely of silumin, Germany's favourite silicon-aluminium alloy. The car was not by any means as heavy as it looked, and was low in relation to its length – or, more precisely, its centre of gravity was low in relation to its wheelbase, reducing pitching moments as well as roll.

Nothing less would have been good enough; the car looked so beautiful that it had to behave beautifully. Promptly pitched into the sporting arena it gave an exemplary

account of itself in the numerous hillclimbs (long Alpine pass-storming affairs, quite different from the briefly explosive sprints popular in Britain) which made up a large slice of the German sporting calendar. Outstanding drivers in these were two: one was Adolf Rosenberger, a wealthy Jewish amateur who had been closely involved with the rear-engined Benz GP cars of 1922 and was at that time probably the fastest driver in Germany; the other was a newcomer, young Rudolf Caracciola.

The two met in the German Grand Prix, held on the very fast Avus track at Berlin in 1926. The official Mercedes-Benz team chose to enter a race at San Sebastian instead, but Rosenberger entered the Avus race privately and Caracciola persuaded the factory to let him run as a semi-official or works-supported privateer. It was the young

LEFT AND TOP A supercharged SSK from 1928. SSK stood for Super Sports Kurz, or in other words it was the short-wheelbase Super Sports. With the supercharger the power output was raised to 225 bhp **ABOVE** *This 1929 SSK engine is rated at 250 bhp merely because the British importers tended to exaggerate....*

man's first Grand Prix (he had been a reserve driver for the team in earlier and less straitened seasons) and he won it – but only after Rosenberger, in the lead on the seventh lap of the rain-slicked track, had lost control at the tricky 105 mph (169 kph) Nordkurve and crashed. Years later, the famous Rennleiter or team chief Alfred Neubauer let the cat out of the bag, saying that the accident had been caused because Rosenberger had been affected by fumes from a leaking ether tank under the bonnet.

So what was he doing with ether? The same as Pierre Levegh was doing with a tank full of a blend containing equal parts of petrol, benzol and alcohol when he crashed his Mercedes-Benz at Le Mans in 1955: he was trying to enlist chemistry as an ally with physics to achieve the best possible performance. Daimler-Benz never missed a trick in the rule-book (they were disqualified from a couple of races in 1928 and '29 for tricks that were not in it) and in those days when racing formulae were pretty free they experimented just as much as some other firms with the fruits of science.

Was this why the works-entered cars

were always so convincingly fast, and why so many private owners were disgruntled by the slowness of their production cars? Not entirely: the customers' cars were always turned out well trimmed and with bodies built heavily enough to be reasonably enduring, whereas the works cars went out stripped nearly naked and no heavier than they needed to be to last the length of the race. Every competent factory in those days did the same, except perhaps Frazer Nash who did not believe in giving the customer more than they had to. The fact remains that there was many an S model, doubtless overbodied and festooned with all the fashionable trappings that induced so much extra drag, that could not do much more than 90 mph (145 kph) – and many more customers who could not drive.

In any case, there was more performance forthcoming in 1928, when the cylinder bores were enlarged to 100 mm to make the displacement 7069 cc. The triple rating told most of the story: the new car, known as the SS, was listed as 27/140/200. At the same time there was a new short sporter, the SSK (Super Sport Kurz), within the 9 ft 8 in (295 cm) wheelbase of which was a more highly tuned engine rated as 27/170/225. As far as the British agents were concerned the 36/220 had grown into the 38/250!

As far as the sporting drivers of Germany were concerned the big blown six had grown almost entirely convincing. Almost? The bonnet was taller, perhaps because the radiator needed to be bigger; the brakes were alleged to be less good than on the S, and, when driven as hard as only maybe five men drove it, it could be heavy on tyres. Fastest man of all was now unquestionably Caracciola, probably the only racing driver in history to rank with Jim Clark for smoothness and equilibrium; he could make a set of tyres outlast anyone else while still going faster, but even he had his problems. Most memorable of these occasions was also one of the most memorable feats ever accomplished by the big Mercs or by Caracciola, when he drove an SSK into third place in the first Monaco Grand Prix. Starting from the back of a grid full of such fancied little jewels as the 2.3-litre Bugatti, the huge SSK was ridiculed; the jeers faded as it fought its way around the houses and harbour of the 'race of a thousand corners' until it was in the lead. Only the need to stop for fresh tyres caused that lead to be lost to a couple of Bugattis. For so big and supposedly heavy a car it was a preposterous performance, suggesting that not only were the steering and roadholding as good as legend would have us believe but also that the brakes were a lot better than some would have us suppose.

The following year saw the car competi-

LEFT Another view of the Lord Cholmondley car which was free of many of the weighty trappings hung on most other examples. Accordingly it was a very fast car indeed

EVOLUTION

1922 Ferdinand Porsche moved to Mercedes and designed the 24/100/140 hp 6-litre Mercedes which featured a Roots-type supercharger.

1926 Mercedes K introduced – the K stood for kurz or short as it was built on a short (134 in/ 340 cm) chassis. It was fitted with a larger, 6240 cc, engine which produced 110 bhp, or 160 bhp with the supercharger engaged. It was the world's fastest production tourer

1927 Mercedes S introduced with engine enlarged to 6789 cc and twin carburettors fitted. Power output increased to 180 bhp, supercharged

1928 Engine displacement increased to 7069 cc to form the SS with a maximum power output of 200 bhp supercharged. SSK introduced on the 116-inch (295 cm) wheelbase with tuned version of the 7-litre engine producing a maximum power output of 225 bhp

1930 SSKL introduced. It was the same size as the SSK but had a much lighter chassis and a larger supercharger to boost power output to 300 bhp

tive there again, but not for long: clutch slip forced retirement. People said that clutch slip was one of the weaknesses of the model, but a lot of people (especially Englishmen and Frenchmen, and worst of all English Francophiles) used to be very sniffy indeed about the big Mercs, casting upon them every imaginable aspersion. Sometimes it was jealousy, more often it was political prejudice and occasionally it was simply an aesthetic distaste for the allegedly aggressive styling of the cars. When, in that same 1930, the lone long SS Mercedes-Benz retired at Le Mans after leading two full teams of Bentleys a very merry dance indeed, the cause was dynamo failure leading to a discharged battery. The way the headlamps faded while the car was in the pits at 2.30 am demonstrated the truth of the official statement, but the British tried to insinuate a gasket failure,

saying that if a Merc was forced to use the blower much its head gasket also blew.

It was a gross exaggeration of the truth. The blower was not to be used except in conjuction with 50/50 petrol/benzol fuel, a reasonable precaution in those days when knock-resistance was a fuel quality little understood. It was not to be used in bottom gear, which was rather low and therefore involved a considerable torque multiplication, which would have been too much for the 'box if the torque were further amplified by the blower. Finally it was not recommended that the blower be kept engaged for more than 20 seconds at a time – but this instruction was for private owners chasing the horizon down the ruler-straight *Routes Nationales* of France, not for racing adepts chasing filigrees up the flanks of an Alp or chasing Bugattis down the echoes of the

FAR LEFT *The 7.1-litre 1929 38 250 SS TT which was driven by Sir Malcolm Campbell in the Ulster Tourist Trophy and at Brooklands where the car held the 7-litre Mountain Circuit record*
LEFT *The rather strange fuel filler cap; the car's thirst was prodigious*
BELOW *The instrumentation included a water temperature gauge, clock, tachometer, speedo and ammeter*
BOTTOM *The view that most other drivers had of the SS. Note the large-bore exhaust*

Nürburgring. In practice, the drill on ordinary roads was imposed by the sheer impossibility of going that fast for long: the top three ratios of the four-speed gearbox were all high (peak rpm were 3200) and after reaching a chosen cruising speed quickly with the blower one relaxed the foot and cruised unsupercharged.

The lie was given to all the snide critics at the end of 1930 when the SSKL was readied for the following season. Dimensionally the same as the SSK, but extensively lightened (most obviously by many holes in the chassis rails), it had an even larger blower known as the Elephant delivering a boost pressure of 0.85 atmospheres to raise the brake horse-power to 300. Caracciola took it out the first time for the last 1930 event, the Schwabenberg hillclimb, winning it and the European Mountain Championship. In 1931 he won everywhere he drove the SSKL: seven hill events (with an outright or sports car record at each one), two closed-circuit road races (the Eifelrennen and the German GP) at the Nürburgring, a track race (the Avusrennen at Berlin) and, most splendid of all, the Mille Miglia road race.

The following year he was beaten at the Avus. He was driving for Alfa Romeo now, and the car that beat him was an SSKL clad in a special streamlined body, the work of Freiherr König von Fachsenfeld, an aerody-

namics formalist of academic authority. The car was timed at 156 mph (251 kph), but the days of the big blown six were fading fast. It could be tossed about in a manner that belied its size but its little rivals kept passing it when it stopped for fresh tyres. Worse, it was out of keeping with the new breed of independently-sprung touring cars put into production from 1931 onwards. Racing an outmoded car did nothing to help sales of the new ones.

In any case, Daimler-Benz had withdrawn from racing. They said they could not afford it because times were hard. Actually they were preparing revolutionary new cars, supercharged, independently-sprung metallurgical marvels with Fachsenfeld-style bodies, for the new GP formula to come into effect in 1934. Soon they would be making times hard for everybody else.

France

For many enthusiasts, it is the combination of sheer splendour, plus its incredible market value today, that places the Bugatti Royale first in the catalogue of great French Cars. Yet some may argue that other cars, including the alternative Bugattis, are worthy of the same, or more, adulation.

Both Delage and Delahaye have produced cars that have seldom been equalled as *Grand Routiers* – powerful imposing machines capable of devouring the kilometres from Paris to the Riviera in great style and comfort.

With regard to the immediate post-war era, the French car

industry was somewhat stunted by a punitive tax system and
the Talbot Lago has been singled out as one of the few high
points of the Fifties.

The Citroën SM of the Seventies, with its distinctive profile,
typified the technical idiosyncrasy that has so marked a Citroën
from the early days of the innovative Traction Avant through
the D-series cars right up to the modern day range. The SM
proved that front-wheel drive cars could be large, fast and
powerful – and, bristling with technical innovation, it, perhaps,
deserved greater success.

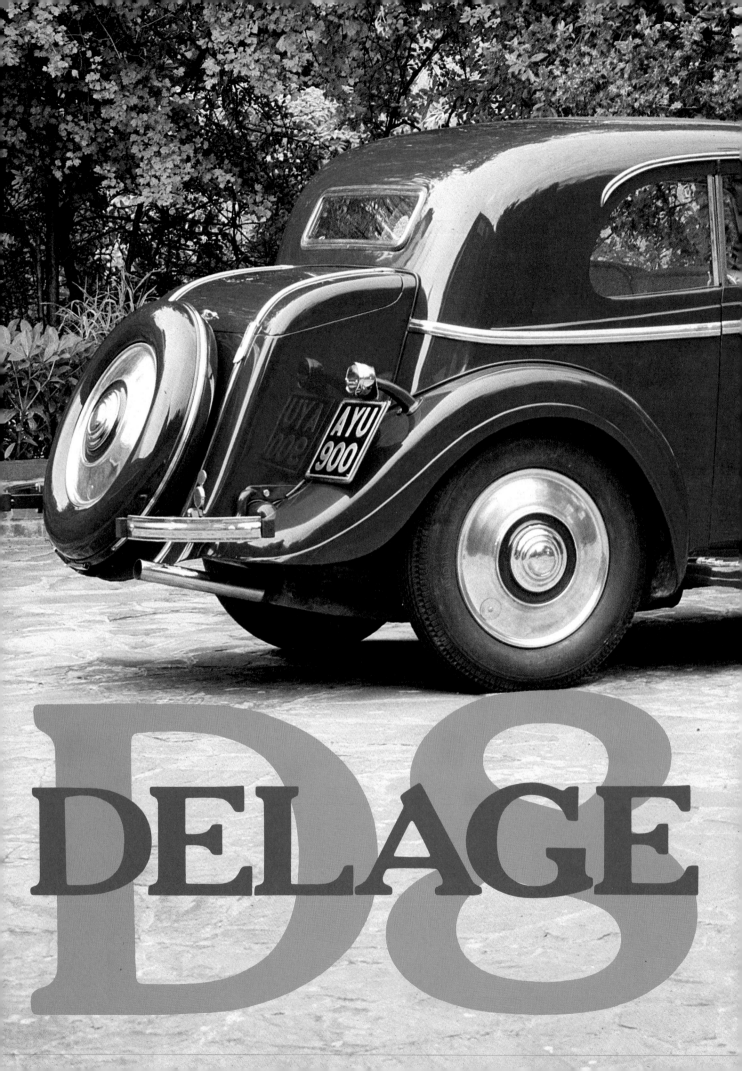

DELAGE
D8

An immaculate Delage D8 15S of 1934
ABOVE *Its splendid Lalique mascot*

Louis Delage was a man of style whose cars, both beautiful and sporting, became the essence of '30s chic, and none more so than the long, low and fast straight-eight D8s

FOR SHEER SMARTNESS at a time when motoring was a fashionable activity the D8 Delage was rivalled only by the Hispano-Suiza and, perhaps, the 5-litre Bugatti. It was a natural winner of concours d'elegance at Nice, Deauville, La Baule and in the Bois de Boulogne, and the perfect accessory for the well-dressed Parisienne. Its low chassis and the immense length·of its bonnet inspired all the best French coachbuilders and a few English ones too, such as Carlton, to feed extravagance into their designs: it was a borzoi amongst cars – very grand, very fast and, as its owners would have said, terribly chic. It also had a certain raffishness which made it a favourite with the demi-monde: as

was often said, one owns a Rolls, one drives a Hispano and one presents a Delage to one's mistress. Perhaps the nearest thing in today's currency is a Jaguar or a BMW – the dream of every pools winner, a glamorous car with a racing pedigree, splendid lines and a fine reputation, but not so magnificent as to frighten away the buyer who has just come up in the world. In fact it was a perfect reflection of its creator, a self-made man from the provinces who became one of France's leading industrialists, with a life-style to match.

Louis Delage was born in 1874, the only son of an assistant station-master at Cognac, and perhaps it was this railway background

which inspired him to become an engineer. When he was only 16 he enrolled at the Ecole Nationale d'Arts et Métiers at Angers, and three years later graduated with a diploma in engineering. After completing his military service in Algeria he stayed on there for a while with a firm of civil engineers before returning and heading for Paris, where he saw great possibilities in the new-fangled automobile industry. After running his own machine-shop and sub-contracting business for a while, he joined Peugeot in 1900, working in the drawing office and experimental department until the beginning of 1905. Then he departed, taking with him a fellow Angers graduate, Augustin Legros, to start his own car manufacturing business, with a one-model policy based on high quality and sound engineering. His cars used the single-cylinder De Dion Bouton engine but were built to large-car standards. These 'big cars in miniature' soon became popular, and tuned versions also did well in

competitions.

The Delage company's first big success came in the 1908 Voiturette (light-car) Grand Prix at Dieppe, which resulted in a first place and the team prize. The winning car's engine had been designed for Delage by one Nemorin Causan, but for rather dubious commercial reasons the credit was subsequently given to De Dion. Causan quit shortly afterwards and Delage decided to move a step or two nearer to making voitures de luxe, lengthening the chassis and installing four-cylinder engines of De Dion or Ballot design. Four cylinders were unusual in small cars at this time, and Delage might well have adopted the slogan flaunted by AC in the 1920s: 'The Rolls-Royce of Light Cars.' Delage adopted the Ballot engine as his own, and the company went from strength to strength. Backed by such a flourishing enterprise, and beginning to enjoy a very grand way of life, Louis Delage decided that the company should embark upon a big competition programme. He employed a new chief engineer in 1910, Arthur Michelat, another Angers graduate, and Michelat soon produced an almost futuristic design for the 1911 Coupe des Voiturettes, organised by the magazine *L'Auto*.

Followers of Vintage Sports-Car Club racing will know the machine well, thanks to 'Denise', an example restored by the late Lord Charnwood and now raced by Sir John Briscoe. Michelat turned his back on the single- and twin-cylindered freaks produced for the Coupe de L'Auto in the past. His cars had four-cylinder, 3-litre engines with hori-

ABOVE *The pleasure of open air motoring in a 1932 Chapron-bodied D8 cabriolet, in this instance being road tested by* Classic Cars *magazine for an 'All Time Great' feature*

zontal overhead valves, two plugs per cylinder and a five-speed gearbox with a high-ratio top gear to take advantage of the long down-hill straights on the Boulogne circuit. His cars finished first, third and fourth. Customers rushed in, proud to be associated with such an exciting design, if only at several removes. Delage built a fine new factory at Courbevoie in the suburbs of Paris and launched his first six-cylinder models, the height of refinement in 1912. Having seen what their success at Boulogne had brought them, Delage and Michelat set their sights on Grand Prix racing.

For the 1913 GP of the Automobile Club de France, Michelat produced a rather similar engine, again with horizontal overhead valves and the exhaust led out through the top of the bonnet, but of 6.2 litres, and with positively-closed (desmodromic) valves. These cars were unlucky in the ACF Grand Prix at Amiens, but in the Grand Prix de France at Le Mans they took first, second and fifth places. Delage was now in a position to purchase a fine country estate. He also sold two of the successful Model Y racers and entered them, all expenses paid, for the 1914 Indianapolis 500 Miles. Here they did more than ring the bell: René Thomas came first and his team mate Guyot came third,

beating all the Americans and, what is more, landing one in the eye of Delage's great French rival, Peugeot.

At the end of World War I, Louis Delage was ready with a new range of cars, the most significant being a stately 4½-litre six (with a 90 mm × 150 mm) bore and stroke) aimed at much the same market as the straight-eights that were to come. Called the Model CO, it was conservative in having a side-valve engine but progressive in offering Perrot front-wheel brakes. The 12 ft (366 cm) chassis would accommodate the most splendid coach work. It was catalogued from 1918 until 1923, and was just the motorcar for Monsieur Delage himself, who now added a town house in the Avenue du Bois de Boulogne, a yacht and a seaside villa in Brittany to his other outward displays of wealth. He was a man who knew how to enjoy himself and he worked very hard to attain the means of affording his comforts. His cars were undoubtedly for similarly minded people.

At 45, however, he was still a *grand sportif,* and unaccompanied, drove the 550 miles (885 km) from Paris to Nice on the war-torn roads of the day in 16 hours, officially observed for the RAC by the English journalist W.F. Bradley. After a lively series of such promotions (including a 3000-mile/4828 km tour of France in five days, he alone driving) Delage turned to other aspects of the sport. The CO was developed into a Grand Sport, later named the CO2, and special cars were developed for hill-climbs and record-breaking; two 5-litre cars also made an appearance, as did the great

ABOVE *This splendid Delage roadster is actually a four-seater, for there is a dickey seat at the rear for two which provides adequate, if a little breezy, accommodation. The interior,* **RIGHT**, *is dominated by the huge four-spoke steering wheel, but it is attractively laid out with colour-co-ordinated red-covered dash and red leather seats*

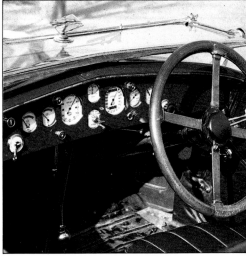

10½-litre V12 which gave Réné Thomas the Land Speed Record in 1923 at more than 140 mph (225 kph) on a stretch of French main road. This car went on to become very well known in England, making famous the names of John Cobb and Oliver Bertram at Brooklands, and it is still active in VSCC events. The big CO2, with tuned engine and underslung chassis, driven by Réné Thomas and Robert Benoist, buiit up a great reputation in sports car racing.

In the mid 1920s, customers had much to keep them amused: Monsieur Delage assailed Grand Prix racing with some of the most ambitious designs of all time. For 1923 he fielded a jewel-like 2-litre V12 engine with a bore and stroke of 51..3 mm by 80 mm, (the tiny Austin Seven's cylinder dimensions were 56 mm × 76 mm). Neither the engine nor the chassis was really ready in 1923 but, reworked by Albert Lory from Louis Planchon's original design, these exciting quadruple-overhead-cam racers finished second, third and sixth in the 1924 French Grand Prix – losing to Campari's straight-eight P2 Alfa Romeo – and proved victorious in 1925 driven by Robert Benoist. Louis Delage received the Légion d'Honneur, and to cap a splendid season the 2-litre cars finished first, second and third in the Span-

ish Grand Prix at San Sebastian.

Two strands can now be described which were to lead to the big D8 series with which we are concerned: luxury and elaboration. During the 2-litre car's domination of Formula One, Louis Delage introduced the Grand Luxe 40-50HP, a model which he hoped would rival the Hispano-Suiza and appeal to the upper crust. His car was a great overhead-camshaft 6-litre (95 mm by 140 mm), longer in the wheelbase than the Hispano, the 45 Renault and the Rolls-Royce. To this was added an utterly charming little 2-litre, the DI, with its sporting derivatives the DIS (DI Sport) and the DISS (Sport Surbaisse) whose refinement, excellent steering and delightful gearbox proved very popular, especially in England. It was followed by a six-cylinder version, with the same bore and stroke – 75 by 120 mm – the DM.

When the two-litre Formula changed to 1½-litres in 1926, Albert Lory, the man responsible for the successful 2-litre cars of 1924–5, designed a straight-eight with its twin overhead-camshafts driven by a veritable cascade of gearing, ball-bearings throughout and twin superchargers. After burning the drivers' feet in 1926 these cars swept the board in 1927, winning Delage the championship of Europe and making such

rivals as Bugatti look very small-time indeed. Monsieur Delage's competition programme, and especially participation in the Grand Prixs, had been very costly, but it helped him to sell his other lines: the DI, DIS and DISS, the silent and stately GL carriages and the 3-litre DM series, basically a six-cylinder version of the DI, designed by Maurice Gaultier, with pushrod overhead valves and seven main bearings, a car of great refinement, which almost out-performed the big 6-litre GL. There was also the DR, a 2½-litre light-six using the DM's lower half but with a Ricardo side-valve cylinder-head and dummy rocker-box. It was a roomy but dull model which sold disarmingly well.

With the success of the 1500 cc racers ringing in his ears it was only natural for

Louis Delage to go for a production straight-eight engine; in this way he could cash in on his own publicity and at the same time follow the example of such exciting makes as Alfa Romeo, Bugatti, Voisin, Isotta-Fraschini, Minerva, Lincoln, Packard and Duesenberg. Straight-eights were very much in vogue in those days, and if the layout entailed a rather long bonnet, that was all the better. Long bonnets spoke power and prestige, and coach-builders loved them.

A long bonnet allowed the stylist's art to be employed to the full with dramatic sweeping wings and an abundance of complex curves fashioned on wheeling machines by the intuitive craftsmen of the day. If such long wheelbases and extensive bonnets sometimes made the cars awkward to manoeuvre, that was a small price to pay for such style.

Accordingly Maurice Gaultier drew out a 23CV (30 hp in Britain) Delage which quickly became known as the D8. Using the same 109 mm stroke as the side-valve DR and a bore of 77 mm, it had a capacity of 4050 cc and there were five plain main bearings. The crankshaft was machined from a solid billet, and by making the detachable block and cylinder head of cast iron, Delage almost assured it of immortality. Two valves per cylinder were operated by a special arrangement of pushrods and valve-springs designed to eliminate noise, so that a well-tuned D8 emitted no sound at tickover other than a gentle hiss from the single Smith-Barriquand five-jet carburettor. Ignition was by Delco-Remy coil, and a single-dry-plate clutch took the drive to a four-speed and reverse gearbox and open propeller-shaft. The cable-operated brakes were assisted by a Dewandre vacuum servo, while steering was by worm and nut. The chassis was of pressed steel, with cruciform bracing amidships, and suspension was by very flat semi-elliptic springs, shackled at their forward ends and assisted by Hartford friction shock-absorbers all round, although more sophisticated dampers were fitted later. Three lengths of wheelbase could be had, ranging from 10 ft 10 in (330 cm) to 11 ft 10 in (361 cm). A very short 10 ft 2 in (310 cm) was also spoken of. The D8 was a large motorcar indeed, despite its rather small engine, which in standard form gave 102 bhp at 3500 rpm and drove an axle with a ratio of 4.6:1.

To prove that his D8 was not just a pretty face Monsieur Delage sent if off driven by Robert Sénéchal, sometime light-car racer and builder, on a trip through the capitals of Europe – Paris, Madrid, Monte Carlo, Rome, Vienna, Berlin and Paris – all within seven days. In 1931 Delage followed this with a record-breaking session at Montlhéry by a light two-seater D8S (S for Sport)). Driven by the British record specialists George Eyston, Kaye Don, Ernest Eldridge and Albert Denly, it broke several world records including 24 hours at 109.6 mph (176 kph). On a later attempt 112 mph (180 kph) was averaged for 12 hours, a very remarkable performance for a touring model in the immediate post-Vintage years when very few

specialised sports cars exceeded the 'ton'.

Early production D8s seem to have been less happy at high speed. Little was understood in those days about the importance of a rigid chassis, and that big, mainly cast-iron engine seems rather to have triumphed over the flexible front springs: the unsprung weight of the front axle bearing big brake-drums and 7.00/18 tyres was at first apt to take charge, but Gaultier made various modifications, including the addition of radius rods to take braking torque, and later cars steered beautifully. A D8S won its class in the 1931 Circuit des Routes Pavées, that most punishing of all races, held on dreadful cobbled roads in Northern France, and nothing could be more revealing than that. However, it was not high speed on the cobbles that sold the D8 series, but that endless bonnet. Leading Paris coachbuilders fell upon it with glad cries: Chapron, Letourneur et Marchand, Pourtout, Fernandez & Darrin and, perhaps the best-known on the English market, Figoni et Falaschi. D8 Delages have been compared to the long-legged fashion models of their day – great for showing off toilette, classic or outrageous, but with no more character than a coat-hanger. A harsh judgment perhaps, but there was indeed a blandnesss about these Delages that one does not find in the contemporary Bugatti, Lancia or Hispano-Suiza. Nevertheless, smart society women, actresses and film stars found a D8 the perfect fashion accessory. Close-coupled saloon, coupé and coupé de ville Delages won the Grand Prix d'Honneur at concours d'elegance – and elegance was the word – in the Bois de Boulogne, at Biarritz, Cabourg, Deauville, La Baule, Monte Carlo, Nice, and overseas – a clean sweep. This was poaching in Hispano territory, like Jaguar rivalling Rolls-Royce, for Delages were remarkably inexpensive. They might compete with Hispanos in the concours, but the price of the D8 was nowhere near the luxury car bracket: its showroom rivals in France were the far more prosaic Hotchkiss, Voisin and Talbot. A Delage saloon with factory coachwork cost 88,000 francs, the same price as the rather dull Renault Nervastella straight-eight. In London in 1931, thanks to a favourable exchange rate, a D8 in chassis form could be bought new for only £685, when the price of a 20/25 Rolls-Royce chassis was £1185. A saloon D8 cost £945, and a close-coupled coupé by Figoni et Falaschi £1180 whether on the normal (11 ft 3 in/343 cm) or short (10 ft 10 in/361 cm) chassis. The long (11 ft 10 in/361 cm) chassis cost very slightly more.

But these price comparisons should still be viewed in context, for although the Delage D8 seemed cheap when set alongside other grand cars such as the Rolls-Royces and Hispanos of the Thirties, compared with the more mundane cars of their day they were still fearfully expensive and far beyond the reach of the average motorist.

When the D8 first appeared it had a rather broad, Hispano-like radiator recalling that of the splendid late-Vintage overhead-cam 5-litre GL Delage six, but this was

gradually narrowed over the years, and often fitted with a stoneguard. Performance rapidly improved, turning what had been an elegant clothes-horse into a formidable sporting machine, raising an original maximum speed of 80 mph (129 kph) to a guaranteed 100 mph (161 kph), a rare performance for the period. This may have been helped by the fact that the radiator was narrower, and the chassis underslung at the rear, decreasing the frontal area. From an original output of 102 bhp at 3500 rpm power rose to 118 bhp at 3800 rpm (with a compression ratio of 6.8:1) on the D8S. Eventually on the D8 SS, equipped with a new camshaft, better oil-cooling, and a 7.5:1 compression ratio the permissible revs rose

ABOVE *This very appealing Delage D8 coupé was bodied in 1937 by the Paris coachbuilders Letourner et Marchand*
RIGHT *This Delage roadster epitomises the height of style and glamorous motoring enjoyed by a few during the 1930s*

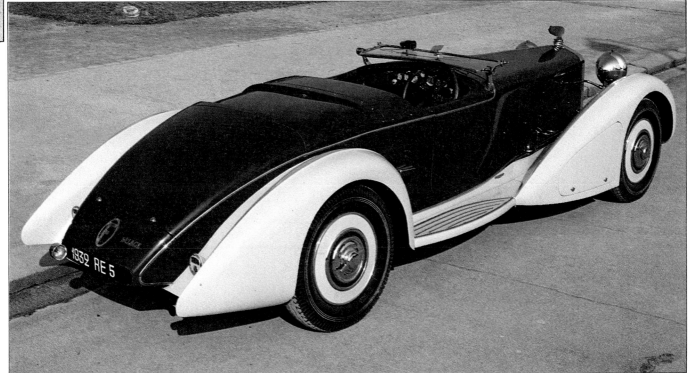

EVOLUTION

The D8 Delage was introduced in 1929 with a 4050 cc overhead-valve straight-eight engine and was available in three different chassis lengths. Power output was 102 bhp at 3500 rpm

1931 The sports version of the D8, the D8S was introduced with an increased power output of 118 bhp at 3800 rpm

1932 The Grand Sport version of the Delage D8 introduced, originally with a 10 ft 3 in (312 cm) wheelbase

1934 The Grand Sport's wheelbase was increased to 10 ft 10 in (330 cm). A completely new and smaller D8, the D8 15, was introduced with a 2668 cc engine and transverse leaf and wishbones independent front suspension

1935 The D8 85 introduced with a 3591 cc straight eight with conventional valve springs. Synchromesh gearboxes and hydraulic brakes were introduced on the six-cylinder models and the D8 range

1936 The D8 100 was introduced with a larger 4300 cc engine

1937 The Super Sports D8 100 was announced with a short 10 ft 10 in (330 cm) wheelbase and a maximum power output of 145 bhp at 4500 rpm

1938 Wheelbase of the Super Sports increased to 11 ft 11 in (363 cm)

1939 The last of the D8s, the D8 120 was introduced with a 4743 ccc straight eight and Cotal electro-magnetic gearbox

ABOVE *The extremely informative dashboard of the 1934 Delage D8 15S,* RIGHT, *which was fitted with its close-coupled sports-saloon bodywork in 1933 and exported to the UK.*

LEFT *The 1934 Delage was fitted with four SU carburettors and a Scintilla-Vertex distributor, with which equipment it produced 118 bhp at modest revs*

to 4500, and the output to 145 bhp. To obtain Customs benefits many cars were imported for completion in the UK; some of these, including a Fernandez et Darrin coupé owned by the late John Bolster, had special manifolding and four SU carburettors. This version was called the D8 SS 100, and had a final-drive ratio of 3.6:1.

From brief trials of Bolster's car the present writer remembers the pleasant, accurate steering and the exceptionally nice gear-change. Bolster himself wrote in *French Vintage Cars* that the gearbox and brakes of the D8 were inherited from the 3-litre, six-cylinder DM, and that 'both were somewhat overtaxed', but they seemed to work all right on his car.

Louis Delage was slightly more fortunate than W.O. Bentley, for the D8, unlike' the 8-litre Bentley, had time to make friends before the slump following the Wall Street crash put an end to this sort of motoring. According to Jacques Rousseau's excellent *Les Automobiles Delage*, the company sold 2001 examples of the D8 and D8S between September 1929, when they were introduced, and May 1933, when production ceased: 819 of the normal chassis, 458 short, 625 long-wheelbase and 99 of the D8S.

The big straight-eight Delage called forth some of the smartest coachwork during a very smart period, a trifle flashy perhaps, but not so vulgar as much French coachwork during the later 1930s when Louis Delage himself had left the scene. The racing budget, an extravagant life-style and the world slump put paid to his manufacturing activities, and he was forced to sell out to Delahaye. Straight-eights with the blue enamel Delage badge could still be purchased during the mid-'30s, but these were Delahayes really and the quality was not the same. One feels though that in Gaultier's D8, D8S, D8SS and D8SS 100, Monsieur Louis Delage had created a car in his own image – *'sportive, très snob, presque cad',* the very car he would have chosed had he followed his father as *sous-chef de gare* at Cognac and come into money. This is no flight of fancy, for when the French National Lottery was instituted in 1932 the first winner of the big prize, a typical *petit bourgeois* (a barber from Tarascon in the South of France), bought himself a chateau and…a D8 Delage. This story has its counterpart in England. One day while in his Fernandez et Darrin coupé, resplendent in two shades of blue, John Bolster met a salesman who had been on the Delage stand at Olympia in 1932. Said John: 'A man in loud tweeds like a bookie came on and, taking one look at the car, said "I'll have that one." Then, rubbing his hands together he cried: "Eeh, but this will knock them f*****s eyes out at Blackpool!"'

BUGATTI

They epitomised the excesses and extravagances of the time, and few cars ever attracted as much attention as the legendary Bugatti Royales

THEY CALLED IT A WHIM, but for a whim it was pretty substantial: 14 litres of engine (twice as big as a Rolls), 180 inches (457 cm) of wheelbase (30 inches/76 cm longer than a long-chassis Phantom) and a bonnet of such length that a Mini could be parked on it. Ettore Bugatti called it Royale because it was to sell mainly to crowned heads, and it carried a lifetime guarantee.

Bugatti had dreamed of making such a car even before the Great War, and his wartime designs for aero engines seem to have further stimulated that dream. During

the early 1920s, while the Brescia and Type 35 were winning races, *le Patron* designed, built and tested the Royale on all the spikiest roads in the Alps, the Pyrennees and the Massif Central, 'in all weathers, at all altitudes with never a moment's trouble.' He continued: 'The minor roads in the Alps, particularly, were calculated to demonstrate the car's qualities – its flexibility and handiness, its ability to...turn like a bicycle'.

The prototype was shown to the Press in 1926. It was an enormous open touring car painted dark green and lined-out in red, the

body of which is said to have come from a Packard in Bugatti's possession; but there was a breaker's yard on the Ile de la Jatte in Paris specialising in used bodywork and it may well have come from there.

Bugatti expected applause and certainly earned it. The greatest compliment, he reckoned, had come from a point-duty policeman in Milan who, staring incredulously at the majestic carriage as it approached, sprang to attention and saluted. Bugatti, delighted, acknowledged this homage by raising his light-brown bowler as he glided

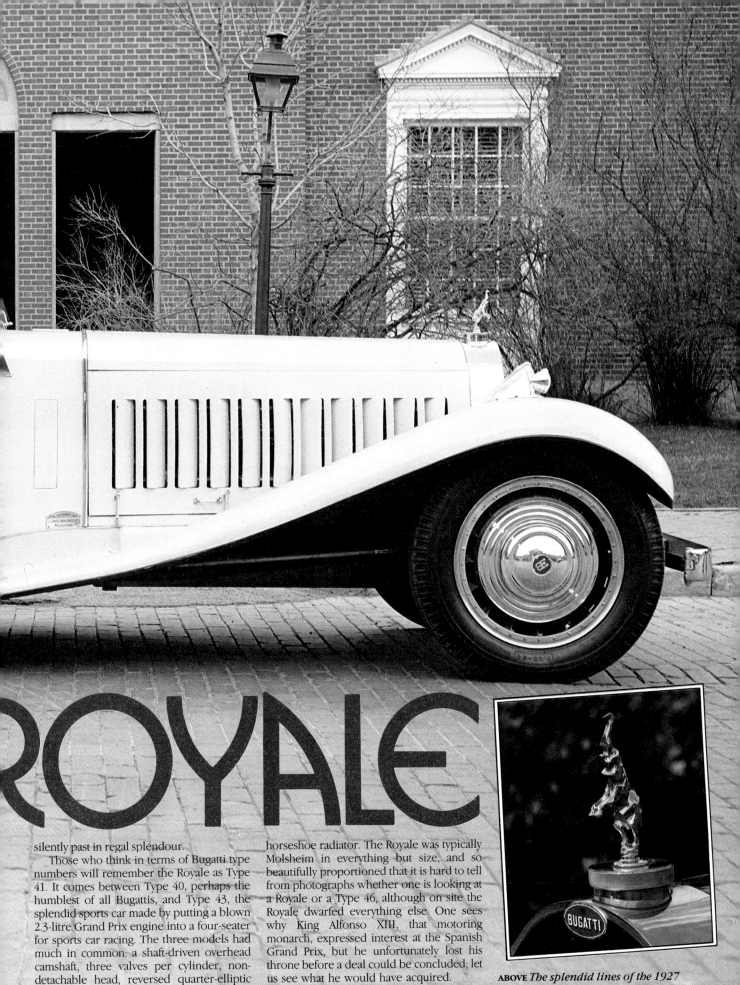

ROYALE

silently past in regal splendour.

Those who think in terms of Bugatti type numbers will remember the Royale as Type 41. It comes between Type 40, perhaps the humblest of all Bugattis, and Type 43, the splendid sports car made by putting a blown 2.3-litre Grand Prix engine into a four-seater for sports car racing. The three models had much in common: a shaft-driven overhead camshaft, three valves per cylinder, non-detachable head, reversed quarter-elliptic rear springing, front springs passing through the axle forging and, of course, the familiar horseshoe radiator. The Royale was typically Molsheim in everything but size, and so beautifully proportioned that it is hard to tell from photographs whether one is looking at a Royale or a Type 46, although on site the Royale dwarfed everything else. One sees why King Alfonso XIII, that motoring monarch, expressed interest at the Spanish Grand Prix, but he unfortunately lost his throne before a deal could be concluded; let us see what he would have acquired.

The prototype chassis beneath that open tourer was slightly larger both in engine and

ABOVE *The splendid lines of the 1927 Royale cabriolet. The elephant mascot was sculpted by Rembrandt Bugatti*

wheelbase than the six 'production' chassis which followed – 20 mm longer in stroke and 10 inches (25.4 cm) longer in its wheelbase. Later cars had a wheelbase of 14 ft 2 in (432 cm) and an engine bore and stroke of 125 mm by 130 mm, giving a capacity of a mere 12,763 cc. The straight-eight engine weighed 770 lb (349 kg), of which 238 lb came from the cast-iron block and integral head, which was 55 inches (140 cm) long. The two-piece crankshaft, which weighed 220 lb (100 kg), had circular webs and ran in nine white-metal bearings, and was so massive that after the prototype none of the cars had need of a flywheel. The main bearings were carried in the huge cylinder-block casting, and the water jackets were extended downwards to provide water cooling for the mains. Unusually for a Bugatti engine of the period, there was room for water between the bores. There were three valves per cylinder as usual, two inlets and one exhaust, in a flat head; they were pretty massive and the whole engine was lightly stressed, which was just as well because to change a valve meant removing that crankshaft.

The camshaft, like the crank, was made in two pieces, and the shaft drive for it was unorthodox. Mr Charles A. Chayne, a senior engineer at General Motors who rebuilt a Royale engine in 1946, has described it thus: 'At the top of the vertical shaft are two bevel pinions having opposite spiral angles. These mesh with two bevel gears, one of which is fixed to the camshaft. The second gear is concentric with the first, but drives through a friction clutch. As the second pair of gears is one tooth off from an even two-to-one ratio, the friction clutch merely loads these gears so that the thrust on the vertical shaft is balanced by the opposing spiral angles. Just one more example of M. Bugatti's rugged individualism.' The engine had full-pressure lubrication except for the gudgeon pins, which relied on splash. It was a dry-sump system, with two scavenge pumps and a pressure pump circulating oil from a tank on the dashboard holding five gallons (23 litres). There was a single duplex carburettor and ignition was by both magneto and coil, with two plugs per cylinder. From the engine a short shaft and heavy fabric

BELOW AND ABOVE RIGHT *When Captain C. Foster bought his Royale chassis in June 1933, he had it fitted with a saloon body by Park Ward, a replica of the one they had previously made for his Rolls-Royce*

universals took the drive to a normal Bugatti multiple-wet-plate clutch under the driving seat, and from there another shaft connected with a cavernous three-speed gearbox in unit with the back axle. The ratios provided low speed for starting, direct drive in second and a geared-up top. Starter and dynamo were mounted on the clutch housing. Much use was made of roller-bearings in the cable-operated four-wheel brake system, and helical turbine-like spokes for cooling the brake drums were a feature of the vast and decorative cast-aluminium alloy wheels. Various types of tyre were fitted from time to time, but were usually of 39 inches (100 cm).

Before discussing performance, we should look at some of the varied coachwork fitted to the Royale. Obviously the 1926 launch was premature: no doubt Bugatti had his reasons for altering the specification, and he was not ready to accept orders until the smaller car was ready. It was his misfortune that the Wall Street crash and subsequent world slump happened just as he was ready. Ettore Bugatti had been convinced that the Royale would sell itself, and perhaps it would have done had he landed King Alfonso as a customer.

Perhaps, too, he was wrong to retain that open body, for quite suddenly at the end of

BELOW RIGHT *The Coupé Napoleon, the last body to be built on the prototype chassis. This car is on display at the Musée National de l'Automobile, in Mulhouse, France*

the 1920s open motoring went out of fashion. The role of the Royale, he now saw, was that of showcar, demonstrator and flagship of the Molsheim fleet. The tourer body was removed and the great man indulged his fancy by building what Regency coachbuilders would have called a chariot and which the French translate as *coupé* because, like a chariot, it comprises the two back seats of a coach with the front part cut off. The first Royale therefore received a closed two-seater body like a brougham – and indeed like the posting chariot in which Napoleon fled from the field of Waterloo. Hence the name (often given to a subsequent Royale body) Coupé Napoleon. The space behind the tiny closed body was filled

in with a free-standing trunk. This car appeared outside the Paris Salon in 1928 and received much attention.

The coupé was not retained long, and was replaced by another Ettore design, again redolent of a carriage. Bugatti had been drawing archaic brougham-like coachwork since 1910 and he saw no reason to abandon this agreeable mixture of straight and curved lines. The 1929 berline, or saloon, might almost have been the coupé re-used with a different back. The same peaked visor recurred, the same curved pillar and 'brougham foot', but the blind quarter panel was replaced by a door, and behind that was a quarter panel featuring a horizontal ellipse.

The next incarnation of the original chas-

sis bore coachwork not by the Old Man himself but by the go-ahead firm of Weymann. C.T. Weymann, airman, engineer and go-getter, had patented a form of very light construction in which the body was free to flex, thus abolishing rattles. Instead of being panelled the structure was covered in leather, leathercloth (the so-called 'fabric' body) or, as in this case, with a glossy patent-leather-like skin called *tôle souple*. Weymann was the father of the two-door 'sportsman's coupé' because his lightweight rattle-proof doors, kept in shape by tensioners, could be of almost any width. So the Weymann-bodied Royale was a two-door close-coupled coupé, very light and smart and with a huge trunk on the back. It won numerous *concours d'élégance*, then a very fashionable diversion at seaside resorts like Deauville, often presented by one or both of Ettore Bugatti's daughters, L'Ebé and Lydia. It was a very pretty car but was unfortunately short-lived, being written off in a crash. Yet this ex-Packard, ex-coupé, ex-berline, ex-Weymann chassis (or at least its chassis-number) was to be reincarnated as a masterpiece by Jean, as will be seen; but before that could happen Ettore had designed another 1910-derived body for the chassis.

The coachwork with which he presented us he called a double berline, a bizarre and uneasy creation. If the coupé had looked like a travelling chariot, this car looked like a *dormeuse de voyage* (sleeper); it was cer-

tainly double, for it looked as though a coach had telescoped into the back of a chariot. There was a curved brougham pillar to each half, front and back, and to fill the gap between and to allow the windows to drop there was a narrow oblong window in between. The car had a small trunk behind; altogether a strange creation, but practical because beneath all the carriage-oriented presentation the body was in fact a Salamanca cabriolet, a style of great versatility created by the English firm of Barker. By dropping the front windows and rolling back the canopy it became a cabriolet de ville; then the rest of the leather top could be folded, creating pretty much the effect of an open touring car. Useful but unattractive, and one feels that Jean would have disapproved.

The four bodies just discussed followed in rapid succession during 1928 and 1929. In 1930, and as though utterly oblivious of the Slump, Jean celebrated the slough of the Depression by designing perhaps the most elegant town carriage of all time, a coupé de ville. This body, no doubt from its nobility, is often referred to as the Coupé Napoleon although there is nothing Empire about it.

For sheer give-the-cat-another-canary luxury there has never been a car to touch it: the cabin aft of amidships (though well within the wheelbase) and chauffeur and footman in the open air. And because Jean Bugatti was the essence of the young sportsman he combined this extreme formality with slim, swept and sporting mudguards and an inclined spare wheel on the back. Furthermore, in order to lighten what might have seemed an undue acreage of sombre paintwork, he relieved it by means of a shallow depression starting from the bonnet hinge line and running back past the scuttle into the door, a horizontal echo, as it were, of the horseshoe radiator shape. Jean was to use the same device often in future, especially on the Type 55, where it became almost a trademark. Another novelty introduced by Jean on the coupé de ville was the transpa-

rent roof, which quite suppressed any feeling of claustrophobia.

By 1931 the clouds were beginning to lift. The Royale had been on offer for six years with no takers, although by equipping the prototype with so many diverse bodies Bugatti had created an impression of movement – a stage army consisting of one extra and a multiplicity of hats. In 1932, however, the till rang for the first time. Evidently impressed by Jean's coupé de ville, a textile magnate named Armand Esders commissioned an equally splendid folly: not a formal carriage but the ultimate sporting two-seater. The front wings were to be very similar to those of the coupé de ville and were to merge into curved running-boards and continue rearwards in a climbing sweep. There was to be a concealed dickey seat for two in the rear decking, complete with disappearing windscreen. The spare wheel was mounted vertically across the tail, but was later inclined. Monsieur Esders saved the designer some work by refusing to have lamps of any kind. He would not, he said, be driving after dark.

Another customer who came forward in 1932 was a Dr A. Joseph Fuchs, who purchased a bare chassis for delivery to the coachbuilding firm of Ludwig Weinberger in Munich, where he lived. The result was a beautifully balanced drophead cabriolet, a style in which German designers excelled at that time. The wing treatment owed something to Jean Bugatti's roadster, but the light-coloured hood, with its landau irons whose slope echoed that of the wings, looked very attractive. There were close-coupled seats for two in the back and a large

ABOVE The graceful Coupé Napoleon was used by the Bugatti family for many years. Its style was much influenced by that of horse-drawn carriages
LEFT Its interior exudes privacy, exclusivity and drawing-room comfort

BELOW The last body built at Molsheim was this Berline de Voyage, an inharmonious but versatile creation, possibly the least successful and least well known of all the Royales

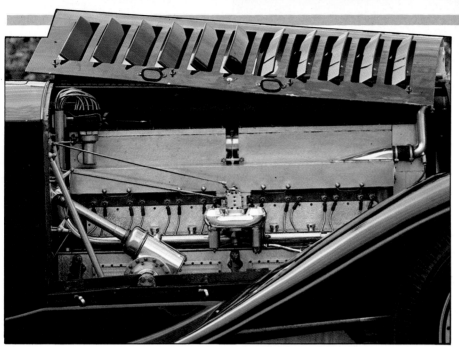

trunk behind. This is the car which Charles Chayne restored, having found it in a junk-yard in New York City, the city where Dr Fuchs had used it for some years until the block was damaged by frost. This car is now in the Ford Museum in Dearborn. The wind-screen and windows are very shallow, in the fashion of the time – one thinks of the Hispano-Suizas and 8-litre Bentleys.

We do have a firm date for the smart owner-driver two-door saloon (a style the French and Americans call coach) which Ettore Bugatti ordered from the Paris coach-builder Kellner, because it was exhibited at the London Motor Show at Olympia in 1932, and won a prize as most costly exhibit. The price would have bought three Rolls-Royces… . Notable for its slim pillars, it remained a favourite with *le Patron* and remained in his stable along with Jean's coupé de ville and double berline.

The last Royale to receive original body-work was purchased new by an English businessman, Captain Cuthbert W. Foster, in June 1933. He sent the chassis to Park, Ward & Co., of London, who built a limousine which was as resoundingly British as Jean's coupé had been French. It is this car, when in the possession of J. Lemon Burton, that the writer has been privileged to try.

Lolling upon the Bedford cord in that stately herse-like interior one felt part Pasha, part corpse. The driver seemed a very long way away, but not so far off as the circus elephant pirouetting on the radiator cap. Symbolically white, this mascot was the gift of sculptor Rembrandt Bugatti to his brother Ettore in 1915. The outside world seemed miles away; and there was very little sound of machinery, but as one looked out at other traffic one recovered a sense of proportion. A Bugatti Royale may be large by car stan-dards, but there are buses and trucks too.

As soon as I was ensconced in the driver's seat I realised that there has never been a finer bonnet to look down; the forward visibility is good. There are sound practical reasons for having the gear-lever and hand

TOP LEFT *The 12.7-litre straight-eight virtually fills the engine compartment* **ABOVE** *The interior of a Royale was not particularly spacious. Note the large steering wheel, necessary for leverage with the large and distant front wheels*

some 1820 rpm at 60 mph (96 kph) in second gear, slightly more than the 1700 rpm quoted as being the maximum-power speed of the engine. None of those on board – Lemon Burton, Cecil Clutton and the writer – felt disposed to believe publicity stories of 'zero to 90 mph in second gear', but all agreed that the car's direct drive was a very practical gear for a three-ton (3048 kg) vehicle. Overdrive was usable when the road was clear, its 2.66:1 ratio giving 43 mph (69 kph) at 1000 rpm and a majestic 70–75 mph (113–121 kph) at peak revs, about right, then, for a ceremonial carriage.

The main question was how well would the Gold Bug handle? The answer came through within the first few yards: the steering was pure Bugatti, typically smooth and precise, although fairly low-geared at 3½ turns from lock to lock. It could hardly have been otherwise with Ettore's own favourite toy: there were three Royales at the family chateau when he died.

One other Royale body remains to be described. The Armand Esdars two-seater came on the market in 1938, when Jack Lemon Burton considered buying and importing it to England despite a British tax rating of 78 hp, but the Munich crisis put him off. The car changed hands in France, the two-seater body was removed (and eventually destroyed by bombing during the war) and a new coupé de ville body commissioned from Binder, the Paris coachbuilder. It looked superficially like Jean Bugatti's masterpiece but lacked its slim elegance.

The Royales were a magnificent folly but far from a waste of time. They brought wonderful publicity and they gave both Ettore and Jean a chance to develop coach-building ideas. From the Type 41 evolved the Type 46 in 1929, a scaled-down Royale with a mere 5.3 litres of engine which, probably to Ettore's relief, siphoned off most the Royale clientele. At that time of crisis Bugatti found a new market for his great lazy 14.75-litre engine – not in boats, as its marine configuration might sugggest, but on the railways. The French national network at that time was developing streamlined rail-cars and Bugatti secured contracts for engines and rolling-stock which kept his factory going for more than 20 years. Powered by either two or four Type 41 engines, Bugatti *autorails* were fast, comfortable and quiet, the latter quality attributable to a layer of rubber between the wheel and its steel rim. The first car entered service in 1933 and was not withdrawn until 1954. Normally they cruised at 70 mph (113 kph), but one day Jean Bugatti startled the railways by covering 70 kilometres (43 miles) at more than 120 mph (196 kph): an excellent performance for these Royale engines

brake central, in the American fashion, but it nevertheless seemed rather atypical of Bugattis. The wood-rimmed steel-spoked wheel however, was perfectly Molsheim in feel and appearance, and it was a good idea to put a finger-tip horn push behind each spoke. The central boss was originally occupied by a beautiful built-in stopwatch.

Jack Lemon Burton then explained the gear positions, which are the same as those of a P3 Monoposto Alfa: a dog-leg change, forward right for first and forward left for second. After moving off in first one changes immediately into second, which gives direct drive and is used most of the time. Bugatti sources and also Charles Chayne, who took the trouble to measure, give the axle ratio as 3.66:1. Chayne used special tractor tyres on the car, and Lemon Burton fitted tyres from a couple of field-guns (retired), 7.50 × 24s, the nearest available size to the original Rapson balloons. These 39-inch (99 cm) tyres give approximately 520 revs per mile (318 turns per km), which means that the engine, with it 3.66:1 axle, would be doing

213

CITROËN

The SM was beautiful, very sophisticated and fast, and, with its Maserati engine and Citroën's incomparable suspension, the last of the French grand tourers. It was also doomed . . .

THERE MUST surely have been, in the early 1970s, more than 12,854 purists in all the world of motoring. There quite certainly were more customers than that who could have afforded the price of a Citroën SM – even though it rose, during that period, from 46,000 to 84,000 francs. Yet that number is all that Citroën managed to sell, of a car that had been acclaimed, by the critics of the international motoring press, with a rare unanimity; that number is all they managed to sell of a car that was tremendously strong, extraordinarily stylish, and uncommonly fast – a car blessed with aerodynamic properties that would be unbeaten for many years, and with steering and lights that have not been beaten yet.

One might think that purists would be attracted by such things. Alas, though many said they liked the car, few actually bought it – and the blame cannot be laid entirely at the doors of the Middle East, whence a mischievously political oil crisis cast its blight upon the world at the end of 1973. Sales in that year had only been half of what they had been in '72. The real fault was probably Citroën's own – not that of the designers and constructors but of the sales and service departments.

The service network was incomprehensibly resentful. They, who could undertake work on the inaccessible complexities of the DS hydraulics without turning a hair or skinning a knuckle, raised no mean outcry over the comparatively simple task of caring for an engine with two more cylinders, three more camshafts and four more chokes than the familiar DS. Maybe they saw it as an opportunity to demand higher rates of payment; in the USA, what was needed was higher education. The typically brutal and deliberately uncomprehending xenophobe, for whose crass ignorance and insensitivity the domestic American car had been de-

signed, having spent the 1950s trashing the SU carburettors of English cars and the 1960s abusing the transmissions of Italian cars, now took the opportunity to do to this French car such things as might have prompted a barbarian to pause and a Vandal to discover finer feelings. Shocked and sickened, Citroën withdrew from the USA market in 1973, after selling about 2000 SMs there. Their feelings about the single examples sold in such places as Bolivia, Liberia and the Philippines must have been similar in kind if not in degree.

Considering the failure of the sales organisation to approach the targets forecast for the SM, one must hold them responsible too. It appears that they were out of their depth, dealing not only with cars but also with customers of a higher class than those with whom they had been familiar. Taking a Renault or a Ford in part exchange for a DS was a comfortable enough process, almost as comfortable as taking a fistful of grimy banknotes for a 2CV; but taking a Porsche or a Jaguar in part exchange for an SM, let alone recognising the qualities in such cars with which the SM had to compete, were ideas above their station.

Yet it was with the very intention of acquiring some glamour, some nobility of lineage and elevation of patronage, that Citroën had set Maserati to producing an engine for their social climber. Citroën had bought the Italian firm – quite cheaply – in 1968, during a wildly expansionist period in which M. Ravenel led them in numerous

LEFT *The Citroën SM must be ranked as one of the most attractive, stylish and well-engineered cars ever produced, yet it was not a great success*

different directions simultaneously, doing various deals with Simca for factories, Panhard for everything, Berliet for a little while, and Fiat, for crying out loud. Maserati fitted easily into his picture: with its reputation for bloodstock engines, it could provide the one thing that Citroën really lacked.

What was foreseen was a new, dramatic, high-performance, high-class Citroën to fill a gap which had grown distressingly obvious since the decline of the upper-crust French firms (Delage, Delahaye and so on) a decade earlier. In the new enthusiasm for refined and redoubtable cars which had blossomed in the 1960s, the scope for promoting Citroën was clear and tempting. The DS or developments of it could provide everything necessary in suspension, brakes, running gear, indeed in everything except an appropriate engine. Because the opportunity was immediate, and because the DS made everything else immediately available, the engine would be needed very quickly. Citroën told Maserati that it must be very light, very short, and develop at least 150 bhp – and be ready within six months.

Maserati told Citroën that a trivial little job like that would only take them about three weeks! Doubtless a sign of hurt pride (they may have been saved by the take-over, but they can hardly have been pleased), this was not to be taken too seriously – but in fact they took less than seven weeks.

They did not have to start from scratch. They had recently created a new engine for themselves, the 4186 cc V8 of the Maserati Indy. Ing. Alfieri sliced two cylinders off it, reduced the bore and stroke of the remainder slightly, and thus produced a 90 degree V6 of 2670 cc, just small enough to get below the 16CV fiscal rating beyond which French cars were punitively taxed and seldom bought. With a choice of camshafts he was able to offer Citroën three alternative power curves, one of which reached 200 bhp. There was work to be done on rearranging the ancillaries and providing for a drive to the Citroën hydraulic clutch and five-speed all-indirect gearbox with spiral-bevel final drive, but when it was done he had created an engine weighing only 309 lb (140 kg) and only a foot (31 cm) long.

It was impressive in its detail. The light-alloy castings were sandwiched together very firmly, the lower supports for the main bearings being integrated with a nether half-crankcase beneath which the sump was a simple and separate casting. The main block of upper crankcase and cylinder

BELOW *The SM interior. Note the unusual brake 'button' rather than a normal pedal*
RIGHT *The crowded engine bay with the Maserati V6 almost hidden under the air cleaners, cables and pipes*

blocks was immensely rigid, despite its open-deck construction, and above its banks a pair of remarkably shallow cylinder-head castings nevertheless accommodated hemispherical combustion chambers in which opposed valves were inclined at an included angle of 76 degrees for operation by paired overhead camshafts.

The drive to these camshafts was an ingenious replacement for that in the original V8. The new three-throw crankshaft (which allowed inertial forces to be balanced out as though the engine were three 90 degree V-twins, though it made unequal firing intervals necessary) drove a chain from its rear to a jackshaft lying in the V of the cylinders. From that jackshaft went two more chains, one to each head and staggered so that the heads themselves were identical and interchangeable; and by being set in the planes of the main bearings, these drives did not affect the engine's length.

It was ostensibly a beautiful arrangement, giving a very short and extremely stiff crankshaft, clear straight porting served by three twin-barrel downdraught Weber carburettors, and minimal torsional flutter in the camshafts. As installed in the car, however, the alternator, hydraulic pump and air-conditioning pump were all carried in a sub-frame well ahead of the engine, to which they were connected by a long and slender torsionally flexible shaft driven from the nose of the jackshaft. Whether that induced torsional flutter of the primary chain, or damped it at the expense of accelerated wear, is not clear; but that chain gave problems, and, too often, very costly ones.

That was the only operational flaw in the entire driveline, which was otherwise remarkable only for the precision of the gearshift and the appropriateness of the gear ratios; this gearbox was later to be used by Lotus in their Esprit. For the Americans Citroën sought Borg-Warner collaboration in confecting an automatic transmission – but that came later, with an increase in displacement to augment the torque as those shiftless customers begged. When the engine was enlarged in 1973 (by reversion to the original Indy bore, giving 2965 cc), European customers continued to enjoy the Bosch fuel-injection system (like that of the DS23i) to which they had been treated since 1972, and which had increased the power somewhat. The fact that the top speed rose without the acceleration being any better was due to the subtle increase in gearing brought about by fitting 205 mm Michelin tyres instead of the original 195 size.

Top speed and acceleration were both excellent without being incredible. About 136 mph (219 kph) was the limit for the former, while the time for a standing-start kilometre was usually an irritating fraction of a second over 30. Both figures must be seen in the perspective of the big and heavy car that the SM was.

Its growth out of the DS was more than metaphorical. The running prototypes actually were DS saloons with the V6 inserted at one end and the wheel arches enlarged at the other. How else do you suppose so complex a car could have been

LEFT AND BELOW *Just nine SM convertibles were built, with bodies styled by Henri Chapron. The rear end treatment was the only weak angle, but Citroën have long had curious style features*

created – from the go-ahead to the debut at the Geneva Salon Automobile in March 1970 – in just 18 months?

As we have seen, the wonderful old DS provided much that was more than satisfactory. It provided a self-levelling self-damping and inimitably progressive-rate suspension system that was already so much superior to anything else in the world that nobody else in the world yet understood it; and there was already proven (but shelved) an active-ride version of it that would eliminate roll, and for which the extra-powerful hydraulics pump of the SM must have been eventually intended. Further, the DS provided a braking system of outstanding power, with inboard discs at the front reducing the unsprung mass (enhancing ride and roadholding) and instant automatic load-dependent modulation of pressure to the rear discs so that they should never lock prematurely.

Further still, the DS provided the basis of a most remarkable steering system. It was developed for the SM by the interpolation of a speed-related negative servo which progressively reduced power assistance from its maximum at standstill to zero at 124 mph (199 kph). Thus the steering was light when manoeuvring slowly, full of feel when driving fast, and as precise as exceptionally high gearing could make it, with only two turns of the handwheel from one lock to the other.

Admirable as the steering system was with so few turns from lock to lock, it was also exceptionally sensitive. Drivers without the necessary feel for the car would move off down the road unable to steer a straight path veering from lane to lane.

Making it all possible was perfect steering geometry, such as no other car but the later (just a few months later, and still going

strongly) GS ever had. With a four-bar linkage (essentially that of the DS) giving strict parallelogram geometry at the front, and with zero camber, caster and kingpin inclination, the SM front wheels went through camber changes equal to body roll but did not suffer camber changes induced by steering, as in other cars, nor any gyroscopic interference.

Strictly trailing rear wheels devoid of toe-in variation complemented this arrangement, accounting for marvellously consistent handling while leaving Michelin with their purpose-built XWX (a derivative of the XVR, and the best 70-series VR tyre then made) to arrange equally impressive roadholding. Only at the limits of adhesion, and especially when reaching them in the course of an S-bend, did the SM begin to reveal the seamy side of front-wheel drive.

The limits of front-wheel drive in this application were vividly shown in the examples that took to the race track where more often than not they could be seen understeering dramatically on the cornering limit in a cloud of tyre smoke.

Mere speed (sheer speed, rather) made no difference to it at all. Today's aerodynamicists might cavil at the lack of downforce, and suggest an abasement of the nose; but Citroën's styling chief Robert Opron (subsequently purloined by Renault) and his assistant Giret extrapolated DS styling to combine low drag with directional stability by keeping close to zero lift – something that the self-levelling suspension maintained by preventing pitch variations. It was a car still visibly descended from the wonderful design created by Opron's predecessor Flaminio Bertoni for the DS of 1955.

Partly because of that, it was a lot of car – expecially in relation to the not extravagantly large interior. In fact the rear seats were derisory; most of the body was full of car, with the boot half-full of spare tyre and the bonnet absolutely crammed with engineering. It was a long body, too, following Citroën's established ideals by being very wide at the front and very narrow at the back; and it was its great length in proportion to its cross-sectional area which played a big part in minimising the drag coefficient.

Citroën took no chances whatever in its construction. The bodyshell was very strongly integrated with the floorpan to create an immensely strong chassis-hull, with little but the doors, lids and front wings removable. It was also heavy – but after all, it was not a sports car, even though it did win its first rally. It was not a town carriage either, even though specialist coachbuilders laboured mightily to make swankmobiles for President, Premier, and visiting heads of state. Nor was it a mean-minded economy car

Henri Chapron was also responsible for the stretched four-door version which is easily as elegant as the standard car. Again only nine were built, exclusive machines which breathe money and style

meant for the parsimonious mobilisation of economists and calculators, although the advent of injection helped its thirst as much as its emissions.

Most of all, it was emphatically not a car such as ought to be doomed never to exceed half its potential speed; but this was what was imposed when the fuel crisis came to cloud all other issues at the end of 1973. With sales already dropping dangerously low, the SM was doomed – a car with no future and very little present. Poor Citroën, sorely overtaxed by the investment in the GS of late 1970 and the CX of 1973, had seen the departure of Michelin who had been major shareholders since the death of André Citroën 40 years earlier. Their new overlords were a hard-headed bunch of Protestants who made cars for a nation of Catholics, and who were unlikely to waste any sympathy on a firm founded by a Jew. They certainly wasted none on the SM: once they had decided that its production should stop, they would not even allow engines to be installed in already-completed body shells. Ligier could have the few engines he had been promised; as for Maserati, they were welcome to put the V6 into their nice little Merak for as long as their new and equally hard-headed owner Alejandro de Tomaso might let them; and as for those SM bodies, they were to be scrapped. Still, we should not be too hard on Peugeot: revivals are all very well, but keeping the dead alive can be more cruel than euthanasia, as they found out with Talbot.

AMILCAR
SIX

In the mid 1920s the French company Amilcar decided to
rival the all-powerful Salmson racers and produced the twin-
cam six-cylinder C6 and C0

THE CASUAL SPECTATOR at the Montlhéry race
track in the Spring of 1925, watching the old
lorry drive up from the Amilcar works at St
Denis, the other side of Paris, might have
thought the little car on the back was just a
lowered version of the Grand Sport model
the factory had campaigned in 1924, for it
had an assymetric scuttle and a very similar
radiator cowl. The fact that the two partners
in the firm, Edmond Moyet the designer and
André Morel the chief driver, were present
might have alerted him to the realisation that
this was a special occasion. But when André
Morel climbed in and the engine was cranked into life, he could have been left in no
doubt that this was an historic event. Here

was Amilcar's answer to the twin-cam Salmsons which were proving invincible in
1100 cc racing.

The origins of Amilcar can be traced back
to the firm of Le Zèbre, which had successfully built light cars since 1909. After the
Great War Le Zèbre was in financial trouble,
and its chief designer Jules Salomon left,
joining Citroën where he met an engineer
named Edmond Moyet. Moyet, like many at
that time, dreamed of manufacturing his
own car, and it seems that Salomon contrived a meeting between him and Morel
who was at that time still working for Le
Zèbre as an engineer and salesman. Over a
meal at the Excelsior, much frequented by

the motoring fraternity of the time, a part-
nership was formed and the first Amilcar
was sketched out on the tablecloth.

There remained the not inconsiderable
problem of financing the venture, solved by
approaching the new owners of Le Zèbre.
The original owners, Borie & Co, had sold
out to one of their directors, Fernand Lamy,
and a wealthy grocer, Emile Akar. They sold
off the Le Zèbre interests but retained the
name and premises of Etablissements Borie.
The money, together with a further considerable sum raised by the erstwhile Le
Zèbre dealers anxious to be in at the birth of
the new marque, went to the founding of the
Société Nouvelle pour l'Automobile. At first

ABOVE *A 1927 type C6 Amilcar with its 62 bhp straight-six engine. It was an 'undersquare' design of just 1094 cc*

the cars were just called Borie, but a new word was made out of Lamy and Akar and the name Amilcar was the result.

From the outset Morel was keen to enter competitions, and as so often happened the wishes of the engineers overcame the doubts of the financiers (who, being both fallible and French, couldn't resist the lure of glory) and competition versions of the little Salomon-designed side-valve engine were made. It seemed that the engineers had been right when Morel won the 1922 Bol d'Or 24-hour race, beating two Salmsons after a race-long battle and initiating the rivalry between the two marques which was to last through the '20s. By the time of their

next meeting, at the GP des Cyclecars at Le Mans, Salmson had produced their twin-cam engine and Amilcar could only manage third and fourth places behind them. Only a matter of minutes behind, it was a creditable performance, but few remember those who come second.

For the next two seasons, Amilcar did their best, trying wind-cheating bodywork, pressure lubrication, front wheel brakes (their chassis engineering was always far better than Salmson) and even supercharging. Despite their best efforts, however, the insurmountable obstacle was the deficiency of power of the side-valve engine, particularly with Amilcar's tortuous inlet passages cast

into the block. Valves were opened out until they almost touched, cylinder bores were extended from 55 mm to 60 mm and the crankshaft was mounted on ball-race bearings, but it was never enough. The marque was selling on its sporting reputation to a large extent, so the decision had to be made: withdraw from racing and face possible loss of reputation and sales, or do something spectacular.

To their eternal credit the management decided on the spectacular. A proper racing

car would have to be constructed, using the very latest technology, and a look was taken at the current fashions in Grand Prix racing. The Henry school, which favoured four valves per cylinder and a barrel crankcase with main bearings mounted on bolted-in diaphragms, was becoming outmoded, and modern design centred on the Fiat racing shop presided over by Giulio Cappa. For 1922 his team had produced the Type 404, a six-cylinder engine with two valves per cylinder, non-detachable head and crankcase split on its centre line with split-cage roller bearings between each cylinder.

That had proved so successful in 1922 that Louis Coatalen lured two of the Fiat engineers away to design his Sunbeam for 1923, and Planchon at Delage had more or less grafted two of these blocks onto one crankcase for his V12. 1924 had seen the advent of the supercharger on what was basically the same Sunbeam engine, making it the fastest car of the year, so when Moyet settled down to produce his racing car it is hardly surprising that was the line he followed. Two assistants were engaged, one from Sunbeam who may well have been Edmond Moglia, and one from Alfa Romeo who had previously been with Fiat. Drawings seem to have started to come from the design office around November 1924, so it can be assumed that the design was laid out in the autumn of 1924.

The new engine was far from being an exact copy of those which inspired it but the basic layout was very similar to the 1923/4 Sunbeam engine. The bore and stroke ratio was almost identical, 55 mm × 77 mm for the Amilcar and 67 mm × 94 mm on the Sunbeam. The twin overhead camshafts were driven by a train of gears from the rear of the crankshaft, with an intermediate gear

driving the water pump. The Amilcar's magneto was driven in train with the water pump, whereas both Sunbeam and Fiat had the magneto driven by skew-gears at the rear of the block. The block followed Sunbeam's principle of non-detachable head with two valves per cylinder, but new ground was broken by making the crankcase integral with the block; this must have added to the weight as the whole unit was cast iron, but it made for a very rigid crankcase with diaphragms cast between each cylinder for the roller main bearings.

The big ends were split-cage roller bearings, the small end following standard Amilcar practice with the gudgeon-pin held by a clamp bolt. The camshafts ran in ball bear-

RIGHT *Jules Moriceau in the Amilcar which raced, and retired, at Indianapolis in 1929 after breaking a conrod at 30 laps, pitching car and driver into the wall*

ABOVE, ABOVE LEFT & RIGHT This 1926 supercharged Type CO won the 1926 Brooklands 200 Mile Race, driven by Charles Martin, and many other races

ings at each end, with two intermediate roller bearings. Finger-type cam-followers were used, valve clearance being set by hardened pads on the valve stems. Dry-sump lubrication was used, with the oil tank set between the front dumb irons. This was soon found to be inadequate (they were always oily engines) and a larger tank went into the cockpit beside the driver. The single sparking plug per cylinder was inclined to the rear, and was fired by a magneto running at threequarters engine speed.

Whatever the origins of the engine, the chassis was pure Amilcar. It had quarter-elliptic rear leaf springs, and drive was by torque-tube from a four-speed gearbox to a straight-cut final drive with no differential. The beautifully-forged front axle had its brakes operated by pushrods inside the king-pins, a principle patented by Moyet and later adopted by Alfa-Romeo. The undertray wrapped round the chassis side-members to provide extra stiffness. A neat (but not very well finished) 1½-seat body with a pointed tail was fitted, made of aluminium panels on a wooden frame.

In its early days the engine was run unsupercharged. Supercharging was something of a black art at the time and Amilcar decided to produce their own. Not surprisingly they had to devote a lot of time to finding the best way to employ the Roots principle. Several configurations were tried; first with the rotors one above the other, then rotors with three lobes, until finally the two-lobe rotors were placed side by side and the tortuous mass of inlet pipework was reduced to one straight manifold with a blow-off valve. A maximum 75 bhp was claimed unsupercharged, and 83 bhp with the blower, but Amilcar were never very informative about the cars so the figures may or may not be true.

This car was given the designation Type CO. 1925 was given over to sorting out the inevitable problems that arise with a new racing car and it was not until the November of that year that the car was considered ready for competition. There was a hillclimb at Gometz-le-Chatel, and Morel drove the little car into second place behind one of the invincible Talbot-Darracqs, only 1.2 seconds slower despite giving away 400 cc to the winner. It was a promising start and no major problems had been encountered which might have led to drastic redesign.

During the winter a second car was completed, and Morel was joined by Charles Martin for the first circuit race for the cars and the first encounter with the Salmsons. This was the Grand Prix de Provence at Miramas, and Morel led his team-mate over the line for a 1–2 victory first time out. At last Amilcar had the necessary machinery, and the two cars were vigorously campaigned during the year. Records were set at the prestigious Arpajon speed trials and the cars won their class at innumerable hillclimbs. The COs were very fast and very reliable. A

third car was completed on a shorter chassis and Arthur Duray joined the others in time for the next clash with the Salmsons, again at Miramas. Unfortunately the cars chose this event to betray a weakness; all retired with broken valves. A redesign of the collets holding the spring cap (the cars were using three concentric valve springs, and were later to use four) was undertaken by Chinoy, head of the drawing office, and the trouble never recurred.

ABOVE *In 1927 the Amilcar team returned to Brooklands and took first, second and third places in the 1100 cc class of the Brooklands 200 Mile Race. The winner André Morel is shown on the left, next to Charles Martin who finished third and Vernon Balls who took second. The cars came second, third and fourth overall*

The scene was set for the third encounter of the 1926 season, the SCC 200 Mile Race (322 km) at Brooklands, in which the 1100 cc class had become a Salmson benefit. The Amilcar team was persuaded to come over by the English concessionaire Vernon Balls, who subsidised them to the then enormous sum of £1000, and he was not even invited to drive despite being a Brooklands expert! From the start the battle was between the three Amilcars and the Salmsons of Casse and Goutte, and after a titanic struggle in which the lead changed no less than seven times, Martin led Duray and Morel (who had had clutch-slip) across the line with the nearest works Salmson a bad seventh. Martin's time was good enough for fourth place overall.

Thought was then given to development for 1927. During the winter the chassis was redesigned and engine and transmission were offset to the left to enable the driver to sit alongside the torque tube. Engine dimensions changed slightly to 56 mm × 74 mm, and the radiator was cowled on some of the cars. A true single-seater had been produced, but Morel only tried it once at Montlhéry and condemned it, perhaps because

ABOVE *An Amilcar MCO single seater, restored and still racing today*
LEFT *The Amilcar driven in a world record attempt at Miramas*

the seat collapsed under him and left him sitting on the torque tube… . It had been designated Type MCO (M for *monoplace*) and the offset cars were called type CO *déporté* (offset), but were usually known as MCOs as they really were single-seaters.

Morel started the season with another win at Miramas, and there was no holding the cars in 1927. Salmson did their best but their cars were nearing the end of their development after five years whereas the Amilcars were still improving. Martin won at San Sebastian, and Duray at Boulogne, while Montlhéry was a happy hunting-ground for the team. At the end of the season Vernon Balls found another £1000 to bring the team over to Brooklands for the 200 Mile Race, and this time was rewarded with a drive, a rare event for anybody outside the works team. The Salmsons were outclassed, and Morel, Balls and Martin finished second, third and fourth in the general category. The cars had done all that could have been expected of them.

It is not known whether the idea of a plain-bearing version of the Amilcar Six was envisaged at the outset, but it was not very long before it was being planned. It may have been inspired by Bugatti who was selling the Type 35A as a more docile version of his Grand Prix car. The factory was interested in competing at Le Mans again, but in order to comply with the regulations production of 50 of the plain-bearing cars was required. The fundamental layout of the engine was the same as the CO, but the new engine had significant differences, chief among them being that the head was made detachable, which made casting arrangements simpler and machining more straightforward. The other basic difference was of course the substitution of white-metal bearings throughout except for ball races at the rear of the crankshaft and camshafts. The bore and stroke were 56 mm × 74 mm and the valves and supercharger were smaller.

The chassis into which this engine was installed was similar to that of the CO, but the side members were much deeper and it was somewhat wider to allow for two people to sit side by side in minor discomfort. All the running gear was identical except that the front springs were mounted at the rear end in slide-blocks, a modification later adopted on the works cars, and a differential was fitted. The oil tank for the dry-sump system lay between the dumb irons and a pressure-limiting valve was introduced into the system. When starting from cold there was at first no oil pressure and then suddenly far too much, which could burst the gauge. As the engine reached working temperature, however, things settled down.

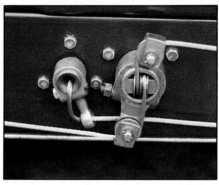

Detail of a 1927 Type C6 Amilcar. Unlike the CO, the C6 had a detachable cylinder head and plain, rather than ball, bearings. The chassis was widened to accommodate two people and the C6 could also be distinguished by its short tail

The limiting valve, operated by a handwheel on the dash, could be adjusted in conjunction with the gauge to keep things within bounds; if it was screwed shut on stopping, the engine remained primed with oil for the next start. Another intriguing detail was the provision of two tachometers driven from the camshafts. The car's body was made of steel on an angle-iron frame with a shorter tail than the CO. Some cars had a small compressor driven from the timing gears to pressurise the fuel tank. Road equipment was available but most owners preferred to buy the new machine as a stripped racing car.

Drawings date from April and May 1926, and the cars, designated Type C6, were available in 1927. Claimed power output was 62 bhp at 5000 rpm, enough to give a top speed of 105 mph (169 kph) on a typical rear axle ratio of 4.5:1: a number of ratios was available between 4:1 and 5.5:1. Much more

power would have been obtained if the revs could have been increased, but the standard connecting rods would not cope with much over 5000 rpm. The roller-bearing engines will actually turn at up to 6700 rpm, and some owners have subsequently modified the plain-bearing variety to rev to 6000 rpm.

Vernon Balls imported the first C6 into England in September 1927, and it excited great interest at the Motor Show. It was priced at £725 and there was a trickle of customers for them, such as W.B. Scott and Beris Harcourt-Wood. In all, Balls seems to have imported seven or eight, and they were soon to be found in most countries on the Continent. Sales can never have been very brisk though as the factory was still advertising the cars as late as 1931.

By 1928 the price of works participation was getting too high. The world was moving into recession and full order books were becoming a thing of the past. A financial reconstruction was necessary that year as Lamy & Akar wanted their money back, and thus a new company was incorporated as the Société Anonyme Française d'Automobiles.

There was still a budget for the racing department, which produced two more

offset cars, smaller and narrower than the previous ones, known as Type MCO Record, as speed was their primary function. At the Arpajon speed trials Morel drove one at a record 206.895 kph (128.56 mph) over the flying kilometre, then climbed into the other car, which had been overbored to put it into the 1500 cc category, and managed 210.77 kph (131 mph) with it. There were other record attempts at Montlhéry, and the previous year's cars appeared in a few selected races, but the good years were over.

Morel and Moyet left the firm, Moyet to return to Citroën where his last task was to lead the design team for the DS19. Martin and Duray also departed, and such racing as was done by the works was in the hands of Jules Moriceau, formerly Segrave's mechanic at Sunbeam. Discreet works assistance was also given to José Searon, a private owner who campaigned two C6s (one of them with an engine converted to needle-rollers) with considerable success up to 1932.

One of the last efforts by the factory was to enter a car for the 1929 Indianapolis 500. Sponsored by Thompson Products, makers of water pumps and other components, driven by Jules Moriceau and painted black and yellow, it broke a connecting rod after 30 laps and the resulting seizure spun the car into the wall, although Moriceau fortunately escaped injury. It was a sad ending.

The C6s kept racing throughout the 1930s. Apart from José Searon, Maurice Benoist gained several victories on the Continent. In Germany Rudi Steinweg and Von Morgen both campaigned cars successfully. A C 6 finally appeared at Le Mans in 1934, unsupercharged and endowed with an ugly 'tank' body, driven by veteran Arthur Duray and the de Gavardie brothers. In Britain many prominent drivers used them at Brooklands and elsewhere. Vernon Balls had ordered one with offset transmission, but when it arrived he decided he needed the money and sold it. It went to Henken Widengren, and he had it endowed with a teardrop-shaped body built by Bertelli, the coachbuilding side of Aston-Martin. In 1933 he took the car to Montlhéry and set a class record for the hour, covering 114.5 miles (186 km). As late as 1937 Harry Clayton succeeded in lapping Brooklands at 121 mph (195 kph) in a car he developed.

About half the cars made can still be traced, although their public appearances are regrettably rare these days. Over the many years of hard use the blocks in particular have become a mass of fatigued stresses and those lucky enough to possess them are unwilling to court disaster. This is a pity, because a generation is growing up which has never heard the song of these beautiful little cars.

LEFT *Lovely front end detail of the C6 Amilcar revealing the quality of engineering that went into producing these fast and effective sporting cars*

Alpine A110

Jean Rédélé's brilliant design came to dominate the rallying world of the late '60s

THERE WERE FEW more stirring sights in the rallying world of the late 1960s and early 1970s than that of a works Alpine A110 in full cry. The car was at its best on tarmac, but it also coped astonishingly well with the rough tracks of events like the RAC Rally. Here the apparently flimsy little machines would grind along, thumping the ground every few yards to add still more noise to the amazing din of their exhausts. Their rear wheels would be set at equally startling negative camber angles and the finish was always patriotic French blue.

It was not only that the A110 looked fast. It really was, and fast enough to win major rallies like the Monte Carlo, the TAP, the Acropolis and the Tour de Corse. Alpine used some foreign driving talent – Ove Andersson was one of their Monte victors in the A110 – but priority was always given to the cream of French rally drivers: Jean-Claude Andruet, Bernard Darniche and Jean-Pierre Nicholas all scored major victories for the Alpine rally team.

This little Gallic masterpiece was remarkable for all manner of reasons. In the first place it gained its major success and fame after being virtually ignored for several years while Alpine's founder and Managing Director, Jean Rédélé, concentrated his competition efforts on pure racing cars. Again, it established itself at a time when its mechanical formula – rear engine, simple suspension, maximum use of standard parts – was already considered outdated. Third, it is perhaps the best-known in Britain of all those cars which have never been (officially) sold here. Certainly it could have been sold because it was for many years France's nearest approach to a true production sports car. The rally-winners were no more than the tip of the iceberg: at the end of the 1960s,

A110s were being built in four-figure numbers per year, and the car was licence-produced in small numbers in Brazil, Mexico, Spain and even Bulgaria!

The history of the A110 must really be traced back to its immediate predecessor the A108, Jean Rédélé's first completely independent design and the first model to wear the smooth and distinctive bodywork designed by Marcel Hubert. The first A108s carried on the Rédélé tradition of making the most of standard Renault running gear, but its structure was neither sophisticated nor successful, a steel-tube confection which made few concessions to the needs of everyday driving. It was only when Rédélé redesigned the chassis completely to take the form of a strong steel platform with a central backbone, welded to a standard Renault front bulkhead and carrying a separate rear subframe for the engine and rear suspension, that the car began to look a more serious proposition. All it needed was more power, and the change from A108 to A110 designation came with the fitting of a 998 cc engine in 1963. This adapted version of Renault's Dauphine engine was soon joined, and indeed rapidly superseded, by tuned versions of the new 1108 cc unit which Renault had developed for the R8.

The formula thus established never changed in essence, however much the details were altered – and in particular, however much the engine grew in size and power. The glassfibre bodywork looked and was flimsy, even though by 1967 Alpine had opened a special factory at Thiron-Gardais to mould its components. Final assembly continued to take place at Dieppe.

The bodywork, however, was essentially decorative and to keep out the weather. The A110's strength lay in its chassis, instantly recognisable when unclothed with its complex assembly of Renault parts at the front and the strong central tunnel running aft to a very distinctive ramp which swept up to a cross-member above the gearbox. Frames

BELOW AND FAR RIGHT *The 1300S Alpine was virtually indistinguishable from the 1600S, and was really just as quick* **BOTTOM** *Jean-Luc Therier on his way to winning the 1974 Ronde Cevenole*

built up on each end of this cross-member located the upper ends of the rear springs and of the twin dampers – one either side of the drive shaft. The front suspension used plain Renault double wishbones with concentric coil spring/damper units attached to the lower member; the rear suspension rather alarmingly retained equally standard Renault swing-axles with fore-and-aft location provided by very long, cranked radius arms attached to the rear of the central chassis backbone. The steering rack was mounted high, and without an engine in the

way it had been carefully positioned to achieve very good steering geometry, commendably free from kick-back or bump-steer.

The engine was of course mounted in-line, aft of the rear-drive transaxle. As we are all supposed to know today, such an arrangement is highly undesirable because of the effect of a rearward weight bias on stability and handling. From Alpine's point of view, of course, it conferred good traction, excellent braking balance, and it also permitted the A110 a super-clean nose shape even though it contained a low-mounted radiator with its air intake beneath the pointed snout. No figure ever appears to have been published for the A110's drag coefficient, for few people in those days worried about such things, but the car's performance with engines of very limited power suggests it can hardly have been more than about 0.35 in standard form (without the customary rash of extra rally lights). However the most important advantage of the engine's position was that there was plenty of room to fit a bigger engine, and eventually this was done.

It was not sufficient that Renault steadily developed the 'iron Cleon' engine from its original 845 cc up to 1289 cc form fitted to the final versions of the Renault 10. It was not even enough when Gordini substituted one of his famous heads with crossed-over pushrods and hemispherical combustion chambers to create the more powerful (103 bhp) unit of 1255 cc which found its way into some versions of the A110 as well as the Renault 8 Gordini. By the end of the 1960s it was clear that successful rally cars needed competitive torque as well as power, and the only way to provide that was to fit a bigger engine. Fortunately Renault had one available in the form of the then-new Renault 16 unit.

This engine had a lot to be said for it. Because it was all-alloy, it didn't weigh a lot more than the 'iron Cleon' despite offering a capacity of 1565 cc. It was of course engineered for in-line installation (although at the front of the car in the Renault 16), and Alpine had to adapt it to five-speed transmission since the 16s of that era all had four-speed boxes operated with one of the world's last column-mounted gearlevers. No such device was needed in the A110 since the gearshift linkage could be run shortly and directly to the gearbox forward of the final drive.

By 1970, the year of the A110's highest production figure, Alpine had more or less completed the development process and offered a range of 1300 and 1600 models for general sale, all of them under the familiar title of Berlinette. The 'base' model was the

85 Tour de France which used a mildly tuned (higher compression, different camshaft, twin-choke Weber) version of the standard Renault 1300 engine delivering a claimed 81 bhp at 5900 rpm: the same basic engine in the Renault 10 was rated at 52 bhp at 4800 rpm, which is some measure of the lengths to which Alpine was prepared to go in the careful tuning of its own units.

For another 7000 francs (about an extra 30 per cent, since the 85 was supposed to retail at 21,600 francs) the customer could have the car fitted with the 'standard' 1255 cc Gordini engine and associated five-speed gearbox, this model being known as the 1300G. Next up the scale, in fact the most expensive version of all at 32,000 francs, was the 1300S. This was effectively the 1.3-litre class competition car, coming with a bored-out and tuned version of the Gordini engine: an extra 1.2 mm of cylinder bore took the capacity out to a convenient 1296 cc, not to be confused with the standard Renault's 1298 cc of completely different bore/stroke ratio. Since the standard Gordini 1255 cc unit delivered its 103 bhp at 6750 rpm, the tuned unit was of necessity a rather wild device, its 132 bhp coming at a 7200 rpm peak. A specific power of over 100 bhp per litre wasn't bad for a pushrod engine, but for rallying the Achilles' heel was the much more modest 90 lb ft of torque which limited the available acceleration. However the sheer power enabled Alpine to claim a

BELOW Bernard Darniche's Alpine receives repairs to the battered front suspension on the way to victory in the tough Moroccan Rally in 1973

LEFT *Therier again, this time he manages to wave at the camera whilst drifting his car on the 1973 Moroccan rally*
ABOVE *Jean-Pierre Nicholas pressing on during the 1973 RAC rally*
BOTTOM *Nicholas again, on his way to second place in the 1974 Tour de Corse*

ber 40DCOE for the standard downdraught Weber 32DAR to give 102 bhp at a very modest 5500 rpm, compared with 88 bhp at 5750 rpm for the 16TS. The high-performance fraternity was naturally expected to opt for the 1600S with a 10.2:1 compression ratio, different camshaft and the huge Weber 45DCOE carburettor helping the engine deliver 138 bhp, still at only 6000 rpm. This version pretty well matched the performance of the 1300S and the much lower power peak rightly indicates that it was far less of a handful to drive, especially with nearly 20 per cent more torque into the bargain. Certainly it was the 1600 which was rapidly adopted by the works rally team, and for a time with tremendous success. In 1971 Alpine won the International Rally Championship, largely due to Ove Andersson's victories but also, in the final analysis, because of Renault's decision in 1967 to give Alpine full support (and a full budget) in the international competition arena.

Autocar ran a full road test on a works Alpine 1600S in February 1971, all the more

maximum speed of 134 mph (216 kph) for the A110 1300S with its standard 4.125:1 final drive ratio (though a check through the gearing calculation reveals this to call for 7900 rpm, so maybe this was achieved with one of the two optional higher final drive ratios designed for roads not rallies).

Extra torque was provided by the 1565 cc engine which came in two forms. The first, which powered the straight Berlinette 1600, was simply a version of the standard Renault 16TS engine with better breathing, mainly the result of substituting the inevitable We-

EVOLUTION

Introduced in 1963 as the Alpine 110 Type 958, a glassfibre-bodied rear-engined coupé with a tubular steel backbone chassis. The 956 cc engine from the Renault R8 produced 44 bhp

1964 Type 1100 '70' was introduced, fitted with the 1108 cc engine from the R8 Major. This unit produced 58 bhp

1965 The Type 1100 '100' was introduced, with the 84 bhp 1108 cc Renault Gordini engine.

1966 The 1300S was introduced, with a 1296 cc bored-out version of the Gordini engine, producing 106 bhp

1967 The 1300G model was introduced, fitted with the 1255 cc 95 bhp standard Gordini engine and a five-speed gearbox. The Type 1500 was introduced, fitted with the 62 bhp 1470 cc R16 engine. Top speed was 112 mph (181 kph).
Total production (1500): 17

1969 Type 1600 introduced, with 1565 cc R16TS engine, producing 80 bhp. Maximum speed was 100 mph (160 kph)

1970 110 '85' introduced, fitted with 72 bhp 1289 cc R12 engine.
The 1600S was also introduced, with a higher compression ratio, improved breathing and better camshaft, and this raised output to 122 bhp, with a maximum speed of 127 mph (204 kph)

1971 Types 1600 and 1300S discontinued. Total production: (1600) 77 (1300S) 185

1973 1600 SCC (carburettor) and 1600 SI (injection) models introduced

1974 1600S discontinued. Total production: 1600

1975 1600 SC and SI models discontinued. Total production: 588

1976 1600 SX introduced, with the R16TX 1647 cc engine, producing 95 bhp, and with A-frame upper and lower wishbone rear suspension.

1976 Type '85' discontinued. Total production: 3343

1977 1600SX discontinued. Total production: 385.

interesting for giving an insight into the car which was going to win the Championship. The recorded performance figures are revealing, even though the ultra-quick works rally car of 1971 would seem almost modest by 1985 standards: the maximum speed was a rev-limited (at 7600 rpm) 124 mph (199.5 kph), the standing start to 60 mph took 8.1 seconds, and the quarter-mile was covered in 17.6 seconds. To be fair, these figures did not reveal the true nature of the A110 because it was not easy to get off the line, as the author painfully remembers: and there were two very smart gearchanges to be slipped through long before 60 mph was reached. In the speed range from 50 mph (80 kph) to 110 mph (177 kph) however the Alpine felt tremendous, and its momentum could be very easily maintained by 'rowing it along' with quick changes between third and fourth. The handling was equally remarkable in that the negative camber of the back wheels, which seemed almost grotesque at a standstill, did just enough to tame the natural oversteer of the car without killing it completely. One was almost encouraged to enter corners too fast for the sheer joy of easing out the tail and then balancing the attitude with the throttle. The brakes were amazingly effective by the standards of the day, much more reassuring than those of a works Escort BDA for instance, and the precision and response of the steering was an education. It was also interesting that after the first five minutes the driver's impression was one of great strength, the fragility of the body panels forgotten because the chassis was so evidently rigid.

There were less pleasant things about the

car too, notably its horrific interior noise level – one wonders how crews ever communicated in those pre-intercom days – its very cramped cabin, several doubtful safety features including the steering column pointing directly at one's chest, and the presence of the fuel tank immediately in front of the scuttle.

Part of the key to the A110's performance and handling can be found in its dimensions and weight. The production 1300 was claimed to weigh only 1378 lbs (625 kg), and the 1600 was reckoned only 22 lbs (10 kg) heavier. The static balance ratio was about 40/60, front-to-rear, although with two people aboard this would have been much closer to 50/50. The wheelbase was less than 83 in (210 cm) and the overall length some 12ft 6in (381 cm), while the car was frac-

tionally under 5ft (152 cm) wide and only 44.5 in (113 cm) high. The reason for the snug cabin becomes evident … as does the low frontal area which complemented the low-drag shape!

As the 1970s progressed, the A110 1600 became outclassed by the increasing power of its rivals, especially the Ford Escorts, and a remedy was sought in the boring-out and further tuning of the Renault engine. Its capacity was taken to 1796 cc by opening out the bore from 77 to 82.5 mm, and by 1973 the works cars had 170 bhp available at 7000 rpm with 141 lb ft of torque at 5000 rpm. In this form the engine ran a

This 1971 1600S road car features a 138 bhp engine. It also sports optional, but de rigeur, factory spoiler and engine lid

10.2:1 compression ratio and had a new camshaft with lots of overlap and increased lift, a reworked head with larger valves, and two Weber 45 DCOEs. The fuel tank had been upped from its original 38 litres (8.4 gallons) to no less than 80 (17.6 gallons), more or less filling the available space, but the weight was still only 1510 lbs (685 kg).

Such measures kept the A110 more or less competitive but there was no doubt the car was losing its edge. One final attempt to keep it a front-runner was revealed in 1974 with the announcement of a Berlinette A110 Prototype. This retained the 1.8-litre engine capacity but with the compression ratio lifted to 11.5:1, an even wilder camshaft (its valve timing was 53-83-83-53 degrees) and Lucas indirect injection. A power output of 187 bhp at 7200 rpm was claimed. Even more important in its way, the Prototype acknowledged that with increasing power, with or without negative-camber settings, the swing-axle rear suspension had become a major handicap. This car therefore became the only Alpine A110 to have double-wishbone rear suspension with double-jointed drive shafts playing no part in wheel location. As a works drawing shows, the wheels were even then set at a considerable negative camber, while the coil spring/damper unit acted on the upper wishbone which also picked up the end of the rear anti-roll bar. The A110 body was also modified, with greatly extended wheel arches to cover the very wide tyres, a deep and ugly beard-type spoiler under the nose and a crude flat-plate rear spoiler propped up behind the tail. The superb lines of the A110 were comprehensively spoiled, and in any

case it was evident that the best way to make a rally car capable of competing with the likes of the Lancia Stratos would be to start with a different chassis and put the engine somewhere else, like in the middle. That philosophy eventually gave rise to the Renault 5 Turbo, but in the meantime it spelled the beginning of the end of the A110. Its planned production successor, the A310, had been shown as early as the 1971 Geneva Show and from then on the writing was on the wall for the older model. It might have departed somewhat sooner had it not achieved its run of rally success. Once it had, its new aura boosted the sales appeal of the production versions and it was not until 1976 that parallel production of the A110 and the A310 finished at Dieppe.

For a time, the A110 had its native French rivals, notably the ugly Ford-engined Matra M530 (indeed mid-engined and able in theory to offer better handling). It says much for the beauty and in most respects the practicality of the A110 that it was able to stave off such challenges and become France's favourite sports coupé. To be sure, it had the advantage of being chosen as Renault's prime rally weapon at a time when interest in rallies was high and results genuinely affected sales, but there was more to the A110 than that. It might be stretching a

TOP *This dramatic side view of the A110 conveys little impression of just how small the car is; waist-high to a normal adult, in fact!*

point to call it France's equivalent of the Lotus Elan, though there are parallels enough. After all, Jean Rédélé set up his own company to exploit the design ideas first tried out in competition with modified production cars, just like Chapman with his Austin 7s; the A110 itself was a nicely stream-lined plastic body on a very strong backbone chassis; you could even compare Gordini's ingenious cylinder head redesign of the Renault engine with Harry Mundy's twin-cam reworking of the overhead-valve Ford.

You shouldn't take the parallel too far, though: in many ways the A110 is very different from the Elan, not only in its engine and transmission position but also in its harsh ride, ultra-cramped cockpit and use of too many standard suspension components to permit good handling without serious compromise of other qualities. That doesn't detract from the car's achievements, or the compensating advantages of being able to exchange one rear-mounted engine for another (bigger) one without significant structural change. On the business side too, Alpine proceeded in its own direction by linking its fortunes ever more closely with those of Renault, so that eventually the A110 was sold and serviced by Renault dealers.

There is one more Elan parallel, of course, in that the A110 eventually gave way to something altogether bigger, more powerful and much more expensive in the form of the A310 V6. But by the time that had happened, the A110 itself had written history for more than a decade and earned itself a niche in the ranks of the great sporting cars, as well as the classic status it now enjoys in its native France.

TALBOT LAGO

Antonio Lago's powerful cars were clothed by France's finest stylists and seemed the essence of European Grand Tourers

AFTER MAJOR ANTONIO LAGO took over Automobiles Talbot in 1935 the French car industry was eventually blessed with some of the most imposing grand tourers ever produced. Some of Lago's creations were almost as striking as those of another brilliant Italian engineer who lived and worked in France. Unlike Ettore Bugatti's cars, however, Lago's were rather more striking than dynamic.

In 1933 Lago moved from his position as general manager of the Wilson Self-Changing Gear Company to become works manager at Automobiles Talbot's Suresnes factory. That gave him two years grace before the Sunbeam Talbot Darracq (STD) combine that controlled Talbot collapsed and was taken over by the English company Rootes Securities. Rootes had no interest in Talbot, and Lago seized his opportunity, raising money from the major French component manufacturers all of whom, of course, had a vested interest in keeping the company afloat, and persuading them to invest in the refloated S.A. Automobiles Talbot, with Lago himself in charge. Bearing in mind that both Sunbeam and Talbot had effectively dissipated a large proportion of their capital on a competition programme which they could no longer afford, it is reasonable to suppose that Lago would have been careful to ensure that his new undertaking steered well clear of the circuits.

On the contrary, Lago, like Bugatti, recognised that motor racing brought not only the benefits of free advertising and marque prestige, but could also serve as a very effective research and development laboratory – par-

ticularly if the competition programme was based on cars developed from production models.

In 1936 the French Grand Prix was changed into a sports car event, a move welcomed by both Delahaye and Bugatti, and this must have strengthened Lago's hand when he sought his shareholder's approval of a racing programme. Back in the 1920s Lago had been involved in marketing his own LAP overhead-valve-conversion kits and was well versed in the art of improving the performance of a basic production model.

He also had some experience of competition driving himself; after service in the Italian army in the Great War and a spell of selling Isotta-Fraschinis, his work for the Wilson company brought him into contact with Armstrong-Siddeley, and he drove in their works team in the 1932 Alpine Trials.

Lago introduced a new line of cars in 1936 which retained the independent front suspension and X-braced frames of their predecessors but incorporated entirely new six-cylinder overhead-valve engines. In 2.7-litre and 3-litre guise the Talbot Darracqs of the old regime had been pleasant but not particularly rapid cars and in many respects

ABOVE & BELOW *Post-war Talbot Lago Grand Sports were particularly striking when bodied by the coachbuilder Saoutchik* LEFT *The cockpit of the 1949 Grand Prix car; particularly unusual features are the pre-selector gear change and the tachometer red-lined at just 4200 rpm*

they resembled the products of Delahaye in Paris. Both marques had passed through a period in which their cars were dependable, but terribly dull, and which finances had declined, and both fielded a range with box-section frames, single transverse-leaf independent front suspension and semi-elliptic rear springing. Like Talbot, Delahaye also had a six-cylinder engine with some considerable development potential, but as one would expect from his background Lago

was a step ahead with cylinder-head design.

Lago's chief engineer, Walter Becchia, was commissioned to design a new 4-litre car based on the old 3-litre Talbot-Darracq K78, and it was this car on which Lago's racing hopes were pinned. Becchia developed a new cylinder head for its engine with cross-over pushrods, the inspiration for which might well have been the contemporary BMW 328. The same engine powered the Lago-Speciale production version, and com-

bined robust construction (it boasted a seven bearing crank) with advanced design and hemispherical combustion chambers to produce 165 bhp and a top speed comfortably in excess of 100 mph (161 kph).

In its racing form, the engine was so impressive that it was easy for Lago to lure race driver René Dreyfus away from Ferrari to run the Suresnes team. The sports racing Talbot Lagos used Wilson preselector gearboxes and were capable of 130 mph (209 kph), enough to set the first lap record in the inaugural Sports-Car GP at Montlhéry.

It took a little while for the cars to settle down and realise their full potential, however, but nevertheless the first season's results included third place in both the Marne and Comminges races. 1937 was a different story, with the Suresnes cars dominating the second French GP for sports cars. Chiron was first home, followed by team-mates Commotti and Divo and with Sommer a

creditable fifth. At Miramas in the same year it was Sommer's turn to lead a 1–2–3 victory for the Lago camp at an average of 112.74 mph (181.4 kph), and when the cars were brought to England for the TT at Donington, Comotti and Le Begue were first and second past the chequered flag.

Possibly as a result of that trip to the UK and the showing at Donington, negotiations were set in progress with the directors of the near-moribund Invicta company, which had made no cars since 1935. At the time Invicta were based in Chelsea and existed as little more than a service depot, Invicta's founder, Noel Macklin, having left to form Railton.

Had plans progressed beyond the discussion stage 1938 would have seen a new range of Invictas built in London in 2.5-, 3- and 4-litre guise; all of which would have been based on the Talbot-Lago range and bodied similarly to the contemporary 3-litre Delage D670.

Since the Rootes-built STD cars differed so greatly from the Lago-built models there were logical arguments in favour of marketing the Talbot-Lago in the UK under the still-respected Invicta name.

Sadly, nothing came of these plans and 1938 proved to be a somewhat less than successful year. Despite an increase in capacity to 4.5 litres for the racing engines, the cars proved no match for the all-conquering Mercedes-Benz and Auto-Union teams at Rheims in the French GP, but no doubt Lago took some consolation from the Le Begue/Morel victory in the Paris 12 Hours and the spirited performance put up by Le Begue and Carriere in the Mille Miglia; there the Talbot Lago was beaten only by three Alfa Romeos and the new V12 Delahaye.

At Le Mans, the 4-litre coupé of Prenant/Morel managed a creditable third place, but it was as a *grand routier* that the pre-war Talbot-Lago (or Lago-Talbot – the 4.5-litre engines certainly carried the former name cast into the valve covers but no hard and fast ruling was ever laid down for the marque name) was best-known.

Bodied both in the works and by bespoke coachbuilders to customer's individual requirements, some quite strikingly handsome cars were turned out – including a two seater coupé by Figoni and Falaschi with a steeply raked screen, pontoon rear wings, a 'spined tail' in the manner of the Type 57 Bugatti Atlantic and an oval grille which anticipated the XK120 by at least ten years.

1939 saw some low-chassis single-seaters prepared in readiness for the coming season, but a projected supercharged V16 got no further than the drawing board. Only German and Italian retirements permitted third places at Pau and Rheims before racing was curtailed by World War II.

It was to be seven years before Suresnes recovered sufficiently from the effects of the war to recommence series production, but pre-war output had been sufficient to ensure that when France's post-war Formula A was being mooted, there were enough 4.5-litre Talbot-Lagos about for the formula to be set at 1.5 litres supercharged and 4.5 litres unsupercharged. During the war Antonio Lago was removed from control of Talbot by

LEFT AND BELOW *Louis Chiron's 1949 4.5-litre Ecurie France Car, the winner of the '49 French GP. The single seaters are still competitive in Historic racing*

the Germans and spent his enforced free time in Paris designing a new sports car for after the war. In 1947, with his factory re-tooled and Marchetti installed as his new chief engineer, Antonio Lago presented his first post-war model range, although a few cars had left the factory in 1946.

The post-war cars were more generally known as Lago-Talbots and the new Lago Record and Grand Sport models used a 4.5-litre 93 mm × 110 mm version of the pre-war engine in what was basically the pre-war chassis. In those austere days, many of the major manufacturers were also forced to re-introduce merely face-lifted models initially, and in France the small luxury sporting marques were hit by crippling taxes.

The 4.5-litre Grand Sport coupé had rather English lines somewhat reminiscent of an Aston Martin DB2 with a similar suggestion of speed and brute force coupled with elegance. It had every right to look imposing too as it weighed a substantial 3740 lb (1700 kg), making it one of the heaviest GTs of the era. It easily outweighed some of its contemporary opposition such as the DB2 while it was even considerably heavier than the Jaguar XK120 thanks to its massive separate cruciform chassis and cast-iron engine. The 4485 cc straight six was introduced in 1946 and looked like a conventional twin-cam but in fact the camshafts were both set high up in the block and operated valves in hemispherical combustion chambers via short cross-over pushrods. It was used in both the Record and Grand Sport models with 170 bhp in Record form and 195 bhp in the more sporting Grand Sport. Despite its interesting specification which even included Lanchester counter-balance shafts to minimise vibration

RIGHT & BELOW *A 1938 4-litre Cabriolet. Its 3996 cc six-cylinder engine produced 105 bhp at 4000 rpm and as usual it featured the Wilson pre-selector gearbox*

it was not really a very sporting engine; its relatively long stroke (93 mm × 110 mm) meant that it did not relish high rpm and above 4000 rpm it began to vibrate sufficiently to keep owners to the factory stipulated rev limit of 4200 rpm. Rather surprisingly in view of its displacement and its reluctance to rev highly it still produced little power at low rpm; under 2500 rpm nothing much happened so the useful power band was somewhat narrow. Nevertheless the Grand Sport accelerated briskly and could cover the standing kilometre in 33.3 seconds and reach a maximum speed of over 110 mph (177 kph). Its high gearing

TOP *A Lago Record of the early '50s with an elegant body clothing what was basically a pre-war chassis fitted with a version of the 4 1/2-litre engine*

also meant that it could reach 90 mph (145 kph) in third gear.

The Grand Sport's grand weight did have one advantage – it was evenly distributed thanks to the engine being set well back in the chassis, helping to balance the car and improve its handling. A modern driver might find the light steering a little imprecise and the road holding rather poor thanks to the Talbot's tendency to wander over less than perfect surfaces, but for its time the Grand Sport was said to handle well.

One of the nicer features without a doubt was the Wilson preselector gearbox, the control for which was mounted on the steering column. Lago had not forgotten his old company and used Wilson 'boxes in all his cars; their great asset was that the driver could select the next gear he wished to use well before the corner in question and then when it came time to change gear he merely had to actuate the clutch enabling him to keep both hands on the wheel.

In the '50s cars were not designed with ergonomics in mind and although the instrumentation was comprehensive the dials were rather scattered on the dashboard. Looking through the very large sprung steer-ing wheel the driver would see three minor dials imparting information about the num-ber of amps, water temperature and oil pressure. Flanking them were the speedo, to the right and marked up to 200 kph, and the tachometer to the left. Neither fell naturally to the eye while the small clock was tucked away on the far right of the dash. The handbrake was also in a rather awkward position ready to impede the driver as he stepped in.

The 4.5-litre racing cars proved to have a distinct advantage over their more advanced Italian blown 1.5-litre adversaries. Their modest fuel consumption enabled them to avoid the constant pit stop refuelling of the smaller cars, and in 1947 Rosier won at Albi, Chiron won the French GP and managed a second place at Nimes, whilst the race of Comminges proved to be a Lago-Talbot be-nefit, the cars taking the first three places.

By 1948 the factory was ready with a new GP car which also used the twin high-camshaft 4.5-litre engine. Its output, howev-er, had been increased dramatically from 195 bhp to 280 bhp, and in its first season Rosier drove to victory in the Coupe du Salon and came second in the Monte Carlo

EVOLUTION

Antonio Lago took over Automobiles Talbot in 1935, producing new 2.7-litre and 3-litre tourers and a new 4-litre 23CV Lago Special in 1936. The Lago Special chassis was a popular choice with the coachbuilders of the day.

1947 New Grand Sport and Record models introduced with the 4.5-litre straight six in what was basically the pre-war cruciform separate chassis. Cheaper Quinze Luxe models were also produced with either the 2.7-litre four cylinder or the 4.5-litre six with disc wheels rather than the Rudge wire wheels of the Grand Sport and Record.

1950 Talbot Lago Bébé introduced. It featured the 2.7-litre, three-bearing, four-cylinder engine from the Quinze Luxe tuned to produce 118 bhp. 1950 production of all cars totalled 433.

1951 Total output for 1951 was 80 cars.

1952 Talbot Lago range restyled.

1955 The attractive 2.5-litre GT introduced with the last new Talbot Lago engine. That was a 2.5-litre, five-bearing twin cam, again with hemispherical combustion chambers and cross pushrods. It was used with a four-speed ZF gearbox.

1957 The GT bodyshell was given the 2.8-litre BMW V8 to form the Lago America built in very small numbers.

1959 Talbot Lago taken over by Simca and the 2.5-litre GT was re-engined with the V8 from the Simca Vedette and formed the last production Talbot Lago.

1960 Antonio Lago died and Talbot Lago production ceased.

Rally and at Comminges and Albi.

The engine proved versatile, powering road cars and Grand Prix racers with equal success, and led to the development of a breed of sports racers equally at home in both Grand Prix or sports car races.

In 1949 the Lago-Talbots apparently had it all their own way. Chiron took the laurels at the French GP, Sommer was first home in the Coupe du Salon, the Paris GP fell to Etancelin and Rosier managed a non-stop performance in the Belgian GP at a creditable 96.82 mph (155.9 kph) which won him the race. At Le Mans, it was Rosier once again; he brought home what amounted to a road-equipped GP car after driving virtually all 24 hours alone. Possibly it was that

LEFT & BELOW *The beautiful lines of the Letourneur et Marchand-bodied Lago America. Only 12 were built, using the BMW 2.5-litre V8 but it was too little and too late to save the company*

performance which inspired Pierre Levegh's attempt to drive for 24 hours without relief in the 1952 event. He almost succeeded, and he would surely have won had be accepted a second driver. None the less Mercedes-Benz were impressed enough to hire him although his 1955 Le Mans drive for them ended in tragedy.

Taken all in all, 1951 was a bit thin for the Suresnes cars in competition. Admittedly, the Dutch and Bordeaux GPs fell to the Lago-Talbot team, but these were the only victories although they also clocked up four second places. By this time, the factory were turning out as many as 1000 cars a year (a total Alvis and Armstrong-Siddeley rarely exceeded for example), a remarkable recovery from the ruins of the old STD days.

Just as Britain's double purchase tax on the higher priced cars decimated the ranks of the 'independent' manufacturers like Lea-Francis, France's penal taxation system gradually whittled down the number of grand

and expensive cars sold. 1952 was the beginning of the end as far as Formula One was concerned – wins in the Finnish and Australian Grands Prix scarcely rating a mention in the press of the day, although Whiteford won the latter event once again in 1953.

In an endeavour to beat the taxation system, Lago introduced a smaller production car in 1950 – the 2.7-litre 'Baby'. Said to produce a creditable 118 bhp it was offered with either synchromesh or preselector gearbox. Most peculiarly, presumably with an eye to export to the UK and Japan, it was produced only with right-hand drive... Its styling, however, was unfortunate and probably prompted unfair comparisons with some of the really elegant models which had left the factory since 1936. It was not a success and the whole range was restyled in 1952 and shown at the *salons*.

The following year a concerted effort was made with a new breed of lightweight aerodynamic competition cars said to produce 247 bhp, but although these continued to be fielded until 1957 they were never successful. Maserati 2.5-litre six-cylinder engines were used for the last two cars entered, one did not start and the other stalled on the grid and refused to restart.

With the Grand Prix team disbanded and production down to about 100 cars a year it

seemed as though the spark was gradually being extinguished in the old company. 1955 was the last year in which a new engine of the firm's own manufacture was introduced. It was a five-bearing 2.5-litre four following the pattern of previous types, and was allied to a four-speed ZF gearbox and attractive GT bodywork, but it was not used for long. By 1957 the firm were buying in 2.6-litre BMW V8s to install in the 2.5-litre chassis to form the Lago America. As the name suggests, it was a last-ditch attempt at earning US dollars.

The recipe of this V8-powered America should have appealed to the American market but that was not to be. Maybe it was because, in a sense, the spirit had gone out of the company with the disbanding of the Grand Prix team after so many years of glory in sports car and single-seater racing. Production progressed only falteringly.

Only 12 Americas were built in all which was something of a shame as the Letourneur et Marchand body was elegant and interesting, with odd features like a glassfibre roof and plexiglass rear screen. Its 2476 cc BMW V8 produced 150 bhp – enough to give the America quite respectable performance considering its bulk. Top speed was claimed to be 124 mph (200 kph), while its 0–60 mph time of 10.5 seconds was good for the era.

In 1958, with production down to a trickle and the workshops hired out to other firms, it was clear that Antonio Lago could not continue unaided for very much longer. 1959 saw Simca in control at Suresnes, although quite what they had in mind when they bought the firm is not clear. Possibly, being a young company, they sought the prestige of an old-established name under which to produce their higher priced models – or perhaps it was Lago-Talbot's sporting image which they wanted.

Whatever the reason, they did little to preserve the reputation of the marque. Since 1947, Ford had maintained a factory at Poissy, Seine-et-Oise, producing 2.2-litre and 3.9-litre V8s, the best-remembered of which was the Vedette. The French Ford company was the result of a pre-war deal between Ford and the ailing Mathis concern of Strasbourg and Asnieres whereby American-type Fords were made in the Mathis factories.

The firm was reorganised as Ford SAF at Poissy in 1947, but never prospered – largely because of the punitive taxes on the higher horsepower models – and in 1954 Ford threw in the towel and sold out to Simca. The Ford Vedette became the Simca Vedette, and at the time of the Simca takeover of Lago-Talbot a fair number of those old V8s were still in stock.

Simca used them up in the 2.5-litre Lago-Talbot chassis, and these pale shadows of the earlier great competition cars were the last model to reach the public, although a peculiar coupé with Simca Aronde engine graced the Talbot stand at the 1960 Paris Salon. It obviously excited no one, since that was the last year of production and, as if to signify the end of an era, it was also the year in which Antonio Lago died.

DELAHAY

In the mid-1930s the gulf between Grand Prix racers and Grand Tourers could be closed – by the right car. The Delahaye 135 did it with consummate ease

135

was such a humdrum lacklustre bumbler, and for a long time after that such a dismal imitation of ill-judged American designs, that to sneer at one would be as superfluous as to complain that crime was sinful. Then, at the 1933 Paris Salon (for the 1934 season), Delahaye produced the Superluxe, radically different from its predecessors, and with developments of it began to do as well in the sporting arena as in the market place; then it was time for people to sneer – and they did, averring that it had a lorry engine.

Delahaye had, to tell the truth, made a lot of lorries. They were good and enduring lorries, as it happens; and if their six-cylinder engine had enough torque to haul a laden lorry up a French Alp, then when installed in a car it would provide ample acceleration in a gear high enough to ensure a decent top speed, so why not? The only rational objection might be that a lorry engine would be too heavy; but since the chassis weight of the Type 135 was only 2061 lb (935 kg) at a time when an other-wise comparable English one weighed on average 2700 (1224 kg), and since the De-lahaye chassis was better behaved than its English contemporaries, the engine cannot have been too heavy.

The chassis of the Superluxe was thor-oughly modern by 1934 standards. Its main longerons were square-section steel tubes, carefully braced by crossmembers designed to give good torsional stiffness; a 1936 press photograph showed the car standing straight and level, with no evidence of distortion in its open (and therefore susceptible) body-work despite one front wheel being up on the camber and the other down in a gutter. The point being made was that the Delahaye had independent front suspension, by an interesting arrangement of transverse leaf spring extending to the bottom ends of the kingpin-carriers, single transverse links to the top ends, and longitudinal radius rods connected at about hub level. Simple fric-tion dampers were fitted, as at the rear where the live axle relied on Hotchkiss drive through very flat leaf springs.

The transmission was modern too – or at least it could be if the customer exercised the option for an electrically-operated Cotal epicyclic gearbox. The alternative was an orthodox cogbox (like the Cotal a four-speeder, but with only one reverse) which originally had constant-mesh gears only for third and top, and did not acquire a full set of synchronisers until 1938.

The gear ratios themselves (1st reason-able, 2nd and 3rd quite low, and top quite high – all in the Continental tradition) indi-cated that the gearbox would not have to be used a lot, thanks to the (dare we say it?) lorry-like torque of that engine. Three en-

'YOU ARE DRIVING ALONG a road at a steady 60 mph and, at the very moment you are passing a driveway, you see a car emerging from it. Before you have gone another quar-ter of a mile, the same car flashes past you. That's acceleration! That's Delahaye!'

More than thirty years have passes since I read that passage in a combined Delage/Delahaye sales brochure, and I may not have remembered it absolutely verbatim; but the message (like the other one: *That's ele-gance! That's Delage!*) was unforgettable. I remember wondering at the time whether the writer of the brochure had been im-pressed, as I was, by a similar descriptive passage published somewhat earlier, where the speed needed to be 100 mph because the car was a Grand Prix Mercedes-Benz....

For all Delahaye's nobly patriotic efforts with the V12 4½-litre car of 1937, they were never really competitive in GP racing. With their less ambitious six-cylinder Type 135, however, they were very effective indeed in sports-car racing, achieving considerable success as soon as they made the effort.

This was quite unexpected, bearing in mind the firm's previous history. It had been engaged in car manufacture since the very earliest days, when in 1894 Emile Delahaye set about making a motor somewhat like the contemporary Daimler. He had been a rail-way engineer – no disgrace, since the same could be said of W.O. Bentley, Marc Birkigt, and F.H. Royce – but nobody sneered at his cars for being built like locomotives. There was no need: for a long time the Delahaye

gines, actually, all of 107 mm stroke: the four-cylinder 2151 cc and six-cylinder 3227 cc versions had cylinders of 80 mm bore, while the 3557 cc six was bored out to 84 mm. The four-cylinder chassis remained a vehicle for semi-formal bodywork, the Type 134, a low-powered six (one carburettor, 85 bhp) did the same as the Type 148, long-wheelbase versions of both were evolved for seven-seater Pullman bodies, and the high-powered six became the 135.

With three carburettors on a manifold designed to pick up some heat from the exhaust (the detachable head with its pushrod-actuated overhead valves was not a crossflow type) the 3.2-litre car developed 110 bhp. Its performance had to be shown off, so a streamlined body with enclosed single-seat cockpit was mounted on a stripped bare-wheeled chassis and sent to the *piste de vitesse* at Montlhèry in 1934. After 48 hours (at over 107 mph 172 kph) and more than 10,000 kilometres (6214 miles) it came away with 11 international and seven world records to its credit.

What about cornering and braking? The car was stable, its suspension combining with a very wide rear track (58 inches/ 147 cm), compared with 55/140 cm at the front and a wheelbase of 116 inches (295 cm) to make it a natural understeerer at a time when most cars did the other thing. It was not too ponderous – that would never do when the worm-geared steering took only 1¾ turns from lock to lock – and because light weight had been carefully cultivated it was decently shod by the standards of its time, with 5.50–17 tyres on centre-lock Rudge-Whitworth wire wheels. They in turn made plenty of room for 14-inch (35.6 cm) drums housing Bendix self-servo brakes. Some contemporary testers claimed better than 1 g retardation from 40 mph (64 kph); their methods were suspect, but obviously the brakes were good, as Ferodo-lined Bendix brakes could be when in adjustment.

To prove all this to the public did not take long. In 1934 Perrot made best touring-car time at the Chateau Thierry hillclimb, and in the following year a works team won

the over-3 litre class in the International Alpine Rally. Thereafter the 3.2-litre Type 135 was known as the Coupe des Alpes model – except by the staunchly ignorant British press, who thought it was the Coupé des Alpes. When *Motor Sport* were able to test a well-used (20,000 miles/32,186 km) example in 1936 they found it '…an extremely hearty and vivid motor car…the car leaps forward in a heartening way and is clearly calling for straight roads and no hedges.'

The steering came in for particular praise, '…one of the best we have experienced, being very high geared with sufficient caster to pull the wheel back through the hands after a sharp corner and, with all that, light to handle…the car behaved beautifully on the various fast bends on

LEFT AND BOTTOM: *This is an example of a 1939 Delahaye 135M with bodywork by Vanden Plas, before the Belgian company became a subsidiary of Austin in 1946* **BELOW:** *A 1937 135 with extremely elegant Saoutchik coachwork*

which we tried it. It was in fact almost impossible even to make the tyres squeal…a car which is thoroughly exhilarating to drive.'

The car did well in several other events of 1934, winning the ladies' award in the Monte Carlo Rally and coming fifth at Le Mans; but the most important happening for Delahaye that year was its amalgamation with Delage.

Some of its new partner's reputation for elegance, quality, and racing ability, rubbed off on Delahaye. From then on, the competition career of the Type 135 was accompanied by no less glamorous a career in the fashion shows, the *concours d'élegance* which were then so popular in France because each car was accompanied (better still, driven) by a lady, and entries were judged according to the beauty of the ensemble. While the ladies dressed in model clothes from Schiaparelli, Patou, Molyneux or Creed, the cars enjoyed the attentions of the best French coachbuilders such as Saoutchik, Letourneur et Marchand, Figoni et Falaschi or Henri Chapron. Quite suddenly, the

Delahaye became not only an athletic 'man's car' but also a cosmetic 'ladies' car', immensely popular among those to whom proportions and styling mattered every bit as much as the sheer speed that the body design implied.

It was in some of these bodies that a modernized echo of the established Delahaye radiator grille first appeared. That was no bad thing: the standard grille had a very dated look about it, being copied (like others on French, English and even Italian cars) from a rather weak American cliché. On the Competition model of the Type 135, however, with its well-balanced body based on the 1935 Alpine Rally cars, the shield-like standard radiator stayed firmly and convincingly, flanked by a pair of low, close-set headlamps. The radiator grille concealed more than most people realised: beneath the heat exchanger for the coolant water was another for engine oil, provision being made for bypassing it in cold conditions. On the other hand, the cooling system lacked a thermostat; such things were not taken for granted, thirty years ago.

The Competition model appeared in 1936, and with its bigger bore it mustered 120 bhp, a figure to be compared with the 110 of the contemporary 3½-litre Bentley, for instance. That was a great year for the

ABOVE *Delahaye used a variety of coachbuilders for their cars, with this 1937 example by Pennock being less extreme than some other designs*

Delahaye in competition, but for serious racing there was a Competition Spéciale version which made no less than 160 bhp available. This engine had the same three Solex downdraught carburettors, but the compression ratio was raised from 7 to 8.2 : 1 and the rpm to 4200, which meant a mean piston velocity of 2949 ft/min. This was not considered an untoward figure then, but the corresponding figure for brake mean effective pressure was 139 psi, definitely healthy. The maximum speed was healthy, raised gearing allowing the makers to claim 125 mph (201 kph) – verified in 1937 when one of these cars lapped the Brooklands Outer Circuit at 126.09 mph (203 kph). The ordinary version was no slouch: geared to give 100 mph (161 kph) at 4000 rpm in top (or 63 mph/101 kph in third, which confirms the point made earlier about gearbox ratios), it could be expected to reach 105 mph (169 kph) even carrying a four-seater body. In those days, that was

RIGHT: *This 1947 example of the Delahaye 135 is of the MS type whose engine featured an 8:1 compression ratio, a six-branch exhaust manifold and some 130 bhp. The bodywork on this car is by the Parisian company of Henri Chapron. Note the elegant and rather unusual steering wheel. Style and performance were very happily combined in the Delahaye:* Motor Sport *described it as 'a hearty he-man's car' with beautiful behaviour on both fast bends and straight roads*

fast indeed for a saloon car.

The 1936 competition season was brilliant. Delahayes filled the first six places in the Marseille 3-hours race at Miramas. The Grand Prix de l'ACF was staged at Montlhéry as a sports-car race that year (to avoid it being a walk-over for the Germans) and Delahaye finished in 2–3–4 order behind the winning Bugatti. In the last Ulster TT, on the Ards circuit, Lebegue's car set a new lap record; in the Monte Carlo Rally, Schell's car finished second.

Opposition was tougher in 1937, as the new Talbot Lago found its feet and the little BMW 328 showed that Germany could also

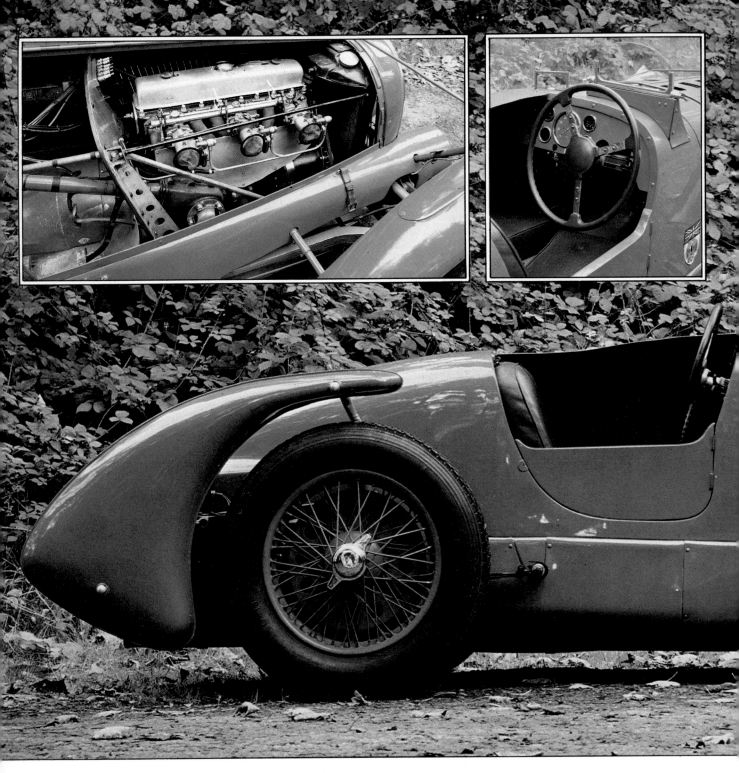

TOP *The engine of Delahaye in Competition Special form with three Solex downdraught carburettors and high-compression engine produced more than 160 bhp*

make a modern sports car. Delahaye had to be content with second and third places after 24 hours at Le Mans, but the end of the 12-hours race at Donington saw the Delhaye of Bira and Dobbs victorious. Third place in the Mille Miglia was even better; victory in the Monte Carlo Rally sounded best of all.

Still, what every sports-car maker really wants is victory at Le Mans. It came in 1938, but it would be wrong to suppose that the Delahaye 135 was the fastest car there. The one driven by Chaboud and Tremoulet was, however, more reliable than its faster rivals (including the V12). The same story was told in 1939 when a curiously half-baked competition was set up at Brooklands to find the fastest road car in Britain. Some obviously

promising candidates were not entered, or did not start; one or two others, such as Hugh Hunter's supercharged 2.9-litre Alfa Romeo and Ian Connell's unblown 4-litre Darracq, suffered troubles, whereas the ex-Bira Delahaye (by then the property of R.R.C. Walker, who entered Arthur Dobson as driver) ran reliably to win. In that year, however, the Type 135 was no longer a front runner in international racing. Rallying was a different

matter: successes were numerous, including first and second in the Paris-Nice event and a tie with Hotchkiss for first place in the Monte Carlo Rally. While Bugatti again won the 24-hours race at Le Mans, the Type 135 could only run with the pack to finish sixth, eighth and 11th.

Ten years later, the Type 135 was running again at Le Mans, finishing fifth, ninth and 10th against opposition that in some cases was fifteen years younger. It was amazing how well the car did in early post-war racing, winning at Brussels in 1946, at Chimay in 1947 and 1948, and at Comminges in 1949. Delahaye had spent the war concentrating on its lorries; when free to make cars again, revival of the Type 135 was the ob-

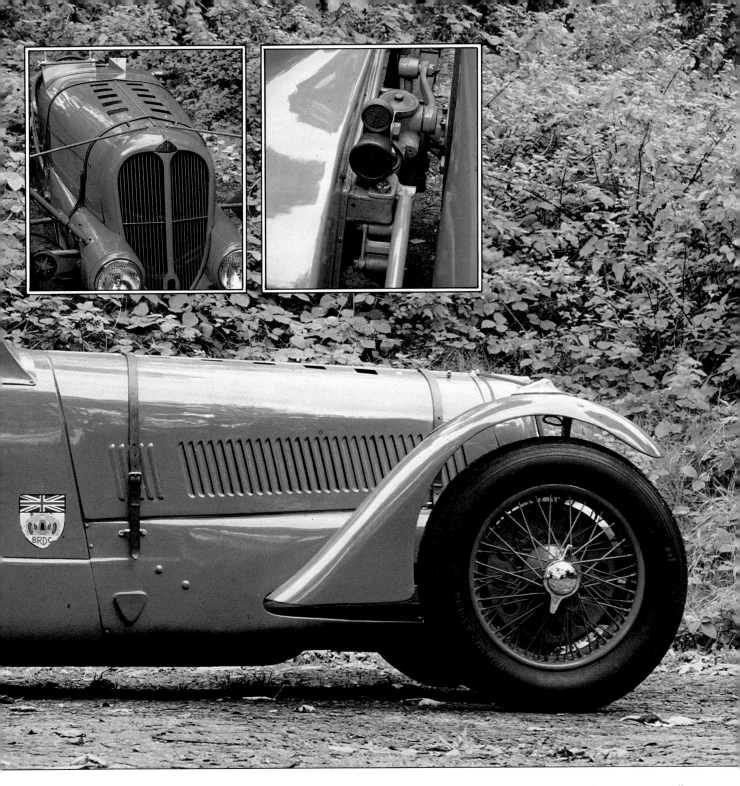

vious course, with new factory-built body-work styled by Philippe Charbonneaux appearing in 1947.

A year later they had a new engine ready. The old 3½-litre six was by now coded MS, the first letter signifying an 8 : 1 compression ratio and the second denoting a six-branch exhaust system, and could be called upon for 130 bhp; but by this time most makers of in-line sixes were under the mistaken impression (though Bristol knew better) that seven main bearings were better than four. The new engine was built accordingly: it had a displacement of 4½ litres, but it was very heavy. In circuit racing it was also unreliable, but the new car (known as the type 175) did win the 1951 Monte Carlo.

This is the Prince Bira of Siam Delahaye 135 which later became the property of Rob Walker, and was the machine entered by Walker for Arthur Dobson to drive at Brooklands to take the spurious title of 'Fastest Road Car in Britain'

What it could not win was customers. The times were not right for something so costly to buy and to maintain; once again Delahaye found it was better occupied concentrating on lorries and things that were truly commercial vehicles. The French army was a good customer, for whom the firm developed a 4×4 neo-Jeep which actually scored the last race success for Delahaye in the 1951 Algiers/Cape rally.

By 1952 the only private car still catalogued was the Type 235. This was in effect a 1938 Type 135 clad in an up-to-date factory-built body, and it was a smart and fast car in the best tradition: a 235 saloon put 113 miles (182 km) into the hour around the Montlhéry banking, convincing support for the claim of 152 bhp from that old engine. Lorries were a better proposition, though, and soon they were the only one: Delage was in the same dire straits as Delahaye, and after nine years of amalgamation they were taken over by Hotchkiss. Very soon an even better proposition was made by the Brandt organisation, which swallowed up the entire group; in 1956 the name of Delahaye was dropped.

Italy

It is almost impossible to make a shortlist of great Italian cars from such a vast number of possible candidates. The car occupies a rarified position in the Italian psyche and the extraordinary wealth of natural talent and expertise within the country has resulted in the creation of some truly glorious machines which are universally admired.

Of the pre-war period, the Lancia Lambda set new standards of handling and performance. This was due largely to the independent front suspension and unitary body construction

which were highly effective and far ahead of their time.
With so many strong and equally matched contenders, such as
Ferrari, Maserati, Lamborghini, Alfa Romeo and Lancia vying for
post-war recognition, the real problem is in deciding which
models to exclude from a truly impressive list.
With their 12-cylinder engines, shattering performances and
massive charisma enveloped in beautiful, handcrafted bodies,
Ferrari's multiple claims are extremely difficult to ignore, and
have been given the accolade of greatness worldwide.

FERRARI
275

Designed to compete against a rising tide of performance cars, the 275 was the first Ferrari with all-independent suspension, five gears and a four-cam, 300 bhp V12

FOR A CAR which remained in production for only four years, and of which fewer than 1000 were built, the Ferrari 275 has had a remarkable impact in the realm of the classic two-seater, high-performance GT coupé. For perhaps a decade after the last 275 was completed in 1968, the car was widely regarded merely as one of Ferrari's stepping-stones on the way to pre-eminence as a builder of exotic road cars. However, by the late 1970s prices of 275s were beginning to rise, and today they command sums as high as you are likely to encounter for any post-war classic car (except one other Ferrari, the extremely rare Daytona Spyder).

In the mainstream of Ferrari development the 275 might be said to have fitted between the earlier 250 and the later Daytona. In fact the Daytona is not the same sort of beast, since the 250 and 275 were really Ferrari's 'light' coupés at a time when the heavier 330s were also on the scene. The 'light' role has since been assumed by the Dino 308s, though these lack the appeal of the 275's V12 engine and the straightforwardness of the front-engined layout.

The 275 was an important design for Ferrari in many ways, for it was the first road-going Ferrari to have all independent suspension, a proper five-speed gearbox and, eventually, a four-cam engine. It also replaced the 250 at a vital moment when Ferrari's reputation was under threat from two quarters: from Jaguar, whose E-type offered highly competitive performance and a quality chassis at an unbelievably low price, and from the upstart Lamborghini, whose factory only a few miles from Modena had started producing GT cars with four-cam V12s of a quality to excite the *aficionado*.

Compared with the 250, therefore, the 275 had to offer three things above all if it was to succeed. Its performance had to be better, its chassis improved and its appearance superb. It succeeded in all three.

The performance aspect was the most easily attended to. There was still some stretch left in the classic Colombo-designed 60-degree V12 which had started Ferrari on his path as a serious car-builder. Not a lot, but enough. There was no easy way in which the stroke could be extended beyond the 58.8 mm of the 250 unit, but the apertures for the 'wet' liners in the alloy block could be further eased out to take the bore to

LEFT *The flowing lines of a pristine 1967 Ferrari 275 GTB/4, capable of 161 mph (250 kph) with its four-cam 3286 cc V12*

257

77 mm. This meant that the capacity was increased from a nominal 3 litres to 3.3; actually to 3286 cc. In those days Ferrari still used the system of naming models after the capacity of a single cylinder of the V12 engine, so that the new car was designated 275 in succession to the 250. It is worth bearing in mind that his choice of engine capacity also had a particular appeal to the American market, since 3286 cc is, as nearly as most people would care to calculate, 200 cubic inches.

Like all Ferrari engines, the enlarged unit was happy to run at extremely high speeds. Its two camshafts, one per cylinder bank, were driven by triple-row chains and operated the valves through stiff rockers. Like its predecessors it was all-alloy (of course) with a fully-machined steel crankshaft and one ignition distributor per cylinder bank, driven directly from the rear end of the camshaft. In standard form it breathed through three twin-choke Weber carburettors and produced a claimed 280 bhp at no less than 7600 rpm! Owners for whom this was not enough could, however, specify *six* rather smaller twin-choke Webers to give them one choke per cylinder and 300 bhp at 7500 rpm.

Quite what this did for fuel consumption is probably best left unrecorded, but then that was not a consideration for the sort of person who was in a position to buy such an expensive car in the first place!

The new car's performance was helped very considerably by a brand-new, Ferrari-designed five-speed gearbox, the first one used in any of the company's road cars (when the need for five speeds had become evident in the late 1950s, Ferrari had plugged the gap by adding Laycock overdrive to the four-speed boxes of the 250 and 400). The new gearbox, lighter and sweeter than the unit being developed in parallel for the 330, was installed at the rear, in unit with the final drive. The object of this, as in the Lancia road cars which had earlier used the layout and the Alfa Romeos and Porsches which came later, was to achieve the best possible static balance in order to help the handling. In practice it also meant that the engine could be mounted relatively far forward, easing design problems in the scuttle area and making for a roomier cabin.

Where the handling was concerned, Ferrari acknowledged – not least under the pressure of the Jaguar E-type – that there was little more to be wrung out of the live rear axle and leaf springs. At least his engineers had a wealth of racing-car experience on which to call, and it was no surprise that the 275 emerged, not with any space- and cost-

RIGHT & ABOVE *Views of the car shown on the previous pages. Pininfarina's lithe and well-balanced design has weathered extremely well, and only its relatively high waistline, quarter-light windows and interior trim reveal its '60s origins*

saving compromise, but with a proper double-wishbone independent rear suspension to match the front-end arrangement. Better still, as far as the road-going enthusiast was concerned, the suspension geometry and the setting up of spring and damper rates was carried out by the late Mike Parkes, who had recently arrived at the factory and was able to make sure not only that each end of the car worked properly, but that the two were well matched – an object not always achieved with all-wishbone suspensions.

The chassis bore few hallmarks of inspiration. It was based on two massive lengthwise tubes which, as has often been pointed out, were very slightly oval in section and made of a special grade of steel, with the result that repairs were almost impossible for anyone but a Ferrari dealer to carry out properly! The tubes formed the sides of a central ladder-frame with simple cross-bracing, and also provided a footing for everything else: the outrigged side extensions which located the body sides, and the multi-tubed sub-assemblies housing the rear suspension and transmission, the front suspension and the scuttle components. None of these was linked to another in the three-dimensional way which would have endowed the chassis with decent stiffness; instead the 275 depended heavily on the body to add resistance to twisting.

One result was that the convertibles – and the competition versions built with lightweight aluminium bodies in place of steel – were notably less stiff than the standard coupé. Nor was the 275 especially light for a two-seater standing on a wheelbase of just 94.5 inches (290 cm): the coupé weighed a claimed 2425 lb (1100 kg), only 200 lb (91 kg) less than the Jaguar E-type with its hefty XK engine and far from lightweight transmission.

Pininfarina designed two bodies for the 275, one the very attractive coupé which owed something to the prettier versions of the 250, the other a less than inspired Spyder. The results went into production in 1964 as the 275GTB, whose body was actually produced by faithful Ferrari coachbuilder Scaglietti, and the 275GTS, for which the Pininfarina factory itself supplied the bodies. During the following 18 months some 250 GTBs and 200 GTSs were produced, along with a handful of special derivatives: 10 GTB/Cs (C for *Competizione*) with lightweight alloy bodies, and reputedly nine Spyder models built for Ferrari's representative in the USA, Luigi Chinetti of NART (North American Racing Team).

Ferrari production figures are notoriously difficult to pin down, and exact totals of some models may never be known. Calculating any such total retrospectively is also fraught with danger since it is sometimes said that the survival rate of some models is more than 100 per cent, due to certain cars being cloned at some point.

In the tradition of the time, Ferrari was loth to let cars anywhere near the European motoring press for assessment. One test was published in Britain, by *Autosport*…after

Patrick McNally had gone so far as to buy a 275GTB with aluminium body! In the USA, Chinetti had other ideas about press testing, and several American publications have 275 road tests on file. The general consensus was that the early 275GTB had a maximum speed of almost 160 mph (257 kph), reached 60 mph (97 kph) in a fraction over 6 seconds and consumed fuel at about 13 mpg when driven with spirit. The handling was universally praised, but the brakes were universally condemned – unless, tactfully, they were not mentioned at all…. The 275 had been given disc brakes all round, but by modern standards they were thin and small, hamstrung among other things by Ferrari's adoption of 14 in (36 cm) rather than 15 in (38 cm) wheels which left that much less room for a decent braking system. Things were made worse by the inefficient Italian-made brake servo, and the usual result was horrifying fade – unless a better servo and harder than standard pads were fitted, when the result was severe overheating of the discs and boiling of the brake fluid!

The brakes were not the only problem to afflict the 275. Two other snags were soon identified, one concerning the transmission and the other the body itself (eventually, of course, there emerged a third problem: the terrifying susceptibility of the body to rust).

The transmission might almost have been expected to give trouble, given the fact that its layout was new and relatively untried. The engine, complete with clutch, was rigidly bolted to the front of the chassis and the gearbox/final drive assembly was equally solidly located at the other end. The propeller shaft which connected the two was thin and whippy – so much so that it was given extra support by a centre steady-bearing to keep its effective length below the critical flailing-point. The idea was that the shaft should have enough flexibility to allow for any misalignment between engine and gearbox caused by chassis flexing (or, indeed, less than perfectly aligned assembly). In that object it more or less succeeded, except that in the process it set up uncomfortable vibrations which were as bad for clutch and gearbox life as they were for cabin comfort.

The second problem was one of aerodynamics. Leaning heavily on competition experience, Pininfarina had endowed the 275 with a highly effective lift-killing back end with a concave Kamm-panel in the tail: its efficiency was proved by the speed with which it collected exhaust-borne oil mist and dirt. The front end of the car looked smooth, with plexiglass headlamp covers

FAR LEFT & BOTTOM *An early 275 GT Spyder, sold in America. Extremely attractive, the convertible was less rigid than the coupé* LEFT *One of the very first 275 GTB/4s, from 1967 – the car which appears on p 1130.* BELOW *Another GTS, a 1967 right-hand drive model built for the British market*

and a pronounced lip above the cooling air intake. In practice, the airflow round and over this lip caused enough front-end lift to make the steering feel light and the stability questionable at speeds over 100 mph (161 kph).

The transmission problem was temporarily 'fixed' by adding a constant-velocity joint to each end of the propeller shaft, but meanwhile work rapidly proceeded on a proper cure which was soon added to the 275GTB. The change was to link the engine and gearbox with a hollow torque-tube containing the propeller shaft (which still retained its centre-steady bearing, now within the tube); this is a layout which finds a modern echo in the Porsche 924/944.

With the proper relationship between the two ends of the transmission thus established, the engine could be located on rubber mountings, which served also to reduce the amount of noise and vibration fed to the cabin through the scuttle. What the torque tube did *not* do, at least as directly as some Ferrari enthusiasts claimed, is add anything to that questionable chassis stiffness. On the other hand, the rubber engine mountings probably reduced the torque-input of the engine to the chassis.

The aerodynamic problem was very simply solved – with the aid of some early wind-tunnel work – by extending the nose and making the cooling air intake into more of a tunnel. The result was the so-called 'long-nose' shape which clearly marks out the more desirable type of 275GTB (and all GTB/4s). With this modification, stability is exemplary up to the highest speeds of which the car is capable. The new nose was fitted to

ABOVE AND BELOW *Two 275 GTBs in action. Making full use of the performance was hindered by the small disc brakes*

the last 200-odd 275GTBs to be built, and apart from helping stability it must also have improved the car's drag coefficient since there is evidence that the long-nose car is up to 5 mph (8 kph) faster.

As always, Ferrari was not content to let the 275 endure a long production run without introducing major changes. The one which had the most obvious influence – and turned the car into such a sought-after classic – was the switch from one to two overhead camshafts per cylinder bank. This move was as much as anything a riposte to Lamborghini, and as had so often been to their advantage, the Ferrari designers had only to dip into their store of racing development programmes and components to

get the job done. It so happened that twin-cam heads had been designed and made for the sports-car racing programme in 1957, and then discarded as that king of racing veered more and more in the direction of fitting Formula One machinery with nominal sports car bodywork. The twin-cam design was, almost literally, dusted off and installed in the 275. Outwardly, the only sign of the new engine under the longer nose was the appearance of a power bulge in the bonnet to achieve clearance over the inboard cam-covers.

The adaptation was simpler than might have been supposed since all the necessary passages and bolt-holes lined up: the camshaft drive was adapted by running the

existing chain round idler sprockets at the front of each cylinder head – thus retaining a nicely symmetrical chain layout with location and tension via a jockey-wheel in each of the three chain runs – and the drive was finally taken to the camshafts by simple gears. The cam profiles were notably sharp in profile and high in lift, which can give rise to problems with the bucket-tappets and adjustment shims if the correct clearances are not maintained.

The four-cam engine carried the Ferrari house designation Tipo 226, to distinguish it from the single-cam Tipo 312, and breathed through six Weber carburettors to produce 300 bhp at a staggering 8000 rpm. At first sight it may appear strange that Ferrari

ABOVE *A 275 GTB/4 convertible owned by NART and shown at Modena in 1983*

should have gone to so much trouble and then failed to produce any more power than is quoted for the single-overhead-cam six-carburettor engine. The answer of course is that mere peak power rarely reveals everything. The 275GTB/4 delivered more power more readily all the way from 5000 rpm onwards and the car proved usefully faster than the plain 275GTB as a result. The gearing was chosen to make the utmost of the power spread available, and the most authoritative GTB/4 test to be published (by the American *Automobile Quarterly*) gave the car maximum speeds of 52, 75, 101 and 127 mph (84, 121, 162 and 204 kph) with an outright maximum of 166 mph (267 kph) in

fifth, and 100 mph (161 kph) reached from rest in 15 seconds. If you prefer, you may calculate on the ratios published by Ferrari for the final year of the 275GTB/4, which suggest that at 8000 rpm the car should have been doing 61, 94, 119 and no less than 150 mph (98, 151, 192 and 241 kph) in the first four gears.

By the time those final cars were in production, many detail changes had been made to the 275's overall specification. The original 6.5 in (16.5 cm) alloy rims and 195-14 tyres had given way to 7 in (18 cm) rims and 205-14 Michelin XWX tyres, accepted as being by far the best tyre choice for the car. The clutch had become a Borg and Beck diaphragm-spring unit, to the benefit of operating effort, while a ZF limited-slip differential – just as efficient, more reliable and certainly much cheaper – had replaced the original in-house Ferrari effort. The single fuel tank had given way to twin tanks with a

capacity of nearly 20 gallons (90 litres). Nothing of any significance had been done about the brakes, which meant that the GTB/4 was almost dangerously under-equipped in this respect, at least by modern standards.

There were of course many areas in which the 275 left much to be desired. It was, by common consent, quieter than the earlier 250 – but the 250 left a great deal of room for improvement in that respect. Its heating and ventilation were rudimentary in the extreme: at least one car was fitted with air-conditioning in an attempt to improve things, but that was one idea which never caught on, at least in Europe.

The overall standard of trim and equipment was far from the best, unless the original buyer ordered something special, like Connolly hide throughout. One must

BELOW *The balance of the styling reflected the even weight distribution achieved with the transmission layout. The 300 bhp V12,* BELOW, *is fed by six Weber carburettors*

remember that at the time, room had to be left for the heavyweight 'luxury' Ferrari 330 to go one better…. It is probably fair to say that in this area, not to mention that of protection against corrosion, most of the 275s which survive are much better today than they were when they left the factory.

The 275 story came to an end late in 1968 with the emergence of the final GTB/4. By that time some 280 of the four-cam cars had been made, bringing the overall total, at an informed guess, to about 950. Yet this was the car which, more than any other, established Ferrari as a builder of road-going cars which combined the highest possible performance with almost equally high standards of road behaviour. And if the brakes were not quite up the job, Ferrari could always have said, like Bugatti in an earlier era, that his cars were designed to go, not to stop.

EVOLUTION

Introduced at the 1964 Paris motor show, the Ferrari 275 was available in GTB (Berlinetta coupé) and GTS (Spyder convertible) forms, both styled by Pininfarina. The car was based on a tubular steel ladder frame braced with tubular outriggers and diagonal braces, and was the first Ferrari to have all-independent suspension, achieved with coils and double wishbones, and the first model to have a five-speed gearbox, which was installed in unit with the final drive. Discs were fitted all round and the 15 in (38 cm) wheels were cast magnesium. The engine was the Colombo-designed V12 with its bore increased to give a capacity of 3286 cc. In standard form, with three twin-choke Webers, it produced a claimed 280 bhp at 7600 rpm; with the option of six twin-choke Webers, power rose to 300 bhp at 7500 rpm. In standard form the car's maximum speed was 161 mph (250 kph), with

a 0–60 mph time of 6.2 seconds. Several competition versions were also built, with all-aluminium bodies

1965 The nose of the 275 was re-shaped to provide extra downforce at high speeds. The transmission was also modified, with a torque tube installed between the engine and gearbox/final drive to improve handling

1966 The 275GTB/44 was introduced, fitted with a four-cam version of the V12 engine and fitted with six Weber carburettors. The engine produced 300 bhp at 8000 rpm, but had a much wider power band than the earlier version. Other changes included the adoption of a ZF limited-slip differential, wider wheels and increased fuel capacity

1968 Ferrari 275 discontinued. Total production: 950 (approx)

De Tomas

They are not quite Italian thoroughbreds, but the Ford-engined Pantera and Mangusta are both exotic and fast

IT WAS THE FASHION, in the Italy of the 1960s, for small-scale car manufacturers to aspire to join the exclusive club founded by Ferrari and Maserati. It might be said that Lamborghini tried and succeeded, that Iso tried and failed, and that de Tomaso tried and tried – and is still trying. De Tomaso's principal claim to club membership lies in the Pantera, a formidable mid-engined GT car which has been in production with remarkably few changes since 1970. It has achieved that feat despite all the financial and political complications which have surrounded it.

The Pantera finds it roots in an earlier de Tomaso design, the Mangusta. This was de Tomaso's first attempt at building a car to a formula which had seemed attractive at the time (in 1965), that of adopting the same mid-engined layout which had so quickly swept the board in Grand Prix racing and applying it to a two-seat GT car, but avoiding the risk and expense of building a suitably

high-powered engine by buying in one of the American 'muscle-car' V8s.

The idea looked promising on paper, the moreso because de Tomaso already had a useful starting point in the form of the Vallelunga, a mid-engined car with a strong backbone chassis, a bored-out Ford Cortina GT engine and a suspension that borrowed heavily from racing car practice. The same basic layout was adopted for the new GT model; it was simply (or so it may have seemed) a matter of scaling the thing up and fitting a much bigger engine. The actual choice of engine was almost inevitable. De Tomaso had admired the Shelby Cobra to the extent that it had triggered his original thinking about how much better a car he could build by combining that kind of power and torque with an advanced mid-engined chassis. Thus the engine which went into the Mangusta was, sure enough, the Ford 289 cu in/4.7-litre V8. De Tomaso had his mid-engined advance on the Cobra and his delight was reflected in his choice of name for the new model. Mangusta is Italian for mongoose, and as everyone knows who remembers the tales of Rikki-Tikki-Tavi, the mongoose eats cobras for breakfast.

There was a lot to be said for the 289 as an engine choice. It was cheap and reliable as well as powerful. It had to be, since it was fitted to the original Ford Mustang in its hundreds of thousands. It was also, naturally enough, fairly heavy even though Ford engineers had already brought thin-walled casting to a fine art. De Tomaso experimented with alloy components to replace the cast iron but the most he could save, reportedly, was 55 lb (25 kg) though reworked porting and other changes were

Views of the Pantera GT5S, a model first shown in late 1984. With its 351 cu in Ford V8 and 350 bhp, the car was capable of over 160 mph (257 kph), with acceleration to match. The neat interior, **ABOVE,** *is sumptuously trimmed in leather*

supposed to have resulted in a power output of 437 bhp compared with the claimed 305 bhp (at 6200 rpm) in standard form.

Because the engine was bulky whichever way you looked at it, even without the encumbrance of overhead camshafts, it was mounted low in relation to the rest of the chassis and the quill input shaft to the gearbox passed under the final drive rather than above it as in most road-going transaxles. As a result the centre of gravity was usefully lowered but the ground clearance was much less usefully reduced. Clearance beneath the vital shaft also restricted the possible clutch size, forcing de Tomaso to use a three-plate clutch which turned out to be extremely heavy in operation. The five-speed gearbox was provided by ZF.

If the mechanical details were interesting, the Mangusta's most substantial reasons for acclaim lay in its body, styled by Giugiaro in one of his first efforts which really caught the imagination. It had a smooth purity of line which only offends the modern eye, if it can be said to do so at all, in the high lip of its nose, needed to make space for the twin headlamps on either side of the grille. Possibly the most remarkable feature of the body was the splitting of its entire back end into two great gull-wings hinged to a central spine. Lifting both panels revealed the total lack of luggage space in the rear: the Mangusta's only toothbrush-stowage was in the shallow nose compartment. The spare wheel was installed above the gearbox, while the battery lived in one rear corner and the tool-kit in the other.

Very few journalists ever got their hands on the Mangusta for any length of time, but a small party visited Modena early in 1969, in the company of de Tomaso's first prospective British dealer. One of that party was the late Mike Twite, then Deputy Editor of *CAR*, and his initial impressions were favourable: he spoke of the car's remarkable quietness and of its very light though low-geared steering (there were 4¼ turns of the wheel between the extremes of a mediocre lock). The handling, however, was something else: 'Going into a bend fast on a dry road the front end ploughs outwards in a strong understeer attitude accompanied by a lateral pitching motion and loads of tyre squeal. Then, as power is applied to make a fast exit

year to the USA, while small-scale production of right-hand-drive cars was shortly to begin for the British market. In fact only about 400 Mangustas were ever built, and the handful that came to Britain all had left-hand drive. Events were overtaking the car and something else – rather more rational – was to take its place.

That rationalisation emerged in the shape of a close tie-up with Ford and a reworking of the Mangusta concept to produce the Pantera. In the first instance, the Pantera was an expression of de Tomaso's realisation that the Mangusta was all wrong when viewed as a large-scale production car. That hadn't mattered in the early 1960s when de Tomaso was working out of a tiny workshop in Modena, but it carried more weight when

LEFT *The flowing lines of the Mangusta were styled by Italian master Giugiaro, and large gull-wing covers,* ABOVE LEFT, *gave good access to the Ford V8*

ABOVE *The Pantera, styled by Tom Tjaarda had a more muscular appearance than the Pantera which it replaced, although mechanically it was similar*

from the corner, the tail begins to whip round and the driver is forced to work furiously on the low-geared steering to catch the slide.'

It may well have been that individual cars varied considerably in their suspension geometry, because other writers, including Paul Frère, are on record with the opinion that the Mangusta handled very well. The chassis exploited the obvious trick of having wider wheels and tyres at the back than at the front to try to balance the handling, but the weight bias was remarkably rearward for a mid-engine car – the claimed front/rear weight ratio of 45/55 is about as believable as the stated 2610 lb (1184 kg) kerb weight – and can't have helped things at all. The Mangusta was almost certainly the victim of the heavy development exercises with high-speed radial-ply tyres: Twite's test car was on German Dunlop SPs, and he mused on the effect of a change to Michelins or Pirellis.

According to Twite's report, orders were in hand for the supply of 300 Mangustas per

he developed visions of boosting his turnover to finance further expansion, after he had bought Ghia's prototype shop, and then Vignale's factory, to find more space.

None of it would have happened at all but for large injections of cash from the American Rowan company, with whose top management de Tomaso's wife Isabel was closely related. That link with the USA was one which proved highly significant. In the late 1960s Ford nurtured ambitions to buy into a prestige European car manufacturer, but it was rebuffed by Ferrari and failed to dislodge the stricken management of Lancia. Next on the list there appeared de Tomaso, a user of Ford engines, builder of the beautiful Mangusta and a company with plans for a much more efficient successor – *and* with an 80 per cent USA shareholding (Rowan's return for all the cash they had put up). The result was that Ford bought out the Rowan shareholding for straight cash.

Ford's plan was that de Tomaso would

build the new Pantera in much larger numbers and ship the bulk of production to the USA, where the model would be sold as a prestige, high-margin operation out of selected Ford showrooms. To make as sure as possible that the programme would be carried through without hiccups, Ford engineers were seconded to Italy to assist with Pantera development.

De Tomaso had a new engineering team of his own, led by Gianpaolo Dallara, and they were more than willing to fall in with the Ford suggestion ('only a suggestion, but let's not forget who's making it') that the Mangusta backbone chassis should be discarded in favour of something nearer to a monocoque shell. That should certainly have led to much better structural efficiency, and no doubt it did, since most of the Mangusta body shell (basically unstressed) was steel anyway; but the eventual quoted kerb weight of the Pantera was a credible 3100 lb (1406 kg), which is why some people cast doubt over the earlier Mangusta figures. There is no way to explain the difference by looking at relative sizes, since the Pantera is exactly as wide and high as the Mangusta (to the millimetre, according to the factory-quoted dimensions) while the Pantera is just 10 mm (0.4 in) longer in the wheelbase but 5 mm (0.2 in) shorter overall!

Despite this astonishing similarity of dimensions, close enough to make one question whether the Pantera really was a completely different car, there is no doubt that Dallara had made it so. It was not simply that the backbone chassis had been replaced by a shell of fabricated sheet steel in which substantial bending and torsional loads were carried through the roof. The whole engine and transmission installation had changed. A new Ford V8, first introduced for the Mustang and allied American models in 1969, now replaced the 289 unit. The new engine, the 351 cu in/5.7-litre V8, offered a reliable 310 bhp at 5400 rpm when fitted with the American emissions gear and 330 bhp when 'stripped' for Europe. The drive was still taken through a five-speed ZF gearbox, but now the transmission was the normal way up, with the input shaft above the differential, and one result was the ability to fit a much more progressive single-plate clutch of large diameter. The suspension was reworked to consist of more conventional double wishbones at both ends (without the very long rear drag links of the Mangusta) and tyre choice settled on the Michelin XWX.

The body certainly looked completely different, chunkier and more aggressive than Giugiaro's Mangusta. It was the work of Tom Tjaarda, working in-house at Ghia, and it differed in many practical respects from the earlier car. The nose line was lower and

TOP *Interior accommodation in the Pantera was much better than the older Mangusta which was very cramped for taller drivers* **TOP RIGHT** *The surprisingly spacious engine compartment swallows the American V8 with ease*

certainly far better aerodynamically, a move made possible by the fitting of pop-up headlamps (which were never powerful enough for the car's performance). The engine cover opened upwards in a single piece, hatchback fashion, and revealed not only the engine but also the principal luggage space. This was created by the removal of the spare wheel to the front, where a slight widening of the track had made just enough room for one of the earliest 'space-savers'. In theory there was a second luggage locker in the nose, but it was so small that few owners can have bothered with it.

The Pantera was officially launched in 1970, and controversy immediately surrounded the question of how many were being made. Ford's intention had been to produce 4000 cars a year, but there is no suggestion from any source that anything like this figure was ever achieved. The controversy really surrounds the years 1971/73, when production was claimed to run well into four figures, but informed yet independent sources estimate that there was a maximum of 300 Panteras a year. It is certainly suspicious that the official de Tomaso production figures suddenly fall from 2718 in 1972 and 2000 in 1973 to 196 in 1974 – the first year in which they were audited by ANFIA, the Italian equivalent of the SMMT.

However, it is entirely probable that Pantera production peaked and fell away rapidly, because the car never had the success that was hoped for in America. Persistent overheating problems were just one of its little nightmares; the energy crisis of 1973/74 was another, and the terminal one as far as its success on the US market was concerned.

There remained Europe, where the car would of course be much more savagely judged against its exotic contemporaries and where the Ford engine would be much less of a perceived advantage (there was no question of every European Ford dealer being 'happy to service it and have all the parts in stock'). The car was quick, but how quick? What did it suffer in refinement through its use of the big V8?

For the author, some of those questions were answered when *Autocar* tested a Pantera GTS in 1972. The car was indeed quick, to the extent that it had the highest maximum speed recorded that year: 159 mph (256 kph). It reached 60 mph (96 kph) in 6.2 seconds and 100 mph (161 kph) in 15.3 seconds, making it at the time the third most

LEFT *A 500 bhp Pantera built for modified GT racing, as full production car homologation was not possible. In this form it achieved only slight success. As might have been predicted, the Pantera was a quick car, but not quick enough when pitted against lighter and better handling competition*

accelerative car the magazine had ever sub-jected to full test (after the Ferrari Daytona and the Aston Martin V8). Not surprisingly, it swallowed fuel at the rate of 13 mpg, which was not nearly so alarming in 1972 as it was two years later. The test car, converted to right-hand-drive by the factory, disgraced itself when the brake-pedal linkage – an appalling piece of slipshod design – fell apart during brake-fade testing, leaving the crew faced with a very short remaining straight into a wire fence, and a handbrake which had already proved almost totally ineffective when used on the move. It says much for the skill of Dave Thomas (the author was cowering in the passenger seat) that the Pantera and fence did not meet.

Like the Mangusta, the Pantera used wider tyres at the rear than at the front in a search for balanced handling. One result was excellent traction. *Autocar* recorded a remarkable 2.3 seconds to 30 mph (48 kph), and the 60 mph result might have been better still but for a baulky gearchange. As far as the handling was concerned, the Pan-tera had been improved by quicker steering than the Mangusta's (3.5 turns of the wheel between locks) without being impossibly heavy to manoeuvre at low speed. The hand-ling balance felt reasonable although there was always the danger, as in any very power-ful car with a limited-slip differential, that too hasty an entry to a corner, or the prema-ture application fo full throttle, could push it into strong understeer from which the re-covery was likely to be untidy. A stronger warning, though, was sounded about wet-road handling: '…over-exuberance can lead to complete front-end breakaway…the re-sponse to [lifting off to correct] can be disconcertingly slow.' Despite the Pantera's four large ventilated disc brakes, the testers were not impressed by the results, quite apart from the worrying failure.

If anything, the real disappointment of the Pantera was its lack of comfort and refinement. As in so many supercars, the footwells were cramped and the problem compounded by the familiar Italian fault of placing the wheel too far forward in relation to the pedals. The rearward visibility was extremely poor, and although the high-speed ride was better than expected, the engine could never have been mistaken for a classic overhead-cam V12, or indeed any-thing but what it was. There was little ques-tion, with the Pantera priced very close to its British and Italian-engined rivals, that the car made little sense except to somebody who wanted to be different. For all de Tomaso's hopes, it had no perceptible superiority.

However, it seems that scattered around Europe there are just enough lovers of the different to keep the Pantera ticking over. It

still trickles along in production alongside the front-engined Deauville and Long-champs, possibly because there seems no serious reason for stopping it, partly because it is de Tomaso policy to run a division of his now-expanded empire, including Maserati and Innocenti, which still carries his own name and, to honour the land of his birth, the badge with the colours of Argentina.

From time to time people have tried their hand at using the Pantera in competition, especially in tarmac rallies like the Giro d'Italia. Cars were prepared by the factory to the old Group 4 (modified GT) formula, since there was no real question of production-car homologation, and later there was a Pantera GT4 to the same speci-fication actually included in the factory price list. Unfortunately, all that the most valiant competition efforts ever proved was that through a combination of less weight and better handling, other cars were faster.

As for the American dream, it faded rapidly. Ford bought out the remainder of de Tomaso's interests and proceeded to close down Vignale, sell off the de Tomaso assembly plant in Modena and turn Ghia into an in-house European styling studio of exceptionally high quality (Tom Tjaarda re-mained there). That left de Tomaso to take his name and designs back to a small factory west of Modena, which is almost where we came in. The only difference is that today, de Tomaso Automobili is just a small part of a large and disparate industrial empire, and one wonders what, if ever, will replace the Pantera.

EVOLUTION

Introduced in 1969, the Mangusta was a mid-engined, Giugiaro-styled two-seater sports car powered by the Ford 289 cu in V8 with a five-speed ZF gearbox. Built on a backbone chassis, it had all-independent coil and wishbone suspension, discs all round and a limited-slip differential. Its maximum speed was 155 mph (249 kph), and the Mangusta was priced in America at $10,950, including air-conditioning.

1970 The Pantera was launched, a similar two-seater sports styled by Tom Tjaarda of Ghia. It was of monocoque construction with double-wishbone all-independent suspension. The Pantera was powered by Ford's 351 cu in V8 with a ZF five-speed gearbox, and was available in two forms, the L and GTS. The engine of the standard Pantera L produced 330 bhp and 326 lb ft of torque, and gave a maximum speed of 158 mph (254 kph); in GTS form the maximum speed was raised to a claimed 174 mph (280 kph), with engine power and torque outputs raised to 350 bhp and 333 lb ft respectively. The Pantera GTS could be distinguished from the L by the addition of front and rear spoilers.

1982 Pantera GT5 announced, with same mechanical specification as GTS but fitted with wider wheels (10 in/25.4 cm front and 13 in/33 cm rear). Claimed maximum speed was 162 mph (261 kph)

1984 Pantera GT5S introduced, with minor styling changes and mechanical specification as that of the GT5

Views of the latest GT5S, introduced in November 1984 at the Turin motor show; a splendid-looking machine, it differs from the earlier GT5 in that the wings and aerofoil have been restyled, and the latter is now made of carbon fibre

EMILIA

EMILIA

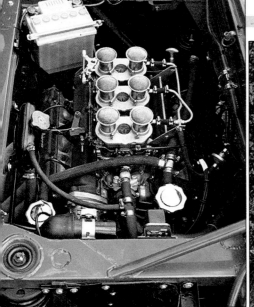

When manufacturers have to homologate rally cars one result is a very small number of spectacularly fast and desirable road cars – the Stratos was one of the best

AN UNASHAMED 'Homologation Special', the Stratos was certainly a true sports car. You couldn't use it for anything remotely practical, although it was not difficult to drive on public roads. It was in fact a gloriously fast car, but maddeningly tricky to *drive* fast. Nevertheless, the Stratos was International rally champion for three years in succession but was then overtaken by rally regulations. It was electrically unreliable, like so many Italian cars, appallingly difficult to see out of, like most Italian stylists' ideas, and its production figures were exaggerated by up to 220 per cent: Lancia's Stratos was quite simply delightfully Italian.

It is extraordinary that the Stratos was a Lancia. This ancient Torinese car maker, which had created what many hold to be the first production stressed-skin chassis (the rakishly elegant Lambda of the 1920s), had changed after World War II into a sort of Italian Wolseley. True, no Wolseley had ever had a narrow-angle V4 engine, nor had Wolseley ever built a Grand Prix team which became the official Ferrari entry, but even the best of the delightful latter-day Fulvia coupés had a staidness about their sporting pretensions. In spite of the successful career of the developed Fulvia in rallying, and its pleasantly mild racy character, in general Lancias were rather old-fashioned.

The company had a devoted following, but devotion in an increasingly competitive market was not enough. Bankruptcy loomed towards the end of the 1960s. Lancia's hugely

ABOVE *Views of an immaculate 1975 Stratos, its engine and dashboard*

successful Turin neighbours, Fiat, who had bought a half share in Ferrari in 1969, came to Lancia's rescue in the same year and bought the company, debts and all. They knew that the name alone was worth preserving and developing, as the up-market, quality end of the Fiat range. A programme of new models to replace the Fulvia and Flavia was quickly started, together with a genuine effort to boost the old name's standing by every means possible, and this included continued competition in international rallying.

If you mean business in any motor sport you must enter the field in which you have the unfairest advantage possible, which means having a car much better than anyone else's – within the regulations, that is. That means extremely specialised machinery and high costs. One way to prevent manufacturers building super-specialised cars regardless of cost is to insist that an awkwardly large number has to be built before the car can be accepted by the racing or rallying authorities: hence the development 'homologation special'.

The change from rally-developed production variants to specialised rally cars began in the late '60s, and the Lancia Stratos may be claimed to have been the first true example of that rare breed which has since spawned the Audi quattro Sport – the Peugeot 205 Turbo 16, the Ford RS200, the Metro 6R4 and Audi's mid-engined replacement for the unsuccessful quattro Sport.

Today's regulations require that 'only' 200 examples of each 'special' have to be made for sale, whereas in 1970 a batch of 500 had to be made of a Group Four car; this may sound worse than 200 but is actually little different, since the economies of mass production do not much apply below

10,000. A company cannot afford to waste money on expensive tooling, and in any case cannot ask a realistic price for something for which there is only a small market. Thus homologation doesn't really work, since if a car-maker believes that the advertising return on winning rallies is worth it, he will spend the money.

The trouble for Lancia in 1970 was that the competition was getting too strong for even the delightful 1.6-litre Fulvia HG coupé. The Porsche 911 was a threat, as was the Alpine Renault – both rear-engined cars and therefore most effective on loose surfaces where traction was critical – and Ford's 16-valve BDA Escort, a front-engined, rear-drive machine, was light and undeniably useful. Lancia's competitions head, Cesare Fiori, knew that something special had to be provided, and, with Fiat's money behind them, that something ideal could be built.

The first requirement was power, since the best that the old Fulvias had been able to deliver was around 130 bhp; the much lighter Alpine Renault had 170 bhp and the Porsche more than 200 bhp. No existing Lancia or Fiat engine was in this league, but there was the Fiat-built, Ferrari Dino unit, a superb double-overhead-cam 2.4-litre V6 which was

BELOW *The privately entered Nico/Barban Stratos, speeding in the '70 San Remo Rally* **BELOW RIGHT** *The Munari/Andruet works car in the '73 Targa Florio in which they came second*

ABOVE *A works car struggling through hell and high water in the '77 Safari Rally*
TOP LEFT *The interior of a rally Stratos. Note the parts drilled for lightness*
LEFT *One of the 1971, Bertone-styled prototypes. Its clean lines had to be modified for reasons of practicality*

ideal for competition.

This engine had an interesting pedigree. It had been developed for the 1967 two-litre Formula Two, which dictated that the power unit had to be a homologated production one, even if racing modifications were permitted. This occasioned Enzo Ferrari's first real contact with Fiat, who agreed to make a road version of the engine for what became the transversely-mid-engined Ferrari Dino 206GT. In less powerful front-mounted form it powered Fiat's own Dino sports car and both cars appeared at the 1966 Turin Show. In the Ferrari, the 86 mm×57 mm 1987 cc motor with its aluminium alloy cylinder heads was highly tuned, turning out a claimed 178 bhp at no less than 8000 rpm, with the torque peaking at 6500 rpm – the characteristics of a real old-fashioned racing engine – whilst the Fiat version was only slightly less exciting, with 158 bhp at 7200 rpm and torque peaking at a rather more civilised 4600 rpm.

To improve driveability by widening the effective power band, Ferrari redesigned the engine by increasing the bore and stroke to 92.5 mm×60 mm, giving 2419 cc for what became one of the most desirable road Ferraris of all time, the immortal 246GT. Its power and torque characteristics were still somewhat wild, with 192 bhp at 7600 rpm and 166 lb at 5500 rpm, and it isn't surprising that when Fiat put the larger unit in their more modest Dino spider and coupé in 1970 for the last two years of its life, it was less highly tuned, with 178 bhp at 6600 rpm and 159 lb ft of torque at 4600 rpm. The engine obviously had plenty of potential for a world-beating rally car. Fiorio realised that if the engine and the Ferrari transmission were used together there was a complete mid-engine drivetrain ready and waiting, and a very compact one too, given the transverse layout. Another help was that the then-current head of Lancia's design office was Piero Gobbato, who had been Fiat's liaison man with Ferrari at the time of the Dino engine's development. Lancia did toy with the idea of turning the 240GT into a rally car, but decided against it because it was too large and heavy, yet not strong enough for rough track rallying.

Fiorio's own design team were responsible overall for what turned into the Stratos, although the then most renowned of Italian styling houses, Bertone, had the job not only of designing the body, but also of detailing the structure from Lancia's general layout work. Italian 'styling houses' are much more than the name implies, easily capable of building complete cars.

In one sense Bertone had been in at the birth of the Stratos even before Lancia or Fiat, since for the 1970 Turin Show they had produced an amazing dream car, extravagent even by the bizarre standards of absurdity for such exercises. It was a razor-fronted, ultra-wedge, closed two-seater with the smoothest upper body and the most optically impractical raked windscreen possible, which was also the only entry to the interior; you raised it from in front, the

tiny steering wheel folded forward out of the way and you stepped in, doing your best to avoid scratching the nose. It was mid-engined, powered by a Lancia Fulvia front-wheel-drive assembly placed behind the cabin. It was a runner, even if one suspects that it would have been more aerodynamically successful as a wing than a car. Because of this Bertone understandably claimed that it looked as though it came from out of this world and called it Stratos (from stratosphere).

The purpose of such exhibits is partly to stimulate, and it is said that the Bertone Stratos did just that for Lancia, even if the real Stratos which made its motor show debut as an incomplete prototype at Turin in November 1971 – just a summer and an autumn after work had started on the project – bore no relation to the styling exercise, other perhaps than its size.

The real thing was incredibly short. It was only 146.1 in (371 cm) long overall (the length of a Ford Fiesta). There was, as there should be on a rally car, very little overhang

BELOW *The Ferrari V6 engine nestling ahead of the rear wheel line was a key factor in the quick and responsive handling of the Stratos, calling for skilled driving*

each side of a wheelbase of only 85.5 in (218 cm), which is 2.75 in (7 cm) less than a Metro's, although the front and rear track (56.4 in/143 cm and 57.4 in./146 cm respectively) were within an inch of that for an XJ12! This unusually close combination of wheelbase and track contributed to the always tricky handling of the car.

Structurally, it was an interesting hybrid design, with a very sturdy stressed-skin monocoque cabin box between the footwell and firewall bulkhead. Fabricated sheet box-member extensions carried the front suspension and steering, and at the rear a high box-beam open-frame was welded to the bulkhead to contain the drive unit and suspension. As first conceived, the Stratos had all-wishbone coil-spring suspension – in front it used Fiat 124 uprights and wheel hubs – but early on during the car's lengthy development the back suspension was changed to strut type, a geometrically less perfect design, but one which fed a much wider spread of loads into the chassis and was much stronger. Anti-roll bars were fitted at both ends, and steering was rack and pinion, very direct with just over three turns lock to lock.

The Girling ventilated disc brakes, nearly

ABOVE *The Stratos ready for inspection. Whilst the windscreen was large and wide, side and rear visibility were not particularly good. The small wing above the roof channelled air over the engine cover and towards the rear lip, increasing downforce and stability. Note the rear suspension – prototypes had wishbones*

11 in (28 cm) in diameter, were unassisted by any servo. The two mid-mounted fuel tanks could carry a total of nearly 19 gallons (85 litres) of fuel – very necessary for a car which could return no more than 20 mpg when touring and a lot less when driven with passion.

It would prove very difficult not to drive the Stratos with passion. The scream of the engine, lightning response of the handling and brakes made a car quite unlike any other to drive. Many cars would be crashed early on in life and most of the rally cars needed rebuilding at quite regular intervals. But that seemed a small price for a winning car.

The body was a mixture of steel for the fixed parts, welded to make part of the chassis unit, and reinforced glassfibre for the moveable nose, tail cover and doors. These latter items had shaped bins to hold crash helmets, and somewhat piggy-eyed side windows which were pivoted at their rear top corners; ingeniously simple in design, you opened each one by undoing a small knob inside and sliding it down a curved guide in the door trim. The pop-up headlamps were electrically operated. Wheels were handsome Campagnolo cast aluminium alloy in a variety of widths – 7.5 in (19 cm) was the standard rim, carrying 205/70VR-14 in Michelin XWX or Pirelli Cinturato CN36 radial tyres.

The power unit, as expected, was the Dino Ferrari 2419 cc V6, with its unusual 65 degree vee angle between the blocks. With its three downdraught twin-choke 40 mm Weber carburettors and the 9:1 compression ratio that was common to all Dino engines,

Fiat or Ferrari, 2-litre or 2.4, the engine was claimed to provide around 190 bhp (DIN) at 7000 rpm, with 165-lb ft torque at 4000 rpm. That this is a relatively flexible spread can be confirmed by talking to any Stratos driver, all of whom enthuse about the engine's marvellously wide range of power. This wonderful V6 was mated to a five-speed close-ratio transaxle gearbox, and had to propel a car with a kerb weight of 2160 lb (979 kg), a figure which doesn't sound particularly light until you remember that the Stratos was designed from the word go for all classes of rally, including the East African Safari. It was good enough to produce a shattering performance for the time, including such statistics as 0-100 mph (161 kph) in around 18 seconds, having reached 60 mph (97 kph) in less than seven seconds. The maximum speed was of course dependent on gearing, which, since acceleration was always more important, was invariably artificially low.

Full testing did not begin until 1972, the year after the prototype's show launch, and although the Stratos won its first international rallies in the following season, it was not until October 1974 that it achieved homologation. The first competition entry was in Sandro Munari's hands in the Tour de Corse of 1972, but it retired after the rear suspension broke. Its first victory was at its fourth event, when Munari won the 1973 Firestone Rally of Spain. It followed these red letter days for Lancia with outright wins in the subsequent Tour de France, the Targa Florio, and the Tour of Sicily. The 1974 homologation was succeeded with wins of the San Remo, the Tour of Italy and the Tour de Corse again, followed in 1975 by the Monte Carlo, Swedish and San Remo rallies. It was a similar story in 1976, the last of Lancia's three successive world championships for

RIGHT AND BELOW *Views of a Group 4 Stratos rally car, delivered in July 1974. Its four-cam Dino engine has been tuned to deliver 270 bhp, its suspension stiffened and 12 in (30 cm) wide wheels fitted at the rear. Accessibility is good, and with engine cover removed, the substantial engine frame is apparent*

makes, when the Stratos took the Monte Carlo, Portuguese, Tour de Corse and San Remo events.

1977 was the last year when the Stratos really competed, for Fiat were then keen to push the rally version of their 131 Abarth, and the near invincibility of the Stratos was threatening to frighten away the competition. A third Monte Carlo win for Munari and a win in the South African Total Rally were the only major trophies, although the Frenchman Bernard Darniche won a fifth (and final) Monte Carlo for the Stratos two years later, whilst other non-works cars did well in isolated European Championship events right up to the end of 1982, when its homologation ran out.

What *didn't* the Stratos win? The answer is, very little, for it was so extraordinarily superior. It never won an RAC rally (it came third in 1974), or a Safari (although Munari nearly made it, finishing second in 1975), but the fact that both of these are loose-surface events is only part of the story. The Stratos' shortness, the rather 'square' track wheelbase proportions and the always tricky cornering behaviour of a mid-engined car certainly contributed in such conditions, but an element of bad luck was also involved.

Whether or not Lancia ever actually made 500 Stratos for homologation is still uncertain, but the best-informed guesses put the final figure at between 450 and 490 cars. You won't find them easy to buy now, and a good one fetches an astronomical price. The Stratos is not an easy car to run, for obvious reasons, but if you have the money and the patience to treat this amazing machine properly, and the skill to drive it you will have a car that is still, over 10 years later, a standard-setter.

BELOW *The surprisingly traditional-looking large flip-top aluminium filler cap is neatly recessed into the glassfibre tail section allowing the 19-gallon tanks to be replenished quickly*

LAMBORGHINI COUNTACH

OF ALL THE SUPERCARS which have blazed their way up and down the autobahns, autoroutes, autostradas, motorways and freeways of the world, one stands decisively apart from the crowd: the Lamborghini Countach.

Fourteen years after its launch it is still the most eye-catching and outrageously styled supercar of them all, with its sharp wedge shape and its crazy yet surprisingly attractive amalgamation of scoops, wings and slats. It still radiates pure aggression and muscle from every curve on its aluminium body. The Porsche 911, another classic supercar, has also aged well, but whereas it is unmistakably a design of the past, the Countach is still a car of the future. The Lamborghini also has the best high-speed handling of any road car, helped by the biggest set of tyres ever to adorn a production machine (they are 12 in/30.5 cm wide at the rear!) and in its latest quattrovalvole form its V12 engine produces more power than any other – 455 bhp. This propels the machine to what is probably the highest top speed of any road car, for the Lamborghini factory *guarantee* all Countach Quattrovalvoles can do 183 mph (295 kph), and the word is that close to 190 mph (306 kph) is possible with patience and a long road.

On the debit side, however, the Countach is also probably the least practical supercar of all, with ridiculous rear visibility, costs, interior room and noise. But again that strengthens its case as the ultimate supercar; all supercars are crazy, so, if you're in the market, why not buy the craziest of them all?

From the start the Countach had to be an extraordinary car. Its job was to replace the Lamborghini Miura, the world's first mid-engined supercar, a fabulously attractive and incredibly fast machine. People desired the Miura from the day it made its debut in 1966. That its handling was flawed and its reliability atrocious did not seem to matter: demand was strong. Yet when the Countach first went

LEFT AND BELOW *The outrageous lines of the Lamborghini Countach LP 500S*

The Countach is built to do two things very well: look sensational and go faster than most other cars. It does both, with consummate ease

on display at the Geneva Show in 1971, few doubted that it was up to the job of succeeding the Miura.

Built and designed by three of the people responsible for the Miura, engineer Paolo Stanzani, Bertone stylist Marcello Gandini and development engineer Bob Wallace, the original Countach was an 'ideas car' prototype that encapsulated Lamborghini's thoughts on how the fantastic but flawed Miura could be improved. The body was not

only more eye-catching than that of the Miura, it was also more aerodynamic with better anti-lift properties (the old Miura had a nasty tendency to go light at the front at speed). The chassis, like that of the Miura, was a sheet steel semi-monocoque. The original Geneva Show prototype, known as LP500, had standard Lamborghini wishbone suspension but with much of the traditional flexibility – which could lead to handling sloppiness – removed thanks to the fitting of metal bushes instead of rubber ones. The engine, too, was more powerful than that fitted to the Miura, and had undergone considerable development. Of 5 rather than 4 litres capacity, it produced a staggering 440 bhp. Apart from being bigger, the engine was also mounted differently, for whereas the Miura had had its V12 installed transversely, between the cockpit and the rear wheels, the Countach's was mounted longitudinally (hence the LP model name, for *Longitudinale Posteriore*). Nonetheless, as with most things in the Countach, there was nothing conventional about this layout. In order to get as much weight forward as possible, the Lamborghini engineers devised a novel system of placing the gearbox in front of the engine, which then delivered the power to the rear wheels by means of a driveshaft running through the centre of the massive magnesium sump casting to the rear final drive.

The forward-mounted gearbox had other advantages apart from helping to give an excellent 43/57 front and rear weight distribution. The gearbox was directly underneath the gear lever, thus avoiding the long linkages which invariably give problems with rear-mounted boxes, or the tortuous linkages necessary with transverse engines. The inconsistent gearchange of the Miura had taught Lamborghini a lot about that particular problem. About the only unfortunate corollary of this unusual front-

mounted gearbox system was that, in order to accommodate the through-the-sump driveshaft, the engine was placed a little higher than originally planned, thus raising the centre of gravity.

The revised engine had a displacement of 4971 cc, achieved by opening up the bore and stroke of the Miura V12 to 85 mm and 73 mm respectively. The massive V12 was cooled by another unusual piece of Stanzani engineering: twin radiators horizontally placed in the rear wings, cooled by smooth ducts well integrated in the flanks. The warm air was expelled through horizontal louvres either side of the rear boot lid.

Lamborghini did not go to great lengths to tout the Countach as the Miura's successor when it first appeared on the Bertone stand at the 1971 Geneva Show – it would have been foolish in any case, for Lamborghini themselves unveiled their latest SV version of the Miura at the same show – but for those with any motor-industry insight, the message was clear. The Countach, named by Bertone after a Piedmontese expletive meaning amazing or incredible, would be Lamborghini's supercar of the future.

It did, however, take quite a while to reach production. Although the LP500 show car was fully roadworthy, and development engineer Wallace actually drove it from Lamborghini's headquarters at Sant'Agata Bolognese to the Geneva Show, it was nevertheless an undeveloped beast, in need of the Wallace touch. Three years of work went into the Countach before it replaced the Miura, and was eventually launched in 1974, during the worst of the oil crises. The timing was as crazy as the car.

Many changes had been made, although the basic concept of the Countach was intact. The production machine had just as much naked aggression about it as the show car, but with a few sensible touches. The front-end ducting had been altered, the nose angle had been made a little less acute (to overcome high speed nose heaviness discovered during testing), the roof line was smoother and air scoops had been placed on top of the wings to cool the redesigned radiators. The original idea of horizontally located radiators worked well enough at speed but hardly surprisingly was susceptible to overheating at low speeds. The production car had vertical radiators, positioned on top of the wings, and new scoops partially spoilt the cleanliness of the original Gandini design, even if they did make the car look more muscular.

The production car retained the pop-up headlights, which emerged like four huge

ABOVE LEFT *When the Countach was first shown at the 1971 Geneva Show it was fitted with this 5-litre 440 bhp V12. Note the transmission output at the rear of the sump*

eyes from the acutely angled front wings, but in addition it featured a pair of grille-mounted spotlights for flashing. The production car also had more attractive tail-lights; in fact all the cosmetic details were generally tidier. The extraordinary doors, which opened vertically (supported by single struts) were retained. In sum, none of the potential buyers courted at the Geneva Show was to be disappointed with the looks when the car went on sale, priced, in 1974, at £18,000.

No one was to be disappointed with the performance, either, even though the original 5-litre engine had given way to the ubiquitous 4-litre V12 on which Lamborghini fortunes had been resting for some 10 years. Despite the 5-litre unit's protracted development Lamborghini did not feel sufficiently confident about its reliability to offer it on the original production Countach: instead the 3929 cc Miura engine was fitted, with additional crankcase webbing and a revised sump. The familiar engine produced 375 bhp in the LP400 and fed its power to the rear wheels through the forward-mounted all-indirect five-speed gearbox. A limited-slip differential was standard. Maximum torque was 266 lb ft at 5000 rpm, and the V12 breathed through six 45 mm dual-throat Weber carburettors.

Many changes had also been made to the chassis. The semi-monocoque steel structure used on the Geneva Show car was replaced by a lighter yet more complicated shoe-shaped spaceframe, designed by one of Italy's foremost chassis experts: Marchesi, from Modena. This incredibly complex chassis was enormously difficult to produce, and highly skilled craftsmen were needed to weld the tube sections together to form the

LEFT *The original 1971 Countach had cleaner lines than the production model. Note the rear horizontal radiator*
TOP *The Countach production line*
ABOVE *The bare bones of the Countach*

Countach's backbone and to add the unstressed alloy body panels. Eleven years after it first went on sale, the Countach is still being built the same way. Ferrari models, by comparison, are built on far more 'modern' assembly lines. It is one of the essential differences between the two firms, and is one of which Lamborghini are rightly proud.

The Geneva Show car's suspension had also been changed, although, once again, the design was not adulterated merely for ease of production. The steel-bushed suspension on the LP500 (incidentally that car, known in Lamborghini language as 'the yellow car' due to its colour, ended its days in Britain during crash testing at MIRA) was replaced by a new system borrowed from racing technology. There were immensely strong unequal-length tubular wishbones at the front, wide-based and lightweight, and single upper link and lower reversed wishbones at the rear with bushes made of a new nylon material. Front and rear hubs were cast in magnesium, adjustable racing-specification Koni dampers were used all round and twin coil springs were fitted at each side at the rear (along with twin dampers) to keep the springs as short as possible and thus keep the rear as low as possible. The car reeked of uncompromising racing-car design in a way which few road cars ever have. Little thought was given to the ease of manufacture or to the cost. The only goal was to build the ultimate sports car, and few doubted that Lamborghini had done it when, after its three-year gestation, a production car appeared at the 1974 Geneva Show.

The entire first year's production of 50 cars was already sold by the time the world's ultimate performance machine starred at Geneva, amid gloomy prognostications about the future of the car in the post-oil-crisis era. While most manufacturers were talking of frugality and cut-backs, here was little Lamborghini unveiling an optimistic, some would say arrogant, answer to the world's legislators and to the prophets of gloom: and the company had a full order book to boot! However, it wasn't all optimism at Sant'Agata where changes were affecting confidence.

Ferrucio Lamborghini was finding that even his considerable resources were being strained by the continued demands of the car-making factory. Also, he appeared to be losing interest in the process of building cars, preferring to spend time developing his vineyards and marketing his own wine with that memorable name on the label.

The Countach had been, originally, the dream of Ferruccio Lamborghini, who wanted it, quite simply, to be the fastest road car in the world, as well as easily manageable and well appointed. Yet when the development of the car had been about to start, Lamborghini had been steadily reducing his direct involvement with the company. He had already sold 51 per cent of his interest to a Swiss businessman, Georges-Henri Rossetti, although he stayed on as executive director. In 1972, he gave up his day-to-day involvement in the factory's affairs to concentrate on the production of his other great passion, wine. By 1974, when the Countach entered production, Lamborghini's remaining shares had been sold to an associate of Rossetti's called René Leimer.

Nothing breeds apprehension faster among employees than changes of company ownership and, thanks to financial insecurity and strained relations with the new Swiss owners, both Bob Wallace and Paolo Stanzani left Lamborghini in 1975. The terrible labour problems in Italy at that time, which affected Lamborghini's craftsmen just as much as it did the less skilled workers, increased the sense of insecurity. Wallace emigrated to America where he set up his own garage and Stanzani started his own design studio.

Yet, amid the union problems, cars continued to be built. What a sight it was to see a Countach being produced! It was one of the few cars during the '70s and '80s to be built totally under a single roof. At the Sant'Agata works – so spotlessly clean that you could

ABOVE *A Lamborghini Countach 500 S which was introduced in 1981 with the 4754 cc V12*

RIGHT *The Countach was one of the very few cars that could actually use such a large rear wing. It was an option which aided handling at the expense of speed*

happily eat your tortellini off the floor – a pile of tubes, aluminium panels and castings started, almost magically, to take shape. The chassis was welded together, the aluminium panels were attached to it, the engines and gearboxes were built, the upholstery was trimmed and fitted and a host of minor assemblies were created. It's still the same, 11 years after the Countach began to emerge from the production line. The car might be futuristic but the manufacturing process is rooted firmly in the past.

Despite the Countach's buoyant start, Lamborghini sales were hit by the recession in 1974. Demand for the Espada and Jarama – the 'old school' front-engined models – had waned considerably, although the little V8 Urraco was selling well in America. The Countach continued to have a full order book but the inevitable labour problems did hit production: making a Countach was a time-consuming process which required high levels of skill, and production was seriously disrupted by a shortage of sufficiently skilled workers and dispute-free working hours. The result was that by the mid-'70s Lamborghini were in dire financial trouble.

They battled on, though, and 150 Countachs were built between 1974 and 1977. In 1978 came the first major revision to the car in the shape of the LP400S, blessed with Pirelli's new high-performance P7. It had always been reckoned that the main limitation of the original Countach was that its chassis could handle more performance than its Michelin XWX radials. The new lower-profile P7s were much wider than the more prosaic Michelins, and to house them properly, wheel-arch extensions were needed. A deeper nose spoiler and a boot-lid wing added to the Countach's extraordinary shape. To compensate for the greater grip, and the stiffer sidewalls of the new Pirellis, Lamborghini's consultative engineer, Giampaolo Dallara (one of the men behind the Miura, who had been persuaded to rejoin the company by Rossetti and Leimer) made a number of changes to the Countach's suspension. The geometry was totally revised, the wishbone mounting points at the front were moved, at the rear the lower wishbones were replaced by twin parallel links and the front and rear hub castings were altered. The car's interior (never one of the best parts of any Countach, old or new) was also changed on the LP400S,

LEFT A 500S Countach from 1981, regarded by many as the classic of the breed, without large bumpers or excessive aerodynamic additions to spoil the line

with more leather and fewer interior reflections. The LP400S went on sale in 1978.

At that time, however, Lamborghini's fortunes were at their nadir. Owners Rossetti and Leimer were fed up with the amount of money the firm had absorbed and they had run out of patience with the labour difficulties. They wanted out. In August 1978 the Italian government took over to prevent closure. Their most significant – and most sage – action was to appoint former Maserati engineer and executive Giulio Alfieri, first as a consultant and then as works manager. He guided the firm through to their eventual sale to the wealthy Swiss Mimram family, and then stayed on as manager. The Mimrams gave Lamborghini the sound financial base they lacked from 1974 to 1980, and the company began to look to the future with hope and increased vitality. The next step, inevitably, was the further improvement of their Countach flagship.

In 1981 the Countach reverted to the

original 1971 show-car form and was fitted with a 5-litre engine. It actually had a capacity of 4754 cc, thanks to increasing the bore and stroke of the V12. The power was thus increased by seven per cent and torque by 14 per cent. Top speed and acceleration, however, were not greatly affected.

In the Countach's most recent guise, Lamborghini have most certainly upped supercar performance parameters. In 1985, in response to Ferrari's latest Testarossa, Lamborghini fitted the Countach with a four-valve-per-cylinder V12, stroked the engine to increase the capacity to 5.2 litres and boosted horsepower to a blood-curdling 455 bhp. Power, torque and top speed were all above the new Testarossa with the factory claiming that the Countach can cover the standing metric quarter mile (400 m) in a staggering 12.9 seconds and reach 60 mph (97 kph) in a mere 5 seconds! Sant'Agata's timeless classic also remains more eye-catching than Ferrari's altogether more modern and more sensible Testarossa.

Driving a Countach is a whole new experience, no matter what type of car you are used to. Despite the massive area it takes up (it is shorter than a Ford Orion yet 8 in/ 20.3 cm wider than a Ford Granada!) it is a cramped car inside. If you are over 6 ft 2 in (1.80 m) tall, forget about filling out an order form at your nearest Lamborghini dealer: you simply won't fit inside. Even anthropomorphically average folk will find themselves in difficulties. The driving position is very much 'knees-up' and quite unlike any other car. The rear vision is appalling. Changing lanes in city driving is as much

good guesswork as good judgement – a sobering thought when you are driving a car which, in four-valve form, is now worth £68,000! In sum, this is a car better suited to the Oxford road than to Oxford Street.

Out on the open road the Countach is an extraordinarily able beast. Its power is enormous but its general road behaviour is no less impressive. Whereas, in the author's experience, supercars like the Porsche 911 Turbo and Ferrari Boxer do start to lean and pitch at high speed on corners, the Countach continues to display impeccable track-car-like handling, even at absurdly high velocities. It is more of a racer than its rivals, and is built more as an *absolute* performance car. It has fewer compromises and is built to do just two things well: look sensational and go faster than any other car. It does both – even if its failures as a sensible mode of transport are too numerous to list. It is difficult, too, to see how Lamborghini could ever improve the Countach (apart from its build quality) although they will probably make it faster and more high-tech. It's hard to visualise a successor which could be any more eye-catching or exhilarating. There will undoubtedly be better supercars than the Countach in the future but there is unlikely ever to be a more extraordinary one.

This member of the Countach line appeared in 1985 in the form of the Quattrovalvole with the 5.2-litre four-valve-per cylinder V12 which produces 455 bhp

Ferrari Dino

The mid-engined 206
and 246GT Ferrari Dinos were not
only a break with front-engined Ferrari tradition
and breathtakingly beautiful but a tribute to Enzo's only son

ONE OF THE MOST sought-after of all Maranello-built cars did not, strictly speaking, carry the Ferrari label at all. At the time the Dino was conceived in the mid-1960s Ferrari's reputation was that of a V12 builder and nothing else, yet the factory – with the considerable assistance of Scaglietti's coach-building works – produced, between 1967 and 1974, well over 4000 examples of a relatively small and light V6-engined car, a model which has come to be regarded as one of the most beautiful post-war coupés.

The origins of the Dino are linked to some grievous Ferrari domestic history. Enzo Ferrari had but one son, baptised Alfredo but who was almost always the affectionate 'Dino' to those who knew him. Dino showed every sign of becoming as gifted an engineer as his father, and after his graduation he joined the Maranello works and took a special interest in the engine and cars then being planned, in the early 1950s,

for an assault on Formula Two racing. Then he contracted leukaemia and in 1956 he died, aged just 24.

It was Enzo Ferrari's decision to name the whole series of smaller racing engines after his son. The original unit was designed by Vittorio Jano, who elected to meet the need for a 1.5-litre engine by making a V6 – in effect, half of one of the much-admired Ferrari V12s and with the advantage of compactness. In the event things did not transpire quite like that because Jano was worried about the amount of space available inside the vee of the engine to accommodate

ABOVE *The Ferrari Dino Spyder is surely one of the most beautiful road cars ever built by Ferrari*

adequate breathing arrangements between the twin overhead camshafts. In order to gain space he opened the vee angle from the theoretically ideal 60 degrees to 65 and restored equally spaced firing intervals by juggling with the crankpin angles.

This was the start of an engine series which was developed through all the vicissitudes of racing and hillclimbing for 10 years. In some versions its vee-angle was reduced to 60 degrees, while in others it was extended to 120. Whatever the changes, it remained a V6, and it was there in 1965 when Ferrari decided he needed to widen his market, if only to generate enough profit to keep all his racing programmes in operation. There was also the new and real threat of the Porsche 911 to meet, since the then-new car from Stuttgart added beauty to the promise of formidable performance.

By stages a road car was devised. The bodyshell was designed by Pininfarina, who

drew much of his inspiration for it from the sports-racing and hillclimbing bodies made for Ferrari by Piero Drogo of Modena. It was designed to fit over a multi-tube chassis which carried the V6 engine installed transversely, immediately ahead of the rear wheels. Thus, among other things, the road-going Dino was a mid-engined car at a time when all the 'proper' V12 Ferraris were front-engined: the Dino's big brother was indeed the magnificent Daytona.

In the established Italian manner Pininfarina softened up the market by exhibiting one-off prototypes at the major motor shows. His first effort, seen at Paris in 1965, was virtually right first time. By the time of the 1966 Turin show he had reacted to initial opinion: the entire body had been raised slightly, which also gave the car some much-needed headroom, and the headlamps had been transferred from a completely streamlined (and illegally low) plastic fairing in the extreme nose to recessed fittings in the front wings. Farina also tidied up the big airscoops in the rear wings which fed air to the carburettors and rear brakes and complied with the factory's chosen engine installation, for the Paris show car had had its power unit

LEFT AND ABOVE *A 1974 246 GT. Engine accessibility is not a strong point with this type of mid-mounting*

installed in-line rather than across. This meant that the fit was a little tight but gave more scope for rear styling and left room for a reasonably-sized boot.

Before then the road-going engine had also undergone a major redesign. The engineer, Franco Rocchi, had adapted it to be more suitable for production needs, and fixed its capacity at the desired 2 litres. The original 65-degree angle between cylinder banks was retained so that three Weber 40DCOE carburettors could be installed without compromising the inlet manifold passages. Inevitably, the engine had dimensions well over-square with a bore of 85 mm and a stroke of only 57 mm to give an actual swept volume of 1987 cc. Such figures made it no surprise that the Dino V6 was a high-revving unit, producing its claimed 180 bhp at no less than 8000 rpm. Ferrari was extremely reticent about quoting a torque figure, but working back from known figures for the later, larger version of the engine, it was probably about 140 lb ft, with a peak that could hardly have been less than 6000 rpm. The twin overhead camshafts per bank were driven in true Ferrari tradition by gears from the crankshaft to an intermediate

RIGHT *Close-up of the Dino's dash panel showing the clear instrumentation. Note the classic gated gearchange*

sprocket and thence by short chains. The valves opposed each other in a 46-degree vee and were operated directly through bucket tappets.

The five-speed, all-indirect gearbox was mounted beneath the engine, with spur gear drive aft to a limited-slip differential. A single very complex alloy casting served as engine sump, gearbox lower casing and final drive housing.

Suspension design allowed little compromise, since the Dino used double wishbones at both ends. The front upper and lower assemblies were of very nearly equal length, with the very short concentric coil spring/damper units squeezed between them. The steering geometry included a very large positive offset. At the rear the lower wishbone was considerably longer than the upper, and the spring/damper unit (with notably longer stroke) had to act on the upper member to leave the way clear for the drive shaft. Any possible shaft-locking problems were overcome in advance with the use of constant-velocity joints at each end.

For the first time in a production Ferrari, rack and pinion steering was adopted, a decision no doubt made easier by the light load on the front wheels. The latter were alloy of course, and shod with 185–14 in tyres. The relatively large wheel size left room for massive brakes, and 10.6-inch diameter discs were used front and rear, more than sufficient for a car whose kerb weight was under 2000 lb (907 kg). The spare wheel was housed in the car's sloping nose where, in company with such items as the washer bottle and the master cylinder, it left scant room for any luggage. The luggage locker was actually housed at the extreme rear of the body, behind the engine compartment, and whilst not exactly large, any contents, as some early testers pointed out, were kept nice and warm by the exhaust system.

In this form the Dino entered production in 1967, but at an extremely cautious rate. Enzo was certainly worried about whether the world's enthusiasts would accept the idea of a 'poor man's' Ferrari, although at the advertised price indigence in this context was strictly relative. It may have been that this worry, just as much as the desire to make the car into a mobile monument for his son, led Enzo to insist that the Dino was a marque in its own right.

The late 1960s were a fraught and complicated time for Ferrari. Fiat effectively bailed Maranello out of financial trouble, and one of the results was that Fiat inherited the Dino V6 technology and set about rationalising it, not least for use in two of their own sporting models – the Fiat Dino Coupé (Bertone-styled) and the Fiat Dino

Spider (by Pininfarina, but by no means with the flair and assurance which marked Ferrari's 'real' Dino 206GT). For this purpose Fiat put the V6 into production at its own Turin works, using castings from Fiat foundries, some of which bore the Fiat imprint even in the Ferrari-built cars!

While Fiat Dinos are still not as highly regarded as their true Ferrari counterparts, it should be said that nowadays they are still highly sought after cars, and are regarded by many enthusiasts as the closest they will ever come to owning a Ferrari. The Spider, in particular is undeniably an attractive and fast car.

In order to provide Fiat's models with the torque and reliability which the company felt was needed, substantial changes were made. The 2-litre engine was opened out to 2418 cc by the process of boring to 92.5 mm and lengthening the stroke to 60 mm. This actually made the bore/stroke ratio even greater than before (increasing it from 1.49 to 1.54) but by retaining the same carburettors and changing the camshaft profiles

the peak torque was boosted to 166 lb ft at 'only' 5500 rpm, while the power output showed a modest rise to 195 bhp at 7600 rpm.

From the purist's point of view, the worst thing abut Fiat's rationalisation of the V6 was their changing the cylinder block material from light alloy to cast iron. This had many advantages – of cost, block rigidity and even noise level – but it made the engine substantially heavier. On the other hand, since the unit now offered a little more power and substantially more torque the changes might be said to have paid for themselves.

Meanwhile, back at Maranello, the ultra-slow pace of early 206GT production was about to quicken. It is worth noting that to

powerful but heavier engine there was another change to the 246GT which offended the purist. The 206 body had been of aluminium panels, hand-shaped in the Scaglietti works and applied to the chassis tubing but although the 246 shell was fabricated in exactly the same way it was made in sheet steel. The result yet again was a weight penalty with the 246GT, even by Ferrari's figures, scaling nearly 450 lb (203 kg) more at the kerb than its predecessor, bringing the power/weight ratio back to close to where it had started.

That was not quite as bad as it seemed because in the process of transition the Dino had gown substantially. In the kind of move which one only dares undertake in a car blessed with a fairly simple steel-tube skeleton under a hand-crafted body, the 246GT gained 2.3 inches (5.8 cm) in its wheelbase and 3.7 inches (9 cm) overall, while its height went up by a further three inches (7.6 cm) to silence complaints from Ferrari's taller customers! It is a tribute to the skill with which the operation was carried out that short of parking the two models side by side the only way most people can tell the 206 from the 246 is by differences in the wheels – the knock-on type on the 206 – and the fuel filler cap, which on the 206 is a protruding chromed device rather than the flush-fitting flap of the later model.

The Dino production process was complex to say the least, and hardly aided the car's resistance to corrosion (Dinos have a

ABOVE AND LEFT Pininfarina presented this be-spoilered Dino at the Frankfurt Show in 1967. Public reaction was mixed
BELOW A 1966 prototype. It had a longer nose than the production car

underline the Dino's nominal independence from Ferraris proper, its designation was based on a new system. Whilst the V12 cars had always been numbered for the cubic capacity of a single cylinder (thus for instance any 250 had a 3-litre engine) the Dino was numbered for its total engine capacity and the number of its cylinders. During two years of production only 150 206GTs had been wheeled out of the factory (according to Maranello, although researchers who have investigated engine numbers are convinced there must have been more). Now the picture was about to alter with the appearance of the 246GT.

The change was needed not only to bring Ferrari practice closer to Fiat's, but because the acknowledged rival, the Porsche 911 (which had already been in production for four years!), was rapidly growing up. Stuttgart was offering bigger engines with more torque, simultaneously achieving better performance and handling. To maintain its challenge the Dino had to be developed.

Apart from the adoption of the more

BELOW The first prototype, shown at the Paris Salon in 1965 had a full-width transparent nose section which was heavily revised before production

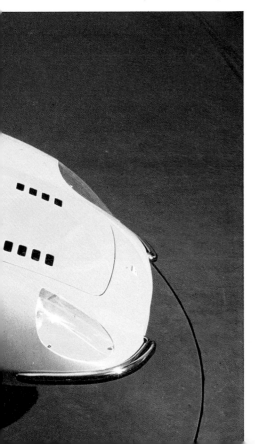

295

fairly evil reputation in this respect). The entire chassis/body assembly was made by Scaglietti in Modena, shipped down the road to Ferrari for engine, transmission and suspension installation, and then taken back to Scaglietti for equipping, trimming and finishing. Regardless of the complications the production really got under way when the 246GT replaced its smaller brother, and in the six years from 1969 to 1974 the factory built 2700 of these classic little coupés.

As late as 1972 the coupé was joined by a sister GTS cabriolet, its roof cut away and replaced by a stiff, removeable Targa panel. The GTS proved popular and Pininfarina was supposed to have been especially proud of it; the conversion was no great technical problem because the Dino body was essentially unstressed, the loads being taken by the tubing beneath. In only two years of production alongside the coupé nearly 1200 GTS cabriolets were made.

The rarity of the 206GT and the extreme reluctance of the factory during the mid-1960s to provide cars for road tests meant

BELOW The air intakes for the V6 were attractively sculptured into the body sides to create a pleasing styling point

that no authoritative performance figures for the model were ever published. *Motor* had better luck with the 246GT and established a maximum speed of 148 mph (238 kph) and a 0–60 mph (96 kph) time of 7.1 seconds. These are near-supercar figures and may have eased the pain of near-supercar fuel consumption, measured by the magazine at 16.1 mpg. The 246GT had a capacity of 14.5 gallons (66 litres) in its twin tanks.

The real joy of the Dino is that it goes and handles as well as it looks. Partly by virtue of its greater weight the 246GT was given wider tyres of 205–14 section, which if anything improved the ultimate roadholding without a deleterious effect on the delicacy and precision of the steering. Certainly the

ABOVE AND BELOW A 1973 GTS Cabriolet. The GTS was introduced in 1972 and 1200 were built during its life until 1974

feel of the steering belied its moderate gearing, for over three turns of the wheel are required lock to lock, and the car has a poor 36-foot (11 m) turning circle.

The gearbox is an acknowledged delight (except in old cars with ultra-worn synchromesh on second gear) and the gear ratios are well chosen for quick road driving even though second presents professional road testers with a familiar nightmare, falling fractionally short of 60 mph at the 7800 rpm red line. By Italian standards the driving position is well suited to tall, long-legged drivers, but the Dino is, of course, strictly a two-seater. The low-speed ride is usually criticised: given the angles of damper installation, it is not surprising that they suffer from 'stiction', or binding, at town speeds, but the Dino smooths out beautifully when driven with the appropriate verve.

Naturally, the 246GT has its drawbacks. The engine noise is a matter of taste: a beautiful sound to many enthusiasts' ears but probably too much of it in the long term. Although the driving position is well laid out for the most part the two main instruments are always half-hidden by the steering wheel rim, especially for tall drivers. Rear visibility is extremely poor and the headlights are in no sense matched to the car's performance. The heating and ventilation system is a joke. Owners admit to such faults, as well as to long-term rust problems and the notorious reputation of Italian electrics – British-market Dinos had electrically-operated windows as standard equipment – yet they insist that the pleasure of driving a 206/246GT ranks ahead even of looking at it parked in your driveway. In every sense the car rates as a classic, possessing in nimbleness what it might have lost in outright performance when compared with the mighty V12s.

There was a real sadness when production of the 246GT ended in 1974. The car was replaced by a new Dino, the 308GT, a 2+2 more in line with the tastes of the market, and powered by a bigger V8 engine. It says something for the reputation gained by the 246GT/GTS during its relatively short production life that its replacement carried the Ferrari badge. The Dino concept was no longer something to be treated with caution, at half an arm's length. Later still there emerged the 308GTB, which, returning to the design ideas and concepts of the 246GTB, proved that the Dino had justly earned its reputation amongst the Ferrari classics.

BELOW A GTS in its element, alone on the open road where delicate handling and ample power make it a real driver's car

EVOLUTION

1965 Prototype shown at Paris Show with longitudinally-mounted V6

1966 Second prototype introduced at Turin Show. It was higher than the first car and featured revised headlight design and smaller side airscoops

1968 Dino 206GT entered production with 2-litre V6 mounted transversely

1969 Dino 246GT replaces 206GT. The car was introduced at the German Show and featured a larger version of the V6 with bore and stroke increased to give 2.4 litres. The block was now in cast iron and produced by Fiat. The 246GT was longer overall and in the wheelbase than the 206GT.

1972 GTS Cabriolet introduced with Targa top

1974 Dino production ceased. Total production was 2700 coupés and nearly 1200 cabriolets

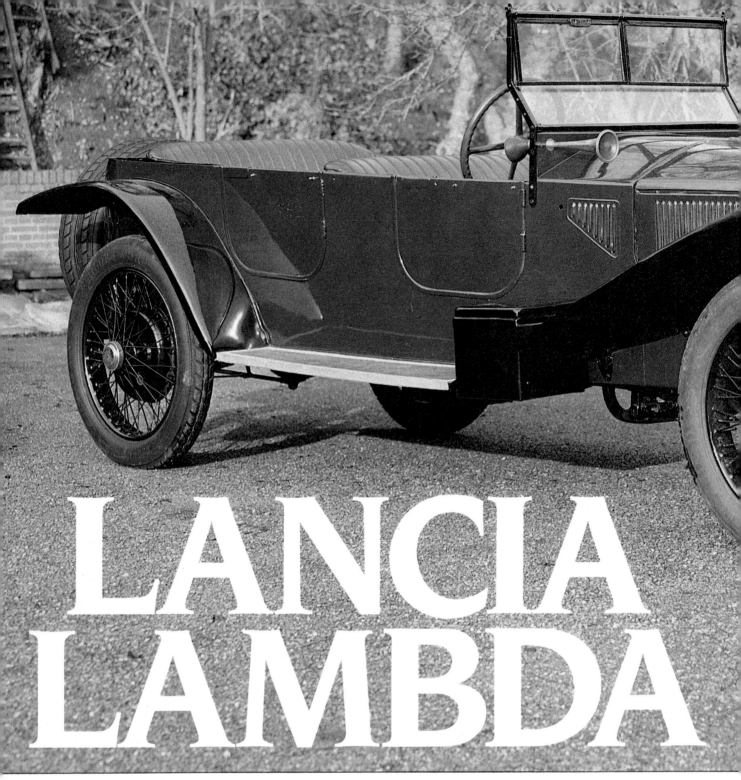

LANCIA LAMBDA

The prophetic design of Vincenzo Lancia's monocoque-hulled Lambda of the '20s has influenced cars ever since

THE LANCIA LAMBDA was one of the great cars of all time, and one of the most prophetic. In an age when Renault, Sunbeam and Rolls-Royce were still offering side-valve Edwardian models to a car-hungry post-war world the Lambda had an all-steel body-cum-chassis, overhead-camshaft V4 engine and independent front suspension. It was that rarity, a car designed from first principles, and because those principles were right, Vincenzo Lancia's touring car would see off many a powerful sports car on long cross-country runs. Launched in 1923 the Lambda remained in production throughout the vintage decade, and the sliding-pillar independent front suspension which it made famous was not superseded in the Lancia range until

1958 (on the Flaminia) when fashion at long last decreed greater deflections and softer springs and suspension.

The idea for a *scocca portante* or load-bearing all-metal hull came to Vincenzo Lancia towards the end of World War I, and he was granted a patent (no.171922) in March 1919. This patent covered 'a type of

car in which the chassis is eliminated, the connection between the back axle and the front axle comprising a rigid shell' and 'also the special form of this shell, which allows of its being lowered below the plane of the axles, and also confers strength'. In other words, Lancia had invented the propeller-shaft tunnel and was using this as a backbone for an all-steel shell. Passengers sat alongside the prop-shaft instead of on top of it, so that the whole car could be lower, with tremendous savings in weight and wind-resistance.

Independent suspension was added to the development programme during 1921 after a front semi-elliptic on a Lancia Kappa had broken while Lancia was taking his

This early series Lambda of 1923 is typical of the type, being a standard Torpedo. It featured a 2-litre V4 engine with overhead camshaft and a narrow angle of just 13 degrees, making it extremely compact both in width and length

mother for a drive. He discussed alternatives with Zeppegno, his chassis engineer from the beginning; also present was a young draughtsman named Falchetto, and the latter is on record as saying that he was so excited that he sat up all night, producing no fewer than fourteen suggestions for an 'independent' front end, including the one finally adopted.

Here an interesting historical point arises, which may explain why that particular system was chosen. Before starting his own company Vincenzo Lancia had been with Fiat, a member of their Grand Prix team and the fastest racing driver of his generation. In 1905 his Fiat had been all set to win the Vanderbilt Cup on Long Island when it was

run into by Walter Christie's unorthodox front-wheel-drive racer. He was thus brought into forcible contact with two original features of that car. One of them was independent front suspension by coil springs and sliding pillars, the other was a V4 engine. Did Christie memories linger in Lancia's mind for fifteen years, to be incorporated in his own masterpiece; was this why he chose this independent front suspension rather than one of the others in Falchetto's notebook?

By mid-1923 a definitive Lambda was ready for production. A first series of 500 cars was laid down and the model made its debut at the motor shows of that year, a low-built rakish four-seater touring car equipped with more interesting features than most journalists could comprehend. They passed over the independent front end for example, the virtues of which were not obvious at the time, but were intrigued by its novel engine and monocoque hull.

The all-steel hull which made the Lambda unique in its day was built like a ship. The sides of the body, from radiator to tail, comprised a skeleton framework of flanged 2 mm pressed steel members riveted together and covered on the outside with steel panels. Like a ship, too, it was crossbraced at frequent intervals. A channel-steel framework surrounded the radiator; next came the scuttle bulkhead. The backrest of the front seats was integral and used as crossbracing, giving immense strength amidships, and the rear seats acted in the same way, while aft of those seats the panelling converged to form a blunt pointed tail. The body in fact was a great steel box. Uniting the rear end with the scuttle bulkhead was the deep propeller-shaft tunnel mentioned in the patent – a most rigid backbone further strengthened by the seat pans and back-axle tunnel. All this was further stiffened by the engine-bearers, a stout pair of tubes running from bulkhead to radiator frame and front suspension assembly. A stout tube attached below the channel-section radiator frame was the bottom member of what Lancia literature calls the 'trapezoidal' framework which carried the jaws of the steering-head in which the telescopic oleo legs of the front suspension were held. Coil springs to control vertical movement of the wheels had been used several times in the past – by Christie, by Morgan and, in fact, by Decauville as long ago as 1899 – but it was Lancia who married the idea to the oleo legs of an aeroplane undercarriage. When he found that the front end of his original experimental car required damping, he added a dashpot, thus inventing the 'Lancia front end'.

For a description of this one cannot do better than quote Mr Geoffrey Robson, of the Lancia Motor Club. The suspension members consisted of 'a long hollow king-pin pivoting and sliding in guide tubes top and bottom, and integral with the stub axle. Two coil springs in compression bore upon a thrust-race above the stub-axle, and a short snubber spring in the bottom guide socket prevented the king-pin from bottoming'. By filling the king-pin with oil and installing suitable valves, Lancia arrived at the system which remained standard practice for as long as he remained in command. The steering-arms emerged forward from the stub-axles and were united by a one-piece track-rod in front of the radiator, and although theoretically this should have

ABOVE *No, these are not early low-profile tyres fitted to this brand new Lambda but wooden 'tyres' fitted in the factory to allow the car to be wheeled around with ease* BELOW *Vincenzo Lancia, seen second from the right, with the prototype Lambda near Turin during early trials*

ABOVE *An Eighth Series car on which the innovative sliding pillar front suspension is picked out with chrome; surely not a good idea since this process can reduce the strength of metal which is thus treated. Eighth Series cars saw the standardisation of a separate platform chassis*

caused tremors and kick-back, nothing of this sort occurred provided the tyres were good and the wheels in balance. Steering was beautifully sharp and precise, making a Lambda delightful to drive. Thanks to its independent front suspension it held the road far better than its contemporaries, especially when the going was rough.

In true vintage style the driver was seated amidships, his eyes a little aft of the mid-point of the wheelbase. Before him, scarcely higher than the lamps and wings, stretched a long and imposing bonnet; and beneath this great expanse, serene and isolated like a castle within its moat, was Lancia's strange but effective engine. The unit was certainly compact: the block was only 16.5 inches (41.9 cm) long and the whole thing, from flywheel to fan measured 22 inches (55.8 cm) overall, so that there was room under the bonnet for the gearbox as well. Perhaps this was to allow for growing; at least one surviving experimental car (known

as S1) is fitted with a 3-litre V8 engine.

Lambda production began in 1923 with a batch of 500 First Series cars, quickly followed by two further 500-car series. All these had the *Tipo* 67 engine, devised by designers Rocco and Cantarini, assisted by Scacchi, head of the experimental department, and no doubt by the *Padrone* himself. For whatever reason they chose a narrow V configuration, the bores converging at an angle of 13 degrees. Bore and stroke were 75 by 130 mm, giving a capacity of just over 2 litres (2120 cc) and the popular R.A.C. (British taxation) rating of 13.9 hp. Initial handouts claimed only 45 bhp (on a 5 to 1 compression ratio) but this power was soon exceeded. Production methods showed a mastery of foundry technique. Four flanged cast-iron cylinder liners were arranged in a mould in staggered V formation, and molten aluminium was poured round them to produce a single cylinder-block and crankcase casting complete with oil-filler, breather and

oilways. The sump, too, was a single light-alloy casting. Having no external oil-pipes the engine was clean and architectural like most Italian engines. On the port side a magneto, dynamo and water-pump driven in tandem gave it a pleasantly powerhouse air, while to starboard there was nothing to mar the symmetry except the oil-filler.

The crankshaft had four throws (to avoid a need for forked connecting-rods) and was

machined all over, a truly delightful artifact. It ran in three white-metal main bearings and the big-end bearings were plain too, with tubular con-rods. For his overhead valve gear Lancia and his team used a vertical shaft at the front of the engine with bevel gears top and bottom to drive a single overhead camshaft operating two vertical valves per cylinder via needle-roller cam-followers and rockers. This was a clear reminder of the Grand Prix Fiats that so often had earned him fastest lap.

The *Tipo 67* cylinder head, like the block, was a piece of virtuoso foundry work. No manifolding was to be seen, all inlet and exhaust tracts being internal and hence water-jacketed. A Zenith triple-diffuser car-burettor was bolted direct to the rear of the head feeding the inlet valves in the centre of the V, while two pipes emerged alongside it carrying away the exhaust. The lower face of this head finished flush with the valves so that it was flat-bottomed like that of the contemporary RL series Alfa Romeo. The combustion chambers were formed in the liners, and sparking plugs screwed into the aluminium block.

First, Second and Third Series cars had three speeds. The gearbox was not in unit with the engine but mounted close behind and braced to it by a strange 'overarm' casting. Ratios were 11.9, 7.3 and 4.16 to 1, or about 25 mph, 40 mph and 65–70 mph (40, 64 and 104–113 kph). It was fitted with a heavy flywheel to give the slow top-gear running that was so prized at the time. The clutch was a multiple dry-plate, and the gear positions were odd, with first and second in the front half of the gate. All Lambdas had right-hand drive and a central remote-

BELOW *A Seventh Series car with unusual English saloon bodywork fitted. The Lambda was never a small car, but the fitment of such bodywork made it very large indeed*

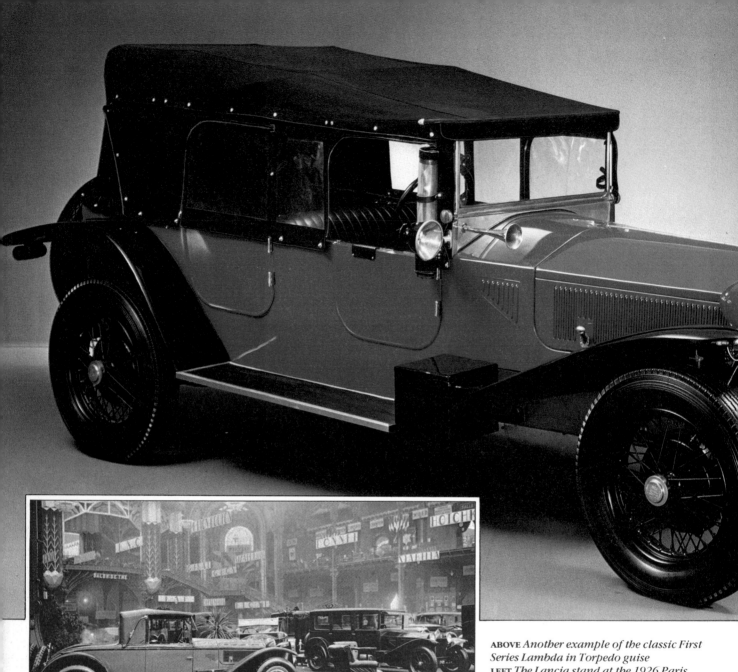

ABOVE *Another example of the classic First Series Lambda in Torpedo guise*
LEFT *The Lancia stand at the 1926 Paris Show with a Farina-bodied Roadster next to a Weymann six-light saloon; both are Eighth Series cars*
BELOW *Another Weymann saloon, this time a Ninth Series example*

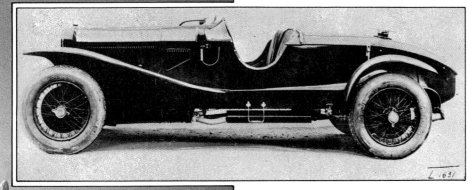

it Lancia brought out a long-chassis on a wheelbase of 123.6 inches (314 cm) which gave room for occasional seats amidships. The long-chassis is perhaps the best remembered Lambda recognisable by its length, its tail-high stance on the road and a phenomenal lock, which allowed U-turns in quite a narrow road and gave the impression that the car was describing a circle about its own back axle. The tourer cost £675, the saloon (a final version of the 'greenhouse' top) £750. The former weighed 2688 lb (1219 kg) and could do 70 mph (113 kph).

At car no.15501, ie, after 5000 cars had been made, the Lambda underwent another transformation. This was the start of the Seventh Series. To accommodate true coach-built closed bodywork the structure was re-thought once more. By boxing the sides of the chassis Lancia was able to do away with the cross-bracing which had come from the structural front-seat squab. He could now use bucket seats and fit normal closed bodywork. Weymann fabric saloons were especially popular because their lightness

ing 22, 37, and 49 mph (35, 59, 79 kph) at the revs corresponding to 70 mph (113 kph) in top, and a delightful change. The fan drive was now taken from the crankshaft instead of from the nose of the camshaft, and the fan itself was now aluminium instead of being carved from wood like a vintage aeroplane propeller. Shorter valves and rockers brought a change from a flat rocker-box to a domed one. During the Fifth Series, too, Lancia went from narrow beaded-edge 675 × 105 Michelins to the new-fangled low-pressure 775 × 145 Michelin *Confort* 'balloons', which was achieved without causing the 'shimmy' or wheel-wobble which beset so many competitors.

The Fifth Series of 1925–6, last of the lightweight slimline Lambdas, was the nicest of all, being the final incarnation of the

BELOW *This heavily revised Ninth Series car seen at Lake Como has bodywork by Farina and is altogether an imposing machine*

TOP *One of the rare Sport Spyder cars built for the 1927 Mille Miglia and subsequently used for several later races. The privately entered Lambdas finished fourth and fifth in the 1927 event, prompting Vincenzo Lancia to research the route himself to find out how to make the cars more competitive*

control gear lever.

In the early 20s motoring was still mainly an open-air pastime. The Lancia hull was so uniquely rigid however that the factory supplied various bolt-on greenhouses to convert one's Lambda into a saloon or indeed into a sedanca de ville. *The Autocar* tested a Third Series saloon conversion costing £695 complete in May 1925. They gave it a top speed of over 70 mph (113 kph) and a minimum speed of 5 mph (8 kph) in top thanks to that heavy flywheel. The weight, remarkable for a closed 2-litre car, was only 2464 lb (1117 kg). They found the four-wheel brakes wonderfully effective, giving a stopping power of almost 1 g.

With the Fourth Series (in the spring of 1925) the Lambda acquired a four-speed gearbox, with nicely spaced gear-ratios giv-

original stressed hull. Lancia now had other plans for the Lambda, and without changing the name or the silhouette, subtly upgraded it. The market was changing. People wanted more room to spread themselves and were less interested in sport. The Sixth Series therefore was virtually a new car, although the engine and 122-inch (309.8 cm) wheelbase remained the same. Introduced in 1926, the Sixth was three inches (7.6 cm) wider in track and no less than 13 inches (33 cm) wider overall. It was quite different in other respects too; the famous stressed hull, with its panelled steel pressings gave place to a stressed skin construction in 16-gauge steel, the metal being doubled below the doors, which were wider, deeper and closer together. The structure was even stronger than before, and as though to prove

matched that of the chassis; they often had wicker front seats. Even on these bodies the tail was still boxed, for reasons of stiffness.

Weight had been creeping up and so, more importantly, had frontal area. Seventh Series cars therefore had a new engine, *Tipo 78*. Piston stroke remained the same but the bore went up to 79.37 mm, giving 2370 cc and increasing the RAC rating from 13.9 to 15.6 hp, so that the annual tax went up by £2. This may not sound much, but in 1926 would have bought some 30 gallons of petrol. On *Tipo 78* engines the vee angle was 14 degrees and there were other changes: counter-balanced crankshaft, an added camshaft-damper, and the tubular con-rods replaced by I-section rods of nickel-chrome steel. At the same time the 'flat-bottomed' cylinder-head gave way to a

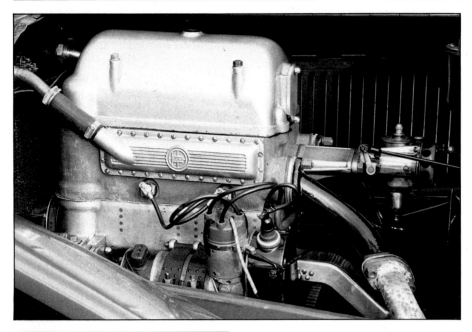

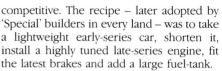

competitive. The recipe – later adopted by 'Special' builders in every land – was to take a lightweight early-series car, shorten it, install a highly tuned late-series engine, fit the latest brakes and add a large fuel-tank.

Very different from these delightful specials was the Eighth Series, which came out the following year, 1929. There was now a platform chassis with stout lateral box longerons, plus the famous tunnel of course, and the boxed boot. An Eighth Series on the long chassis was a car of formidable size, almost as long as a Phantom II Rolls-Royce at 189 inches (480 cm) overall, and carrying luxurious coachwork. The Eighth looked

Cazaro were a Torinese coachwork company who worked exclusively with Lancia. This is one of their Spyders based on a 1924 chassis and one which was first owned by Count Zborowski of 'Chitty-Bang-Bang' fame
RIGHT *Note the primitive 'dipping' mechanism on its Carl Zeiss lamps*

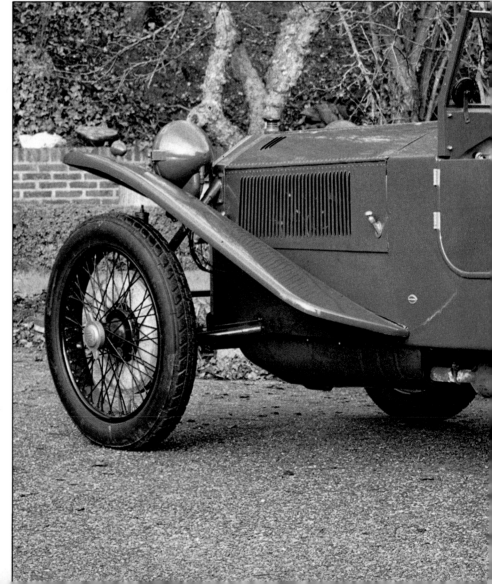

normal one, complete with combustion chambers and sparking-plugs. The carburettor was mounted further away from the head to keep it cooler, and maximum-power revs rose from 3000 to 3250. Maximum output went up from 50 at 3000 to 59 bhp at 3250. More important, in view of the weight and frontal area, the *Tipo 78* had almost one-third more power at maximum torque revs – 48 bhp at 2250 instead of 38 at 2125. What is more, the new crank and rods allowed a rev limit of 3600. All these changes brought their due reward: more than 3000 Seventh Series cars were sold, half as many as all the previous series put together.

The year of the Seventh Series, 1927, was the year of the first Mille Miglia. Although officially against racing, Vincenzo Lancia was delighted when privately entered Lambdas finished fourth (Strazza/Varalla) and fifth (Pugno/Bergia) behind three works OMs. In January 1928 he drove round the course himself at racing speeds with Gildo Strazza, seeking ways to make the Lambda more

more massive than the Seventh because the radiator and scuttle were three inches (7.6 cm) higher.

With the Eighth Series came the *Tipo 79* engine, largest of them all, although still only 2.6 litres. The bore had gone up to 82.55 mm, bringing the fiscal rating to 17 hp and the capacity of 2570 cc. The V angle was now 13 degrees 40 minutes, and other changes had been made: thicker valve-stems, modified con-rods, improved lubrication to the main bearings, a 38 mm Zenith instead of a 36 mm and a better exhaust manifold. All this raised the power to 69 bhp at 3500 rpm, gave a respectably flat

torque curve, peaking at 2300 revs, when there was 53 bhp available for acceleration, and pushed the rev limit towards 4000. Maximum speed (maker's figure) was 75 mph (121 kph), maximum gradient climbable 1 in 3½, and fuel consumption 19–20 miles per Imperial gallon.

Once again Lancia had his sums right. Although its launching coincided with the Wall Street crash of 1929, the Eighth sold better even than the Seventh had done and by 1931 despite the Depression sales totalled 3929, not counting Ninth series cars which differed only in having coil ignition.

And so the Lambda advanced into the post-vintage period – larger, roomier, more imposing but still very similar to that remarkable signpost the First Series tourer. Production continued into 1931, by which time 12,530 had been made, not counting the Ninth Series.

When finally the Lambda was withdrawn it took three models to do the same job: the Artena, the Astura and the Dilambda, respectively a 2-litre four, a 3-litre eight, and a majestic 4-litre eight. They all had the narrow-V engine layout and the independent front suspension which Lancia pioneered. The world was slow to catch up. In 1931 virtually no other manufacturer offered independent front suspension; today there is virtually none that does not.

EVOLUTION

Introduced in 1922 at the London and Paris motor shows, as a four-seater torpedo-bodied touring car with monocoque body and chassis. It also had independent front suspension and an overhead-cam V4 engine which produced 50 bhp. The engine was so short that the three-speed gearbox was mounted under the bonnet. First, Second and Third Series were mechanically identical

1925 Fourth Series Lambdas were fitted with a four-speed gearbox. Fifth Series cars were fitted with low-pressure balloon tyres and Marelli electrics instead of Bosch

1926 The Sixth Series Lambdas were wider and roomier, with a new and stronger stressed skin construction.

1927 The Seventh Series was introduced, with a separate chassis offered as an option. This model was fitted with the new 2370 cc Tipo 78 engine, which produced 59 bhp

1929 The Eighth Series was introduced, with platform chassis as standard, and long-wheelbase version available as an option. The new 2570 cc Tipo 79 engine was fitted, producing 69 bhp

1930 Ninth Series Lambdas introduced, identical to Eighth Series cars except for coil instead of magneto ignition

1931 Production ended. Total sales: 13,000

IT WAS, IN MANY WAYS, an unlikely cast, but together its members built the most stunning supercar of the '60s. There was Ferruccio Lamborghini himself, the short, thick-set Italian industrialist who started amassing money by rebuilding war surplus armoured vehicles into tractors, and there was his physical antithesis, Bob Wallace, a blond-haired, lanky New Zealander who went to Modena to be a racing mechanic and ended up chief test driver and engineering troubleshooter with Italy's newest, and probably most exciting, exoticar manufacturer.

Wallace was only 25 when he joined Lamborghini, in the summer of 1963. Even younger was the brilliant Parma-born engineer Gianpaolo Dallara, the holder of a degree in aeronautical engineering who had worked for both Ferrari and Maserati. He was in charge of chassis design and development. Dallara's assistant, Paolo Stanzani, was only one year older. Wallace, Dallara and Stanzani nurtured the idea of building a mid-engined supercar for the road which, in 1964, would make it the world's first. Lamborghini, a born showman who himself had long dreamt of building the ultimate road car, agreed with alacrity and enthusiasm. And, finally, there was another young man: 25 year-old Marcello Gandini. Following the departure of Giorgetto Giugiaro to Ghia in 1965, Gandini was reckoned to be Bertone's best stylist. He clothed the dream and made it the most sensational looking sports car of its day.

Rumour has it that Lamborghini went into the supercar business because he was dissatisfied with the service he received as a Ferrari customer and especially because Enzo Ferrari once made him wait a long

Twelve cylinders, four cams and 350bhp all clothed by one of Bertone's beautiful bodies – it was no wonder that the Lamborghini Miura outshone even Ferrari in 1968

BELOW AND RIGHT *Two views of the P400 Miura, which burst onto the scene in 1967 after a debut at the 1966 Geneva Show*

time for a meeting. The story is almost certainly untrue; Ferruccio built supercars because they were to him the most exciting machines. When asked why he became a sports car manufacturer, Lamborghini once answered: 'In the past I have bought some of the world's most famous *gran turismo* cars. In each of these machines I have found faults – too hot – too uncomfortable – not fast enough; now I want to make a GT car without faults. Not a technical bomb; very normal, very conventional, *but perfect.*' A factory was set up in Sant'Agata Bolognese, a village between Bologna and Modena. And because Lamborghini was a young car manufacturer, Ferruccio – who liked to think of himself as 'Cavaliere Lamborghini' (as opposed to 'Commendatore Ferrari') – recruited keen young men.

The first Lamborghini, the 350GT, was previewed at the Turin Show in the same year as the new company was formed. A strange looking, some said downright ugly, front-engined *gran turismo* machine, the GT offered 155 mph (249 kph) top speed with 0–60 mph (approximately 0–100 kph) acceleration of some 6.5 seconds. Its most notable feature was its 3.5-litre engine. From the start Lamborghini insisted on manufacturing his own power unit rather than buying it in (which he rightly thought would spoil the new car's pedigree). More than this he wanted nothing less than a V12 and gave former Alfa Romeo and Ferrari designer Giotto Bizzarrini a commission to build one. It so happened that Bizzarrini had already done preliminary work on a four-cam 60-degree engine which ideally suited Lamborghini's requirements, the four-cam arrangement appealing to Ferruccio as a piece of

LAMBORGHINI MIURA

one-upmanship over the contemporary twin-cam Ferrari layout.

Thus was born the first of the breed, but the classic work was yet to come. The three youngsters – Dallara, Stanzani and Wallace – wanted to build the ultimate GT car, one that could also be used for racing. Lamborghini himself persistently said no to sporting involvement, but the three got their wish and the Miura was on its way.

In the event, very few Miuras would ever take to the race track but that is not to underestimate the degree of racing experience that went into their construction. Quite clearly Mr Lamborghini saw the carrot of a racing programme as a very fine way of keeping his design team hard at work until the car was in production.

Dallara, the most important member of the team, was greatly impressed by the styling and construction of the Ford GT40 which appeared in 1964 and decided that a mid-engined car with a central monocoque was the way to go. Even more innovative was his idea of mounting the V12 and its transmission transversely with the latter behind the engine and direct cog drive from one to the other. The arrangement would take less fore-and-aft room (the same argument used by Alec Issigonis for the Mini) and thus leave more space for passengers and luggage. It was also argued that it would provide better access to some key mechanical items, not that access was ever a prime consideration in supercar design.

It obviously made sense to use as many parts as possible from the front-engined GT car and the suspension geometry and most of the parts were the same as on the 350GT. There were front and rear wishbones, with integral coil springs and dampers. 12-inch solid Girling discs were used at front and back, as were anti-roll bars. The chassis, of course, was quite different from that of the front-engined machine. The Dallara design had a deep central monocoque of light-gauge steel to which were bolted box sections to support the drive-train and front suspension.

The power-train was a mechanical work of art. One of its most extraordinary features was the single aluminium alloy casting which combined the block, crankcase, transmission and final drive, with cast-iron wet liners for the cylinders. The engine itself was based closely on that of the 350GT, soon to have a name change to 400GT, thanks to a capacity increase. It was the new 4-litre version of the V12 that actually went in to the Miura. The four camshafts were chain driven and actuated the valves through inverted steel bucket tappets. The valves themselves were inclined at 35 degrees to the cylinder centre-line, and operated in hemispherical combustion chambers. The crankshaft was nickel chromed, machined from a solid billet, and ran in seven main bearings which gave it ample strength and location.

The 350GT had six twin-choke Webers, but Dallara, who was most responsible for the development of the V12, decided to fit a quartet of three-choke units to the Miura.

The carbs were downdraught Weber 40 IDL3Cs as used by Porsche on their 911 of the day. Wet-sump lubrication was chosen in preference to the dry-sumping as seen on the 350GT. The end result of this Dallara deliberation and Bolognese brilliance was a claimed 350 bhp at 7000 rpm and 271 lb ft of torque at 5100 rpm, but like all power output figures quoted by Italian supercar makers of the day that was rather optimistic! This Sant'Agata power was transferred to Lamborghini's own five-speed gearbox (with synchromesh on all gears, *including* reverse) by a three-plate clutch, placed before the input shaft of the gearbox. When production started, however, this arrangement was superseded by an arrangement more like that of the Mini. The clutch was changed to a simpler single-plate affair, placed at the end of the crankshaft, which drove the gearbox input shaft through a pair of helical gears. A very small pinion and large ring gear took the drive from the gearbox to the in-sump

final drive, and then to the wheels via conventional splined halfshafts. Originally a hydraulic gear linkage was envisaged, but this was soon scrapped and a conventional metal linkage used.

The first Miura chassis, complete with engine and gearbox, was ready by November 1965, in time for the Turin Show. Even with no bodywork it attracted a vast amount of attention thanks to its transverse layout. Lamborghini admitted during the show that production would be strictly limited, and the boss himself told a gathering that he was making 'a dream car for a few crazy people'. Although many sceptics dismissed the display as a publicity stunt, others started to get out their chequebooks. Lamborghini took ten Miura orders in Turin. For a car still some twelve months away from production, and with no body, that was quite a feat.

Not only were the motoring press and the general public intrigued by the Lamborghini display, but Italian coachbuilders also took more than their fair share of interest in it. The identity of the stylist had still not been

made public and there was no doubt that the exciting new low-slung chassis offered real aesthetic possibilities. Touring of Milan, who built the 350GT bodies, would have been a strong candidate and had even begun work on a design but serious financial problems, resulting in bankruptcy, prevented their carrying on. After their demise, Bertone were considered the most likely candidates. The Grugliasco firm not only had a distinguished reputation, and the facilities, but they also had the important qualification of not being linked with either Ferrari or Maserati. Nuccio Bertone knew that a really stunning set of clothes on Ferruccio Lamborghini's new baby would act as a great boost for his company. And although his star designer, Giorgetto Giugiaro, had recently left to join Ghia, Bertone had another great young designer he could trust to come up with the goods: Marcello Gandini The Italian youngster and his small team worked crazy hours during the latter part of 1965 and early '66 as

ABOVE *An S model of 1969 with 370 bhp engine. Later cars featured improved braking*

the design moved from paper to the wooden model stage. Early in 1966, the chassis and body were coming together at Bertone's factory with the Geneva Show of that year as the target. Lamborghini made it – just; but not only did the car have to be finished, a name had still to be decided upon. Until the '66 Geneva Show, the car was known as the P400: P for *posteriore*, and 400 for 4.0 litres. Miura, the name of one of the greatest strains of Spanish fighting bull was finally decided upon.

Quite simply, the Miura absolutely dominated the Geneva Show. Not only was it the first mid-engined supercar designed specifically for the road, with a claimed top speed of 187 mph (300 kph), but it already had the look of a future classic. Both the front and rear body sections were made from aluminium, with the centre monocoque and the doors of steel. There was no glass fibre anywhere in a Miura's bodywork. There was even practicality to match the beauty. The bonnet was hinged at the front, the rear engine cover at the rear. Both gave excellent access, and both could be removed totally to improve matters further. Although mid-engined cars have never been renowned for their luggage space, the Miura did have a useful, if hardly capacious, boot behind the engine. In overall length this Gandini masterpiece measured 171.6in (436cm) – about 2.0 in (50 cm) shorter than a Ferrari Boxer, or about the same as a Ford Cortina. It was certainly not as wide as modern exotics, being only 4.0 in (102 cm) broader than an everyday Cortina. If there was any one extraordinary specification of the Miura, however, it was its height – or rather lack of it. From just behind the windscreen to the bottom of the specially made Pirelli tyres it was barely higher than a dining room table – some 2 in (2.5 cm) lower than the ground-

They *looked* imposing but were poorly sited, just a little too low for the driver's natural line of sight. In the central cowled console were six additional instruments, all angled towards the driver. There were gauges for water temperature, oil temperature, oil pressure, fuel level, the ammeter and a clock. Mounted in the roof, behind the rearview mirror, were six toggle switches for lights, wipers and the like.

Getting the Miura ready for the 1966 Geneva Show had been a monumental task – but the really hard work was still ahead. Real testing began in May '66 with Bob Wallace doing most of the hard driving. The most common route for Wallace and the Miura was the highways between Sant'Agata and Florence, which combined *autostrade* with winding mountain roads. Wallace soon discovered that his work should be concentrated on two main areas: adjusting the suspension and solving engine and cockpit cooling problems.

the occupants' ears and one bank of exhausts perilously close to the driver's rear. Wallace later admitted that the engine's location did cause serious heat and noise problems – and, to be sure, the Miura was always a noisy and fairly hot car. These early problems were partly remedied by a special perspex sheet (instead of the original glass) between the cockpit and the engine, by the slatted rear cover (which extracted heat from the engine), and by four inches of polystyrene insulation behind the sheet metal bulkhead.

By the end of May the Miura had progressed well enough for Ferruccio Lamborghini to gamble on giving his new charge its second public airing. The Monaco Grand Prix was approaching. The Boss knew full well that among the Pierre Cardin set, who flock to the Grand Prix like aristrocrats to Royal Ascot, were prospective Miura owners. So Bob Wallace and a mechanic were dispatched to the Principality as Lamborghini had the Miura accepted as the course marshal's car. An equally overt publicity coup was arranged for the night before the Grand Prix. Ferruccio Lamborghini knew that the Place Du Casino was the place to be seen on that Saturday night and managed to park the prototype Miura right in the centre of the square, amid all the other exotic machines which assemble there. Naturally the striking rarity with the charging bull motif stole the show that evening. In case anyone had failed to notice the car, Ferruccio Lamborghini fought his way through the crowd surrounding the Miura to start up the V12 for a curious friend. The snarling buzz of the twelve trumpets drew even more inquisitive glances and doubled the size of the crowd. Ferruccio didn't bother to take sales orders that evening, but it is a fair bet that when the new Lamborghini finally hit the streets in early 1967 a number of those Monaco Grand Prix goers were the first to part with the 75,000 Swiss Francs required.

One of the corollaries of this protracted development period and continuing pre-production publicity was that the order book suddenly became much bigger than the intended production run, envisaged at something like twenty a year. As it turned out, during 1967, the first year of proper production, 108 Miuras were delivered to increasingly impatient customers. Most stayed in Italy, but cars were also delivered to rich enthusiasts in the USA, Britain (where the price in 1967 was a whopping £8050 at a time when an E-type Jaguar cost nearly £6000 less), Sweden and even Venezuela.

The fact that in many countries no after-sales network of any sort existed did not deter many well-heeled owners from taking delivery of a new Miura. Among the super rich it became quite common practice to send the car back to Italy should major work become necessary. It should be said that major work was quite often necessary; not unusual for a specialized supercar.

In late 1968 the first major improvement to the Miura was effected when the P400S Miura went on sale. First shown at the Turin

ABOVE *The interior of the S was rather more luxurious than that of the P400*

hugging Turbo Esprit of today.

Visually striking features of the Miura included the uncovered headlights with their curious 'eyelash' surrounds, which were raised and lowered electrically, the vast raked windscreen (which made the cockpit of the Miura like a sauna on a hot day) the big rear three-quarter air intake louvres, novel ducted alloy wheels for brake cooling and (later in 1966) the Venetian blind-like heavily slatted rear window cover which helped extract hot air from the engine, helped cool the interior and did not restrict rear vision too badly.

The interior was equally striking. It was – like most Italian exotics – not lacking in instrumentation. Directly in front of the driver, but placed in separate circular housings, were the tachometer (to 10,000 rpm) and the speedo (to 200 mph or 320 kph).

Wallace soon found that the car was prone to rather sudden oversteer when pushed hard and also had rear toe in/toe out problems. Under acceleration there was excessive rear toe-in; under braking too much toe-out. Many of these problems were never in fact fully rectified until production was well and truly underway. They were eventually partially overcome by larger Pirelli tyres and reinforced rear trailing links. Front end lightness was also a problem when running at the sort of high speeds of which the Miura was capable. This was never fully cured either although it was partly solved by the introduction of a chin spoiler, by the larger tyres and by more efficient expulsion of the radiator air (which cured a pressure build up under the nose). A ZF limited-slip differential was tried but abandoned because of oil viscosity problems with the common engine/transmission lubricant.

When the car was shown at Geneva, critics were also dubious as to how noisy and hot the new Lambo would be – with all those Webers gulping for air only inches behind

ABOVE *An SV variant of 1972 vintage. The SV is readily identifiable by its rather bulbous flanks, which were incorporated to cover wider wheels and tyres. With 385bhp, a stiffer reinforced chassis and improved suspension, it was the most desirable of the Miuras*

Show of that year, the S, besides getting 70 series Pirelli tyres which greatly increased the predictability of the handling, had more power, thanks to larger-diameter inlet porting and modified combustion chambers. The claimed output went up by 20 bhp, to 370 at 7700 rpm.

The carpeting and the upholstery were improved, with electric windows replacing the terribly low-geared window winders. The overhead toggle switches were replaced by rocker switches, as demanded by American safety standards. Externally the S was nearly identical to the original Miura – the main differences being chromed window and windscreen frames and headlight surrounds.

During the S's 2½ year life, ventilated discs were adopted to replace the solid variety, reinforcing links were employed on the lower rear wishbones to help overcome toe-in changes (although this was only done to a few cars) and the equipment level was increased.

In March 1971, when demand still easily outstripped supply, the most desirable of all the Miuras hit the showrooms. The Miura SV (V for *veloce*, or speed) was intended to be

released in the late '60s but was held up by the labour problems which racked Italian industry at the time. Although it was somewhat overshadowed at its Geneva Show launch by the Countach show car on the Bertone stand (which was rumoured to be the Miura's successor), the SV still caused an enormous amount of interest. More different from the S than the S had been from the original P400, the Miura SV had modified styling (with wider hips to cover the wider Pirelli 60-section tyres; new tail lights; a different grille with new side lamps and

different headlamp surrounds – without the eyelashes), some interior modifications and a number of mechanical ones. The most important mechanical change was the increase in horsepower (to 385 bhp at 7850 rpm) and torque thanks to an increase in the inlet valve diameter, modified cam timing and revised Webers (with bigger main jets). Miuras suffered from a lack of chassis stiffness when going very hard, so the SV had reinforcements put on both the front and rear extensions. Broader quadrilateral lower suspension arms replaced the

LEFT *The opening front and rear body sections were made in aluminium, while the rest of the body and chassis were in steel*
RIGHT *The black air vents of the P400 turned to silver for the later cars*

A-shaped lower rear wishbones, further to reduce toe in/toe out changes. A ZF limited-slip differential was also specified, necessitating a separate oil supply for the gearbox, but many SVs were built without the limited-slip diff. Some of these Miuras also had dry sumping.

Great car though it was, the Miura P400SV could not rightly claim to be the ultimate Miura. That honour must go to the Miura Jota. Initially conceived as a one-off, as the definitive high-performance Miura, the Jota project happened after Dallara had left the company.

His second in command, Stanzani, had assumed the role of chief engineer, and asked Bob Wallace to build a special car which could, if necessary, be raced successfully. Built to the Appendix J rules of the FIA (one of the reasons it was called Jota), the machine became a mobile test bed to evaluate a number of new components, some of which found their way on to the Miura SV. The project started in late 1970 and was much more than just a modified Miura. The suspension was pure racing car (with fabricated wishbones at the front), the chassis had a narrower and less massive backbone,

and both the front and rear subframes were different. Inside, the beauty of the Miura was discarded and replaced with a starkly functional alloy-sheet dash, gutted doors and fewer instruments. The wheels and tyres were also genuine sports car racing ware.

The beauty of the Bertone shape was sacrificed in the pursuit of better downforce (particularly for the sometimes suspect front) and a more slippery shape. The headlights were placed upright, behind perspex cowlings and canards (or small wings) were placed around the front corners of the nose

to increase downforce. An increased compression ratio (11.5:1, up from the 10.5:1 of the road car) and racing cams helped boost power to 440 bhp at 8500 rpm.

The original, and greatly prized, Jota was eventually sold in late 1971, never managing to turn a wheel in racing.

Naturally, some people wanted copies made. The factory, although initially uncooperative, eventually acquiesced and built what became known as SVJs, or Jota replicas. In most cases these cars were rebuilt versions of existing SV Miuras, although three

real SVJs were built from scratch (on SV chassis). These machines developed just over 400 bhp (thanks to larger inlet ports and free flow exhausts), and had a chin spoiler (as opposed to nose canards). They looked somewhat tamer than the original Jota but were far more practical road cars than the 'Wallace Wonder', albeit slower.

Miura production finished on 15 January l973 when the last P400SV – painted white – left the modern Sant'Agata factory. 750 cars were manufactured during the six year production run, with 1968 being the most successful year (184 deliveries).

On the road, it should come as no surprise to learn that the Miura was one of the most exhilarating road cars ever built, as well as being one of the most trend-setting. *Autocar,* during a test on the P400S variant in August 1970, quoted its top speed as 172 mph (277 kph) which was then the highest speed they had ever attained on road test. It's doubtful whether an SV variant would have achieved a better terminal velocity (the extra power was counterbalanced by the bigger wheels and tyres), although the SV would probably have done better than *Autocar's* 0–60 mph time of 6.7 sec for the P400S. The maximum speeds in the first four gears were 59, 86, 121 and 153 mph, or 95, 138, 195 and 246 kph.

These speeds were combined with an uncanny poise on the road by virtue of the engine layout and the aerodynamic qualities of that stylish body. What left a lasting impression on those road testers fortunate enough to push the Miura to its considerable limits, was the sound of fury of that 12-cylinder engine at full power.

There were faults, of course. The driving position left a lot to be desired, particularly for those over about 5 ft 10 in (183 cm). Head room was very limited for tall men (the highest part of the car was actually just behind the windscreen rather than above the seat) and the steering wheel was angled a little too much, in typical Italian fashion. Quality control on the Bertone made coachwork was rather suspect – certainly inferior to the quality of contemporary hand-made Aston Martins and Rolls-Royces. Glue stains, for instance, were quite common in the

interior. Apparently a number of British buyers took their cars to local coachmakers for an interior refit. That's rather a sad commentary on the motto on the Lamborghini factory wall, *'Il prossimo collaudatore e il cliente. Fate in modo che resti soddisfatto'* (The next test driver is the buyer. Build it so he'll be satisfied).

The handling, in most situations, was as good as the mid-engined layout, with its perfect weight distribution, promised. Road test after road test lauded the high-speed behaviour of the mid-motored marvel and the ride, although firm, did show surprising suppleness over all except badly broken roads (when the low-slung Lambo would bottom). The Miura's cornering behaviour, when a driver was *really* motoring, however, could be a bit uncertain at the limit. This was largely rectified by the bigger tyres and rear suspension modifications which came with the P400S series, and was further improved with the SV – the sweetest handling Miura.

That V12 engine, apart from offering superb ultimate performance, was a gem in other ways too, particularly for its low speed tractability. You could pull away in top gear at 1000 rpm without any complaint, and keep accelerating until the 170 mph (273 kph) mark. Few cars have ever offered such flexibility. What was particularly impressive was the way the Miura would keep thrusting forward well after 125 mph (200 kph) had been registered.

As *Autocar* put it 'At 3200 rpm on the

TOP LEFT *The roadster version of the Miura appeared first at the 1968 Brussels Show*
TOP RIGHT *Extra compression and racing cams helped boost the Jota's power output to 440 bhp, which pushed the top speed to 200 mph (320 kph)*
ABOVE *The Jota racer was the ultimate in Miuras, with even sleeker bodywork and revised chassis*

accurate Jaeger rev counter the exhaust becomes a spitting spiteful, rasping bark and the car races forward. It stays like that unrelentingly all the way to 8000 rpm, the only change is that the noise is almost a scream at the top end'.

The engine was noisy, of course, but not unreasonably so for a motor that sits so close to the driver. Even at high revs, with the blended cacophony of cam chains, valve chatter, carburettor hiss, drive gear whine and the inevitable rumble of the wide Pirellis underneath, conversation was still possible and a radio was still considered a useful option.

The view out of the front of the Miura was nothing less than panoramic, with the large windscreen giving an extensive view of the sky as well as the road. Rear vision was a different story. Straight behind in the rearview mirror, a driver got a better view of the air cleaner on top of the Webers than he did of the road. Rear three-quarter vision was even worse and enthusiasts soon found out how inherently impractical mid-engined cars were.

It was a heavy car to drive, too. The steering was the only control which was reasonably light to operate. The brake pedal and the clutch both required tree trunk-sized thigh muscles to operate effectively. Even the throttle pedal was heavy, not helped by the tortuous throttle linkages, which made the job of opening the twelve throttle butterflies a real test of strength. The American magazine *Road & Track* criticised that aspect of the Miura in their first road test of the car, complaining that the gearchange from second to third was 'particularly slow. The 5-4 downshift was also slow and so clumsy as to require considerable diversion of attention'.

The worst aspect of Lamborghini Miura ownership, however, was undoubtedly the maintenance needed to keep one of these charging bulls on the road. Bob Wallace later admitted that the car went on sale well before all the development work had been carried out. 'They had a very, very bad maintenance life,' recalled Bob. The later cars – built in the early '70s rather than the late '60s – were much better, as development improved the quality of materials used.

Even though it did not always continue to run reliably on the road, there is no doubt it will be remembered as a classic. It was the first mid-engined supercar and as such sired a breed of exotics which began with the Ferrari Dino of 1967 (Ferrari's first mid-engined road car) and continues today with the likes of the latest Lamborghini Countach,

Ferrari Boxer and Lotus Turbo Esprit. It was also the fastest road car of its day, able to beat anything else on the road by a good 10 mph (16 kph) in ultimate speed, even if its claimed 187 mph (300 kph) top end was a bit optimistic. There is also little doubt that it was the fastest mid-engined car ever built specifically for the road.

Ferruccio Lamborghini himself, who sold the firm after financial problems some ten years ago, puts the Miura above all the cars he produced – including the Countach. Thanks to the Miura his infant company, with far more temerity than tradition, started to be recognised as one of the great Italian exoticar manufacturers able to compare with older firms whose, histories were steeped in racing successes rather than tractor manufacture.

EVOLUTION

Introduced in chassis form at the 1965 Turin Show and available in 1967 as a two-seater, 4-litre, V12 mid-engined coupé.
Early production changes included the fitting of a chin spoiler at the front to help cure front end lightness at high speed. The glass section between the cockpit and engine was replaced with Perspex and insulation added to rear bulkhead to help reduce noise levels.

1968 P400S Miura, introduced at Turin Show with larger (70 section) Pirelli tyres and more power thanks to enlarged inlet ports and modified combustion chambers. Power now up to 370 bhp at 7700 rpm. Other changes included the introduction of electrically operated windows, improved trim and upholstery and rocker switches to replace the 'unsafe' toggle variety. Later the Miura S received ventilated disc brakes and a reinforced rear suspension to overcome toe-angle problems at the rear.

1971 Miura SV introduced at the Geneva Show with revised and wider bodywork to accept even wider (60 section) Pirellis. Other external differences included new tail and side lights, different headlight surrounds and a new grille. The inlet valve size was increased, bigger carburettor jets installed and the camshaft timing changed to produce a claimed 385 bhp at 7850 rpm. To cope with the extra power the chassis was reinforced further and the rear suspension changed as a new quadrilateral link replaced the lower wishbones. Some SV's were built with limited slip differentials and some with dry-sump lubrication.

1971 Miura Jota appears as a one-off prospective sports racer with narrower chassis, fabricated wishbone suspension and different subframes, and a more aerodynamically efficient body.
Compression ratio was raised to 11.5:1 and different cams installed to produce 440 bhp at 8500 rpm. The Jota spawned a number of Jota replicas with slightly less power (400 bhp) and chin spoilers rather than the canard wing of the true Jota.

1973 Miura production ends in January after 750 cars are produced.

GIULIETTA
Alfa Romeo
GTV

Most of Alfa Romeo's postwar success can be traced to their stylish Bertone and Zagato coupés – twin-cam powered they were fast as well as attractive

---

THE LAST of the Giulia GTV coupés left the production line in 1976, marking the end of a pretty well direct line after 20 years, true testimony to the high quality of the original design.

The first Giulietta coupé had been introduced in very limited numbers during 1954 and the range really made its debut at the 1955 Turin Show. Giuliettas were small cars, designed chiefly to be popular and affordable but also to be versatile enough to be built as practical, indeed dowdy, saloons,

LEFT *A rare Giulietta Sprint Zagato, only 200 of which were built between 1960 and 1962*
BELOW *The Giulietta SZ was powered by the 1290 cc twin-cam which produced 100 bhp at a high 6500 rpm*

elegant coupés and even efficient race winners.

At the heart of the Giulietta was a twin-cam engine, essentially the one that's still in production in the '80s. It marked a return to pre-war Alfa practice in some ways, being built in alloy with wet cylinder liners (although with shimmed rather than threaded tappets). Its slightly undersquare dimensions of 74 mm × 75 mm resulted in a displacement of a mere 1290 cc from which no less than 80 bhp was extracted at 6300 rpm. Much of that power was due to the top end design of the engine which featured two overhead camshafts, chain driven and operating two valves per cylinder inclined at 80 degrees, in hemispherical combustion chambers. That amount of power naturally gave the coupé impressive per-

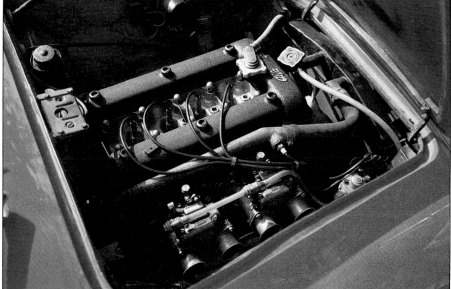

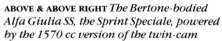

ABOVE & ABOVE RIGHT *The Bertone-bodied Alfa Giulia SS, the Sprint Speciale, powered by the 1570 cc version of the twin-cam*

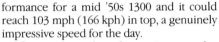

RIGHT *The same engine was used in the Giulietta Sprint of the mid '50s which was mechanically identical to the SS*

formance for a mid '50s 1300 and it could reach 103 mph (166 kph) in top, a genuinely impressive speed for the day.

Almost as good as the engine was the suspension, a strong thoroughly engineered and relatively simple design of double wishbones and coil springs at the front and a live rear axle. The axle sounds very much in keeping with the '50s except that great pains had been taken to locate the axle very securely to eliminate tramp and hop. Two stout pressed steel lower trailing arms were complemented by a triangular upper bracket connected at one point to the differential carrier and at two points to the body in front of the axle. Again the springs were coils and the dampers telescopic.

Although the Giulietta saloons were the incarnation of dullness the coupé was fortunate in having a body styled by Bertone, a neat two-door 2+2, compact and graceful. Everything in its design gelled; it was light and nimble, quick and graceful – the only oddity was the column mounted gearchange but that soon migrated to the floor.

Bertone's design seemed hard to improve on yet he managed it quite dramatically in 1957 with the lower and strikingly flamboyant Giulietta Sprint Speciale. The body was originally in alloy but later of steel and for once some overtly aerodynamic lines did not lie – the SS could cleave its way through the air at speeds of up to 125 mph (200 kph) on just 100 bhp. That extra power had been extracted from the 1300 engine simply by raising the compression ratio to 9.7:1 and fitting double twin-choke Webers. Unfortunately the SS was never built in huge numbers (2755 in all) but it did live on until 1965 as the Giulia SS with the larger 1570 cc twin-cam of the later cars.

A modern critic has condemned the Giulietta SS as having overly soft suspension

and (surprisingly) rather imprecise steering as well as very weak drum brakes which could '…provoke a heart attack in any attempt to bring that beautiful body to a standstill.'

Inevitably the Giulietta coupés were raced, and very successfully too, particularly the short and light Zagato-bodied cars. It was partly the search for even greater success that eventually led to the slightly larger and more powerful Giulia range. The 1290 cc engine was fine but there were more laurels to be won with bigger engines and by 1962 the twin-cam had been rejigged with a bigger bore, longer stroke and slightly revised block. It was now just slightly more undersquare than before with a bore of 78 mm and stroke of 82 mm, giving a displacement of 1570 cc; Alfa's engineers obviously got it just right as there has been a 1570 cc twin-cam ever since. In its first coupé application the 1570 produced only the same output as in the saloons, namely 92 bhp at 6200 rpm but that was soon increased to a far better 106 bhp at 6000 rpm for the Sprint.

Just to confuse matters (and the constantly changing Alfa line up and name changes can be extremely confusing) the first Giulia coupés used the old Giulietta body, but by 1963 the definitive Giulia coupé appeared, the Giulia Sprint with the body style that lasted until the mid '70s. Again it was by Bertone who seemed to be keeping his best work for Alfa – the coupés were actually the work of Giorgetto Giugiaro before he became famous in his own right and showed that he mastered curves before moving on to straight lines and angles.

Whereas the exaggerated styling of the earlier Sprint Speciale had been striking, the Giulia Sprint was simply perfectly proportioned – gone was the slightly hunchbacked look of the ordinary fastback Giulietta

coupé, replaced by a large gracefully sloping rear window and boot. In some ways it should not have looked so good, after all the doors were very deep, the car quite short and the windows fairly tall. The result should have looked short and too upright but instead was just right. Photographs are deceiving, making it look like a larger car whereas length and width are no more than that of an Escort RS.

Suspension had evolved along with the engine. The live rear axle was retained but its unsprung weight had been reduced thanks to the alloy differential casing used. The pressed trailing arms continued but sideways location was improved by a uniquely Alfa feature, a curious, almost 'T'-shaped forged arm mounted in front of the diff and attached to it at the side and to the body in two places. It was pivoted to allow the axle to move freely up and down and yet it improved location equally as well as more complicated systems such as four trailing arms and Watt linkage.

It wasn't long at all before the Giulia Sprint became the Sprint Veloce, or GTV for short. The main change sounded trifling yet it apparently made all the difference; the Veloce was given an extra 3 bhp, bringing output up to 109 bhp at 6000 rpm, along with 100 lb ft of torque at 4500 rpm. As Alfa claimed, perhaps accurately, that the GTV weighed only 2200 lb (990 kg), that gave it a good if not spectacular power to weight ratio in the order of 20 lb/hp. Obviously that meant the car was no rocket off the line, reaching 60 mph in 1.5 seconds, but once properly underway it came into its own, mainly due to that wonderfully free-revving and flexible twin-cam.

Although its specification might lead you to expect peaky performance from a narrow rev band the engine's character was quite different. It would potter around in fifth gear at surprisingly low rpm and still be able to pull the car, albeit without briskly accelerating it. Usable power was there after 1500 rpm and past 3000 rpm the engine soared happily towards the red line, although making a good deal of noise in the process. One of the problems with having chain-driven overhead camshafts in an alloy engine is an inescapable whirr and clatter. Alfa never really tried to suppress it either – after all, it was all part of the image.

To anyone who has only driven one of the later Alfas with the rear-mounted transmission and necessarily remote gear linkage it's hard to imagine just how satisfying the GTV's change was. The lever was surprisingly long and the up and down throws equally long although the movement across the gate was short. Fifth was out to the right on a dog leg with a strong spring action to bring the

lever back to the third-fourth gear plane. The best results were achieved by almost leisurely changes savouring the movement of precision engineering while bearing in mind that Alfa synchromesh was never that strong, particularly on second gear!

By the time of the GTV, Alfa had adopted disc brakes all round (the rears had little drums inset, just for the handbrake) and they worked very well indeed as long as corrosion hadn't attacked the master cylinder which was cunningly located *below* the car just behind the front wheel where all the mud, snow and salt could be sprayed over it in winter. That, and the Bertone body's propensity to self destruction through rust proved, to put it kindly, that Alfa had not really thought seriously about all their export markets.

The GTVs took a little getting used to as the driver sat low in the car, short people having serious difficulty, while the driving position was irritatingly Italianate requiring

extremely short legs and long arms. Normal people would find their legs annoyingly splayed if they wished still to be able to reach the steering wheel and the result on long journeys could be that rather unusual complaint of cramp in the buttocks, not helped by the awkward angle of the pedals sprouting from the floor. There was, however, a hand throttle which one could use as a crude form of cruise control to allow the legs to stretch out for a while… .

Despite the lack of rack and pinion steering, the action was quite precise, albeit extraordinarily heavy at parking speeds, needing a definite heave on the wheel. As the speed rose, so the steering improved, being quite beyond reproach at high speeds. For all these quirks the GTVs were very safe cars to drive, very predictable and with no vices – if you really overdid a corner the car seemed to take over of its own accord, with the steering self-centring itself vigorously. In ice or snow, however, the cars were frustration personified, their very light rear ends having next to no traction, easily leaving one stranded. As almost all photographs of the GTVs racing show, they cornered with con-

ABOVE RIGHT *The famous alloy twin cam engine, so effective in the GTV*
RIGHT *One of the racing GTAms at Spa Francorchamps in 1971*

ABOVE *The GTC was a convertible version of the 1600 Giulia coupé. Around 1000 were built in the mid '60s*

siderable lean, an indication of suspension supple enough to give a reasonably compliant ride. All the Giulia coupés were raced and with considerable success even against far larger displacement opposition. Their racing career really took off in the mid-'60s after touring car race regulations changed, basically requiring the manufacturers to keep much closer to the car's original specification than before. That spelt the end for the far more specialised racers like Alfa's TZ (*Tubolare Zagato*) with, as the name implied, tubular spaceframes. Luckily the Giulia coupés provided a good base; the main problem was not more power, which could be fairly easily obtained from the basic twin-cam, but weight and that was solved by the creation of an alloy body fixed to the standard floorpan. Visually the alloy bodies were identical to those of the Giulia Sprint

GTV but a crucial 700 lb (317 kg) lighter at just over 1700 lb (771 kg). At the same time the 1570 cc twin-cam was uprated to produce 115 bhp at 6000 rpm, giving a far better power to weight ratio of around 13 lb/hp.

The car was the GTA (A for *allegerito*, or lightened) and homologation requirements led to 500 being manufactured for sale to the general public or the keen private competitor. With 115 bhp the 'production' GTAs were obviously not up to being Alfa's frontline racers – the works car featured far more radical changes than simply the higher compression ration (9.7:1) of the homologation cars, going back to pre-war racing practice in having two spark plugs per cylinder. That was not on belt-and-braces reliability grounds but to speed combustion in those large hemispherical chambers. With a further increase in compression ratio, up to 10.5:1, 170 bhp was possible at a higher 7500 rpm. Given their light weight it wasn't surprising that the works GTAs could get within sight of 140 mph (225 kph). To help put that power on the road, the GTA had a limited slip diff, wider wheels and uprated rear suspension.

Alfa's aim was the European Touring Car Championship – a series they still compete in successfully with the V6 GTV6 but somehow without the same publicity or impact. The GTA plan worked to perfection and Alfa took the ETC Championship three years in succession, 1966, '67 and '68. Apart from beating the Lotus Cortinas in '66 the GTA put up such fine performances as Jochen Rindt's in Florida where he took the Sebring 4 Hours. 1967 saw the works cars victorious again and the hat-trick came in '68 with the bonus of class wins in the prestigious 24-hour races at Daytona and Spa.

Naturally the GTA approach was widened to bring even more success; a GTA Junior appeared with an extremely powerful fuel-injected short-stroke version of the 1270 cc engine and there was even a twin-supercharger GTAS. It too was a short-stroke development, this time of the 1570 cc engine, the idea being to let the engine rev more freely and indeed maximum power, all 220 bhp of it, came in at 7500 rpm. The drive to the superchargers, by hydraulic pump, chain driven (of course) from the engine sounds power-sapping but obviously wasn't and the car became the ideal hill-climb contender. 220 bhp was also extracted from the next GTA, without the help of blowers but with the aid of more cubic inches and bigger valves. To confuse the issue it was called the 1750 GTAm but was actually almost a 2 litre; the 'm' stood for *maggiorate* so in other words it was a 1750, only bigger… . It proved to be just as competitive as the others taking over where they left off, winning the ETC Championship in its first and second years (1970 and '71).

Early GTVs featured an interior just as elegant as the Bertone body with a large black and silver steering wheel and large, round and clear instruments. As the car developed however the interior design suffered somewhat, particularly in the 1750 GTV introduced in 1967. The fuel and water temperature gauges were moved to a large fake wood console or binnacle shrouding

ABOVE & BELOW LEFT *The alloy-bodied GTA was produced between 1965 and '69 with the 1570 cc twin-cam slightly tuned to give 115 bhp at 6000 rpm*

ABOVE *The GTA's interior was starker than the standard coupé's, but it was a functional car and saving weight was critical to its high performance*

EVOLUTION

The first Giulietta coupé, the Giulietta Sprint, was built in 1954 making its official appearance at the 1955 Turin Show, powered by an 80 bhp 1290 cc twin-cam engine.

1957 Bertone-designed Giulietta Sprint Special introduced with the 1290 cc engine but with the power increased to 100 bhp at 6500 rpm, giving a top speed of 124 mph (199 kph)

1962 The twin-cam engine was stretched to 1570 cc and fitted in the new Giulia range. The first Giulia coupé however retained the old Giulietta Sprint style bodyshell, with the larger engine

1963 The Giulia Sprint Speciale was introduced with the 1570 cc engine, now producing 112 bhp at 6500 rpm. Its bodyshell was the same as the earlier Giulietta SS. Production of both SS versions totalled 2755 between 1957 and 1964. Giulia Sprint GT introduced at the Frankfurt Show with disc brakes all round, the 106 bhp version of the 1570 cc engine and a top speed of 111 mph (178 kph). It introduced the Bertone body style which remained in production until 1975

1966 Alfa GTV introduced with 109 bhp version of the 1570 twin-cam. A little later that year the GT Junior appeared with the 1290 cc engine

1965 The GTA was developed for homologation, 500 being built in all between 1965 and 1969. It was a lightened version of the GTV with aluminium body panels and a high-compression version of the 1570 twin-cam. Works cars were far more highly tuned with twin spark plugs per cylinder

1967 The 1750 GTV introduced with 1779 cc engine which produced 118 bhp at 5500 rpm. The bodyshell could be distinguished through having four head lights and no step below the leading edge of the bonnet

1970 The 1750 GTV received the GTA treatment but the engine was enlarged to 1985 cc to produce the 1750 GTAm

1971 The largest of the GTVs introduced, the 2000 GTV with the 1962 cc version of the alloy twin-cam. Power output increased from 118 to 132 bhp at 5500 rpm. Top speed rose to 122 mph (196 kph)

1972 A 1600 version of the coupé was reintroduced in the form of the GT Junior

1976 Production of GTVs ceases. In all 40,826 1600 coupés were produced along with 42,040 1750 GTVS and 36,385 2000 GTVs

---

that long gear lever where they were by no means as convenient, while the binnacle itself made the interior seem far more cramped and claustrophobic. At the same time some curiously ribbed seats were introduced which were neither very attractive, nor very comfortable.

On the other hand the engine was an improvement. Despite its name it wasn't a 1750, Alfa merely employed the evocative name of their pre-war sports tourers much as they were to do later with the Alfetta and Alfa 33. The genuine displacement was nearer 1800 cc than 1750, 1779 cc to be precise, achieved by increasing the bore to 80 mm and lengthening the stroke to 88.5 mm. That made the twin-cam more undersquare than before which appears a retrograde step in theory. In practice the configuration was almost ideal as it was still willing to rev freely yet had more pulling power. Up went the power, to 118 bhp from 109 while torque increased to 138 lb ft at 3000 rpm, helping to reduce the 0–60 mph sprint time to an impressive 9.3 seconds, the standing quarter to 18 seconds and increasing top speed to 116 mph (187 kph).

Externally the 1750 GTV could be identified by its four headlights and the lack of that curious step in the leading edge of the bonnet which distinguished the 1600 cars.

Curiously the 1750 wasn't the sales success those improvements suggested and it was not that long before Alfa decided on the final stretch of the twin-cam to its greatest displacement of 1962 cc for the 2000 GTV which appeared in 1971. Only the bore was increased this time, from 80 mm to 84 while the stroke stayed at 88 mm. With no other changes other than obvious things like rejetted carbs, the power rose substantially to

132 bhp at 550 rpm, a most impressive figure for a mass-produced vehicle.

A certain number of GTVs were exported to the United States, never as many as Alfa hoped as their distribution network and after-sales back-up certainly wasn't what it could have been and even then was far overshadowed by BMW's. In the USA and Canada, the Weber and Dellorto carburettors were replaced by Alfa's Spica mechanical fuel injection which undoubtedly made the cars far thirstier but did enable them to keep the same high (9.0:1) compression ratio and yet run on low (91) octane gasoline. In the GTV 2000's case maximum power was very slightly down at 129 bhp at 5800 rpm along with 132 lb ft of torque at 3500 rpm.

Road & Track tried the car and basically liked what they saw although they had to admit that its time was really up. 'The GTV is a good 1964 design, overdue for a change (but) still a good car and capable performer…'. What had seemed outstanding before, now seemed only adequate. The brakes for example were once regarded as the best around, '… but evolving standards of performance find them not as outstanding as they used to be.'

Despite the power increase the acceleration times of the 1750 and 2000 were not really all that far apart; *Motor* had managed to squeeze a 9.3-second 0–60 mph time from their 1750 GTV while *Road & Track* took 9.6 seconds with their 2000. Just as you would expect, however, the larger engine was enjoyed for the extra flexibility and quicker response making the car more driveable.

The interior of the US spec 2000 was an improvement over the 1750 and the European version of the 2000; the minor dials

were back where they belonged, between the tach and speedo, while the ugly central binnacle had been chopped down to size. The two main dials in the European versions were rather unfortunately given a tach and speedo with white dials having a broad black band with the numbers inset in white and a similar treatment was given to the three minor dials in the centre of the fascia. Elegant it was not, and yet another indication of just how needlessly Alfa Romeo could play around with a given design.

In the end the scope for change ran out and the Bertone GTVs were replaced by another Giugiaro design, the cleverer but more clumsy Alfetta GTs.

Ferrari 250

The 250 series, with its extended range of body styles and models, contains some of the greatest Ferraris ever

THE EARLY FERRARIS were all identified by a number which represented the capacity of a single engine cylinder, and thus the 250 was by definition a V12 with a nominal capacity of 3 litres. Until the development of the V6 Dino engines, Ferrari power units, with the exception of the Grand Prix racing in-line fours, all used the classic 60-degree V12 layout – which perfectly balances all the principal unequal forces.

In the 1950s there were two such engines in production at Maranello – if production is the right word for a process which involved such small numbers and so much skilful assembly by hand. For want of any better description, they tend to be known as the 'short' and the 'long' V12s. The short engine,

LEFT & BELOW *A splendid 250GT Lusso Berlinetta, a model launched in 1962*

designed by Gioacchino Colombo, was a little jewel and the first Ferrari power unit of all; it had started life with a capacity of only 1.5 litres in the original Tipo 125 sports car of 1947. The long engine, physically much bigger, was the work of Aurelio Lampredi, and began life in 1951 as a 4.5-litre GP power unit aimed at wresting supremacy from the Alfa Romeo Alfettas (which, of course, it did).

When it came to a 3-litre engine, the choice lay between these two, because the short engine could be opened up all the way to 3-litre capacity while the long one could be sleeved down. It really depended upon the design priorities: the bigger engine promised greater reserves of strength and reliability, but inevitably it was much heavier and needed to be installed in bigger chassis.

It is hardly surprising, given the way in

which Ferrari's product planning was carried out in the 1950s – which is to say that broadly speaking, there wasn't any – that the 250 emerged by confused stages and with versions of both the available engines before finally settling, many years later, into the configuration which was to gain status as perhaps the most desirable of all Ferraris – the 250GTO. One of the seeds was sown in 1952 with the appearance of the 250 Sport, in which the short engine for the first time reached 3-litre capacity with a bore of 73 mm and stroke of 58.8 mm, giving an actual capacity of 2953 cc. The real point of interest here was that this engine replaced the long engine which had hitherto been used in Ferrari's larger sports models, the 340 America and Mexico.

Both the America and the Mexico in their various guises were massively powerful and fast cars, yet the restrictions placed on their handling by the mass of the long-block engine were such that the appeal of the displacement-increased smaller engine began to grow. Production of both the America and Mexico ended in 1955.

Such was the improvement in handling achieved by the adoption of the smaller, lighter engine that the 250 Sport won the 1952 Mille Miglia, with Bracco defeating the might of the Mercedes 300 SLs. Eventually, this line of development led through the 250 Mille Miglia and thence to the deservedly famous 250 Testa Rosso. Yet the definitive Ferrari 250, the road-going GT car which first appeared in 1953, began life with a shrunken version of the long engine!

In essence, the original 250 Europa was seen as a version of the 375 America. While the more powerful car's 4.5-litre engine achieved its actual 4522 cc capacity with a bore of 84 mm and stroke of 68 mm, the 250 saw it sleeved down to the square dimensions of 68 mm × 68 mm. giving 2963 cc. The engine in this form was reputed to deliver 200 bhp at 6000 rpm. Though this looks suspiciously simple arithmetic when you realise that the 4.5-litre 375 – half as much engine again – was rated at 300 bhp! Whatever the truth of the case, it didn't

matter much because the 250 Europa was a fairly awful car. It had perforce to use the America chassis, a huge device with a 115 in (292 cm) wheelbase and 54 in (137 cm) track, with suspension of rather doubtful merit (by Ferrari standards), consisting of front double wishbones with a single transverse leaf spring, and a live rear axle with simple leaf-spring location.

It is perhaps as well that this first 'production' 250 ran to no more than 20 examples, including the one seen on the stand at the 1953 Paris Salon where the model was announced. Probably the lesson of the 250 Sport was already being taken aboard, for by the following year the so-called Second Series 250 Europa had already appeared. This used the short engine first seen in the 250 Sport and was in effect a wholly new car, sitting on a much shorter wheelbase of 102 in (260 cm) and looking infinitely more handsome in its Pininfarina bodywork. The entirely different character of the engine can be seen in its power output of 220 bhp at 7000 rpm, achieved when breathing through three Weber 36 DCZ twin-choke carburettors – a choke for each pair of cylinders, in effect. As in the former engine, there was a single chain-driven camshaft for each cylinder bank, operating the opposing valves

by rockers. Drive was taken through a four-speed gearbox, and the chassis too was much improved, with coil springs in place of the front transverse leaf and a rear Watt linkage to relieve the leaf springs there of the strain of locating the axle in the side-to-side sense. Since it was still only the mid-1950s, the brakes were of course drums all round, a major shortcoming in a car capable of excellent performance. In those days, even more than now, press road-tests of Ferraris were very hard to arrange, and one can best judge the potential of the 250 by dividing its 220 bhp output by its kerb weight of just over a ton (1016 kg).

The new, much improved 250 Europa officially lasted little longer than its clumsy predecessor, Perhaps 35 had been made when, in 1955, there came a shift of designation to 250GT. To some extent this reflected the needs of the moment: the Le Mans disaster of that year caused a welcome switch of emphasis away from long-distance racing with thinly-disguised GP cars and back to something like genuine road-going machinery. This pitched the Ferrari 250 against the Mercedes 300SL (and the Jaguar C-type) and it was understandable that Ferrari wished to emphasise the civilised GT nature of his car.

ABOVE LEFT & RIGHT *A 1962 GTO, and* TOP & LEFT, *another '62 GTO, but with three sides louvres instead of two; the former was a feature on later cars. Introduced by Ferrari at a press conference on 24 February 1962, only 39 were built during the next two years. The GTO was very successful in racing and is today one of the most valuable and sought-after classics in the world*

Whatever the reason, the 250GT became outstandingly successful for Ferrari, in competition and in production terms. It stayed in production until 1964, when it was replaced by the 275, and even that was little more than a bigger-engined 250 with the vital modification of independent rear suspension. However, in the years on either side of 1960s, the 250's handling was quite good enough with its well-located live rear axle.

What did happen through those years was that in true Ferrari fashion the basic 250GT was refined, chopped about, fitted with different bodies and generally treated in a way that could only have happened at Maranello.

The 250GT was quickly launched into racing: indeed, it had already collected its first victory by the time it made its official debut at the Brussels Motor Show early in 1956. From then on it was never really bettered in 3-litre GT racing until the 1960s appearance of the new generation of mid-engined racing cars. In particular it made a habit of winning the then-prestigious Tour de France; its nine wins in a row in this event speak volumes for the effort Ferrari was prepared to put into its development, for its rivals certainly did not stand still.

Those early race-winners retained the standard 260 cm wheelbase but were (naturally) substantially tuned and lightened. Much

of the weight-saving came from a new light-alloy body by Scaglietti; power output was eased up to 260 bhp, still at 7000 rpm. These cars, the 250 Berlinettas, were remarkable not only for what they achieved, but for the handicaps under which they did so: for they retained four-speed gearboxes and drum brakes as well as the live rear axle.

Technical innovation in these peripheral spheres was not a Ferrari trademark at this period. While racing Ferraris would typically have the best engineered engines and probably the most attractive bodywork, gearbox, brakes and final drive would often lag behind other manufacturers. Nevertheless, the cars were still effective packages.

It was clear, though, that steady development of the existing car would not keep the Ferrari flag flying for ever, even in the Tour de France. Something altogether lighter and more nimble was needed: something which would, however, still be identified as a 250GT. There would be every justification, for the main mechanical elements would be retained. What was done, quite logically, was to chop a lump out of the wheelbase – easily enough done with a simple tubular chassis frame – and commission new bodies for the result. One body (built by Scaglietti again, to a Pininfarina design) would serve for the new line of Berlinettas, while Pininfarina himself (again) would come up with an equivalent road-going car.

The actual choice of wheelbase was equally logical. If the original was 102 in, the shortened version would be 94.4 in (240 cm) which was quite sufficient to allow the design of a snug two-seat coupé – or even a generous one, given the greater front and rear overhangs permissible in a road car – while making the 250 substantially lighter

325

and quickening its steering response. The results of these labours emerged in 1959 and met with deserved acclaim. It was not just that the car was lighter and more nimble, or even that the Berlinetta at least looked very pretty: at last the 250GT had been given Dunlop disc brakes, and this was enough to sharpen their competitive edge – being worth a good deal more, in terms of lap times, than the further engine tuning which lifted power output to 280 bhp.

If the short-wheelbase Berlinetta was almost an instant classic – and there are Ferrari enthusiasts who today rate it the best of the entire breed – the Pininfarina road cars were less of a success. There were two, a coupé and (for the first time) a convertible Cabriolet whose body was certainly not stiff enough: despite their use of chassis frames, Ferraris also depended on the extra torsional stiffness contributed by the body. The earliest road-going cars were also hampered by retaining drum brakes.

However, these cars were relatively short-lived, for the development bandwagon was really rolling and Ferrari had plans to split the 250 line far more positively between racing and road-going cars (it is worth noting, in passing, that while the Berlinettas were the 'racing' as distinct from 'road-going' models, they were in keeping with the spirit of their age and were entirely capable of being driven legally, if not always easily or quietly, on the road). The results of these further deliberations emerged in 1962 with the 250GTO and the 250GT Lusso.

Those letters GTO have, in recent years, assumed almost mystical status with examples of the breed changing hands for millions of pounds. Rarity and the charisma of the Ferrari name means that all other Ferrari models are following in step, with even the mundane cars worth considerable sums and reaching ever higher prices.

The GTO designation resulted from one of the more famous linguistic accidents. Ferrari needed his new lightweight coupé to be homologated for GT racing: in Italian, 'omologato'. Thus the car was named the GT

TOP LEFT & LEFT *A 1963 Ferrari 250 LMB: in fact most LM models had 3.3-litre V12s and should have been called 275 LMs*
TOP & ABOVE *The 250 Testa Rossa had a 300 hp V12 and was successful in the World Sports Car Championship*
BELOW *A 250 GT Pininfarina Cabriolet,*
BOTTOM RIGHT *A 250GT Pininfarina Coupé*

the stability. Bizzarrini used the University of Pisa's wind tunnel, plus a good deal of cut-and-try track testing, to achieve a shape which says much for the innate Italian ability to make cars look good even when working within this kind of technical constraint. Even so, the final touch remained to be added as an afterthought: having solved the problem of front-end lift, Bizzarrini discovered at a very late stage that the back was going light instead, and the final solution was to add two rear spoilers. The first, easily visible above the Kamm-type tail panel, became a kind of GTO trademark. The second, beneath the fuel tank, was equally valuable but much less obvious. The production GTO bodies were yet again built by Scaglietti.

It was Scaglietti also who built the corresponding road-going car, the Berlinetta Lusso. This was an extremely beautiful machine, but with none of the hard-won aerodynamic refinement of the GTO. In some ways it resembled a stretched version of the Alfa Romeo GTV of the same period, but was none the worse for that; its real drawback lay in the shape of the elegant but high-set nose which must have been worth a substantial amount of Cd all by itself. Against that, it is probably one of the easiest of the classic V12s to see out of, with extremely slim pillars all round and none of the blinkered tightness of modern exotics.

The GTO engine was itself an interesting unit, since in effect it was the famous Testa

Omologato, or just plain GTO.

Unlike any previous Ferrari, the GTO was not styled as such. Bizzarrini, then Ferrari's chief development engineer, had realised the need for proper aerodynamic research – since even GT races were already being fought out at speeds above 150 mph (241 kph) on the longer straights. It was already accepted that the existing Berlinetta body had a nose shape that caused both drag and front-end lift at high speed, and these faults needed urgent rectification, as did the narrow rear track which did nothing to assist

EVOLUTION

First tested in 1952, the Vignale-bodied prototype 250 Sport was the earliest Ferrari fitted with a 3-litre version of Colombo's V12. also shown that year was the 250 MM, based on the Sport. In all, 17 Pininfarina coupés, 13 Vignale Spyders and one coupé were built

1953 The road-going version of the Sport was introduced, the 250 Europa, fitted with a 3-litre, sleeved-down version of Lampredi's 4.5-litre V12. Approximately 20 were built

1954 The Second Series 250 GT Europa was announced, fitted with the short Colombo engine and with a shorter wheelbase; styled by Pininfarina, about 32 were made

1956 The 250 GT Boano 'low-roof' coupé was announced, of which 70–80 were made, along with the 250 GT long-wheelbase Tour de France Berlinetta Coupé, of which 74 were made over the next three years

1957 The 250 GT Pininfarina Cabriolet was launched at the Paris Salon; in all about 45 were built. The 250 GT 'high-roof' Ellena coupé was introduced (of which 50 were made), as was the sports-racing 250 Testa Rossa, designed for the 1958 World Sports Car Championship. This it won, as well as in 1960 and '61. In all, 34 were built. Also introduced was the long-wheelbase, Pininfarina-styled 250 GT California Spyder, 46 were made

1958 The 250 GT Pininfarina Coupé was launched, a highly successful model of which 350 were built

1959 The short-wheelbase GT Berlinetta was launched for racing. 162 were made

1960 The short-wheelbase 250 GT California Spyder was launched. 55 were built

1962 The 250 GT 2 + 2 was introduced; styled by Pininfarina; about 900 were made. Also offered was the 250 GT Berlinetta Lusso, styled by Pininfarina, of which 400 were made, and the 250 GTO of which 39 were built

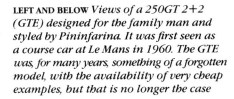

LEFT AND BELOW *Views of a 250GT 2+2 (GTE) designed for the family man and styled by Pininfarina. It was first seen as a course car at Le Mans in 1960. The GTE was, for many years, something of a forgotten model, with the availability of very cheap examples, but that is no longer the case*

Rossa racing engine but without the red cam-covers which gave it its name. This retained the familiar short 3-litre engine dimensions but was revised in many respects. Most important was the change in breathing arrangements, the siamesed inlet ports of the standard 250 V12 being replaced by six separate inlet ports per head (and by six Weber 38 DCN carburettors to feed them!). This was not as simple an exercise as it sounds, since the existing spark-plug positions could no longer be used and the plugs had to be switched to the other side of the heads. The whole bottom end of the engine was also stiffened through the adoption of seven main bearings for the crankshaft instead of the previous five.

In this form, the GTO engine delivered a genuine 295 bhp at 7500 rpm. At this point the power curve was still climbing, but that was the maximum officially stressed speed of the engine. It is possible that drivers brave enough to go past the red line may have seen the 310 bhp sometimes claimed for the unit…for a while! The drive was taken through another innovation, a proper five-speed gearbox (later road-going 250s had offered an overdrive, but never a genuine five-speed box) driving through a ZF limited-slip differential. As befitted the car's competition status, various final-drive ratios were available ranging from a 'sprint' 4.85:1 to a 'Le Mans' 3.55:1. With the latter ratio and standard tyres, the theoretical maximum speed at the red line in fifth gear worked out at 180 mph (290 kph), though it seems unlikely that the GTO would ever have exceeded 165 mph (266 kph) in practice. Acceleration depends even more on the final-drive ratio fitted, but the GTO's ratio of torque to weight suggests that it should have bettered 6 seconds to 60 mph (97 kph) without too much trouble.

There was just one problem with the 250 GTO. Although it was Omologated on the understanding that the requisite number would be produced, they never were. The most authoritative record suggests that 40 GTOs were built in total, and three of those certainly didn't count because they were powered by vastly stretched 4-litre engines. The FIA countenanced this failure but made sure it wasn't repeated when Ferrari presented his planned GTO replacement, the mid-engined 250LM. It was three years before the necessary papers were issued – and in just about that time, the 250 GTO itself had made the transition from front-running GT racer to sought-after classic.

FERRARI

As successor to the 275, the Daytona cured many of its ills without being greatly different from it. Its 4.4-litre V12 engine endowed it with shattering acceleration and a 175 mph top speed

THE DAYTONA – or as Ferrari always insisted on calling it, the 365 GTB/4 – was a remarkable car in more than one way. In the first place, authoritative road tests of the early 1970s made it beyond doubt the fastest road car of all time, until the advent of the most exotic beasts of the mid-1980s, turbocharged or otherwise. Yet it achieved this feat with chassis engineering which some critics decried as old-fashioned even when it first appeared!

In essence, the Daytona was a replacement for the Ferrari 275. By the mid-1960s, Ferrari had clearly established its presence in the market for nimble, ultra-fast GT coupés as well as that for heavy but prestigious sports cars like the 330. The Ferrari GT reputation had been established with the much admired 250 and 275 models, culminating in the classic 275 GTB/4 with its four-cam engine. The question was where the company should go next. With the 275 becoming longer in the tooth, and the competition becoming keener (none more so than from the upstart Lamborghini) there was an obvious need for something both quicker and even better-looking. Yet at the same time there was the looming threat of exhaust emission regulations in the USA, long since Ferrari's principal market.

It was the birth of the emission requirements which quickly killed the 275GTB/4, since there was no way its engine could beat the regulations without emasculating its performance. It was simply too highly-tuned to survive. That argued strongly that the 275 replacement should be bigger-engined; it would then have the margin to achieve decent performance with such additions as an air pump and exhaust gas recirculation, while in Europe that margin could be put to better use in a search for really shattering performance by road-car standards. Since

the engine had to be bigger, it followed that the car as a whole would grow; but not too much, since it had after all to follow the GT tradition of the 275. Perhaps it was a risk to place any great restraint on Pininfarina when he addressed himself to the problem of coming up with a shape to attract even greater admiration than the 275; but it is beyond question that he succeeded.

The 275 had represented the last practical stretch of the Colombo-designed 'small-block' Ferrari V12, and the engineers therefore turned to Lampredi's 'big-block' unit whose own origins stretched back to 1951. The basic power unit was used in the hefty 330s and had been stretched even further to 4390 cc for use in the 365 GT 2+2. As always with Ferrari designations of the time, the 365 referred to the cubic capacity of a single cylinder: bore and stroke were 81 and 71 mm respectively, making the engine far less over-square than the 275 unit whose dimensions were 77 mm bore and 58.8 mm stroke.

However, the 365 had but one camshaft per bank (and a power output of 'only' 320 bhp at a leisurely – for Ferrari – 6600 rpm) and it was clear from the reception accorded the four-cam 275 GTB/4 that its replacement would likewise need four camshafts. The development process proceeded mainly in the straightforward manner of most Ferrari exercises, save for a brief mad excursion into a ·prototype unit with three valves and twin plugs per cylinder and Heron-type combustion chambers, all in

The Ferrari Daytona Spyder is rapidly becoming one of the most collectable of Maranello cars. It provides wind-in-the-hair motoring with true 170 mph performance, provided by its V12 engine which spins effortlessly up to 8000 rpm

search of better exhaust emission. In the end however the 365/4 engine retained its classic hemispherical head and opposed valves and the process of its adaptation closely followed that by which the 275 had been turned into the 275/4. In particular, the same camshaft drive train layout was used, with the chain drives to the original single camshafts retained but used instead to drive idler wheels which in turn drove the twin camshafts via gears. The result, after due attention had been paid to breathing and fuel delivery, using twin Bendix electric pumps and the then standard Ferrari installation of six twin-choke Weber 40DCN carburettors, was a power output of 352 bhp at 7500 rpm.

That may not seem a great deal by comparison with the 300 bhp of the 275 GTB/4 – just 17 percent more power for a 35 percent increase in engine capacity – but power is not everything even in a Ferrari. It was clear enough that given a body with better aerodynamics than that of the 275, which itself had a maximum speed of more than 160 mph (258 kph), an extra 52 bhp would be enough to push on past 170 mph (274 kph). On the assumption that 170 mph ought to be fast enough for any road car, and with an eye to the need for differences between the European and USA-specification cars not to be *too* great, the engineers therefore spent their margin of tuning on extra torque. This is where the Daytona's superiority – 318 lb ft at 5500 rpm, compared with the 275's 217 lb ft at 6000 rpm – really showed. Its torque advantage was therefore a massive 47 percent; and it is torque which governs acceleration.

In some senses the extra torque was needed, since whether or not the Daytona-to-be turned out bigger than the 275, it would inevitably be substantially heavier. The bigger engine alone, with other compo-

DAYTONA

nents to match, would make sure of that. It was in any case decided in principle to build the new car on the same 94.5 in (240 cm) wheelbase as the 275 since this would ensure sufficient cabin space to take two people in comfort, and there was no question of the Daytona being a four-seater even in the most occasional way. It was further, and crucially, decided that whatever the appeal of the mid-engined layout, by then already dominant in racing, the Daytona would stick to a front engine driving the rear wheels; and that like the 275, the drive would be taken to a five-speed gearbox at the rear, in unit with the final drive but linked to the engine by means of a torque-tube. This was the layout which had cured the 275 of its original problems of vibration and short-lived gearboxes. There was indeed no question but that the Daytona would be a kind of 'grown-up' 275 rather than breaking new ground as far as mechanical layout was concerned.

These decisions naturally had a lot of bearing on the styling approach adopted by Pininfarina. In many ways they made his job easier. While Bertone was struggling, though with outstanding success as it turned out, with the mid-engined Lamborghini Miura, Pininfarina had merely to take the familiar

The ex-Ecurie Francorchamps Daytona which came 20th in the 1973 Le Mans 24-Hour race in the hands of Andruet and Bond at an average of 95.147 mph

dimensions of the 275, adopt the same general body-construction technique of carefully welded, relatively small panels adding little extra rigidity to the strong tubular frame (the sort of construction Ferrari's body-builder Scaglietti was throughly at home with, in fact), make allowance for some necessary extra width and space around the engine bay, and clothe it with something really stunning.

ABOVE *The Andruet/Ballot-Lena Daytona on its way to fifth at Le Mans '72*
BELOW *Clay Regazzoni's own '69 car which is fitted with hand controls*

Stunning it certainly was, but not merely in the aesthetic sense. With the earlier experience of the 275 in mind – its need for subtle nose reshaping to kill front-end lift – Pininfarina resorted to wind tunnel studies at an early stage. This also gave him a chance, as his vision of the car grew, to ensure that its aerodynamic drag was cut to the minimum. The characteristic horizontal blade of a nose (aerodynamic cleanliness ensured in the early cars by faired-in head-lamps, and later by retractable twin units) was pitched at a height to ensure more air went over it than under it. The concave tail panel neatly killed back-end lift just like that on the 275, but did it without sticking a spoiler up at right angles to the airflow: the whole thing was more subtle. So were the lines joining front to rear. Pininfarina studied various different lengths of tail, though all with the same general shape, and eventually settled on one which was seen essentially practical: it resulted in the Daytona being virtually the same length overall as the 275, and it provided just enough space for a full-sized spare wheel to be installed flat between the final drive housing and the rear bumper.

The bumpers were light quarter units front and rear, and they were never intended to serve much more than an aesthetic purpose; they were the only real concession to decoration and appeared to 'hover' in the narrow air intake, complementing the handsomely-styled front end.

The overall shape was exceptionally clean and devoid of needless scoops and frills. The main cooling air intake was tucked beneath the nose; two plain extractor vents in the bonnet sucked hot air from beneath

the engine compartment.

The Daytona in its final form might have been little bigger than the 275 physically (less than an inch longer, an inch and a half wider) but the car was a great deal heavier. Just how much heavier is a matter of some discussion. Official Ferrari figures at the time of the 1968 introduction speak of 2825 lb (1280 kg) which made the Daytona 330 lb (151 kg) more than the 275 GTB/4; but when *Autocar* came to put its test Daytona on the weighbridge in 1970 the kerb weight emerged as 3530 lb (1600 kg)! Whatever figure you take there is no doubt that the Daytona carried a substantial handicap by comparison with its predecessor – but then it had ample torque available to make light of it, quite literally.

Compared with the 275 in another sense – that of creature comfort – the Daytona was in another class. Its cabin was quite roomy for two occupants, with notably more width. Ferrari chose to provide adjustable pedal pads for small drivers (they could be set 2 in 5 cm nearer) rather than an adjustable steering wheel. Heating and ventilation was tre-

ABOVE *A brace of Daytonas worth maybe a million pounds, or more. The closed coupé is a later model with the retractable headlamps in place of covered items. The open car is a rare beast indeed, being an original right-hand drive version, one of only a handful made and not a converted closed car*

ated in the usual cavalier fashion but while air-conditioning was rarely if ever installed in the 275 it became a popular option in the Daytona and was well worth it in hot weather. The seats were superb, and so were the instruments, the main speedometer and rev counter dials exceptionally large and easily read.

Unlike the 275, the Daytona suffered no major changes of specification during its production life, and far fewer questions arose concerning such matters as the gearing actually fitted. The ratios within the

five-speed gearbox were unashamedly chosen for high performance: in conjunction with the standard 3.3:1 final drive ratio and 215/70–15 Michelin XVR tyres, they gave maximum speeds of 59 mph (95 kph) in first, 86 mph (139 kph) in second, 116 mph (187 kph) in third and 146 mph (235 kph) in fourth! Maximum speed in top gear was of course a matter of great debate. The *Autocar* figure of 174 mph (280 kph) represented 7100 rpm, still 400 rpm short of the power peak, suggesting that the Daytona was ideally geared for a 184 mph (296 kph) maximum. It is certainly true that the *Autocar* test car was suspiciously heavy – it was fitted with air conditioning, for one thing – and that it suffered the aerodynamic intrusion of two auxiliary lights under the nose (and wired up to replace the flashing function of the retractable headlamps). It may well be that more would have come with a completely 'clean' car but the author – who was heavily involved in the *Autocar* test – doubts that the difference would have amounted to anything like 10 mph (16 kph). In any case, does it matter? The 174 mph (280 kph) was

LEFT *The formidable V12 engine which produces enough power to propel the Daytona at speeds of up to 175 mph, making it one of the fastest cars of its time*

(241 kph) and still have room to brake before the end of a 1-mile (1.6 km) test straight.

While the brakes on the 275 had been without doubt the worst engineering feature of the car, those of the Daytona were beyond serious reproach. The difference lay partly in a move from 14 in (35 cm) to 15 in (38 cm) wheels – itself made possible by the introduction of low-profile 70-series high-speed radial-ply tyres – which made room for bigger discs, and partly in the arrival of the ventilated disc which made all the difference when it came to stopping anything with Daytona performance. The car used ventilated Girling discs of more than 11 in (28 cm) diameter all round, and the *Autocar* fade test failed to shake their composure in any way; but the handbrake, in the manner of so many supercars, was diabolically weak.

The Daytona suspension, again like that of the 275, was all-independent but relatively simple, using unequal-length double wishbones at each corner together with concentric coil spring/damper units. The front springs bore on the long lower wishbones in order not to intrude on the limited nose height, but those at the rear ran from the upper wishbones up to fabricated towers which formed part of the frame – thus leaving space for the drive shafts each with twin constant-velocity joints to run between the wishbones. Anti-roll bars were fitted at both ends of the car, their stiffnesses chosen to fine-tune the handling as close to neutral as possible, aided also by pronounced negative static camber on the rear wheels. The

enough for the Daytona to remain the fastest road-going production car ever authoritatively tested from 1971 until 1985.

It was not, however, the maximum speed which was so instantly impressive as the acceleration. Despite the problems of getting away from a standing start with wide and grippy tyres, that exceptionally high first gear and a rather soft clutch, the Daytona proved capable of passing the kilometre post in 24.3 sec (very much in line with the factory's brochure claim of 24 sec) at a terminal speed of 139 mph (224 kph). Such was its acceleration even at this speed that it proved possible to take times to 150 mph

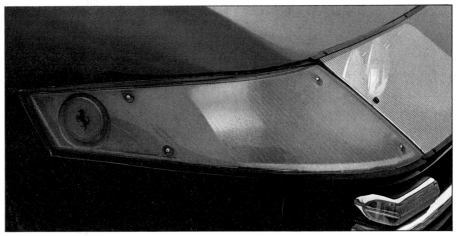

Two examples of earlier Daytonas, distinguishable by the perspex covers over the headlamps. The low-slung hammock seats were fixed but provided an excellent driving position with a good view forward over the vast expanse of bonnet. Some very early models featured a Ferrari-esque chromed gearchange gate – later covered

steering, though not power-assisted, was high-geared at three turns lock-to-lock (though admittedly one is talking about a 40 ft/12 m turning circle, to put the thing in proper perspective). A very large positive steering offset, almost half the width of the tyre, resulted in lighter efforts at very low speed at the cost of heavy kick-back over bumps and potholes.

Driving the Daytona was not, therefore, pure unalloyed pleasure but it succeeded better than the 275, and better than most of its rivals in putting the utmost levels of road performance within reach of those who were prepared to sacrifice money, but not comfort or convenience, in order to have it. One of the author's most vivid memories of the Daytona, oddly enough, is driving it at a rock-steady 30 mph (48 kph) to obtain a steady-speed fuel consumption figure (which, for the unlikely record, turned out to be 24.5 mpg). The car's docility, the ease with which it could be held at exactly the right figure, was all the more remarkable when taken together with the acceleration figures it had just recorded. For that matter, there was also the astonishing ease with

which the fuel flowmeter could be installed on the magnificent-looking engine.

What this rightly implies is that in areas where mid-engined rivals have their almost inevitable drawbacks – in cabin space, visibility from the driving seat, smoothness of driveline and lack of town-driving temperament, interior noise level, luggage space, engine accessibility – the Daytona excels. That in itself seems to condemn it in some eyes, expecting to see all practicality compromised for the sake of performance and handling, as 'not a *real* supercar'; yet the performance speaks for itself, and so indeed does the handling as long as you do not allow yourself to be dragged into the perennial argument between mid-engine and front-engine. One might perhaps quote the *Autocar* comment that the Daytona's 'handling is everything you expect of it, and the limits of adhesion are well beyond what is sane and rational on public roads'. It goes almost without saying that wilful misapplication of 319 lb ft of torque while cornering in second or third gear will have dire consequ-

ences, but that is equally the case in any of the Daytona's rivals (and even more quickly and devastatingly in some).

As always in the case of major Ferrari models, there is some confusion about the number of Daytonas actually built. The total must however approach 1500 of which well over 100 were Spyder convertibles completed from 1970 onwards. Extreme rarity has made the Spyder the most expensive and sought-after of all Ferrari road cars, and one result is that many crashed Coupés (especially in the USA) have been converted to Spyder form as part of the 'repair'. The main Daytona chassis frame is renowned for its strength and rigidity – another lesson learned from the over-flexible 275 – but the body follows the usual Ferrari pattern of being terribly vulnerable to rust; Scaglietti applied no corrosion protection at all during building.

Daytona production continued until 1974, by which time it was clear that whatever the merits of the car, the pressure for any current Ferrari GT car to be mid-engined became irresistible, and the result was the 512BB, the Boxer. The front-engined layout lives on in the big but remarkably civilised 400i, but that cannot have the cachet of the Daytona: probably the most instantly recognisable Ferrari model even to the non-enthusiast, and one which for so long could lay claim to being The Fastest Road Car.

United States of

The American automobile industry is marked by extreme highs and lows, for some of the very best and worst products have come from the USA since the earliest days of the car. Fortunately, we do not have to concern ourselves here with either the worst looking or the worst performers but to concentrate totally on the high points. Beginning with the pre-war greats, these include the extraordinary 16-cylinder Cadillacs, the Hollywood-favoured supercharged Duesenbergs

A638 VTW

America

and the amazingly styled but instantly recognizable Cord. The post-war era has seen many high points, with the 'muscle cars' staking a major claim to fame with their power output and straight-line performance that will probably never be equalled. Only recently has appreciation of these cars started to grow significantly outside the United States of America, but they are now acknowledged by most discerning enthusiasts as being on a par with many mainstream European greats.

FORD TH

When America fell in love with the Thunderbird, back in 1954, it was a lively, compact two-seater, but during 30 years it's been through many changes

THUNDERBIRD is undoubtedly a fine name for a motor car, with its connotations of power, flight and a hint of mystery, and it's also a truly American one, being a magical totem for the Pueblo Indians of the South-West United States. That's appropriate, because the Thunderbird was – and still is – the essence of the American car, illustrating over its 30-year history most of the foibles and many of the strengths of that peculiar breed.

Every story on the Thunderbird begins with the idea that the car was conceived as an 'answer' to the Chevrolet Corvette. This is not entirely true, for both designs evolved in response to the growing demand in the post-war American market for cars with more style and performance, cars best typified by the stunning Jaguar XK120.

The birth of the T-bird was surely hurried along by the introduction of the Corvette. One story among the many holds that Louis D. Crusoe, vice-president of design for Ford, and George Walker, then a design consultant for the company, saw a prototype for the Corvette at the 1953 Paris Motor Show. Crusoe told Walker that he liked it, and Walker replied: 'We have something like that already going.'

Bill Boyer, who worked in Ford's Design Centre at Dearborn, Michigan, picks up the story: 'That same evening Walker called our Design Studio from Paris with instructions to "put some clay on that thing" and build that car. That telephone call gave us instant authority,' said Boyer, who at the time was senior designer on the yet un-named project car.

Boyer's boss, Frank Hershey, tells it differently. Quoted by Dennis Adler in *Car Collector* magazine, Hershey says that he and Boyer had worked out the design, but that Production Planner Chase Morsey actually sold Ford management on the project.

In any event a prototype appeared on 20 February, 1954, at the Detroit Auto Show, to thunderous acclaim, although at this point the car was still nameless.

A 'name-that-car' contest resulted in a Ford car-stylist winning a new suit of clothes for submitting the winning moniker. A new suit of clothes! Hang the expense.

Following a remarkably short gestation period, the first T-Bird rolled off the line on 9 September, 1954, as a 1955 model. The two-seater drop-head coupé had an overall

ABOVE *The now-classic Ford Thunderbird coupé of 1956, an American compromise of performance and comfort. The badge,* **RIGHT** *is part of the V8's rocker covers*

UNDERBIRD

length of 175.3 in (445 cm) and weighed in at 2833 lb (1285 kg). That these dimensions made it the smallest Ford to be built in decades says a lot about American cars of the period, if any reminder is necessary.

Throughout its history the Thunderbird has seldom been a technological leader – unless you count sequential turn-signals and Swing-A-Way steering wheels as technological leadership. It had no innovations like the Corvette's glassfibre bodies, fuel injection or fully-independent suspension. Nor was the Thunderbird to be a blood-and-thunder sports car like the Jaguar which helped spawn it. In fact, it was to be a 'Personal Luxury' car – one with sporty styling and acceleration but with no sacrifice of creature comforts. Where it has broken new ground has been in styling and marketing rather than engineering.

The 1955 model was quite lovely, largely due to the simplicity of the lines. It came with a removable glassfibre hardtop. A rayon folding top was available for $75 instead of the hardtop, or $290 in addition to it.

Aside from the unique cruciform frame and body, the Thunderbird consisted largely of bits from the parts bins of Ford's sedan models. The front suspension was a ball-jointed, unequal-length A-arm arrangement, and the rear was a leaf-sprung live axle. The 256 cu in (4195 cc) 160 bhp overhead-valve V8 that appeared in the prototype was enlarged to 292 cu in (4785 cc) in the production cars. It was rated at 193 bhp with a three-speed manual gearbox and a steering-column-mounted selector, and 198 bhp with the two-speed automatic.

Like most sub-teenage car freaks in North America at the time, your scribe was duly enchanted, but the love affair went unrequited until many years later. I finally drove a 1955 T-Bird at a press preview for the 1981 Fords.

How illusions can be shattered. This particular car wasn't cherry, but it wasn't trash either, and the shape certainly looked as good as ever. The V8 produced the pre-emission-controls burble that promised excitement. The dashboard had Ford's odd tinted perspex panel behind the instrument nacelle – an attempt to generate some 'available light' illumination, but something which succeeded more often in generating some magnified sunlight that left more than one Ford owner with melt-down of the speedo needle.

The gigantic steering wheel operated slack and feel-less power steering in spite of which the car felt extremely heavy and unwilling to move off dead ahead. The engine's power was there, but the rather stiff ride and unprepossessing handling were quite a disappointment. Such an excursion

ABOVE & RIGHT *The 1957 Thunderbird was given rocket-style fins and a wider, more chomium-bedecked grille and front-end treatment. The portholes were optional*

in an older classic is illuminating – we do tend to forget the degree of progress that has been achieved in even the most mundane of today's vehicles. Nevertheless, the T-Bird's road manners were certainly no worse than those of contemporary cars, and it looked a hell of a lot better. A fairly stiff price tag of nearly $3000 – nearly double that of a low-line Ford sedan, yet several hundred less than the more radical but less luxurious Corvette – didn't deter some 16,000 customers, and the car was deemed a success.

From the start, Ford executives realized that the market for luxury two-seaters was very limited. As the first T-Bird hit the streets, plans were already in place for a four-seat car, the first in a series of 'longer, lower, wider' Thunderbirds. Did I mention earlier the foibles of the American car?

While the four-seater was being planned, the two-seater continued for two more years. 1956 saw the introduction of a deep-dish steering wheel, padded dashboard and optional seat belts, as Ford tried vainly to sell safety to an unimpressed American public. Dual exhaust pipes were re-routed from the bumper overriders through the ends of the bumper, and the spare tyre was mounted 'continental-style', behind the rear bumper. This artifice improved boot capacity, but the added weight hanging out there did little to improve the car's handling. Portholes became a no-cost option on the hardtop, and a wider choice of V8 power became available.

In 1957 the Thunderbird succumbed to the tailfin craze, as canted appendages graced the rear wings. It worked better than most such attempts, and in any case was a thing of beauty in comparison with what was to come, for in 1958 the four-seater reared its ugly head.

That was a landmark year, in a sense, for auto styling in America. Never, before or since, were so many hideous designs offered in one model year. It was as if all the car stylists in the country conspired to give the American public just what they felt it deserved. There wasn't a single car in the

catalogue that year, from any manufacturer that wasn't gross in a hatful of ways.

The new Thunderbird was no less guilty than the rest. It was immediately dubbed the 'Squarebird', largely because of the rectangular roofline which nevertheless defined 'formal roof' for all time (cf. any current General Motors sedan). The huge air intake – all chromed, needless to say – made the car look like an automotive vacuum-cleaner. There were tailfins, of course, and the rear aspect looked like a Buck Rogers intergalactic cruiser. Dimensionally, the new car was 205 in (520 cm) long, on a 113 in (287 cm) wheelbase.

How did the public react to this monster? With renewed gusto, proving once again that there's more of them than there are of us. Retail deliveries of the Thunderbird reached 48,482, nearly equalling the total of the three years of the two-seaters.

Two models were offered: a coupé with a

FAR RIGHT *By 1961 The Thunderbird drophead had grown into a four-seater of rather different style to the original car, but popular nonetheless*

ABOVE *The 1983 Ford Thunderbird was a compact and aerodynamic two-door car*
LEFT *The 2.3-litre 1985 Turbo Coupé has a maximum speed of 115 mph (185 kph)*

permanently attached roof, and a convertible which accounted for less than one-third of total sales. Sportiness had been replaced by luxury as the *raison d'etre* of Thunderbird, and it would be a long time before that direction would be reversed.

The V8 became larger and more powerful as the horsepower race became more important. A three-speed automatic called Cruise-O-Matic was offered for the first time.

For many enthusiasts today, Thunderbird means solely the two-seaters of 1955–57. At the time, the lone defender of the faith within Ford seems to have been Frank Hershey, the original design chief on the car. He resigned in 1956 after losing the battle to keep the T-bird a two-seater. Can 48,000 Americans be wrong when it comes to designing a car? Hershey says yes, and today he gets a lot of support. Where was it when he needed it?

The years 1959 and 1960 witnessed few changes in the Thunderbird, aside from the

EVOLUTION

Introduced in September 1954 the Thunderbird was powered by a 292 cu in (4785 cc) V8

1956 The 312 cu in (5112 cc) V8 was offered as an option, and the dashboard was padded

1957 The car was restyled, and tailfins added

1958 The four-seat Thunderbird appeared

1961 The car was restyled, and offered with a 390 cu in (6390 cc) V8 with outputs of 300, 375 and 401 bhp and Cruise-O-Matic transmission

1962 A two-seat roadster was reintroduced, and a 406 cu in (6653 cc) V8 was offered

1965 Sequential turn signals were introduced and disc brakes fitted at the front. Engines ranged between 390 cu in (6390 cc) and 427 cu in (6997 cc) V8s

1966 The last convertible model was offered

1967 A four-door model was offered, and the range made with body-on-frame construction

1970 The Thunderbird was restyled, with a long bonnet. It was powered by a 429 cu in (7030 cc) V8 and Cruise-O-Matic transmission

1972 A new, two-door range was offered. The millionth Thunderbird was sold

1975 Similar in appearance, the new models were longer – overall length was 224 in (596 cm) – and heavier, and the cars were powered by a 460 in (7538 cc) V8

1977 New, smaller, Thunderbird range offered, fitted with a 302 cu in (4949 cc) V8

1980 Smaller still, the Thunderbird was fitted with a 200 cu in (3277 cc) in-line six

1983 Restyled, the Thunderbird became an aerodynamic two-door coupé with engine options of the 200 cu in six, a 302 cu in (4950 cc) V8 and a turbocharged 140 cu in (2300 cc) in-line four

than the last, were offered. One, a 427 cu in (6997 cc) fire-breather, later distinguished itself in several racing venues, although not in this car. In T-Bird guise it produced 410 bhp with the assistance of two Holley 4-barrel carburettors.

It might be said that the Thunderbird had truly arrived by 1963, for it was in this year that General Motors launched its counter-attack in the form of the attractive Buick Riviera. GM had few qualms, apparently, about borrowing either the personal luxury car concept or the T-Bird roof for this newcomer.

The Big Deal for Ford in 1964 was the Mustang. It was supposed to be an affordable sporty car based on production compo-nents. Where had we heard that before? You might think that the Mustang would have stolen some of Thunderbird's thunder, but it was not so. The restyled 'Bird lit up the lives of some 92,000 people in 1964, nearly a one-third increase over 1963.

Longer hoods, shorter rear decks and sculptured body sides were the trend in the mid-1960s, and the T-Bird was front and centre. The 1965 season saw the introduc-tion of the sequential turn signals, a fairly radical departure from accepted practice, and of front disc brakes, which was not. Engine choices ranged from a 300 bhp, 390 cu in (6390 cc) V8 to a twin-four-barrel 427 cu in (6997 cc) V8 with 425 bhp. Attempt-ing to drive one of these limply-sprung behemoths quickly on anything but a dead-straight road was a stylish way to kill your-self, but we didn't worry as much about those things back then. Nevertheless only 15,631 1965 T-Birds were built – the lowest number in the history of the marque.

The year 1966 was important in T-bird history only because it was the last year in which a convertible was offered. Ragtops were beginning to lose favour, not only because the safety crusaders were working their way into the minds of the American public, but because increased urban polu-tion, the threat of forced entry and theft and higher highway speeds had made open-air motoring less pleasurable. The public began to appreciate the sounds of a stereo radio more than the burble of a well-tuned motor.

The following year saw yet another leap for Thunderbird into the realm of luxury and opulence. Chief among the innovations of 1967 was a four-door model with 'suicide' rear doors, built on a 117 in (297 cm) wheel-base, 2 in (5 cm) longer than the two-door model. This was an idea from Lee Iacocca, who was heading the Ford Division at the time, and like most of his ideas, it sold – nearly 25,000 units, far more than the con-vertible model had done in 1966. The 1967 cars also reverted to separate body-on-frame

first sliding sun-roof on a post-war American car in the 1960 model. Ford's sales wizards luxuriated in the success of the larger car. From a marketing perspective they had clearly made the right decision.

The 1961 Thunderbird styling was again all-new, retaining little but the roofline. 'Pro-jectile styling' was what they called it, and it was shared by all Fords that year. A chrome character line ran up from the grille along the belt line, incorporating the door handles and terminating at the end of the tailfins on the rear wings. The huge, round tail-lights looked like Siamesed jet planes going the other way.

A new 390 cu in (6390 cc) V8 was intro-duced in three forms, producing 300, 375 and 401 bhp. The Cruise-O-Matic transmis-sion and self-adjusting power brakes were standard equipment. An electric windscreen wiper motor, the first fully-transistorized radio and – wait for it – the Swing-A-Way steering wheel were also offered. Again, the coupé outsold the convertible, this time by six to one.

As if in response to the ghosts of desig-ners past, a two-seat Sports Roadster model was offered in 1962. There is no record of whether or not Frank Hershey approved. The car was little more than a standard

convertible with a glassfibre tonneau cover over the rear seat area, moulded to create a twin-headrest effect and leaving a limited-access storage area underneath.

It was the model everyone said they loved, but few of them spoke with cash. Only 1427 examples were built, compared to over 8000 regular convertibles and over 78,000 hardtops.

If folding tops and roadsters weren't what the public wanted, Ford tried another approach – a vinyl-covered hardtop with chome 'landau' bars on the C-pillar.

The 390 engine continued in 1962, but was supplemented by a 406 cu in (6653 cc) V8 with a maximum output of 405 bhp. By this time the famous Swing-A-Way steering wheel was a standard fitment.

The last season for this style was 1963, and by this time a three-year styling cycle was part of the Thunderbird tradition. The sports roadster was still offered, but only 455 were made, and the model was dropped in mid-year.

An example of styling change for the sake of change was the 'feature line' pressed into the body sides. It started at the front and terminated for no particular reason half-way along the door.

Seven V8 engines, each more powerful

FAR LEFT *The fussy, overstyled 1978 Thunderbird here fitted with a T-roof, having lost most of the charisma of the early cars. It sold well, however*

ABOVE *Views of an immaculate 1955 Thunderbird convertible, powered by a 4785 cc (292 cu in) V8 and driven through a three-speed automatic transmission. This car has electric seats and windows and power-assisted steering and its number plate is entirely appropriate: the owner's initials are T.T.*

Jack Telnack, had just taken over his position, returning from a stint in Europe, and he had to introduce this thing to the motoring press. I recall him looking and sounding very nervous during this presentation. I thought he may have been apprehensive since this was his first North American introduction in his new capacity. I also suspected that Telnack, a man of evident personal taste and style, might simply have been aghast at what he had to offer – and it wasn't even his fault!

When asked about this episode at the January 1985 presentation of his own, and quite lovely, Ford Taurus and Mercury Sable, Telnack said of the 1980 Thunderbird, 'It was pretty awful, wasn't it?'

Among the many oddities about the car was the fact that its widest part was not the rear-view mirrors, but the arches over the rear wheels. You would squeeze the car into a tight spot, thinking you had it made when the mirrors got through, and then crunch.

The 1980 car did have some technological importance, returning the marque to unitized construction and being the first Thunderbird to offer other than a V8. A 200 cu in (3277 cc) in-line six was standard, with a 225 cu in (3687 cc) six and a 302 cu in (4948) V8 as options. The ugliness was unrelieved for two more years, and the less said of those years, the better.

Many enthusiasts still claim that the T-bird died in 1958, but they could take some heart from the fact that the 1983 models at least restored some of the style and dash of earlier years. The 1983 Thunderbird was the first shot in Ford's aerodynamic barrage – at least for the North American market. The car was as beautiful as the immediate predecessors were grotesque, and had actually been designed after the even more radical Lincoln Continental Mark VII, but was introduced first to help cushion the market.

In the UK too, the pre-'58 Thunderbirds are widely considered as the epitome of USA-style motoring. Having passed through a phase of being regarded as rather second-rate classics, they are now eagerly sought after and several firms specialise in their sale and maintenance. Later examples have a small but growing market.

If the six-cylinder engine of the 1980 model was a surprise, imagine the reaction to a four-cylinder being offered in the 1983 car. This was a turbocharged 2.3-litre Brazilian-built overhead-cam design that turned the Thunderbird Turbo Coupé into an exciting performer. Equipped with stiffened suspension, a slick five-speed manual gearbox and Goodyear Eagle GT tyres, the Turbo Coupé was – and remains – the best handling, best performing of them all.

The Thunderbird has completed its first 30 years as a stylish, comfortable, well-equipped car, which is pretty much how it began. In retrospect, all the changes may not appear to have been for the better, but like it or not, they have been the history of the American Motorcar Dream. And at this point it is once again a car which is worthy of that fine name.

construction, the then traditional method.

During 1968 and 1969 only minor changes were made, but in 1970 the last trace of sportiness in the Thunderbird was abandoned, and it became just another big luxury car. It still sold well, but to a different clientele. The competition had long since ceased to be the Corvette, and was now the Buick Riviera, Oldsmobile Tornado and even the Cadillac Coupe de Ville.

The Thunderbird's three-year styling cycle was broken in 1972 when the car was enlarged for the last time. This variation soldiered on for five years of mostly declining sales. As the first oil crisis in 1973 changed the industry forever, Ford began working on a smaller, more fuel-efficient Thunderbird.

Introduced in 1977, this car was really nothing more than a rebodied intermediate sedan, and, what was worse for the Thunderbird's image, its shape was shared with the Mercury Divison's Cougar. But what was even worse, from an enthusiast's point of view, was that the car sold better than ever, recording some 318,000 units. Ford had taken an exclusive name, with tremendous appeal, and moved it into the mass market. A great victory for marketing, a great defeat for purists.

Believe it or not, it went downhill from there. In 1980 came the debut of one of the truly ugly automobiles in my experience. Based on the Ford Fairmont chassis, the 1980 Thunderbird was angular, had a track far too narrow for its body, and exhibited some of the most heavy-handed detailing since the Daimler SP250. Ford's Chief Stylist,

CHEVROLET CAMARO PONTIAC FIREBIRD

For nearly 20 years the Camaro and Firebird have rivalled, and sometimes beaten, Ford's Mustang as America's most popular sports coupé

HOW DO YOU define a sports car? Is it the distillation of everything that a brilliant engineer has learned after years in the business? Or maybe a mildly softened version of a competition car? In truth, unfortunately a sports car is more likely to be a pretty body grafted onto an ordinary saloon.

If that strategy was good enough for MG, surely it was good enough for GM. And General Motors followed that plan perfectly with their Chevrolet Camaro and Pontiac Firebird. But is it justified for cars like the Camaro and Firebird to be called sports cars? It depends.

Does a sports car have to be in the garage half the time being fixed? Does it have to leak when it rains? Does a fifty-mile trip have to mean kidney dialysis for driver and passengers alike and does the presence of more than two seats or a steel top disqualify it?

Then how about trend-setting styling? How about competition successes in every major venue available for production-based cars? How about accolades like 'The Best Handling Car in North America', conferred by the most respected automotive publication on that continent?

It seems clear that however mundane the genesis of the Camaro and Firebird, the end results surely merit the label.

The Camaro and Firebird – collectively known as the 'F-car' in General Motors' alphabet nomenclature – are usually thought of as GM's response to the resounding success of Ford's Mustang in 1964. The realities of lead time in the car business mean that this is not strictly true. GM stylists and engineers had been working on small, sporty cars almost continually during the late '50s and early '60s.

In fact, GM had started the US trend toward affordable sporting machinery by dropping bucket seats and a floor-mounted four-speed into their rear-engined Corvair. The resulting Monza coupé and roadster were the only bright spots in the Corvair's otherwise sad story. It was Ford who recognized the vast potential of the youth market which the Monza had barely scratched. They responded with the Mustang in the spring of 1964. One year and 418,000 sales later, the world was convinced that Ford indeed had a better idea.

The world, that is, exclusive of General Motors. In spite of the public's reaction to the Mustang, GM nabobs sniffed. 'It looks just like a down-scale big car – all square and angular. We would never build something as stodgy-looking as that.' Judging by what happened to the curvaceous Corvair, however, GM had no room to be so arrogant.

Eventually, GM couldn't ignore the Mustang, so a styling exercise that had been hanging around the advanced design studios

An early Chevrolet Camaro V8 Z28

for some time was given the green light.

It was primarily a Chevrolet project. Chevy had been shut out of the previous 'personal luxury car' programme that became the 1964 Buick Riviera, so they got the F-car as compensation.

There is some dispute over Pontiac's desire to be part of the deal. According to one report, Pontiac boss John De Lorean lusted for a two-seat roadster, and had several unsuccessful stabs at trying to convince GM's top brass of the wisdom of his approach. He was given a share of the F-car to keep him quiet, but De Lorean was later quoted as saying that he really wanted the F-car all along – asking for the two-seater was just a diversionary ploy. De Lorean is the only one who knows the real story here, and he's too busy these days to return 'phone calls and letters.

The Camaro appeared in September 1966. The beautifully-styled body was deliberately more *Italiante* than Ford's baroque Mustang. The convertible version even had hints of the lovely BMW 507, with its extended bonnet, short boot and graceful curves over the rear wheels.

GM stylists had wanted a fastback configuration for the coupé, a battle that was only to be won three years later. They settled for a 'semi-fast' roofline that allowed vestigal access to an equally vestigal trunk.

Underneath the pretty sheet metal was the 'Mum and Dad' saloon. The chassis was based heavily on the revised Chevy II which was being engineered concurrently with the F-car but wasn't scheduled for production until the 1968 model year.

The semi-unitized body structure had a separate front sub-frame bolted to the cowl which carried the unequal length A-arm front suspension and formed a cradle for engine and transmission mounting.

At the rear, the Camaro made do with the Chevy II Hotchkiss live axle on mono-leaf semi-elliptic springs. There was widespread concern that failure of the single leaf would leave you limping along like a dog with a broken leg, but the real problems of this design were limited suspension travel, poor spring rates that caused severe tail dragging with four people on board, and considerable road noise.

The Firebird's introduction was delayed until the following February, due to Pontiac's late involvement in the project. The car was clearly Camaro-based, with a Pontiac-style twin-nostril grille and revised rear-end styling. There were three tiny 'bird' emblems, one on each front wing and one at the rear.

Pontiac engineers added a pair of trailing links to the rear axle on all but the least powerful models. These were supposed to cure axle tramp on acceleration, but contemporary reports indicate that the trick wasn't entirely successful.

A wide range of engines was available in the F-cars. The Camaro started with a 230 cubic inch (3.8-litre) in-line six with pushrod overhead-valve gear which developed 140 bhp at 4400 rpm. At the same time, a three-speed manual transmission was standard.

The most powerful Camaro option was a 375 bhp 396 cu in (6.5-litre) V8, an engine far more powerful than the car's simple suspension could really cope with. That did not concern the drag racers, who soon discovered the wonderful power-to-weight ratio of the new GM cars.

Pontiac's most interesting engine was an overhead-cam variant of the Chevy six. With 4-throat carburettor, dual exhaust manifolding and moderately radical valve timing, this engine generated a healthy but relatively

TOP *A '73 Pontiac Firebird 400, capable of reaching 60 mph in just six seconds. The Chevrolet equivalent of this car was more powerful still with 375 bhp which made the car very popular with sprint and drag racers all over the USA*

FAR RIGHT *The interior of the 400*
ABOVE RIGHT *A 1975 Pontiac Trans Am, top of the Firebird range*
RIGHT *The shape of the second generation Firebirds was universally admired. This is a 1974 Trans Am 455*

EVOLUTION

The Chevrolet Camaro was introduced in 1966 in both coupé and convertible form, based on the Chevy II chassis. Standard equipment was a 3.8-litre straight six with a three-speed manual transmission. The top Camaro performance option was a 6.5-litre V8 with a four-speed manual transmission

1967 The Pontiac Firebird was introduced with a 'twin nostril' front grille and different rear end treatment. The more powerful Firebirds also featured trailing links on the rear suspension, supplementing the simple leaf springs of the Camaro. Top Firebird engine option was a 400 cu in (6.6-litre) V8 producing 335 bhp. Power-assisted front disc brakes were an option on both Camaro and Firebird

1968 The Z28 performance package became available on Camaros; it included a 4.9-litre V8, heavy duty suspension, four-speed gearbox and power-assisted front disc brakes

1969 The Camaro and Firebird were restyled and enlarged and an 'egg crate' style grille introduced on the Camaro. Pontiac introduced the Firebird Trans Am with the 6.6-litre V8

1970 The definitive Camaro and Firebird shape was introduced, in coupé form only

1974 Both the Camaro and Firebird facelifted with more prominent nose sections

1975 Wrap-around rear window added to Camaro and Firebird

1977 Another restyling saw the Firebird receive four rectangular headlights

1978 The Camaro was face-lifted, with a new, more aerodynamic nose

1980 Pontiac introduced a 4.9-litre turbocharged V8 to the range

1982 Third-generation Firebird and Camaro introduced. They were smaller and lighter than the second-generation cars but retained rear-wheel drive with live axles. A four-cylinder engine was standard with V6 and V8 options. Z28 and Trans Am performance options were still available, using a 155 bhp 5-litre V8. Performance of the V8 engine was increased steadily over the next few years, reaching 190 bhp by 1984

1984 IROC Camaro Z28 introduced with high-output fuel-injected V8

peaky 215 bhp at 5200 rpm. The overhead-cam unit was probably another of De Lorean's attempts to infuse GM in general and Pontiac in particular with some European flavour.

A flock of Pontiac-built V8s was also offered in the Firebird, culminating in a 335 bhp 400 cu in (6.6-litre) monster that could propel the 3000 lb-plus car from rest to 60 mph (97 kph) in under six seconds.

Drum brakes were standard equipment on the Camaro/Firebird – not surprising given the prosaic nature of the cars' forebears. Power-assisted front discs were optional, and used by most serious drivers.

Road tests published at the time indicate that from a handling perspective, the Camaro and Firebird were little more – and certainly nothing less – than typical North American saloons. As such they went pretty well in a straight line, had generally insufficient braking stamina, cornered fairly well when the roads were smooth, and fell apart (handling-wise) when the road surface deteriorated.

So where does that leave the sports car label applied to them earlier? Well, when modified to the extent that traditional sports cars always are for production-class racing, the results were convincing. It had previously been great fun for Euro-car fans to watch Mini-Coopers beat the big American cars on tighter tracks, but as soon as racing tyres became available in sizes commensurate with the Yank-tanks, the writing was on the wall for the small fry.

The key phrase in production class racing in the United States and Canada soon became Camaro's Regular Production Option Z28. Coding RPO Z28 on your Camaro's order form got you a hybrid engine: the block of the 327 cu in (5.4-litre) V8 with the crankshaft from the 283 cu in (4.6-litre) mill. The resulting 302 cubic inch (4.9-litre) displacement was, no coincidence, just under the 305 cubic inch (5-litre) limit that the Sports Car Club of America (SCCA) had set for its up-coming Trans-Am saloon-racing series. Z28 also served up a heavy-duty suspension, front disc brakes, metallic linings for the rear drums, quick-ratio steering, wider wheels and tyres and a modified bonnet with air scoop. To get the Z28 you also had to order a four-speed manual transmission.

Chevy built just enough of these to homologate the package for the Trans-Am, which soon became the most important production-based racing series in America.

The public soon caught on to a Good Thing, and Z28 became part of the performance car language in North America.

Mark Donahue and Roger Penske, two fabled names in American racing, took on the task of making the Z28 into a competitive race car. Their 1967 results were spotty – they had early handling problems, not unexpected with a brand-new race car derived from a brand-new road car. But two wins late in the season set the stage for 1968 – which the Camaros absolutely dominated.

Where was the Firebird during all this? Left on the side lines. Pontiac's attempt to do a V8 engine under the 305 cubic inch (5-litre) limit led to a 303 (4.9-litre), but it never breathed well enough to develop sufficient power. Various attempts were made to make the overhead-cam six competitive, but were doomed to failure. At the time there really was 'no substitute for cubic inches'.

Aside from the Camaro's competition success, there was little new about the 1968 versions of the F-cars. The usual slight modifications in exterior styling – changed parking lamps and the like – were made purely for model year identity.

1969 saw the first major styling changes. True to American form, these were mostly for the worse. The American Dream was to get bigger and better – in this case, one out of two wasn't bad.

The cars were indeed a couple of inches longer outside, with none of the badly-needed improvement in interior space. The wings acquired eyebrows, a misguided attempt to capture the flavour of the Mercedes-Benz 300 SLR of the mid '50s. They added a fussiness to the cars' smooth flanks that looks even worse today than it did then. The grille on the Camaro was recessed and converted to a large egg-crate pattern. The Firebird too got a new grille, heavier and ungainlier than before.

The most significant F-car event of 1969 was the name chosen for Pontiac's high-performance Firebird. Pontiac has a sordid history of assigning totally inappropriate names to their models, witness Grand Prix for a chrome-bedecked barge, Le Mans for a prosaic mid-size family saloon, and as for the GTO....

Their choice for the new Firebird model was Trans Am. Now the Firebird had been a total failure in the Trans Am racing series but that didn't seem to bother anybody. In fact, within a couple of years, the racing series had dwindled to a shadow of its former self, while the namesake Firebird went from marketing strength to marketing strength.

RIGHT First of the third generation Firebirds, a 1983 model Trans Am, smaller and lighter than the older cars but mechanically similar

What's logic got to do with anything?

The Trans Am model got the 400 cubic inch (6.6-litre) 335 bhp V8, and revised suspension that finally allowed some of the car's power to be applied to the road. Functional hood scoops, front wing vents and a rear boot-lid wing gave the car an aggressive appearance, and the only available colour scheme was white with blue go-faster stripes – the official United States racing colours. Only 697 1969 Trans Ams were sold, but the stage was set.

There were no new F-cars announced when the rest of GM's 1970 product line appeared in the fall of 1969. A completely new design had been taking shape in the styling studios, and it wasn't quite ready. When it finally hit the streets as the 1970 Camaro/Firebird, it was the public that wasn't quite ready. For this car turned out to be one of the most spectacularly successful designs in US automotive history.

Bill Mitchell, the slightly outrageous chief of GM Design, had not liked the first-generation Camaro. He complained about the constraints of working with the Chevy II internal structure, about that car's high cowl, about the committee nature of the beast. He

ABOVE The 1985 Pontiac Trans Am with, ABOVE LEFT its electronic dashboard BELOW In a bid to replace the performance lost due to emission controls, Pontiac launched a turbocharged Trans Am in '81.

convinced GM top brass that the F-car was worthy of its own structure, so the stylists had a freer hand. A coupé was the only body style considered – convertibles were on their way out in America thanks to increasing urban pollution, improved air conditioning and stereo radio systems, and the threat of complete banishment of open cars by the government. Tooling costs of a separate convertible F-car would also have been prohibitively high.

Among the trickier details to be worked out on the fastback-but-not-hatchback configuration were the rear quarter windows. The resolution came about when they were simply abandoned. The resulting doors were very long and heavy – a real treat to open in crowded parking lots. But they gave the Camaro/Firebird a clean uncluttered side elevation that is its most endearing and enduring aspect.

The Camaro had two different front ends, depending on model. The low-line cars had a square grille opening bisected by a thin chrome bumper. The sportier RS model dispensed with the bumper, using instead a hard-rubber 'Endura' moulding, with two small bumperettes protecting the outer cor-

ners of the front end. The RS also sported round parking lamps mounted inboard of the headlamps, a detail admittedly inspired by the Jaguar XJ saloons.

Firebirds for 1970 had a massive body-coloured Endura grille, again with huge twin nostrils. This styling theme had been a Pontiac stand-by since 1959, and still is.

The Trans Am model received two styling tricks that soon became trademarks. One was the 'shaker' hood scoop. The inlet for the intake manifold was so tall it needed to protrude through the hood. When the engine idled, the hood scoop shook, hence the name. It was to remain a Trans Am feature for nearly 12 years.

And remember the bird emblems mentioned before? This motif re-appeared as a decal on the Endura grille just ahead of the hood opening. Inspired by some Indian jewellery that a Pontiac stylist had seen in the Phoenix Arizona airport, the 'dead chicken'

grew larger and more garish moment by moment until it soon became a self-parody. But the kids loved it, and that's who Pontiac were after with this car.

On the engineering side, the 1970 F-cars were clearly slanted towards comfort. Engine choices still ran the gamut from modest in-line sixes to lusty V8s, but increasingly the cars were viewed as an American answer to a Grand Touring car rather than an all-out sports car. The US government's push for stricter exhaust emission controls plus the growing safety lobby had also made performance cars harder to sell.

The result was a smoother-riding, much quieter car. The low-mounted seats gave a slightly submerged feeling to the occupants, and while the car was only a couple of inches longer than the 1969 model, it looked, felt and drove like a much larger car.

The dashboard featured an oval instrument panel that was curved around the driver for ease of viewing. It was so successful that it remained essentially unchanged until 1979.

While performance was de-emphasised, it wasn't completely lost. Pontiac's Trans Am continued, acquiring even more aggressive-

The third generation Camaros and Firebirds were downsized to the extent that GM considered it worthwhile trying an export version of the Camaro Z28, the Z28E. It did not enjoy the same success outside North America, however. The instrument panel was influenced by European styling and is notable for the interesting speedo with contra-rotating needles for mph and kph. Enterprising Americans soon learned how to switch the system so that mph appeared on the kph dial, thus overcoming the regulation 85 mph speedo…

looking hood scoops, front wing vents and trim tabs ahead of the rear wheels. These were not mere decoration according to GM, who supplied lift and drag measurements to a sceptical motoring press to prove that the aerodynamic add-ons really were functional.

Because the 1970 model had been such a radical change, and because it had come out late, there was little need to do much different for 1971 or even 1972. But three years was the normal product cycle at GM in those days. It was suggested that the F-car had lived its life and should be dropped at the end of 1972. Declining sales in the sporty car market and a crippling strike at GM in 1972 made the future look glum indeed. But Chev and Pontiac executives launched an internal public relations campaign and the car was saved, with minimal changes, for 1973.

1974 saw a tougher bumper standard, and the second-generation Camaro and Firebird received their first major facelifting to meet this regulation. Both cars gained more prominent noses, to provide a larger crumple zone. Camaro made do with a simple but surprisingly effective beam of extruded aluminium. Pontiac retained the twin-nostril effect, again in body-colour Endura, with black rubber-faced bumpers below it.

In 1975, a wrap-around rear window was added to both cars. 1976 saw the introduction of a T-bar roof, with twin removable glass hatches. These things leaked when it rained, rattled when it didn't, but in fact they were very popular, since it was as close as

of the first magnitude. It was slow and wheezy – a pale imitation of the mighty 6.6-litre V8s of the past. It was not a fitting finale to this line of cars, which came to an end in 1981.

The number of styling changes that were successfully rung up on the second-generation F-car are a testimony to the integrity of the original design. In 1982 *Car and Driver* conducted a poll of international car designers, automotive experts and the magazine's readers, searching for the 'Ten Best-Looking Cars of All Time'. The '70–'81 Camaro Z28 tied for fifth with the Porsche 911 in the eyes of the designers, and was second only to the Jaguar E-type in the experts category; the readers preferred the Trans Am as Number 2 behind only the 911. A weighted average had the E-type first, the Cord 810 second, and a four-way tie for third between the Camaro, Trans Am, Porsche 911 and Ferrari 308. Nice company. One independent designer said the Camaro 'looked like it had been designed by an Italian on a good day'. Could there be higher praise?

1982 saw the introduction of the third-generation Camaro and Firebird. To some, these cars are relics, retaining as they do the old-fashioned front-engine rear-drive configuration with its attendant inefficient use of space. But no-one can argue the brilliance of their styling. The Camaro and Firebird have never looked more different than each other, yet the bodies are more interchangeable than before. The 1982 Firebird has curved, high-crown wings while the Camaro has a linear 'wedgier' shape. Yet the lines are so carefully contrived that identical door panels can be used.

Both cars use a Pontiac-built 92 bhp four-cylinder engine as standard equipment – how are the mighty fallen. A Chevy-built V6 is optional as are a couple of variations of Chevy's famed 302 V8.

Nevertheless, the base model is very definitely a boring car these days. In common with so many other cars sold in America, they have been hounded on all sides by safety and environmental lobbyists, perhaps rightly so. Nevertheless, the memories of those earlier cars still rub off on the newer versions.

General Motors is still selling a performance image for these cars. A new-for-1984 IROC Z28 Camaro model is based on the race-prepared cars used in the International Race of Champions, promoted by long-time Camaro mentor Roger Penske. With 'High Output' fuel-injected V8 engine and exceptionally capable suspension these are easily the most road-worthy F-cars ever.

And the Trans Am lives on, with similar mechanical specification to the Z28 and a complete aerodynamic kit with side skirts, deeper front air dam and rear spoiler.

But time marches on. GM will not commit themselves as to how long the F-car will continue in its present form. The next generation will very likely be a front-drive car, probably about the general size of an Audi 80 Coupé. Whatever form it takes, it will have quite a legacy to live up to.

you could come to a Camaro/Firebird convertible without spending a king's ransom getting the top chopped off by some automotive butcher.

Throughout the '70s, engine power was dropping in response to fuel crises, exhaust emissions controls, public safety clamour and ski-rocketting insurance rates. But the image of performance got a tremendous shot-in-the arm when the movie *Smokey and the Bandit* was released in December 1976.

Eric Dahlquist, whose product promotion company handled Pontiac's account in those days, supplied a black-with-gold-trim Trans Am for Burt Reynolds to use in the movie. The smooth-talking Reynolds rapidly became the macho man of the decade, and his car acquired similar shine. It was perhaps the slickest Public Relations ploy since Pontiac got Ronnie and The Daytonas to record a little rock 'n' roll ditty called *Little GTO* over a decade earlier.

The 1977 Firebird got yet another front-end re-do, using quad rectangular headlamps for the first time and another variant on the twin-nostril theme, this one derived from a 'Banshee' show car. This lasted just two years. Then the quad headlamps found individual resting places and the nostril idea was dropped.

The Camaro waited until 1978 for its face-lift. The shovel-nose was more aerodynamic and looked right with the new body-colour bumpers. Tail lamps with amber turn indicators and body-colour bumpers enhanced the rear view as well.

By the start of the '80s, F-car engines had become standardised, with mostly Chevrolet hardware being used. The last Pontiac gasp was a turbocharged version of their 4.9-litre (303 cubic inch) V8. This thing was a disaster

LEFT *The styling of the third generation cars perhaps lacks the appeal of the earlier cars, but its lines are clean and aerodynamic*

PIERCE ARROW V12

The Pierce-Arrow V12 engine proved its worth in endurance runs; but the promise it afforded was not enough to survive the Depression

THE ORIGINS OF PIERCE-ARROW are as bizarre as any in motor manufacturing history, for George N. Pierce of Buffalo, New York, started in business in 1865 making cages for birds and squirrels. He then met the needs of a new, and potentially more profitable, industry by translating his wire-forming skills into the manufacture of cycle spokes; thus he progressed, step by step, to the building of complete shaft-drive cycles.

From there, Pierce's cycle company stepped into uncharted territory in 1900, building an unsuccessful steam car designed by Overman. This was followed by a more successful De Dion-engined quadricycle, which persuaded Pierce that petrol had a surer future than steam, and led directly to the first production Pierce, the diminutive De Dion-engined Motorette. This was designed by Yorkshireman David Fergusson, who had arrived in America in 1899 as part of the entourage of the 'motor charlatan', E.J. Pennington, returning to base after a concerted attempt to stitch up the infant British motor industry.

The 'Arrow' part of the company name first appeared in 1902, on a 15 hp twin-cylinder car; then, in 1904, Fergusson launched the 3770 cc 24/28 hp four-cylinder Great Arrow, directly inspired by the Mercedes, and joined, in the following year, by 28/32 hp and 40/45 hp Great Arrows.

The Pierce company was moving steadily up-market, and proved its credentials by winning the arduous 1000-mile Glidden Tour reliability trial four times in succession, starting in 1904 when a 28/32 hp Great Arrow driven by George N. Pierce's son Percy scored 996 points out of a possible 1000.

Pierce launched its first six-cylinder model in the 1906 Glidden Tour; four years later, the company offered no kind of power unit other than the six-cylinder engine.

The marque officially adopted the name Pierce-Arrow in 1909, when the company was offering a range of sixes of 36 hp (5686 cc), 48 hp (7423 cc) and 66 hp (10,619 cc). The distinctive 'trademark' of Pierce-Arrow – headlamps set into the front wings – first appeared on the 1913 Second Series, which also marked the end of annual model changes for Pierce-Arrow.

Having established an enviable reputation as one of the most patrician of American cars, it was a quite uncharacteristic act for Pierce-Arrow to merge with the plebeian Studebaker company in 1929. However, the poor sales of the 1928 Series 81, styled in Art Deco mode by James R. Way, had caused blind panic among the Pierce-Arrow stock-

ABOVE *The arrow of Pierce-Arrow*
LEFT *Futuristic styling was not restricted to the outside of the car alone! This is the strangely attractive and very well equipped Silver Arrow dashboard*
BELOW *The Splendid 1933 V12 Silver Arrow*

holders, whose Pavlovian reaction was to vote for the ill-starred merger, which saw Studebaker investing $2 million in a reorganisation of Pierce-Arrow's facilities. The head of Studebaker, Albert R. Erskine, became chairman of the Pierce-Arrow board, while Myron Forbes, the incumbent Pierce-Arrow president, continued in office.

In 1929, too, Pierce-Arrow brought out an excellent new 5998 cc straight-eight, to counter the dilution of the marque's exclusive status by the wholesale adoption of six-cylinder engines by lesser makes. During its first season, Pierce-Arrow sold 8000 examples of the new Eight; even in the Depression year of 1930, some 7000 were delivered.

It was with this background that Pierce-Arrow began developing a new luxury model as a riposte to the introduction of the V16 Cadillac. Although the Cadillac was promoted as the ultimate in smoothness, the

LEFT *A menacing view of the Silver Arrow*
ABOVE *Ab Jenkins in the salt-encrusted V12 Pierce-Arrow used for the 1933 24-hour endurance run*
TOP RIGHT *This is the compact 1932 Series 52 V12 cabriolet*
BELOW *1702 chassis which offered 'mechanical excellence and greater safety'*

Pierce-Arrow engineers decided that any nominal advantage of the 16-cylinder engine was more than outweighed by the drawbacks, like increased complication and extra weight. A 12, they stated, was virtually as smooth, weighed 15 to 30 per cent less than a 16, used less fuel, accelerated better (because the crankshaft was lighter) and, because it had fewer bearings, incurred fewer frictional losses.

The Pierce-Arrow V12 went into production on 9 November 1931, built to the impeccable standards that the company promoted in its advertising: 'The micrometer, not the clock, governs the building of each Pierce-Arrow. The engine… goes through 350 skilled hands and nearly 100 inexorable tests. Instruments as sensitive as seismographs attest the balance of many of its parts. Even when it is running with whisper silence on the dynamometer, Pierce-Arrow experts may dismantle and reconstruct to correct some microscopic irregularity. The clock means nothing, the micrometer everything.'

The original 1932 range of Pierce-Arrow's V12 cars was available with a choice of two engine displacements – 6524 cc and 7035 cc – and three wheelbases – 137 in (348 cm), 142 in (361 cm) and 147 in (373 cm). There were three models – 51, 52 and 53, the first having the largest engine in the longest wheelbase chassis, the second offering the

7035 cc engine in a choice of chassis – 147 in (373 cm) and 142 in (361 cm) – and the third using the 6524 cc engine in the 137 in (348 cm) or 142 in (361 cm) wheelbase chassis.

The configuration of the V12 Pierce-Arrow engines was unusual, in that the cast-iron cylinder blocks were set at the particularly wide angle of 80 degrees – the contemporary Cadillac, Packard and Lincoln V12s used included angles of 45 degrees to 67 degrees – in order to make the single central camshaft easily accessible. In theory, this should have induced engine vibration, but the engines were fitted with a specially-tuned vibration damper and a separate induction system for each bank of cylinders, and were remarkable for their smooth running.

These power units were set in a particularly rigid chassis, with the front portion composed of welded and rivetted box girders, and bonnet, scuttle and radiator designed to contribute to chassis stiffness.

A choice of wire, wooden or steel artil-

BELOW *A long-wheelbase 1936 Pierce-Arrow which boasted big brakes and ample power, but sales were sliding and the firm closed a year later*

lery 7 in × 18 in wheels was given, and the V12s were particularly well-equipped, with dashboard levers controlling both freewheel and ride control, the latter varying the setting of the Delco hydraulic shock absorbers from a hard setting for high-speed driving to a soft 'boulevard ride' for towns. The 1932 Pierce-Arrow V12 was one of the first cars to be offered with a purpose-designed radio installed at the factory.

Studebaker obviously thought the new models would sell well, for in February 1932 they announced: 'Arrangements have been completed for the production at the Studebaker works at Walkerville, Ontario, of Pierce-Arrow cars. The eight- and twelve-cylinder cars will be manufactured as well as trucks.' Unfortunately, nothing more seems to have come of this proposal.

The Pierce-Arrow company offered an impressive line-up of cars for 1932, with the straight-eight Model 54 range priced from $2850 to $3450, and the V12 ranges beginning where the eight left off. The cheapest 1932 V12 was the Model 53 convertible roadster, selling at $3900, and the most costly, the Model 51 Enclosed Drive Seven Passenger Limousine, which sold for $4800 and scaled an impressive 5336 lb (2420 kg); in all, the factory offered 12 different body styles on Model 53, five on Models 51 and 52.

Nevertheless, despite this wide choice,

Pierce-Arrow sales fell dramatically during 1932, probably more as a result of the Depression than from any other cause. The company's 385-strong dealer network only managed to sell a total of 2692 cars that year, a 25 per cent drop on 1931, which was itself only half the level of 1930.

The Pierce-Arrow company decided that something spectacular needed to be done to demonstrate the qualities of the new V12, and accordingly charged one of their senior engineers, Omar J. Diles, with preparing a roadster, fitted with a prototype 1933 engine, in which a 0.125 in (3.2 mm) increase in the bore size brought displacement up to 7566 cc, for a 24-hour endurance run on the Bonneville Salt Flats, with the famous 'Mormon Meteor', David Abbott 'Ab' Jenkins, as driver. The aim was to crack the World 24-Hour Unlimited Speed Record of 113.50 mph (183 kph), held by a Voisin.

During the development of the big Pierce, the engine put in a remarkable 150 hours running at 4000 rpm on the dynamometer, which represented a theoretical 127 mph (204 kph) with the special 3:1 final drive fitted to the record attempt roadster.

A circular 10-mile (16 km) course had been marked out on the Bonneville Salt Flats under the supervision of George M. Haley of the Utah State Road Commission and marked out by steel stakes driven into the hard-packed surface of the salt – small oil

flares picked them out at night – for Jenkins's drive, which started on the morning of Sunday 18 September 1932, with a standing lap at 114 mph (183.5 kph), timed by stopwatch – sufficient under Automobile Association of America regulations for runs exceeding 10 miles – by W.B. Rishel of the Utah State Automobile Club, G.P. Backman of the Salt Lake City Chamber of Commerce, R.J. Ashton and J. Allen. The AAA, sceptical of the feasibility of 24-hour endurance runs on the salt at Bonneville, had declined to send an official team to supervise the record attempt, claiming that they had been given insufficient notice of the event to make preparations.

Jenkins, his face greased against the 120 degree daytime temperatures on the salt flats, was circling the record track with great consistency, covering 115.9 miles (186.5 km) in the first hour. It was claimed that the remarkable Jenkins remained in his seat during the entire record attempt, even during pit stops. Claiming that 'The car was virtually stock except for removal of the

BELOW One of the aluminium-headed 1937 cars, a survivor of the 167 units sold that year as the company was falling into debt and insolvency

ABOVE *Another view of the same 1937 car. It was a fast and elegant machine and the company deserved to survive to build cars post-war*

fenders,' Ab Jenkins reported that: 'The car was stable at all speeds, more like a racing chassis... tyres were Firestone smooth racing, four did the job... gas about 9 mpg...' (which was equivalent to about 11 miles to the Imperial gallon, 25.6 litres/100 km.)

And, since the big Pierce-Arrow was running with the silencers removed, Jenkins' ear was also mentioned: 'I was as deaf as the Statue of Liberty!'

At the end of 24 hours and virtually 2710 miles (4363 km), the engine was still running smoothly; Ab's average speed of 112.91 mph (182 kph) had been almost 12 mph (19 kph) faster than that at which Fred Frame's Miller racer had won that year's Indianapolis 500.

It was, indeed, the fastest ever 24-hour run by an American car, but could not be claimed as an official record because the AAA hadn't been present to sanction it.

The 1933 Pierce-Arrows went into production in November 1932, with a redesigned power unit that featured hydraulic tappets – the first direct-acting hdraulic tappets to go into production in America

EVOLUTION

The first Pierce-Arrow V12 range was introduced in 1932. Three different models were offered, the 51, 52 and 53, with a choice of two engine displacements, 6524 cc and 7035 cc, and three wheelbase lengths. 12 body styles were offered for the 53 and five for both the 51 and 52

1933 The V12 engine was modified to include hydraulic tappets, a US first, and the smaller V12 discontinued while a larger, 7566 cc, unit was added. Safety glass was introduced for all the windows and the smaller V12 featured underslung worm drive. By this time 45 body styles were on offer. The Silver Arrow was introduced at the Chicago exposition on the 7.5-litre chassis. Five were built

1934 Five 'production' Silver Arrows were built

1936 The Model 1602 and 1603 V12s were introduced with new X-braced chassis and extremely efficient servo-assisted brakes. Overdrive and automatic restart were standard features and the V12's output was boosted to 185 bhp with the introduction of alloy cylinder heads

1938 All production ceased after just 17 1938 models were built

(although the principle had already been patented and produced by Amédée Bollée *fils* of Le Mans for his Type E model).

The smaller V12 power unit offered during 1932 was discontinued, and a new, larger V12 of 7566 cc added to the range; all windows were now fitted with safety glass, while the headlamps – still mounted in the wings – had lenses designed on a new 'crossbeam' principle, which was claimed to improve visibility on dipped beam. The nearside beam dipped, while the offside beam was simultaneously cast across in front of the dipped beam, away from oncoming traffic.

The smallest V12 range, the 1236 Series, adopted underslung worm drive (also featured on the Pierce-Arrow eights), while the larger 1242 and 1247 Series (the last two digits of the serial number refer to the longest wheelbase available in that series, expressed in inches) retained the hypoid bevel axle. Customers were offered a choice of 45 catalogue body styles, with prices ranging from $2785 to $7200; most of the 1247 Series bodies were built by LeBaron or Brunn.

During the winter of 1932–33, Ab Jenkins toured America promoting the Pierce-Arrow, lecturing on his record run and exhibiting a silent movie of the Pierce at Bonneville made by the Pierce-Arrow adver-

tising manager, William Baldwin. In Washington, the lecture and film were attended by the AAA Contest Board secretary, T.E. Allen, who straightway granted AAA sanction for an official run in 1933.

Meanwhile, in October 1932 Pierce-Arrow vice-president Roy Faulkner had discussed another project aimed at boosting the company image with a 25-year-old designer named Philip Ogden Wright, who had recently gone freelance after working for the Art & Color Section at General Motors since 1928, when he had graduated from the Art Institute of Chicago.

Pierce-Arrow planned a special exhibit at the Century of Progress exhibition scheduled to be held in Chicago between 27 May and 1 November 1933, and Wright was commissioned to design 'the car built in the 1930s for the 1940s'; this Pierce Silver Arrow was built in three months on a 7566 cc V12 chassis, and, of all the luxury cars specially built for the Chicago Exposition, it was the Pierce-Arrow which created the most dramatic impact – even though all the automotive prizes at the Century of Progress were awarded to the conservatively-styled Dietrich-bodied V12 Packard displayed beneath the dome of the entrance hall.

Philip Wright had based the avant-garde styling of the Silver Arrow on wind-tunnel experiments, and indeed the car was a pretty good forecast of the shape that luxury cars would take in the 1940s: while its headlamps, set either side of a discreetly-raked radiator shell, were faired into the front

ABOVE LEFT *Two spare wheels were carried by this method on the Silver Arrow*
TOP *A fabulous array of instruments for driver and passenger alike!*

RIGHT *Note the Silver Arrow's odd rear windows*
ABOVE *Rear-seat passengers could also tell the time of day and the road speed*

wings in the best Pierce-Arrow tradition, those wings then flowed back into the rising belt line of a full-width passenger compartment with a tapered tail, whose smooth curve was broken by the only jarring note of the entire composition, a tiny 'eyebrow' window whose faceted panes were in the shape of elongated triangles... .

Twin spare wheels were hidden behind the panelling of the front wings, and the rear wheels were fully skirted-in.

Inside, the Silver Arrow was upholstered in broadcloth, with birds-eye maple woodwork; in the rear compartment was a radio and a set of duplicate instruments.

The aerodynamic merits of Philip Wright's 'harmonious and impressive' creation were demonstrated by its 115 mph (185 kph) top speed.

Pierce-Arrow built five identical silver Arrows, priced at $10,000 each – a publicity photo claimed that film star Ginger Rogers, billed as 'Radio's Terpsichore' had bought one of them – plus, in 1934, five less radical, 'production' cars, which had little in common with the original Wright design, save the fastback body styling. Philip Wright, who

later freelanced for Willys-Overland, eventually worked for Douglas Aircraft as a technical illustrator, and died in 1982.

The critical acclaim awarded to the Silver Arrow was a fitting starting point for the company's newly-reacquired independence, for a consortium of Buffalo businessmen bought back the car side of Pierce-Arrow from Studebaker, itself in receivership, in August 1933 (Pierce-Arrow's profitable truck activities had been transferred to White, another company within the Studebaker empire, in 1932). In 1933, however, the Depression was at its nadir, and the revival of Pierce-Arrow's flagging fortunes seemed an insuperable task. Against the odds, Pierce-Arrow did record a profit in the third quarter of 1933.

On 6 August 1933, Ab Jenkins was back at Bonneville Salt Flats, this time with a stripped 1933 convertible: its 7566 cc engine had a reground camshaft, gas-flowed porting and a compression ratio raised to 7.5:1. The effect of these modifications was to increase the power output of the engine to 207 bhp, whilst the top speed was over 128 mph (206 kph).

The Pierce-Arrow covered the first 1000 miles (1610 km) at an average speed of 123 mph (198 kph), a new world record. However, as the sun rose the following morning, a rear tyre burst at over 120 mph (193 kph), cut by sharp gravel used to fill a pothole where the salt surface had started to break up. The car slid violently, but was brought back under control by Jenkins, who promptly made a three-minute pit stop for a new wheel to be fitted and the Pierce to be refuelled.

Despite worsening weather during the latter part of the run, with high winds and rain causing further deterioration in the condition of the salt track, Jenkins maintained his speed, and the Pierce-Arrow ran so steadily that Jenkins was able to shave himself with a safety razor while the car was travelling at 125 mph (201 kph).

And although the run was scheduled to finish after 24 hours, Jenkins signalled that he was carrying on running: 'The engine is running perfectly after 24 hours, and the 3000-mile record is there for the taking!'

The 3000 – mile mark was reached after 25 hours 30 minutes 36.62 seconds, giving an average speed of 117.6 mph (189.25 kph); the average for the 24 hours had been 117.8 mph (189.6 kph). Jenkins had broken 14 international and 65 national records, and a 40-minute sound film of the record run, entitled *The Flight of the Arrow*, was used to promote the Pierce-Arrow marque.

Paradoxically, sales continued to decline – only 2152 Pierce-Arrows were sold during

1933 – and there was talk of financial reconstruction. Against this background of despair, the indefatigable Ab Jenkins continued his record-breaking work. During the winter of 1933–34, he and the Pierce-Arrow engineers developed a further V12 record car, this time carrying a hand-beaten aluminium racing body with a cowled-in radiator but no bonnet sides. There were six carburettors, straight-through exhausts and high-compression cylinder heads, bringing the power output to 235 bhp at the remarkable engine speed of 4000 rpm which gave a theoretical top speed in the region of 150 mph (240 kph). In August 1934, Jenkins averaged 127.229 mph (204.749 kph) for 24 hours, covering 3053 miles (4915 km).

Publicity from the record breaking was extensive but the slump in the market had dealt the firm a body blow. A vicious circle developed; falling demand left little money for technical development which made the cars less attractive, lowering demand still further. Desperate attempts were made to reverse the trend in 1934.

By that time, Pierce-Arrow was in deep trouble: 1934 sales were down to 1740, and in 1935 the figure was halved, to 875. Late 1935 saw several merger rumours and some financial reorganisation, which was followed by the launch of an outstanding 1936 range – Model 1601 eight and Models 1602 and 1603 twelves – promoted as 'the safest cars in the world'. They had massive X-braced chassis with vacuum-boosted brakes (which had the largest friction area of any American produc-

tion car – 342 sq in (2206 sq cm), against 284 sq in (1832 sq cm) for the Packard V12 – plus a standard specification which included such items as Startix (automatic restarting of a stalled engine) and overdrive.

Aluminium cylinder heads boosted standard power output of the V12 Pierce-Arrows to 185 bhp, but sales continued to slide: just 787 cars were sold during 1936.

The 1937 Pierce-Arrows were almost identical with the 1936 models, except for minor trim details, but only 167 were sold. Another reorganisation, which was aimed at taking Pierce-Arrow into the medium-priced sector of the market, failed to happen, thanks to a minor recession in late 1937, and although a handful of 1938 models – just 17 of them – was assembled, the production lines had already come to a standstill.

When a major creditor pressed for repayment of his $200,000 debt, a Federal Court judge declared Pierce-Arrow insolvent in April 1938, and the company's assets, valued at nearly $1 million, were auctioned for a mere $40,000.

But those magnificent Pierce-Arrow power units lived on, for the Seagrave Fire Apparatus Company bought all the engine tooling and manufacturing equipment, and began building Pierce-Arrow engines to power its fire-engines.

One wonders whether Pierce-Arrow could have survived the aftermath of the Depression if its truck manufacturing activity hadn't been hived off by Studebaker in 1932….

DUESENBERG
MODEL J

Top: The elaborate chrome-work which is so typical of Duesenberg quality

Above: The Duesenberg emblem adorns the "Model J" hood. A feature of this particular car is the Duesenberg hood speedster styled by Figoni

'THE SUPERLATIVELY FINE has no need to be boastful,' stated the catalogue for the Model J Duesenberg in a welter of hyperbole. 'Always there is devotion to an ideal with: only one thought in mind: to produce the best, forgetful of cost or expediency or any other consideration.'

The Model J Duesenberg, launched at the December 1928 New York Automobile Salon, was born of the fusion two years earlier of two quite remarkable talents, those of Fred S. Duesenberg, a 50-year-old engineer of German origin who, with his brother August, had been working in the motor industry since the turn of the century, and of the 31-year-old Erret Lobban Cord, a remarkable young entrepreneur who had turned round the moribund Auburn company in 1924–25 and then acquired Duesenberg Inc, in 1926.

Cord very soon realised that in Fred

With a 265 bhp twin-cam straight eight, the Duesenberg Model J of 1928 was as powerful as it was imposing

---

Duesenberg the company possessed a rare talent, and instead of ousting him from the company in the wake of the takeover, praised him as an 'acknowledged genius as a designer of both racing cars and high-grade passenger cars'. In 1920, the first passenger car to bear the Duesenberg name had also been America's first production car with a straight-eight engine, aluminium pistons and four-wheel hydraulic brakes.

In addition, following the takeover, Cord promised: 'With the assistance of Fred

Duesenberg, I will build the world's best automobile, a car with superlative acceleration, speed and hill-climbing ability, pleasant to drive and safe, with maximum reliability and exceptionally long life, secured by the finest material and workmanship.'

In an article awash with superlatives, Harold Blanchard, technical editor of *Motor* magazine, welcomed the new Duesenberg as being 'as beautiful as it is powerful…it has the power, acceleration and speed of a racing car together with the size, comfort, flexibility, durability and foolproofness which must be prime features of any outstanding passenger car'.

The heart of the Model J was its power unit, built by Lycoming, another company in Cord's group, to the designs of Fred Duesenberg. But although Lycoming was well-known for its manufacture of propriet-

ary engines, there were no traces of this heritage in the Model J unit, which was claimed to develop a remarkable 265 bhp from 6876 cc.

In fact, the Duesenberg engine bore ample evidence of Fred Duesenberg's experience as a racing-car designer, with twin overhead camshafts actuating four silchrome valves per cylinder; the hemispherical combustion chambers were fully machined and the cylinder head was detachable. It also had Ray-Day aluminium pistons which were carefully designed to compensate for expansion, with a split skirt only attached to the crown at the gudgeon pin bosses so that its expansion matched that of the grey iron block casting.

The double heat-treated, chrome-nickel-steel-forged crankshaft was carried in five massive main bearings each 2.75 in (7 cm) in diameter, and was fully counterweighted and balanced both statically and dynamically. It was fitted with an ingenious torsional vibration damper which consisted of two sealed cartridges 94 per cent filled with mercury and bolted on opposite faces of the crank cheek between cylinders 1 and 2. Each cylinder had two internal baffles, and when the crank started to enter a vibration period, the slight twisting effect on the shaft caused the mercury to flow to and fro across these baffles, the resulting inertia damping out the torsional crank vibration before it became detectable to the driver.

The aluminium con-rods were I-section and designed for maximum heat dissipation, with white-metal bearings spun into the rod.

The engine inhaled through a dual-choke Schebler carburettor, and breathed out down a massive 4.75 in (12 cm) diameter exhaust pipe; the exhaust manifold encompassed the inlet tract, which it heated through twin pipes in which the flow of hot gas was controlled by a thermostat. Both exhaust manifold and pipe were chrome-plated on the first Model Js – although on subsequent models it was coated in green vitreous enamel to match the cylinder block – and the silencer was specially designed for minimum back pressure.

Particular attention was paid to engine lubrication, with pressure-feed to all the bearings, camshafts and timing gear. The oil was filtered both before and after passing through the gear pump in the base of the deeply-finned 12-pint (7-litre) aluminium sump.

The specification of this engine was quite remarkable by the standards of the Twenties and compares dramatically with the simple and heavy engineering of so many post-war American cars. Based on this specification and the exceptional performance that resulted, Cord's claim to be building the best car in the world had credence.

The engine was carried on six rubber mountings, two at the front and four at the rear. The front two were spring-loaded to prevent twisting of the crankcase in the event of extraordinary frame distortion, while the rear four were cone-shaped, set in pairs, one above and slightly to the side of the other, in mounting cups formed in a bracket riveted to the chassis.

The drive was taken through an 11 in (28 cm) twin-plate clutch to the three-speed transmission, unusual in that the middle ratio was obtained through two pairs of constant-mesh internal/external gears, engaged by moving a splined shaft.

The final drive was through a torque tube to a hypoid crown wheel and pinion, used to give a lower centre of gravity.

The chassis frame of the Duesenberg Model J was particularly massive, pressed from 7/32 in (6 mm) steel, with a maximum depth of 8.5 in (22 cm) at the centre, with 2.75 in (7 cm) flanges and six tubular cross-members, the second of which carried the radiator and was 'A'-braced to the side-members of the chassis, while the fourth cross-member was a 4 in (10 cm) square tube riveted and welded into the frame with massive double gussets.

The brakes were hydraulic on all four wheels, acting in finned 15 in (38 cm) steel drums and supplemented by a locomotive-type handbrake at the rear of the gearbox.

The car's performance and handling were of a level to justify the care taken to ensure that the chassis was both rigid and readily stoppable: 'Whether on straight road or curve the Duesenberg traces a true, steady course without the slightest pitching or sidesway – even above 100 miles per hour. Due to perfect weight distribution, low centre of gravity and other factors, the car negotiates curves as though it were on rails. Here its easy, accurate steering is particularly appreciated. Curves may be taken at surprising rates of speed without the slight-

est skidding.

Riding comfort such as no other car possesses is built into the new Duesenberg. Whether the pace be fast or slow, the road smooth or rough, the passengers ride with surprising ease and comfort…Low unsprung weight is a prime requisite for smooth, stable running at high speed. Small unsprung weight involves clever design, plus the willingness to go to the extra expense of manufacturing parts which are both light and over-strong, of the finest, most suitable, costly materials…To state that the maximum speed in second gear is 90 miles per hour is merely to illustrate and to emphasise the unusual superiority which distinguishes every detail of the Duesenberg automobile.

Monitoring that superior performance was 'the most complete set of instruments ever supplied on an automobile'. Set in an engine-turned oxidised nickel panel, they consisted of 150 mph (241 kph) speedometer, petrol gauge, altimeter/barometer, water temperature gauge, brake pressure gauge, ammeter, oil pressure gauge, tachometer, split-second stop watch, ignition control, choke and starter knobs and automatic lights indicating oil change, chassis lubrication and battery care intervals.

These four automatic lights were actuated by the motor industry's first on-board computer, over half-a-century ahead of the trend, even if it was controlled by mechanical, rather than electronic, wizardry.

The heart of the system was the 'timing box', a train of tiny planetary gears, each with a ratio of 4.8:1, driven from the fuel pump shaft. The fuel pump shaft was turned at 1/20th engine speed, and the step-down between fuel-pump shaft and timing box was 1:16, so that the last gear in the timing box turned just once for every 169,870 engine revolutions, equivalent to once every

40 minutes at peak engine rpm.

Thus steadily enumerating the rotation of the engine, the timing box opened a spring-loaded valve on the fuel pump housing which forced oil under engine pressure to all the chassis lubrication points every 75 miles (121 km). A red tell-tale lamp indicated that the system was in operation, a green one informed that there was still oil in the Bijur lubricator's reservoir; every 700 miles (1127 km) the timing box switched on a dashboard light to warn the driver to change the engine oil, while every 1400 miles (2253 km) another light instructed him to verify the battery level.

Erret Cord's recipe for success had always been to clothe the chassis produced by the companies under his control in beautiful bodywork. with the Model J, he announced that all bodies would be custom-built for each purchaser, whether from the company's ample portfolio of designs or on a one-off bespoke basis. To preserve a continuity of style, the Duesenberg Model J chassis was supplied with radiator shell, headlamps, bonnet, wings, running board and bumpers in place, and to coalesce the ideas of the customers who possessed the necessary cash but had no preconceived vision of the bodywork they desired, Duesenberg initially asked America's leading custom coachbuilders to submit design sketches which could be placed in a portfolio and shown to clients.

As early as June 1928 top coachbuilders were sent advance blueprints of the Model J,

RIGHT AND CENTRE *This 1933 Duesenberg Dual-Cowl Phaeton has a seven-seat body by LeBaron. Note the second screen to protect the rear-seat passengers from the wind*

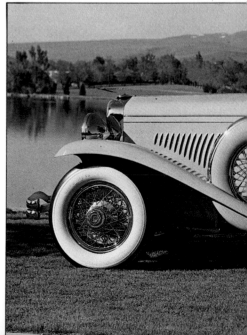

so that when it was launched six months later the portfolio contained such designs as a phaeton and sedans by Derham, a town cabriolet and a two-window sedan by Holbrook, a LeBaron phaeton and a convertible sedan and a convertible roadster by Murphy.

The process of ordering coachwork for a Duesenberg chassis was further refined in June 1929 when a factory body-design department was instituted; its designers would both create new body styles for individual clients and act as a link between the Duesenberg company and the coachbuilder. Chief designer from 1929–33 was Gordon Buehrig, who subsequently achieved fame as the designer of the 'coffin-nose' Cord 810/812; overall control of the department was in the hands of Philip A. Derham, who was appointed body engineer in January 1930. Former general manager of the family Derham Custom Body Company, Philip Derham, had remarkable experience of all phases of the coachbuilder's craft, since he was the son of Joseph J. Derham, an Irish-born wheelwright who had founded his renowned coachbuilding company at Rosemont, Philadelphia, in 1887, but did not build a motor car body until 1907. The Derham company made up for this late start, however, and by 1926 it was making $800,000 annually from custom coachbuilding, particularly for Packard. It was this high level of expertise that Philip Derham brought to his new job at Duesenberg.

Consequently, the company was able to indulge in what looked suspiciously like a spot of boastfulness: 'Duesenberg maintains a custom-designing and body-engineering organisation second to none in the world. They originate more designs and actually build more individual bodies than any other custom company.'

In fact, the Duesenberg factory's role in body construction was restricted to a certain amount of trim and paint, though it did use a local coachbuilder, Union City, to construct 21 bodies. These were mostly phaetons, which were normally delivered without a bodybuilder's plate although the name 'La Grande' was coined for them (and also used on most of the bodies from other coachbuilders delivered to Duesenberg 'in the white' for factory trim and paint). In addition, every chassis had to pass a 500-mile (805 km) test on the Indianapolis Motor Speedway before

it was handed over to the carrossier.

The tally of 'works' coachbuilders used by Duesenberg, Inc, amounted to 14 American and two European companies, although a number of customers, particularly in Europe, bought their Model Js in chassis form for bodying by a carrossier of their choice (or for the transfer of a favourite body from an old car of different make). The price of all this elegance was not cheap – one Torpedo Sedan built as a show car by Rollston was finished in platinum lacquer, upholstered in heather-coloured broadcloth piped in silver leather and had burr walnut door trim inlaid with silver – it was officially named the Arlington, but was more popularly known as the Twenty Grand after its price tag… .

Among the European coachbuilders who built Duesenberg bodies were Saoutchik, Figoni, Franay, Letourneur & Marchand, Hibbard & Darrin and Fernandez (which became Fernandez & Darrin in 1931) in France, Barker and Gurney Nutting in England, Van den Plas and D'Ieteren Frères in Belgium, Castagna in Italy and Graber in Switzerland; of these, Castagna and Hibbard & Darrin supplied a handful of bodies direct to Duesenberg in Indianapolis.

The clientele for the Model J was as glittering as the car itself: film stars Gary Cooper, Clark Gable, James Cagney, Greta Garbo, Joe E. Brown, Richard Arlen, Mae West, Lupe Valez, Marion Davies and Dolores del Rio all drove Duesenbergs, as did Hollywood directors Howard Hughes, Howard Hawks and Walter Wanger; royal Duesenberg fans included King Alfonso of Spain, Queen Marie of Yugoslavia, Prince Serve M'Divani, the Maharajah Holkar of Indore and Prince Nicholas of Romania, who raced one of his Duesenbergs – with great enthusiasm and small success – at Le Mans. Amongst the other celebrities who patronised the Indianapolis marque were William Randolph Hearst, the much-married Tommy Manville, bandleader Paul Whiteman, tap-dancer Bill 'Bojangles' Robinson, Lew Wallace Jr. (son of the author of *Ben Hur*), Mayor Jimmy Walker of New York, evangelist Father Divine, whose 178 in (452 cm) wheelbase 'Throne Car' was provided by one of his female faithfuls, and the President of Syria, Mehmed be Abed. There were also quite a few gangland bosses, who found the 265 horses of the Duesenberg coped very well with the armour plating called for by their nasty, short and brutish mode of life.

Catering for such super-rich clients, who could still afford to indulge their whim for an astronomically-expensive motor car in the midst of a cataclysmic depression, Duesenberg's advertising in magazines such as *Vanity Fair* was a model of understate-

ment – just a pencil drawing of a distinguished-looking man standing on the vast deck of an ocean yacht or seated in the baronial gloom of a timbered hall in which the pipes of a mighty organ gleamed softly in the middle distance, above the simple legend 'He drives a Duesenberg'. The marque's not inconsiderable feminine clientele was represented by another advertisement – 'She drives a Duesenberg' – depicting a *grande dame* issuing orders to a forelock-tugging menial about to tend a formal garden stretching to the distant horizon... .

May 1932 saw a new departure for the Duesenberg Model J, when a supercharged version – known as the 'SJ' – was announced: 'A definite demand for a fast, strictly sports motor car has prompted Duesenberg to design and build, in addition to the present Model J Duesenberg, and to order only, a special 320-horsepower supercharged chassis. Although there are several similar sports cars manufactured in Europe, they are engineered entirely for speed without regard for comfort and quietness. This new 320-horsepower Duesenberg is as quiet as the famous Model J, with the exception of a pleasant, soft singing of the supercharger, and in spite of its tremendous speed you enjoy a comfortable, safe ride.

'This supercharged Duesenberg will throttle down to three miles per hour and will accelerate from a standing start to 100 miles per hour in 20 seconds. A phaeton with top lowered has been driven 129 miles per hour in top gear and 104 miles per hour in second gear. The car steers exceptionally easy, holds the road perfectly, and has no tendency to wander at any speed.'

Apart from seven prototypes which had a one-piece, eight-port stainless-steel manifold emerging from the bonnet side, the SJ had quadruple external chromed flexible exhaust pipes that were, in theory, the hallmark of a supercharged Duesenberg; in practice, twice as many Model J owners bought the external exhaust system as an optional extra.

The supercharger was of the centrifugal pattern, and turned at six times engine speed. That meant that at 4000 rpm, the 12 in (30 cm) diameter impeller was turning at a phenomenal 24,000 rpm, and that its periphery was rotating at the remarkable speed of 14 miles (22.5 km) a minute – or 857 mph (1379 kph), equivalent to over 1.1 times the speed of sound. Claimed to be 'noiseless' in operation, the supercharger

LEFT *The clean lines of a 320 bhp 1931 Convertible Coupé. The green colour was typical of the liveries adopted by owners of Duesenbergs, be they film stars or wealthy industrialists, to whom being noticed was a high priority*

369

delivered air at around 8 psi.

A few weeks after the introduction of the SJ, Fred Duesenberg was returning to Indianapolis from a business trip in an SJ convertible coupé when he hit a slippery stretch on the descent of Ligonier Mountain in Western Pennsylvania, and skidded off the road.

His injuries appeared slight, but, a little over three weeks later, Fred relapsed and died, at the age of 55. His brother Augie took over as chief engineer of Duesenberg.

There was one last spectacular variation on the SJ theme: in 1936, two short-wheelbase 'SS SJ' roadsters were built by cutting down the regular 142.5 in (362 cm) wheelbase SJ chassis to 125 in (317 cm); bodies were by Central, an Auburn-Cord-Duesenberg subsidiary, and the cars were bought by Hollywood's Clark Gable and Gary Cooper.

Augie's tuning skills were amply demonstrated in 1935 when Ab Jenkins, in his Duesenberg Special, 'Mormon Meteor', which had a designed top speed of 200 mph (322 kph) on its 3:1 final drive ratio, averaged 135.47 mph (218 kph) for 24 hours at Bonneville Salt Flats, and took the hour record at 152.145 mph (245 kph), over 17 mph (27 kph) faster than the previous record set by Von Stuck's Auto-Union racing car; the periphery of the blower would have been turning continuously at some 1000 mph (1609 kph) for 24 hours… .

Considering the considerable impact the Model J and SJ Duesenbergs made in their day – for they even gave the spoken language that enigmatic superlative 'It's a duesy!' – it is salutary to realise just how truly minute production was. The contract with Lycoming for Duesenberg engines was just 500 units, and these were delivered at the rate of 203 in 1928–9, 152 in 1930, 50 in 1931, 5 in 1932, 25 in 1933, 26 in 1934 and 25 in 1935, totalling 486 units which were assembled in some 472 chassis (the remainder being for spares, exhibition units or rebuilt cars). Of those chassis, some 36 were SJ Duesenbergs; indeed, the last Duesenberg of all was an SJ, completed in 1938 – after the factory had closed down – in Chicago to the order of German enthusiast Rudolf Bauer. Its Rollson body was finished in 1940, by which time Mr. Bauer had escaped from Nazi Germany and taken up residence in the USA.

The sleek black convertible coupé, a spectacular 20 ft 6 in (625 cm) long, was a fitting postscript to the Duesenberg story And in the five decades since that last

LEFT *Comprehensive instrumentation shamed the Duesenberg's rivals*
BELOW *Figoni's Model J Speedster was commissioned for the Paris-Nice Rally and Cannes Concours d'Elégance of 1931*
RIGHT *A power unit as beautifully presented as the car itself*

Duesenberg was delivered to its proud owner – who already possessed two phaetons of the same make – America has singularly failed to produce another car which could be described as proudly (for hadn't its makers told us they weren't boasting?) as the Model J: 'Just as its speed exceeds by many miles an hour that of any other automobile, so does it excel in all its other features, including fineness of material, strength, comfort, durability…an outstanding automobile from any angle.'

CADILL

J 176

AC V16

LEFT AND BELOW *The Maharaja of Tikari's 1931 V16 Phaeton. The 'goddess and drape' mascot was introduced during the '30s, with several variations*

Designed to reinstate Cadillac at the top, the V16 proved a grand finale to the Roaring Twenties. Unrivalled in engineering refinement and luxury, it appeared just as the Depression began to winnow the American motor industry

---

AT A RECENT CONCOURS in Detroit, the proud owner of a quartet of V16 Cadillacs was asked the obvious question: 'Why do you need *four* V16 Cadillacs?' He thought for a moment, then responded: 'You can never have too many V16 Cadillacs . . .'.

That, I suppose, is a remark that Ernest Seaholm and Owen Nacker, creators of the world's first and most successful V16 car, would have been proud of, for the V16 was intended as the ultimate extravagance, a supreme gesture that placed its owner above the common ruck of motoring.

To find the reason why such an extravagance was launched just as the Depression was gathering momentum, you have to look back to 1925, when Cadillac, top of the American luxury car league, was rudely swept aside by Packard, thus diminishing General Motors' pride in having overtaken Ford in terms of sales. Although General Motors was 21 years old when the V16 was launched, the start of the corporation's irresistible rise began in 1923, when Alfred P. Sloan was appointed President, and began to rearrange the corporate structure.

As conceived by Sloan, the product spread of General Motors was such that it could provide cradle-to-grave transport for Everyman, catering for his economic and social progression from Chevrolet through Pontiac, Oldsmobile, Buick, and LaSalle to Cadillac, each marque a clearly-defined step and status symbol.

Imagine, then, the displeasure that Sloan must have felt when Cadillac suddenly lost leadership of the luxury car class to Packard, who moved ahead in terms of sales by a ratio of over two to one in the mid-1920s.

Plans were laid as early as 1926 for a grand gesture that would reassert Cadillac's place at the top of the league. Packard had established an image as a company who could achieve the ultimate in engineering with its Twin Six, the world's first series-production V12 car, of which over

35,000 were built between 1915-22.

The success of that car partly dictated the way that Cadillac had to go. The new Cadillac had to be faster, more powerful and more refined than anything else on the market. The answer was to enlarge the power unit of the existing Cadillac V8, but this would not do, for a bigger V8 would lose something in terms of smoothness, could have thermodynamic problems and most certainly would possess torque characteristics that would necessitate the development of a new, stronger transmission.

That, for several reasons, was not desirable. Cadillac's existing transmission was generally quite satisfactory; the company was working with Earl A. Thompson to adapt his new Syncro-mesh mechanism to their gearbox and the extra development cost, plus the possible reliability problems that could follow, dictated that the new engine, despite extra power, should possess similar torque characteristics to the V8 and thus share a common driveline.

That meant extra cylinders to even out the torque – but there were strong reasons against a V12, not the least of which was that Packard had been first in the field with an excellent product, and however good were such a unit developed by Cadillac,

there would always be comparisons and charges of plagiarism.

So the die was cast; sixteen cylinders it had to be, a configuration not previously seen in any motorcar, and rarely found even in non-automotive installations like racing motorboats. Even there, the few 16-cylinder powerplants had been composed of two V8 engines, not conceived as a hexadecimal whole.

The V16 project coincided with the arrival at Cadillac of a new engine designer, Owen Nacker, who had previously worked as a consultant with Alanson P. Brush. Though Brush's products had not been renowned for their refinement, Nacker was an exceptionally gifted engineer whose first project at Cadillac had been to develop the 341 Series V8 engine – which initially appeared in the first-ever LaSalle in 1927 – and who then turned his attention to the development of the new V16.

The entire project was the responsibility of Chief Engineer Ernest Seaholm, and the degree of secrecy in which it was developed was quite remarkable. Most of the lower-echelon engineers and outside suppliers – the principal sources of leaks – were convinced that Cadillac was developing a new commercial vehicle, since the

blueprints were mostly marked 'Bus' or 'Coach'.

Body styling too was carried on in-house, as Fleetwood was part of the General Motors organisation.

The launch of the V16 consequently took the press and industry by surprise. The statement by *The Autocar* on the Cadillac's Olympia Motor Show debut, that 'something of a sensation should be caused by the appearance of the sixteen-cylinder Cadillac, showing in practice a type of engine of which more will be heard in the United States in the future' was a masterpiece of understatement. Cadillac was less modest: an early advertisement for the V16 proclaims it merely as 'the very finest of its kind ... a mechanical masterpiece ... there is no power plant in any motor car so

A 1931 Fleetwood Sports Phaeton built for the Maharaja of Tikari – hence the right-hand drive. The lower lights swivel with the front wheels and passengers could monitor progress via the supplementary speedo and clock

374

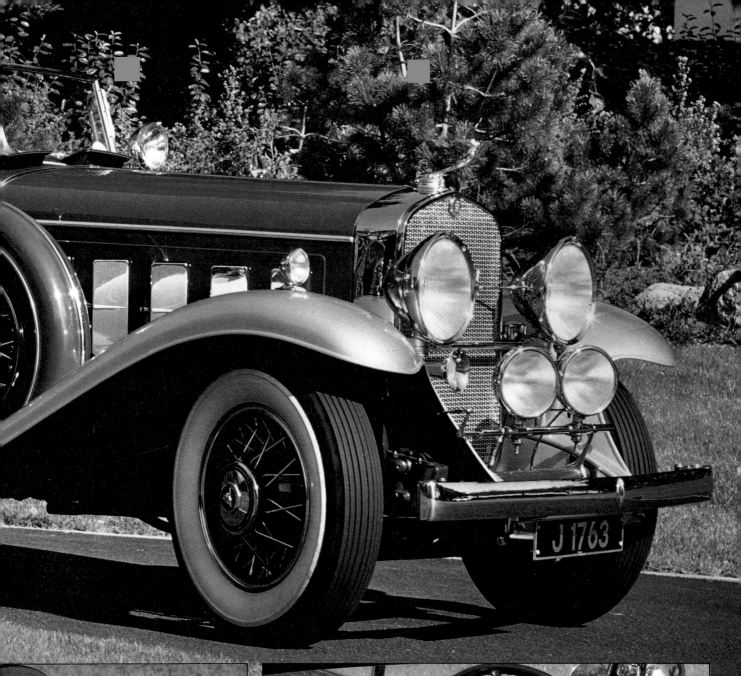

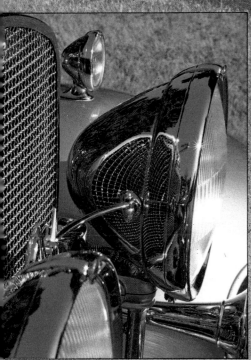

ABOVE *Elegance personified in the form of a 1931 V16 convertible. Note the V16 motif on the wheels and the optional trunk on the rear of this example*

smooth, so quiet, so flexible – or so generally satisfactory – as Cadillac's 16-cylinder engine . . .'

This remarkable smoothness was almost certainly the result of 'automatic adjustment of rocker clearance which requires no attention and ensures silent running'. The Cadillac V16 had conventional pushrod overhead valves, but instead of the hydraulic tappets which are commonly used nowadays, the rockers were pivoted on snail-cam eccentrics with an hydraulic plunger pushing at one end. Thus the centre around which the rocker pivoted was varied by the hydraulic plunger until all the clearance had been taken up at either end. While it wasn't a new idea – it went back to Amédé Bollée *fils,* who patented the idea in April 1910 – the V16 Cadillac was the first production car to use the principle, and it brought an unprecedented degree of refinement to the Cadillac's manner of going.

In 1962, *Motor Sport* tested a 30-year-old Cadillac V16 and remarked that: 'Extreme silence and flexibility is the beauty of this monster from Detroit . . . engine, transmission and back axle are well-nigh inaudible.'

According to Cadillac experts the only sound audible when the engine is ticking over should be the spark at the contact points, augmented when the engine is running at cruising speed by the hiss of the air intake and the sound of the fan blades. Even Rolls-Royce could not match this level of refinement, and it's worth noting that when their Phantom III was launched a few years later, the engine was equipped with

hydraulic tappets . . .

Cadillac however, were particularly interested in Rolls-Royce's renowned riding qualities. Cadillac head, Lawrence Fisher (one of the seven body-builder brothers) had engaged Maurice Olley, who had been working at Rolls-Royce of America at Springfield and had done much work on suspension design, to improve the ride of Cadillacs. Olley brought in Rolls-Royce techniques, such as swinging a car from overhead pivots to determine its moment of inertia, and set up a 'bump rig' – a crude form of rolling road – for the dynamic testing of suspension and ride on a static, and hence more observable, car.

Thus in 1931 came Cadillac's 'K' test vehicle, a seven-passenger limousine equipped with weights which could be moved to vary the moment of inertia and front and rear suspension deflection while the car was in motion. Using this rig Olley was able to show that for a really flat ride

the front spring rate had to be slower than the rear; he then began to investigate the use of independent front suspension to reduce the frustrating front-wheel shimmy and brake wind-up, as well as to secure accurate steering geometry. A Dubonnet system was tried, and then Olley developed a system with unequal-length wishbones and coil springs. This had the advantage that the wheelbase remained constant throughout the suspension travel. This SLA independent front suspension was adopted on 1934 Cadillac V16s.

Also praiseworthy was the braking on the Cadillac V16 which, after some problems with brake fade on early V16s, was the subject of a $200,000 investment which produced fully-machined cast molybdenum iron drums ground to an accuracy of 0.007 in for concentricity. In conjunction with cast aluminium brake shoes which expanded as they heated to counteract brake fade, these modifications gave im-

ABOVE *The 1932 V16 featured a modified chassis, restyled body and choice of two wheelbases. 296 were built*

pressive braking characteristics, particularly with Cadillac's vacuum servo system. Any shortcomings by modern standards can be attributed to the problems inherent in overcoming the inertia of a fast-moving car weighing some two and three-quarter tons (2800 kg) . . .

Though the Cadillac V16 was aimed at a small and exclusive market, sales got off to a good start. The V16 was introduced at the National Automobile Show in January 1930, and by April that year the thousandth car was being shipped; three months later, the 2000th left the factory, and sales volume was reported as having reached $13.5 million. It was a false dawn: some idea of the way that the Depression affected sales can

be gained from the fact that the first six months of V16 Cadillac production represented 52 per cent of all the overhead valve V16s built over the model's seven year life, nearly 46 per cent of total Cadillac V16 output. Only 500 V16s were sold in the latter half of 1930, and in 1931 sales totalled 750, despite big discounts by dealers.

Since the entire market was 42 per cent down that year, the 70 per cent drop in V16 Cadillac sales is perhaps not so startling; production, however, was just 346 cars, since many of the 1931 sales were of cars left over from the year before. That represented a collapse of over 87 per cent in terms of cars actually built: and worse was to come . . . In 1933, Cadillac announced that it would build just 400 V16s – one for each of that legendary top echelon of American society, the Four Hundred? – and in the event made a mere 126. From then on, an average of 50 V16s a year was built until production ceased in 1937.

EVOLUTION

Series 452 V16 introduced in January 1930. High-speed axle dropped 1 June. Annual production: 1826 cars.

1931 Series 452A introduced. Annual production: 1424 cars.

1932 Series 452B introduced in January with restyled bodies, triple-silent gearbox, mechanical fuel pump, air-cooled generator, controlled free-wheeling and vacuum clutch, modified chassis, ride control, 750/18 wheels and choice of 143 in (363 cm) and 149 in (378 cm) wheelbases. Annual production: 296 cars

1933 Series 452C introduced in January with modified axle ratios and 750/17 wheels. Annual production: 125 cars

1934 Series 452D introduced in January with 185 bhp power output, dual X-braced chassis, open propeller shaft, independent front suspension, 154 in (391 cm) wheelbase. Annual production: 56 cars

1935 Series 60 452D introduced in January. Similar to 1934. Annual production: 50 cars

1936 Series 90. Similar to 1935 but with modifications to bodywork. Annual production: 52 cars

1937 Series 90 continues with hydraulic brakes added. Last season for overhead valve V16. Annual production: 49 cars

1938 Series 90 with 135 degree side-valve 7023 cc V16 engine introduced. Dual downdraught carburettors, single-plate clutch, helical gearing, hypoid final drive, 141 in (358 cm) wheelbase. Annual production: 311 cars

1939 Series 90 continues. Annual production: 136 cars

1940 Series 90 production ends. Annual production: 61 cars. Total V16 production amounted to 4386 cars

RIGHT *A splendidly preserved 1935 V16 in California, where so many of them now reside. This is one of the 50 or so examples built that year*

RIGHT *A splendidly preserved 1935 V16 in California, where so many of them now reside. This is one of the 50 or so examples built that year*

To some extent, Cadillac had diluted the potential of the V16 in August 1930 with the announcement that they were to build a V12 of their own, This was a derivative of the V16, but using the biggest of the V8 chassis, and with a bore of 79.4 mm against the 76.2 mm of the V16.

Another factor in the V12's favour – which must have weighed heavy in post-Wall Street Crash America – was that it cost considerably less than the V16. At the launch in late 1930, the V12 models cost between $3795 and $4895; the comparable V16s were priced between $5350 and $9200. Since the V12 was mechanically similar to the V16, and offered almost equal levels of refinement, it's small wonder that right from the start it outsold the V16. By 1937 ten V12s were being sold for every V16.

Nevertheless, the V16 did stimulate Cadillac's rivals into action: Packard retaliated with a new-generation Twin-Six with sleek styling and hydraulic valve lifters, but sold only 549 of them between June 1931 and January 1933 (in the same period Cadillac sold some 7700 of its V12). Lincoln launched its KB V12 in 1932, but again sales were nowhere as good as those of the V12 Cadillac; V12s also came from two declining giants, Pierce-Arrow and Franklin, but only two other firms dared to compete by producing V16 cars. Both failed.

In January 1931 Marmon unveiled a 'car of exceptional interest', an overhead valve 200 bhp V16 with an aluminium-alloy engine which had pressed-in steel cylinder liners. The Marmon was certainly an impressive car, but lacked the ultimate panache of the Cadillac. Few were built.

Then there was the Peerless V16, last-ditch stand of a company which had formerly been one of the greatest American luxury-car makers. It appeared during 1930, and matched the Cadillac V16 in terms of performance, for its 7.6-litre power unit developed 173 bhp. Despite this, the Peerless failed to pass the prototype stage, and production ceased in 1931.

So, in comparison with its rivals the Cadillac V16 was not as unsuccessful as it first appeared, and proved that Cadillac was again a serious contender in the luxury car field.

Of all the early Cadillac V16 models, none achieved greater fame than the 1930 'Madame X' series, which acquired its name as the result of a visit to the cinema by Harley Earl in 1929. He saw a much-acclaimed talking picture in Detroit in which the central character, was 'Madame X ... different, mysterious, exciting and, above all ... intriguing'.

At the time, the GM Art and Color Studios was working on a new body style with

ABOVE RIGHT *The superb 1931 V16. Bore was 3 in and stroke 4 in to give a displacement of 452 cu in (6½ litres) and 165 bhp*

slender pillars and a pronounced windshield rake; it had, thought Earl, the same characteristics as 'Madame X'.

No expense was spared, and some of the early Madame X Cadillacs had stainless-steel coach striping sweated to the bodywork instead of the traditional painted stripes; gold-faced instruments and stainless-steel wire wheels were also featured.

Individual variants were not only legion but rare. For instance, even in 1931, only two right-hand-drive V16s were built, while in the 1934-37 period, the most built with one body style in one year was 24. The majority of body styles were built in ones and twos, and some were truly extravagant, like the one-of-a-kind 1934 Convertible Victoria Coupé which still exists in Chicago. As close-coupled as a coupé riding on a massive 154 inch (391 cm) wheelbase (the longest used by any major American manufacturer), the car has pontoon wings (the rear wheels fully faired in) and a projecting boot; horizontal louvres in the bonnet sides are echoed by louvres on the front

wings for aesthetic reasons.

In 1937 Cadillac announced, not unexpectedly, that the V16 was to cease production; what was unexpected was that its replacement was to be a new V16. As much as any ultimate extravagance could be, the new engine was more in tune with the austere climate of the late 1930s. Its specification had been simplified so that it needed only half as many parts, resulting in a 250 lb weight reduction, yet it was as powerful and smoother than the original V16. It was more compact, yet had nine main bearings against the 1930 V16's five; its cylinders were splayed at 135 degrees for superior balance, yet it took up only about two-thirds of the volume.

And, intriguingly, this new V16 flew in

the face of fashion by abandoning overhead valves in favour of side valves; it was also designed for easy service and, as a result, was not as clean architecturally.

Nonetheless, the 1938 V16 found few customers – just 508 of them in its three-year production life but a distinct improvement over the 50-a-year of its predecessor.

Progress in engine design and installation had rendered the concept of a super-smooth sixteen an anachronism. The V8 Cadillacs of the late 1930s were both smooth and flexible, and developed almost as much power as the V16 (135-140 bhp against 185), yet cost from only $2290 in comparison to a starting price of $5140 for the V16. Since they were also available with as wide and elegant a range of coachwork, what logical choice could anyone have made but the V8? As the late Michael Sedgwick pointed out: 'in the era of alligator hoods, only those who worked on the engine got a clear view of it . . .'

The motorist of the late 1930s was also less interested in mechanical specifications than his predecessor of a decade before, and the concept of paying more than twice as much for eight more cylinders, when the car performed just as well with the V8 power unit, made it generally redundant. The 1930 V16 had set a fashion and established Cadillac in the front rank of constructors; a decade later, the V8 had become perfectly adequate.

Moreover, hadn't Cadillac proved its worth by riding out the Depression, where so many of the other luxury car manufacturers had foundered?

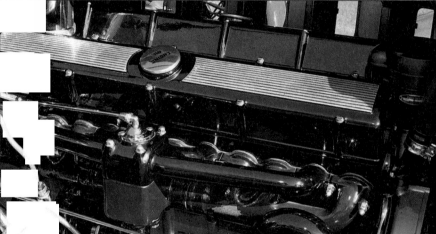

BELOW *By 1937 the hand-built coachwork had given way to pressed steel and a more modern shape, which perhaps has lost some of the elegance of the earlier stately cars*

CHEVROLE

America's sports car started life as a glassfibre-bodied six-cylinder convertible in 1953 and grew in stature to become the powerful Sting Ray muscle car of the '60s and then the high-tech sports car of the '80s

A NAVAL ESCORT as fast as it was uncomfortable – it was truly a stroke of genius to choose the name Corvette for 'America's sports car' in 1953.

It can be argued that the Corvette was GM's riposte to the post-war British invasion of MGs and Jaguars – perhaps, but if you produce the number the General does, the number of sports cars imported then would hardly have raised a corporate eyebrow. No, it wasn't the numbers (how could it be with the production capacity of the British car industry?) but the inspiration that counted.

By the middle of this century Harley Earl had risen to be chief of GM's Art and Colour studio in Detroit, and that made him as important then in North America as Giugiaro is today in the whole world. His admiration for the Jaguar XK120 led him to father a truly American answer, aided and abetted by a figure destined to be just as influential, Ed Cole – the force behind the later '57 Chevy. In 1953 Cole had not long been Chief Engineer at Chevrolet and his burning desire was to improve Chevrolet's staid and rather boring image. That, coupled to Earl's vision, was bound to produce something special. Vision and enthusiasm, however, were not enough to sway one of the most conservative of car companies to produce something speculative and radically different just on a whim; the Corvette would have

to earn its corn as a mobile test bed. It was to be the first mass-production glassfibre car and a relatively risk-free way for the GM hierarchy to evaluate glassfibre for sedan use without committing themselves to 'real' mass production. Although glassfibre didn't take over, the Corvette has continued its test bed role throughout its life, with the current car pioneering the use of lightweight mono-filament transvere leaf springs fore and aft.

Naturally enough, for a low-volume and somewhat speculative mobile test rig GM were not generous in allocating funds, and the first car was largely an amalgam of available production parts, such as Chevy's venerable and stolid 235 cu in (3.8-litre) straight six, suitably modified with solid lifters and different cam timing to produce 150 bhp at 4500 rpm. It was mated to that most sporting of transmissions, the Powerglide two-speed automatic, and drove the rear wheels via a leaf-sprung axle, all mounted on a solid box section X-braced frame.

Although the first cars were anything but elegant compared to the Jaguar (or much

The second generation Corvettes were introduced in 1956 with a 210 bhp 4.3-litre V8 and three-speed manual transmission at a base price of just $3149. It was one of the most elegant of 1950s American cars

T Corvette

else come to that), with their deep slab sides making them look more like freighters that the weapon the name evoked, when the Corvette was introduced at 'Motorama' (GM's travelling extravaganza) public reaction was wildly enthusiastic. That response was enough to put the car into production, briefly on a very small six-car line in Flint, Michigan, before being transferred to St Louis where the car was built for many years until the 1981 move to its present home in Bowling Green, Kentucky.

Unfortunately the American public did not put its money where its mouth was, and by the end of 1954 a mere 3600 of the year's models had been sold, leaving another 1500 homeless. The answer came in 1955, and it wasn't the extra 30 cubic inches but the fact that the new 265 cu in engine was Chevrolet's latest V8, lighter (by 30 lb/14 kg) and more powerful (by 45 bhp) than the archaic six. Nevertheless the damage had already been done for the first generation Corvettes, and it was not until 1956 when the ugly duckling turned, as they are all supposed to, into an elegant swan, that the Corvette took hold of the American imagination.

The combination of V8 power, a manual transmission (albeit only a three-speed) and a body that was exactly right worked wonders, and sales proved it, with 3388 sold in 1956, compared with just 674 in 1955. By

that time the Belgian engineer Zora Arkus-Duntov's influence was beginning to be felt. Up went the compression ratio and the power, to 9.25:1 and 225 bhp respectively. With 270 lb ft of torque at 3600 rpm and a virtually even weight distribution the '56 car was very rapid indeed. It had finally turned into a genuine sports car capable of 7.5-second times to 60 mph (96 kph) and a top speed of 120 mph (193 kph), and measured by the all-important American yardstick, it could cover the standing quarter mile in 14.2 seconds with a terminal speed of 93 mph (150 kph). Performance improved

This 1967 Sting Ray Coupé represents the end of an era, dating from the last year of Sting Ray production. The first Sting Ray Coupés of 1963 featured a split rear screen but that was soon discarded in favour of the wide screen (ABOVE), much to the designer Bill Mitchell's disgust. Mitchell felt the split screen was an essential feature of the whole design. The coupé proved popular, immediately accounting for 50 per cent of Corvette production ABOVE LEFT *Sting Rays were well equipped inside with a plethora of instruments to supplement the large speedo and tach*

even further when the Borg-Warner four-speed transmission became available in 1957.

The second generation Corvette lasted for seven years before the starkly different Sting Ray appeared in 1963, yet during that time it epitomised the traditional open sports car. It was not exactly sophisticated but was strong, looked simply terrific and was *very* fast.

Under that elegant glassfibre, the quality of which had improved dramatically since the first cars, tradition reigned. The stout box frame soldiered on, carrying the live

as well as it went, and by that time it certainly *would* go... That V8 had gradually been getting bigger and bigger, and by '59 it had been bored out to displace 283 cu in (4.6 litres) with power to match its greater size. Rather neatly, the short-stroke V8 (3.87 in × 3 in/98.3 mm × 76.2 mm) gave one horsepower for each cubic inch of displacement, with the 283 bhp (SAE gross) being delivered at 4800 rpm. Admittedly that was with the high-performance Rochester-built GM fuel injection, which unfortunately proved to be every bit as troublesome to GM as Lucas fuel injection had on the Triumphs of the late '60s. When it worked properly, however, the results were spectacular and it would power the '57 Corvette to 60 mph in just 5.5 seconds; it was hardly surprising that at the end of the standing quarter mile the car would be touching 100 mph (161 kph).

Such impressive power and speed should obviously be raced, and the second generation 'Vettes were quite successful in the SCCA Class B Production class in 1958 and '59. Sadly for sports-car development in the United States, however, the National Safety Council managed to convince the Auto Manufacturers' Association (AMA) that direct involvement in racing was tantamount to endorsing death on the roads, and in June 1957 the infamous AMA ban on factory involvement came to pass. The AMA edict did

was replaced by a rear end with strong overtones of the Sting Ray to come in 1963.

Bill Mitchell had become Chief of GM Design in 1961 and his ideas spelt the end for the '50s styles. To his credit however, Mitchell did not stop developing the second generation cars until his favoured form appeared in '63, and some critics consider the 1962 models to be among the best. By that time the Corvette sported a 327 cu in (5.3-litre) V8 producing 360 bhp and a top speed approaching 150 mph (242 kph). In retrospect perhaps Mitchell was right; that sort of power deserved to be housed in something more up to date than an obsolescent braced frame with semi-elliptic rear leaf springs and a live axle. Sales figures for 1963 seemed to prove the point; the new car, the Sting Ray, prompted a 50 per cent rise in sales, with half of the 21,000 sold being the new hardtop Coupé.

What was so modern about the Sting Ray? In the early '60s there was a clear worldwide trend towards rear-mounted engines, a fashion that inspired cars as disparate as the Porsche 911 and the Hillman Imp, the Renault Dauphine and the Chevrolet Corvair, and thus Zora Arkus-Duntov was strongly tempted to follow with the Corvette. In the end the Corvette tradition won, and the front V8 remained in a car strongly modelled on one of the fragile fruits of Chevrolet's racing Corvette programme. Duntov's stillborn Sebring SS of 1957, with its magnesium body, steel space frame and de Dion rear axle, had been remodelled by Mitchell to form the Stringray racing car, successfully campaigned by Dick Thompson in SCCA C-Class Sports during 1959 and 1960. In 1962 Mitchell turned the car into his personal road car, which exists in a pristine silver to this day, and it illustrates just how much it influenced his design of the third generation cars, although they, naturally, did not feature the racing style hump behind the driver's seat...

The Sebring SS cost more than 100,000 dollars to build. It was fitted with a 310 bhp version of the 283 cu in engine. With a dry weight of 1,850 lb, it was a handy performer indeed and with such a favourable power-to-weight ration and ample torque it accelerated fiercely too.

The looks may have been similar but there was no chance of the alloy bodywork or spaceframe chassis being put into production, and the mechanical changes were far less radical than the styling. The major difference lay with the rear suspension. It wasn't the racer's de Dion arrangement but a rather odd device using something almost as traditional as a live axle, a transverse semi-elliptic leaf spring, which gave the Corvette independent suspension for the first time. The differential was bolted to two of the cross members in the new upswept ladder perimeter frame with the spring bolted to the diff carrier. Transverse location for the wheels was provided by two lower tubular radius arms and double-jointed drive shafts, while longitudinal location came via two trailing arms.

rear axle on leaf springs, although Duntov had revised the spring mountings to give more precise handling. The front suspension was a wishbone and coil spring arrangement with positive recirculating ball steering (with just three turns lock to lock).

By 1959 Chevrolet were starting to cater for serious drivers by offering a performance suspension option, consisting of a front anti-roll bar and uprated springs and dampers all round, complemented by quicker steering and a limited slip differential. That, allied to a wide track and a 52:48 front/rear weight ratio meant a Corvette that handled

not slow down the NASCAR stockers all that much, and somewhere deep in the bowels of Ford and GM racing parts continued to be built and delivered to favoured teams. The Grossman/Fitch Corvette that finished an extremely commendable 8th at Le Mans in 1960 did not exceed 150 mph (242 kph) down the Mulsanne straight with a stock engine...

Nevertheless, at the beginning of the '60s the Corvette was hardly the child of the race track. It had grown bigger and started to sprout too much extraneous chrome until finally, in 1961, that graceful rounded tail

ABOVE LEFT *The original Sting Ray, transformed into Bill Mitchell's road car*
LEFT *Many Corvette prototypes never made it into production, including this 1970 V8 mid-engined example*
ABOVE AND BELOW *A fourth generation Corvette of 1976 vintage. By 1976 the 5.7-litre V8 produced just 185 bhp*

That transverse spring had no intrinsic merit other than it saved space – there was simply no room for coils in the new design – but that hardly seemed to matter, for the new rear proved a great success, putting an immediate end to two of the earlier car's faults – terminal oversteer and axle tramp.

In the 1960s there really was no substitute for cubic inches, and when the Corvette entered the horsepower battle it did so in full, with the 427 cu in (7-litre) engine. With solid valve lifters and an 11:1 compression ratio, that engine didn't need fuel injection to impress; with a four barrel Holley carburettor it produced 425 bhp at 5600 rpm and a massive 465 lb ft of torque.

That spells performance in anyone's language and Corvette customers could choose exactly how much of it they wanted; usually there were four engine options, and in 1966, for example, the range was wide, from the mundane base 300 bhp 327 cu in (5.3-litre) V8 to the top performance 427 cu in (7-litre) V8. If one chose the 427 with the 4.11:1 final drive then the car would break the 5-second barrier to 60 mph and still reach 140 mph (225 kph) while with a more conservative rear end 160 mph (257 kph) was theoretically possible. That extra power was cheap too; in 1966 the 427 engine was a $312 option.

A huge V8 is guaranteed to make your progress rapid but it's a lot of metal to stop, and for years that was the Corvette's main problem. By the early '60s the Corvette's massive alloy drum brakes had been given special sintered iron linings, but even they could not cope, as the racers discovered. The solution, long overdue, appeared in 1965 with disc brakes – 10 years after Jaguar's D-type proved their effectiveness. Strangely, when *Autocar* tested a Sting Ray in 1963 they did not find the drum brakes a problem, declaring that they were 'light in operation, very powerful at all speeds and free from fade…', although they did lock prematurely. Otherwise they quibbled at the car's lack of refinement compared to high-performance European GTs. On a more positive note they liked the gear lever's

action ('smooth, short and extremely light') and were surprised by the comfort above 50 mph (80 kph) despite the hard spring and damper settings that made the rear step out of line through bumpy corners.

Overall the tone was grudging, even though the test car out accelerated the E-type, Jensen CV-8 and Maserati Sebring which they compared it to, both to 60 mph and over the standing quarter (which the Corvette managed in just 13.5 seconds).

When the American magazine *Sports Car Graphic* tried a '65 427 with disc brakes they were far less stilted: 'We didn't even bother to take it to Riverside or Willow Springs for acceleration runs…all you need is a two-

block-long straight. From a 70 mph cruising speed you can accelerate to…140 mph in roughly a mile. Sixty to 100 mph in top gear takes a mere 7.2 seconds. Tell us you'd like a hotter performing road machine than this and we'll call you some kinda nut!' Like *Autocar* they noted the initial understeer which turned into slight oversteer with the power on. 'The limit is reached with the rear end breaking loose all of a sudden and, even though it takes quick reflexes, a slight twitch of the wheel and an instant lift with the accelerator foot will bring it back under control. But you have to be going gawdawful fast to reach the limit – very near competitive racing speeds.'

Even more exciting were Arkus-Duntov's Grand Sports, built to rival Carroll Shelby's AC Cobras in SCCA Production racing. The original plan was to build 125 for homologation and to take the car to Le Mans in 1963. Duntov was confident that his twin-plug per cylinder, fuel-injected experimental alloy 550 bhp 377 cu in (6.1-litre) V8 would push the Corvette to 180 mph (290 kph) along the long Mulsanne straight. GM spoiled the fun, forcing Chevrolet to veto the project, citing the old AMA ban. That also meant an end to the 125 production run, but the Grand Sport did have its moment of glory when three of them went to the Nassau Speed Week in the Bahamas in 1963 and proved themselves dramatically quicker than a host of Cobras. Perhaps the oddest thing about the Sting Rays was that they lasted only five years before the fourth generation cars took over, and yet those cars were around until 1983, when, by common consent, it was hardly a classic. The exaggerated coke-bottle styling, with the wasp waist and long front and rear overhangs, was certainly not as striking as the original Sting Ray's, the car was never as fast, and to top it all, was more cramped.

Part of the explanation for its over-long life lies in the troubles the American auto industry had to face through the '70s, with oil crises and the increasing tide of Japanese competition. A new Corvette was hardly a priority, and despite the numerous cosmetic styling updates the basic design stagnated as proposed replacements fell by the wayside. The Astro Vette was no great loss but the Astro II of 1968 showed what the Corvette should have looked like in that era. In the late '70s, the Aerovette very nearly did make it into production for 1980. Its transverse V8 was mid-mounted with a complicated drive arrangement involving chain drive to the differential. Before the energy crisis finally killed off GM's interest in the Wankel engine the Aerovette became a test bed for both two and four rotor rotaries before reverting to the 400 cu in (6.5-litre) V8. It was in V8 form that it would have entered production had not three of the Corvette's most influential figures, Ed Cole, then GM President, Bill Mitchell and Zora Arkus-Duntov, retired at the same time.

By the time the 'new' Corvette finally did appear in 1983 it was long overdue and marked a dramatic shift in policy. The first Corvette's base price was $3513, and that level was maintained through the years, to the $7600 of the '76 model and the $16,300 of 1981, as inflation took its toll. The '84 model was aimed at a significantly more wealthy clientele, with a base price nearer $30,000.

What could possibly make a Corvette worth so much? After all it was still only a front-engined, rear-drive V8, as the model had been for so long, albeit clothed in an attractive and sleek, modern-looking body. Under the skin, however, the car was much better than its predecessors in many ways and would get better still as GM-owned Lotus reworked and improved the suspension, giving the car a much more European driving feel.

EVOLUTION

Introduced at the GM Motorama Show at the New York Waldorf-Astoria in January 1953 as a two-door, two-seat convertible with glassfibre body on separate chassis. It followed English practice in having no exterior door handles. Engine was in-line six-cylinder with two-speed Powerglide automatic transmission.

1955 V8 engine became available with three-speed manual transmission.

1956 Second generation Corvette introduced with restyled body.

1957 Four-speed manual Borg-Warner transmission introduced. Rochester-built fuel injection available, along with Positraction limited slip diff.

1960 Aluminium cylinder heads and radiator introduced.

1962 327 cu in (5.3-litre) V8 introduced.

1963 Third generation Corvette introduced as Sting Ray with new ladder frame, lighter body and independent rear suspension with transverse leaf spring introduced. Coupé available for the first time.

1965 Four-wheel disc brakes introduced as standard equipment. Close-ratio four-speed transmission optional.

1966 425 bhp 427 cu in (7-litre) V8 available.

1967 Sting Ray discontinued and longer fourth-generation Corvette introduced.

1969 350 cu in (5.6-litre) V8 introduced and Corvette known as the Stingray.

1970 Turbo Jet 454 cu in (7.4-litre) introduced along with 350 cu in 'small block' V8.

1972 Power outputs appeared to decrease as SAE net standard replaced SAE gross.

1975 Catalytic converters introduced and maximum power falls to 205 bhp. Roadster discontinued.

1977 Leather seats became standard equipment.

1979 Low profile tyres became available.

1981 Glassfibre monoleaf rear spring introduced.

1982 Throttle body fuel injection introduced along with four-speed automatic transmission. Manual gearbox no longer available.

1983 There was no official '83 model but the fifth generation Corvette was introduced as an '84 model with glassfibre springs front and rear and completely new chassis and body. 5.7-litre V8 continued with power output of 205 bhp. Choice of four-speed automatic or computer-controlled overdrive on four-speed manual gearbox. Alloy wheels with special Formula One-derived Goodyear low profile tyres.

The '84 Corvette was a quantum leap forward in design, handling… and price. At one stage the car cost £28,000 in the UK (partly due to a weak pound it's true). Enormous care was taken to make the under-bonnet area as attractive as possible with careful colour matching of all leads, pipes and wires. One of the most attractive features of the new 'Vette was its electronic dashboard – it changed from metric to imperial at the flick of a switch

That, claim the Chevrolet engineers, was a deliberate policy, a reaffirmation of the American way… The engine itself is certainly nothing special; even with throttle-body fuel injection (known as 'cross-fire injection' at GM) its 350 cu in (5.7 litres) delivers only 205 bhp at 4300 rpm, but, as Aston Martin or Rolls-Royce would put it, the power output is 'adequate'. This Corvette has been built for handling rather than outright performance, the goal being to equal the best of the Europeans, like the Porsche 928.

Naturally, with that level of ambition some new suspension was called for, and the rear has been remodelled with two short trailing links per side with an extra control arm to enable toe in and out to be set precisely. The transverse plastic leaf spring introduced in 1981 was retained; Chevrolet have been so pleased with its performance that they decided on a similar system at the

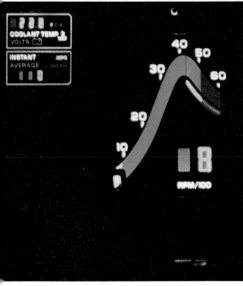

moulded on the company's FI rain tyres. The massive 'gatorback' 255/50VR16s are unidirectional and thus can only be used on one side of the car. Allied to those stiff damper settings they mean that 1 g cornering is almost within reach.

European GTs are meant to be nimble, so very 'quick', precise steering was regarded as essential, and the '84 Corvette has the most precise rack and pinion system ever seen on an American production car. Basically the Corvette engineers, under chief engineer David McLellan, had free rein, and the end result is a car with superb reactions and response on the race track, where its prodigious grip and massive disc brakes come into their own. McLellan claims that 'With its totally new suspension configuration, this car will be at home and respected on the interstate, the autobahn, or any highway in the world.' That may have been the intention but the reality turned out to be rather different. On the ordinary road the unfortunate '84 Corvette driver finds that refinement has fled, to leave him fighting a heavy and wilful car that seems to have a mind of its own, with steering that's really too sharp and a tendency to follow every crack and undulation in the road.

It's a major mystery why the Corvette is not tuned to the road, and equally puzzling is the car's weight. The new car is significantly smaller than its predecessor in every dimension except width, its perimeter chassis uses lightweight high-strength steel, the bonnet is in SMC (sheet moulding composite), the springs are in plastic and the drive shafts, propeller shaft and even the radiator fins are in aluminium. The net result is...a car weighing nearly 3200 lb (1451 kg).

As it stands at present the car has rather too many rough edges to make it one of the world's great GTs, which, after all, is what is claimed for it. The manual gearbox, for example, is clearly inferior to that used years ago and praised in road test after road test; the present GM four-speed has a truly trucklike action almost requiring two hands to change gear. When queried about it a GM engineer argued that easy-shifting gearchanges just couldn't handle the power... It is rather more sophisticated than a straight four-speed in that it's blessed (if that's the right word) by a computer controlled overdrive (0.67:1) operating on the top three ratios, linked to the engine management system which tells it when to engage overdrive for optimum fuel economy. That change is automatic unless the car is under hard acceleration. In principle it's a good idea but it has proved to be nothing but trouble.

Nevertheless, despite the problems with transmission and normal road handling the Corvette will prove a worthy successor to the '60s Sting Rays.

Corvettes are among the most popular American classic in the UK with a thriving British branch of the Corvette Club catering for needs of hundreds of enthusiastic owners who find the enforced left-hand drive and a thirst for fuel a small price to pay for a car of this speed, power and eye-catching looks.

front, working with short double wishbones and an anti-roll bar. All the suspension arms are beautifully forged in aluminium, a material also used for the propeller and drive shafts and the central chassis beam connecting differential to gearbox.

One of the most time-honoured ways to achieve reasonable handling characteristics is to stiffen the suspension to the point where the wheels can hardly move out of their ideal plane, and if you choose to use ultra-low profile 50-section tyres as GM have, it becomes even more critical to keep the contact patch flat on the road. The Corvette's ride has become, to put it mildly, firm, and if you choose the Z51 performance suspension option, damn near solid.

An even easier route to a handling heaven is through modern tyre technology and Chevrolet commissioned Goodyear to build Eagle GTs specificaly for the Corvette,

FORD M

It was America's first muscle car, and the Mustang's sales grew as rapidly as did the options list and power output. Today's models are different, with brains as well as brawn

'DESIGNED TO BE DESIGNED BY YOU' went the advertising slogan in the '60s and '70s, and for once the advertising did not lie. Anyone could, and many did, design into the simple pony car exactly what they wanted; Ford deliberately made the option list so long that you needed a computer to keep track of it. As the publicists claimed, the Mustang was a state of mind....

Bottom of the range when the cars were introduced in 1964 was the cheap and cheerful 170 cu in (2.8-litre) straight-six with a three-speed manual. With just 101 bhp and soft suspension it hardly represented a performance breakthrough. What it did represent was a new image; the (relatively) small nimble 'personal' car was a reaction to the chromed opulence of the '50s, and the products of the post-war baby boom bought it in huge numbers. Ford's vice-president Lee Iacocca saw them coming – his salesman's intuition told him that a car which looked sporty, could carry four people and cost (just) under $2500 would have a huge market. The Mustang was so exactly right for the times it sold 22,000 on the day it was introduced and 417,000 in its first year of production, prompting the opposition to rush out their own personal-size performance cars. The Mustang was responsible for the Camaro and Firebird from General Motors and the underrated Javelin from American Motors, while even Chrysler tried to fight back with the Barracuda before bringing out the fearsome Charger.

Like the Corvette, the history of the Mustang from the mid-'60s to the mid-'80s reflects the state of the American motor industry. Brash enthusiasm characterised the early models and that rapidly began to focus on the serious pursuit of pure power until the second generation Mustang II appeared in 1974, by which time things were getting gloomy for Detroit and Dearborn. Ford's

USTANG

Mustang II was gloomy too, a quantum leap backwards compared to the European and the increasing Japanese competition. So mediocre was it in fact that it's safe virtually to ignore the whole range and the early examples of the third generation too. It was really only in 1983-4 that the Mustang regained some appeal.

In the early '60s, although those who knew their way around the option list could order themselves a genuine high-performance muscle car, Ford decided that some racing exposure would do wonders for sales and who better to coordinate the effort than Carroll Shelby, whose Ford-engined Cobras were almost unbeatable?

The Shelby programme got underway as early as late 1964 and the Mustang he chose

The '85 Mustang GT convertible is powered by a 5-litre V8 producing 210 bhp and is capable of 0–60 mph in 7 seconds

to rework was the aggressive-looking fastback rather than the ordinary hardtop or the convertible. Shelby had to abide by SCCA (Sports Car Club of America) rules, which specified that either the engine or the suspension had to stay essentially standard. Believing, like a good Texan, that power was the answer, Shelby chose to retain, more or less, the standard suspension and rework the engine.

The standard suspension was exactly what you would expect of the times – double wishbones at the front with the coils mounted above the top wishbone, an anti-roll bar and a live rear axle located by semi-elliptic leaf springs. That all stayed put but the standard anti-roll bar was discarded in favour of a thicker one, the bottom wishbones were lowered and the standard dampers thrown away in favour of vastly superior Konis. Top-mounted traction bars were

tang had the largest engine available, the 289 cu in (4.7-litre) V8 mated to the four-speed manual. Like every other contemporary American V8 it was a cast-iron pushrod engine, which sounds mundane in the extreme but Ford's advanced thin-wall casting techniques meant a relatively light engine to go with the compact layout. With suitably modified valve timing Shelby raised the output of Ford's High-Performance short-stroke (4 in × 2.87 in/101.6 mm × 72.9 mm) V8 from 271 bhp at 6000 rpm to over 340 bhp. That was measured in SAE gross terms of course and in race trim but it was enough to give the Shelby Mustang the 350 GT designation even though the road-going cars produced just over 300 bhp....

Shelby's revisions were so successful that his Mustangs took the SCCA B-Production class national title in '65, '66 and '67, beating mostly Corvettes and the odd hybrid like the V8 Sunbeam Tiger.

In 1964 *Motor* tested the car on which the GT-350 was based, the High Performance 289, and found it capable of a maximum 128.5 mph (206.8 kph). Only its low gearing held it back as that top speed needed nearer 7000 rpm than 6000 rpm, but that same low gearing meant excellent acceleration which

BELOW *By 1968 the Mustang had already grown to house increasingly large and powerful engines. This is a 1968 GT version with the distinctive sloping tail*

installed at the rear to help control the axle with its rather crude limited-slip differential, and quicker steering was installed to help keep it all on the road or track. Stopping was improved too with larger front discs although the rear had to soldier on with drums.

Shelby was lucky in one respect. The standard chassis, described by *Motor* as a 'welded punt frame with high torsional rigidity', was indeed very stiff and an ideal platform on which to build a performance car. Some of that torsional rigidity was accidental; in the '60s there was no computer-aided design and as Ford had very little experience of building small cars they erred on the side of caution, knowing that some heavy and powerful engines would find their way into the new car.

Naturally Shelby's building-block Mus-

saw the car leap to 60 mph (97 kph) in 7.6 seconds, to 90 mph (145 kph) in 15.9 seconds and cover the standing quarter mile in 15.2 seconds. With less wheelspin the figures would have been a great deal more impressive!

Strangely, given the popular prejudices about American cars, *Motor* liked the gearchange and the suspension, even finding the powerful synchromesh gearbox '...delightful to use though it requires a fair amount of energy as the light flywheel dictates a quick change.' The suspension was found to be '...quite firm without having the rigidity associated with some British sports cars.... It strikes a pleasant balance between firm handling and good ride over indifferent surfaces, at the same time keeping roll down to a comfortable minimum.'

On the other hand the brakes (which

ABOVE *The classic shape of the early Mustang; this is a 1966 289*
LEFT *The interior from the '66 289*
BELOW LEFT *The original Mustang I resembled the production Mustangs very little. Ford vice-presidents H. C. Misch (left) and Gene Bordinat admire the car*

were drums all round as optional front discs did not become available until the next year) were found to be 'quite inadequate' and the handling as tricky as they expected in the wet. Even so the appeal of a V8 with 312 lb ft of torque was revealed in their nicely understated conclusion: 'Perhaps the greatest safety point of the Mustang is the ease with which a skilful driver can accelerate out of trouble.'

Americans, of course, were not prone to understatement and Dan Gurney let his enthusiasm get the better of him to the extent of claiming the High-Performance Mustang had 'the feel of a 2+2 Ferrari' – an unusually soft Ferrari presumably.

By 1966 Ford had dropped the huge and heavy 390 cu in (6.4-litre) V8 into the Mustang, leading *Car and Driver* to expect the nose-heavy 350 GT (the weight split was 60/40) to suffer terminal understeer, to 'plow like an Ohio farmer' as they put it. It didn't but its handling was best described as clumsy. Performance was another matter as the happy road testers went on to recount: 'Driving as laconically as we ever do in a car like this, we knocked off 15.2-second quarter-miles with the air-conditioner and the sterio tape deck going full blast and letting the XPL 3-speed automatic shift when it felt like it'.

The Shelby programme continued until

1969 by which time Shelby's independent spirit was becoming tired of working with large corporations. He felt he had gone about as far as he could go, which if you take a look at his GT 500 KR (for King of the Road, what else?) seemed reasonable. The GT 500 KR was built in limited numbers in both fastback and convertible form and boasted a truly staggering performance. Its four-barrel Holley carburettor pumped air into the 428 cu in (7-litre) V8 at the rate of 735 cubic feet a minute, producing over 400 bhp – just about the right amount of power when you recall that the weight had crept up with the power to as much as 3700 lb (1680 kg).

The Shelby versions of the Mustang, usually with distinctive paintwork, have become easily the most collectable of the whole Mustang range. In the UK they have proved themselves formidable historic racing cars capable of showing a clean pair of heels to many lighter and more agile cars with brakes that don't fade!

When Shelby had finally had enough Ford brought the really high-performance Mustangs in-house. In 1969 the whole range had been restyled, becoming longer (by four inches/10 cm), lower and slightly wider. That distinctive scalloped side treatment of the early cars disappeared to the detriment of the whole design, although the Mach I did have simulated rear three-quarter scoops to show it meant business. It also had the strange feature of an air scoop mounted directly to the air cleaner and poking out through the bonnet where high rpm vibrated it enough for Ford engineers to christen it The Shaker… . That would have been merely amusing if the car had only had pretensions to performance but speed was guaranteed even with the standard engine, the 250 bhp 351 cu in (5.7-litre) Windsor V8.

The 351 was regarded as a far better and smoother engine the the 289s and 302s but as *Motor Trend* observed in late '68, 'No matter what you say about the 351 it is not a Cobra Jet and if you're going to be in the Mach I dream you may as well have the genuine article.' The heavy 428 cu in (7-litre) V8 referred to meant that 'of course there is understeer but you can easily, very easily, bring the rear end into line with the throttle'. Of course you could, with more than 355 bhp on crossply tires. At that time American companies still measured horsepower in SAE gross terms (in other words power at the flywheel discounting any of the energy-absorbing ancillaries like the water pump or dynamo, let alone the transmission). The 355 bhp quoted would be more like 300 bhp in European terms. Nevertheless it was still a healthy power output although obviously nowhere even near the street limit for such an engine despite the high (10.6:1) compression ratio. No, the Cobra Jet's potential was indicated by the torque output of 440 lb ft at 3400 rpm.

That torque was fed through a three-speed Cruise-o-Matic transmission although a four-speed manual was available as an option. Either way the top speed was quoted at 127 mph (205 kph) and the standing quarter mile took only 14 seconds to cover with 60 mph coming up in 5.7 seconds.

Although the Mach I still had basically the same suspension as the very first models the rear was transformed by a simple trick lifted from the Shelby cars. The rear dampers were staggered, one mounted ahead of the axle, the other behind with both inclined toward the centre of the axle. There was a new and much improved Traction Lok limited slip diff to go with that modification and the excessive liveliness of a live axle was overcome.

By this time, however, Americans were obviously becoming blasé about horsepower alone as *Motor Trend's* Eric Dahlquist went into raptures about the interior, '...your hand reaches out to see if the teak-

TOP *The Mustang II could be made attractive, like this 1977 Cobra*
ABOVE *A late version of the Mach I, from 1972. The '71–'73 Mustangs were the largest of all, 8 in (20.3 cm) longer, 6 in (15.2 cm) wider and almost 600 lb (272 kg) heavier than the first Mustangs*
RIGHT *Early Mach Is were not quite so gross. This is a 1969 example being put through its paces on the test track*
BOTTOM *400 bhp of real muscle in the form of the 1968 Shelby GT 500 King of the Road*

dinosaur age; they were well developed, extremely powerful, ponderous and doomed. They roamed around for a few years and then died in the ice age of the first energy crisis. Evolution only took a step sideways when the Mustang II appeared in 1974. It was a foot shorter than the '73 car and even five inches (12.7 cm) shorter than the original Mustang, but the fuel fright meant that the standard power plant had become the small 2.3-litre overhead-cam four-cylinder. When the Mustang II first appeared the new Mach I had to be content with a 2.8-litre V6 which reduced its 0-60 time to a yawning 14 seconds plus. Discerning critics disliked the Mustang II and consequently it led a quiet life until the next generation of Mustang appeared in 1979. That had far cleaner styl-

wood grain panels are real…. It is as if some native had gone off into the forest and felled a teak and carried it back through the undergrowth to the river where it was lashed to others of its kind and floated down to the saw mill.' As he implied, and presumably as most of America agreed, who needs natural materials when the world has plastic?

The Mustangs grew yet larger in 1971, but for the performance cars, the Mach I and Boss 351, the increase in track (3 inches/ 7.6 cm at the front and 2.5 inches/6.5 cm at the rear) far outweighed the increase in weight. Not surprisingly it made the handling of the new Boss 351 with the Cleveland engine far more secure than that of the Boss 302; the 351 went through most corners with virtually no roll and had so much power that it over- rather than understeered.

As America entered the '70s the Mach I and Boss Mustangs were entering their own

ing, almost as exciting as that of the last Cortina. A live rear axle was retained as was the rack and pinion steering that had come with the Mustang II, but the new styling and strut front suspension were sufficient excuse for Ford to dub the range 'A New Breed of Mustang'. There was nothing new about the engines as the lifeless 2.3 struggled on and although the 302 V8 was still available it was strangled by emissions controls.

Nevertheless the high-tech that was eventually to rescue the Mustang had begun to make an appearance in the form of a turbocharger for the four-cylinder engine, and low-profile Michelin TRX tyres. Unfortunately the turbo installation was a disaster of the first order and Ford's first excursion into turbocharging for the masses was quietly buried.

As worries about fuel supplies receded and the new breed of electronic engine

EVOLUTION

Mustang I prototype introduced in 1962 to test public desire for a small sporty Ford. It was an open two-seater powered by a mid-mounted 90 bhp 2-litre V4 and had front disc brakes, magnesium wheels and a top speed of 115 mph (185 kph)

1964 Mustang production car introduced as a '65 model with a 2.8-litre in-line six-cylinder engine as standard with three-speed manual gearbox. Optional engines included the 3.3-litre six and 4.3- and 4.7-litre V8s. The large V8 was available with a four-speed manual gearbox as standard. Three body styles were available – hardtop, convertible and coupé

1965 Shelby Mustang GT-350 introduced with 289 cu in (4.7-litre) V8

1966 Base engine became the 3.3-litre

1967 Optional 390 cu in (6.4-litre) V8 with 320 bhp introduced. Track and body widened by 2.5 in (635 mm) and fastback body redesigned to eliminate the awkward step in the earlier design. Front suspension modified. Shelby GT-500 introduced with 400 bhp 428 cu in (7-litre) V8 and either four-speed manual or three-speed automatic transmission

1968 302 cu in (5-litre) with 230 bhp and 390 bhp big-block 427 cu in (7-litre) V8 introduced as options. Later in the year the 428 cu in Cobra Jet V8 became available. Suspension slightly modified

1969 Mustang Grande introduced as luxury version. Mach I introduced as new high-performance variant. Styling revised once more, making the Mustang longer, lower and wider with the distinctive body side-scalloping removed. Mach I was available with either the 250 bhp 351 cu in or the 355 bhp 428 Cobra Jet V8 and included the GT Equipment option package which featured staggered rear dampers. Two ultra high-performance models were introduced – the Boss 302 and Boss 429

1970 GT suspension package discontinued except on Boss and Mach I models. The big-block 390 cu in (6.4-litre) V8 discontinued

1971 Mustang range restyled and the cars grew longer, wider and considerably heavier. Boss 302 and 429 were dropped and replaced by the limited-production Boss 351 with Traction-Lok limited slip differential and four-speed Hurst transmission

1974 Mustang II introduced. It was far smaller than the '73 model and even shorter than the original Mustang. Base engine was the overhead-cam 2.3-litre four while the Mach I was powered by a 2.8-litre V6. Rack and pinion steering introduced

1979 Third generation Mustang introduced with completely new styling and MacPherson strut front suspension. Base engine was still the 2.3-litre four with the 2.8-litre V6 and 5-litre V8 as options.

1982 Mustang GT reintroduced with 5-litre V8

1983 Mustang Convertible reintroduced with 3.8-litre V6 or in GT form with the 5-litre V8. Five-speed manual gearbox standard on GT

1984 SVO Mustang introduced with turbocharged 2.3-litre four with intercooler

1989 Mustang in improved form celebrates 25 years in production

management control systems meant that Ford and GM could meet the Federal fuel economy requirements known as CAFE, North America and the Mustang began to re-discover high performance.

By 1985 the Mustang GT was once more a reasonable car and Ford brochures were allowed to mention power outputs once again. The four-barrel 302 produced 210 bhp (SAE net) at 4400 rpm, a figure that's grown steadily from the trough of around 150 bhp just three or four years before. Some judicious strengthening of the bodyshell meant that it was even possible to have a Convertible GT once again (introduced in '83 as an '84 model) and although the chassis still felt rather more flexible than a purpose-built open sports car it was acceptable and its performance even more so. Once again there was a Mustang that could turn in 7-second 0-60 times and reach a top speed near 120 mph (193 kph).

The five-speed manual gearbox was de-lightfully light and precise to use and the

power steering direct and not overly boosted, although it was still rather insensitive.

The years since the Shelbys and Mach Is have seen some rear suspension development too. From staggered dampers and semi-elliptic springs Ford have progressed to a full belt-and-braces affair in locating the GT's axle. Two lower trailing arms are supplemented by two upper angled torque arms, a Panhard rod, an anti-roll bar and four dampers cunningly arranged to form what Ford call their Quadra Link system. The second set of dampers is inclined almost to the horizontal, like upper trailing arms, to cushion the shock of fierce gear changes and mask axle tramp.

BELOW *The distinctive lines of the SVO Mustang. The SVO is the most sophisticated Mustang built so far, with a 2.3-litre intercooled turbocharged engine producing 175 bhp*

Although the GT convertible looks the part and has a superb powertrain offering smooth and instant acceleration, the driver is seated far too high and the car is still too vague for European tastes. That problem was addressed (and almost solved) with the SVO Mustang introduced in 1983. As rear-drive Mustangs are scheduled to go out of production in '86 or '87 the SVO represents the pinnacle of Mustang design, its creators trying to achieve through 'high-tech' what was done with cubic inches years ago. Ford's electronic engine management control has permitted the use of up to 14 psi of turbo boost, enough to force 175 bhp out of the 2.3-litre four at 4400 rpm along with 210 lb ft of torque at 3000 rpm. Fuel injection and in-

tercooling also play their part, the intercooler bringing down the temperature of the air flowing into the engine down from around 300 degrees Fahrenheit to 175 degrees F to make that air more dense. That alone gave the turbo 2.3 a 20 per cent power boost. That makes it very slightly slower than the 5-litre GT with 0-60 times nearer 8 than 7 seconds, but it's faster over the standing quarter (15.8 seconds, 89 mph/143 kph) when the engine really gets going. There are echoes of Shelby in the use of Koni (gas-filled) dampers all round (even in the Quadra Link system) while braking is by ventilated discs, reflecting the growing impatience of American car buyers with cars incapable of braking strongly without suffering bad fade. There are other notable features. Its cast alloy wheels are covered by 225/50VR16 Goodyear Eagles, the same unidirectional 'gatorback' design pioneered by 1984 Chevrolet Corvette. Such low profile tyres give

LEFT *Another view of an SVO Mustang. The turbocharged engine is very effective and the car is little slower than some of its larger-engined counterparts. The handling is good too*

the Corvette and the SVO incredible grip.

Although the power peak is only 4400 rpm the 8.0:1 compression ratio means that the engine has to be kept boosted and certainly over 2500 rpm to produce the sort of performance the chassis craves. On the ordinary streets with a new car where the Hurst gear change is still stiff and notchy the result is extreme frustration as the revs drop. Around a test track such as Ford's Dearborn handling course where stop-start motoring is hardly called for the result is far more pleasing, the only mild criticism being that the SVO's small engine cannot match the wide spread of torque from the GT's 5-litre V8. While it lacks the GT's sheer punch, it fortunately lacks the larger-engined car's propensity for terminal understeer, making it almost the equal of the '84 Corvette through the slalom course. *Road & Track*, however, were prompted to wild enthusiasm, concluding that the Ford SVO team '…could hardly have done a better job of improving the car to world-class GT standards. This may be the best all-around car for the enthusiast driver ever produced by the US industry…'. They may be right – after all not many American cars can boast such sophistication or its ability to reach over 130 mph (209 kph) and still return near to 25 mpg. At least the Mustang will go out with its head held high after 20 years.

CORD

The Cord of 1935 was regarded as one of the finest examples of styling of all time, yet its futuristic body shielded a host of obscure problems

'THE NEW CORD proves that it *is* possible to build a radically different motor-car which is still in absolute harmony with the highest standards of beauty and good taste.'

That was how advertisements of 1936 promoted the 'new, original and ornamental design for an automobile' which had been patented by Gordon Miller Buehrig in May 1934 and which later went into production as the Cord 810. In fact the car should have

been a baby Duesenberg.

In 1933 Erret Lobban Cord's Auburn-Cord-Duesenberg Corporation was laying plans for future models, and because of the decline in sales of luxury cars during the Depression and the fact that those who could still afford them wanted less outwardly ostentatious means of transportation, it was determined that work should start on a lower-priced Duesenberg line.

810/812

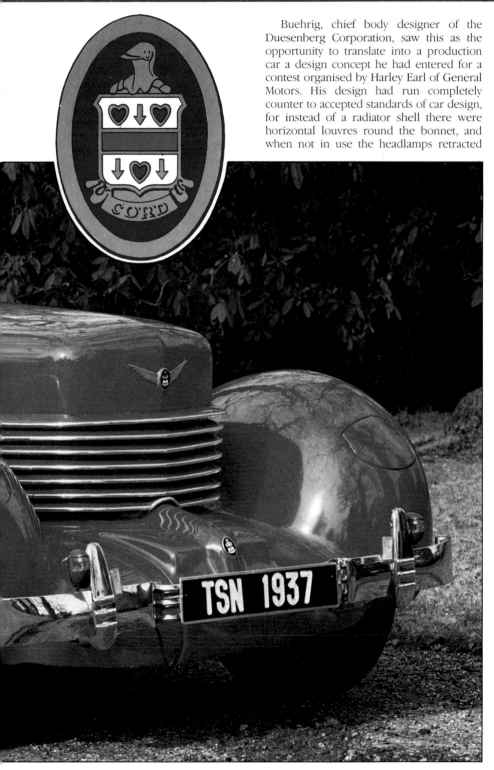

Buehrig, chief body designer of the Duesenberg Corporation, saw this as the opportunity to translate into a production car a design concept he had entered for a contest organised by Harley Earl of General Motors. His design had run completely counter to accepted standards of car design, for instead of a radiator shell there were horizontal louvres round the bonnet, and when not in use the headlamps retracted into the front pontoon-type wings; on this early design study the twin coolant surface radiators were mounted in the airstream between wings and bonnet.

A prototype body was built and fitted to an experimental Auburn chassis early in 1934, and Buehrig then applied for a patent. He was, however, now working for Auburn, having been transferred in an emergency move to restyle the Models 850 and 652 Auburns for 1935, the 1934 models having proved a dismal failure.

After creating the classic Model 851 and 852 Auburns, Buehrig returned to his baby Duesenberg project, which had been put on ice in the interim. He discovered that the car would now be a Cord, a spiritual successor to the grandiose L-29 Cord of 1929–32, and like its predecessor it would be front-wheel-driven. He started work on a quarter-scale model of the revised project, and it was completed by the late summer, when Buehrig took a brief honeymoon.

On his return he found that the baby Duesenberg project had been shelved once again; the Auburn-Cord-Duesenberg management was instead attempting to promote a stop-gap project using components from the Auburn V12. The design staff responded to this suggestion by producing a stupendously ugly mock-up, and the ill-considered idea was quickly dropped. Nevertheless, time and money were rapidly running out, and Auburn president Roy Faulkner believed that the decision should be taken to resume the front-wheel-drive Cord project. He persuaded Buehrig and his assistant Dale Cosper to prepare a presentation in a day so that it could be laid before the Auburn-Cord-Duesenberg board of directors at their imminent meeting in Chicago, when a decision would be made.

Faulkner made the presentation and the board was persuaded to give the project the go-ahead. Only four months remained before the first show opened, and for the car to be eligible as a production model in the eyes of the Automobile Manufacturers' Asso-

LEFT A 1937 Cord Beverly Sedan, instantly recognisable with the wrap-round radiator grille and side exit exhausts of impressive dimensions

397

ciation, a minimum figure of 100 cars had to be built. To meet this almost impossible deadline within the desperately tight financial constraints of the Auburn-Cord-Duesenberg group, certain short-cuts had to be taken; dies, for instance, were only made for right-front and left-rear doors, for the doors were symmetrical apart for the cut-outs for the rear wheelarches, which were removed afterwards by an extra cutter die. Again, the Auburn-Cord-Duesenberg corporation did not possess a large enough press to stamp out the roofs of closed models in one go, so this panel was welded together from smaller pieces.

The interior door handles were bought cheaply at a bankruptcy sale and fitted with showy plastic knobs to make them look expensive; instruments were acquired cheaply, too, and mounted in an engine-turned aircraft-type control panel designed by Buehrig.

Those retractable headlamps were another economy turned to good effect, for they were actually landing lights from Stinson aircraft (Stinson was yet another Cord group company, as was Lycoming, who built the Cord's V8 power unit), though the fact that they had to be cranked up and down manually can hardly have endeared them to Cord owners. By fully utilising such economies the necessary 100 Cords were built in time for the New York Show, although these

398

lacked the complex front-wheel-drive transmission, in which the gears were selected electro-pneumatically by a miniature lever moving in a gate on the steering column.

With its unusual styling, the new Cord proved an instant sales success. Many orders were taken at the show with promises of delivery by Christmas, but the inevitable problems with the transmission retarded the development programme, and all that those hopeful customers received for Christmas was a tiny scale model Cord mounted on a block of marble.

Perhaps surprisingly, unlike its contemporary, the Chrysler Airflow, the Cord didn't frighten customers away with its avant garde styling; instead, it proved embarrassingly attractive. Even those two hard-boiled critics, Montague Tombs and Freddie Gordon Crosby of *The Autocar* felt that 'The radiator must be subordinated to the design of the whole job, and the design of the whole must first be practical, and it is not practical unless the forward vision is unimpeded, which means a lower scuttle and bonnet and a sloping front… Just about this time the Cord projected itself into range of the companionate vision, and was instantly met, not with contumely, but with a real appreciation of a fine piece of bold and original designing work

LEFT The Cord 812 chassis provided the basis for this 1938 Phantom Corsair with quite extraordinary bodywork that looks to have given minimal visibility
BELOW A 1937 supercharged 812 Phaeton

…the writer and the illustrator fell to unalloyed appreciation of original work, not forgetting the clever details of the trapdoors for lamps in the streamline wings and the manner in which the bottom edges of the wings are not left straight down, but are neatly curled inwards.'

There were other clever design details, the petrol tank filler was concealed under a faired-in hinged flap, the hood was completely hidden when folded down, and the advantages of front-wheel-drive were exploited to the full in providing a 'step-down' entrance and a flat, uncluttered floor. The

BELOW A 1936 Cord Westchester Sedan, named after the exclusive New York town to give an idea of the car's status value to the company's image-conscious clientele

twin tail lights were faired into the 'fastback' tail and the door hinges were completely concealed. Tenite plastic was extensively used for trim hardware, and there was a choice of interior colour and trim designed to complement the external finish.

Buehrig's design for the Cord was so far ahead of its contemporaries that it was subsequently honoured by the Museum of Modern Art in New York as one of the 10 finest examples of industrial styling of all time, the only car to be so recognised.

When *The Autocar* tested a production 810 saloon in 1936, priced then in Britain at £880 (including tax), their report was highly favourable. They wrote: 'An unusual performance is automatically expected from so unusual a car, and one is not disappointed, for this Cord is really fast and the acceleration is very good indeed…'. At Brooklands the testers managed 0-60 mph in 20.1 seconds and achieved a top speed of

92.8 mph (149.3 kph). 'Exceptional average times are possible,' they continued, 'for this car has no speed that can be called a cruising rate, and is virtually as happy at 80 mph as at 60 mph where conditions allow. Certainly it is as fast as most people ever wish to use or our roads permit.'

The gearbox on this car was trouble-free and simple to operate: 'A pause is necessary, with release of the throttle pedal momentarily, to secure engagement of each gear, the action usually being devoid of any noise provided it is not hurried, or at the most there is a mild "clonk".' The finger-tip control was so positioned that once accustomed to it, the driver did not need to look at it to select gears.

The writers found the engine extremely smooth and quiet, 'free from thrash or thump when being accelerated, likewise from mechanical fuss or carburettor intake roar. High praise can be given to the Cord for the manner in which it is able to propel itself slow or fast without giving the occupants any real impression of the speed at which they are travelling. This results from the qualities of the engine…and the high gear ratios that are used. The top gear of 2¾ to 1 is among the very highest ratios employed on production cars of recent years; very few cars have had such a ratio…the performance is astonishingly effortless'.

Whilst the styling and performance of the Cord were collecting plaudits, its mechanics were still causing problems. That front-wheel-drive transmission, with its electric preselection of the gears by a tiny gearlever moving in a miniature gate on the steering column, was an attractive concept that failed to live quite up to its promise. It was beset by a host of obscure problems. Even when properly adjusted, there was sometimes a timelag between operating the clutch pedal and the engagement of the pre-selected ratio by a complex arrangement of electromagnets and vacuum-actuated diaphragms. It was clever but over-ambitious.

The transmission was only part of the Cord's mechanical problems, however, for early examples of the 4.7-litre V8 Cord FB engine, specially built for the car by Lycoming of Williamsport, Pennsylvania (yet another member of the Auburn-Cord-Duesenberg group), had restricted water passages in the aluminium cylinder heads, which frequently overheated and cracked.

The Cord power unit was, otherwise, a carefully-designed three-bearing V8 with main bearing inserts, poured connecting rod bearings and a counterbalanced crank. Valves were set horizontally between the blocks, and operated by cam-and-roller mechanism. Domed aluminium pistons were used. The rest of the car was just as

ABOVE RIGHT Auburn Automobile Company president Roy Faulkner (centre) with the first supercharged Cord 812 outside the factory; a car built for the New York Salon

carefully designed. The front suspension featured a novel arrangement of trailing arms sprung by a transverse semi-elliptic leaf spring while the rear was taken care of by a light 'dead' axle and two longitudinal semi-elliptics. All told that meant a reduction in unwanted unsprung weight of around 40 per cent compared to a conventional rear-drive car and the trailing-arm front suspension had the advantage of keeping the wheels vertical, eliminating the camber changes found with other independent systems. That was a very important considera-

tion with front-wheel drive.

All 'the mechanical failings of the Cord had a debilitating effect on the proposed rhythm of production: the target had been for 1000 cars a month, while in reality the Cord factory could only manage to build 1174 cars in the first 12 months.

It seems likely, too, that E.L. Cord had lost interest in the project; during 1936 he unloaded the greater part of his holdings in the Auburn-Cord-Duesenberg corporation for $4 million and the next year was to be found in Nevada pursuing a new-found interest in

ABOVE *The elegant lines of a 1937 Cord 812 Phaeton, prepared for US concours events*
RIGHT *A British-registered 1936 Cord 810 Phaeton*

radio and television. In his absence the Auburn-Cord-Duesenberg management decided to apply the same tactics that they had used to boost flagging sales of Auburns and Duesenbergs during the Depression: fit the car with a supercharger and outside exhaust pipes....

The result was the Cord 812, introduced for 1937 with an improved Lycoming FC engine. A Schwitzer-Cummins centrifugal supercharger was fitted, driven at six times crankshaft speed by a ring gear in the centre of the camshaft; at high loads the friction drive to the impeller was designed to slip to relieve torque loads on the blower drive gearing. The faster, more flamboyant 812 could be distinguished by twin flexible exhaust pipes protruding from either side of the bonnet which then vanished into the pontoon wings to merge into a single tailpipe.

As originally produced, the 812 engine developed 170 bhp at 3500 rpm; on later models the boost pressure was increased, lifting peak output to some 195 bhp at 4200 rpm. It was claimed that a well-tuned Cord 812 was capable of developing more than 200 bhp, while the Bonneville record breaker Ab 'Mormon Meteor' Jenkins said that during AAA observed test runs on the Utah salt flats his car was developing

225 bhp. Jenkins recorded a top speed of 121 mph with a stock Cord sedan but couldn't maintain it because the standard tyres threw their treads.

The Autocar testers were extremely impressed with the supercharged 812 when they drove a Westchester-bodied sedan, priced then at £1025 (including tax): '...there is no question that a terrific performance is given... Fine and easy though the performance of the unsupercharged car proved to be last year, this present machine unquestionably excels it... Yet in no sense

have the softness, quietness and smoothness of an excellent type of eight-cylinder engine been impaired...the general effect is of an exceedingly quiet, easy running machine. It is superlatively good in these respects at medium and high speeds, even to as much as a genuine 80 mph, wafting along with hardly a suggestion of mechanism working. The speeds shown by the speedometer seem quite unbelievable...the acceleration of this machine is tremendous...'. They reported that only by careful listening would' one detect the sound of the supercharger.

ABOVE, RIGHT, BELOW RIGHT *A 1937 Cord 810 Beverly Sedan. Note how far back in the car the engine is mounted, contributing to the car's good weight distribution. The instrumentation was almost excessive. The flexible exterior chrome exhaust pipes were a hallmark of many 1930's American cars*

The acceleration was certainly much improved, and in trials at Brooklands the 812 travelled from rest to 50, 60 and 70 mph (80, 96 and 113 kph) in 10.5, 13.2 and 19.6 seconds respectively, reaching a top speed of over 102 mph (164 kph). On this car the testers noticed some of those transmission-selection defects: 'A "plonk" sound frequently accompanies the actual engagement of a gear, but this is not serious, and occasionally a gear is missed and does not engage instantly. First and second make no more than a subdued note, while third and top are to all intents and purposes quite dead.' More than that they did not say, but motoring journalists were more forgiving in those days. The third and fourth gears were widely spaced ratios, giving respectively 19 mph (30.6 kph) and 28.2 mph (45 kph) per 1000 rpm. The latter, they wrote, 'is a sort of super top, intended to·be the fast cruising gear, though it can be kept engaged for considerable periods of time…'.

The ride and handling of the 812 and 810, were praised, the cars being found comfortable, stable and easy to take through corners at speed. 'It can be cornered fast confidently, and does not seem to mind whether bends or even sharper turns are taken with the engine pulling or on the overrun, though for a quick corner there is something to be said for keeping the engine on the drive. Generally, however, one is very apt to forget that

front wheel drive is utilised… it introduces no disadvantage or special difficulty. Tyre "scream" can be produced on a very fast corner, in which case there may also be some tendency to sideways motion of the body, but the car basically feels steady even then.'

With the introduction of the remarkable 812, Cord also attempted to woo the luxury market with a 'Custom Series' of two new long wheelbase models. These had longer, higher bodies with greater head and leg room than the standard Westchester and Beverly sedans, and attempted to conceal their larger overall dimensions with a taller 'coffin nose' incorporating eight horizontal louvres instead of seven. Unfortunately, the general effect was slightly overblown, though nowhere near as unsightly as the one-off long-wheelbase six-light limousine

EVOLUTION

Cord 810 introduced at the 1935 New York Motor Show, but the first 100 prototypes were not fitted with front-wheel drive. The unusual and attractive appearance attracted many orders, but development problems with the transmission and engine delayed the commencement of production.

1936 Production began of 810, available in Westchester and Beverly sedan form (identical but for upholstery) and four-seat Phaeton and two-seat Sportsman convertibles. The 810 was powered by a 4.7-litre Lycoming V8 driving the front wheels through a four-speed transmission with Cotal finger-tip electro-mechanical selector

1937 Production began of Cord 812, similar to 810 series but with Schwitzer-Cummins supercharger fitted to the Lycoming V8, which raised output to 195 bhp. Production also began of Custom Series Cords, with larger, longer bodies, intended for the top end of the market

1938 Production ended when the receiver sold off the Auburn-Cord-Duesenberg group. In all, 2320 Cord 810 and 812s were produced. The body dies were sold to Hupmobile who switched to rear drive, producing the unsuccessful Skylark.

which had louvres in the bonnet and looked ridiculously high and narrow!

The Custom Series cars were well-equipped; the Custom Beverly had normal pleated upholstery, plus an integral luggage boot, while the Custom Berline was designed for the chauffeur-driven end of the market. Therefore it had a wind-down glass division between front and rear compartments, and the rear seat passengers had built-in vanity case, smoker's companion, additional radio loudspeakers and an electric telephone for communicating with the chauffeur. Not surprisingly the Custom Series accounted for only a small part of total Cord 810/812 production, which reached 2320 units before the receiver was called in.

Just before the end, the LeBaron coach-building company produced some conventionally-styled design studies on the front-wheel-drive chassis: these had radiator grilles, side-hinged bonnets and running boards, but all they did was to prove just what a skilful design job Gordon Buehrig had performed with the coffin nose design.

In 1938 the receiver sold off the remains of the Auburn-Cord-Duesenberg group for what he could get – sadly it was to one Dallas E. Winslow of Detroit, who was not interested in reviving car production.

The body dies for the 810/812 Cords were sold to Hupmobile, another once-great company in financial straits. They adapted the bodies to fit their normal rear-wheel drive chassis and had the cars built as the 'Hupmobile Skylark' by Graham, who were by this time renting a large part of the Hupmobile factory. Graham, in return, were permitted to fit their own power units into the same chassis/body combination, and sell the result as the 'Graham Hollywood'. Neither car proved a success, and production of both Skylarks and Hollywoods petered out in 1940-41. It was predictable, said Buehrig, for the Cord body dies hadn't been designed for mass production (in that case, were those early production targets of 1000 Cords a month realistic or just wishful thinking from the start?).

The Cord dies were eventually thrown out as scrap, but by some devious route found their way to Japan – this was still before Pearl Harbor – where they were bought by Nissan, which couldn't bring itself to put the hammer to the old Cord dies. So there they remained, crated in a warehouse at least until the 1960s.

Although some attempts were made to revive the marque they never amounted to very much and as for the famous Erret Lobban Cord he died in January 1974, having long severed all connection with the car that bore his name

With such classic styling Cords have made the connection between cars and works of art, examples of the marque appearing in automotive and art museums. Their value has increased dramatically too with their milestone status guaranteeing that they will remain very expensive and very exclusive, exactly as they were when new.

PACKA

With the help of their brilliant designer Jesse Vincent, Packard built some of the finest V12s the world would see in the '20s and '30s

IF THE TRUE HALLMARK of the classic car is a V12 power unit, then Packard must surely deserve the supreme place of merit in the annals of classicism, for not only did this most patrician of Detroit marques popularise the V12 but in all Packard built a remarkable 40,790 of them, mostly under that celebrated Packard model name, Twin-Six.

But it's unlikely that there would ever have been a Packard V12 had it not been for Sunbeam of Wolverhampton and their brilliant Breton-born chief engineer Louis Coatalen, for it was he who first put a V12 engine in a motorcar, back in 1913, when he built a racing car – Toodles V – as a mobile testbed for a prototype V12 aero engine. A successful racer, capable of lapping Brooklands at some 112 mph (180 kph) Toodles V was shipped to America to continue racing when World War I broke out in August 1914, frustrating Sunbeam plans to put a V12 car on the market. But, claimed Coatalen, Toodles V 'was bought by a firm of perhaps the highest reputation in that continent. In consequence, that firm copied the engine and standardised the twelve-cylinder car.'

Whether that allegation of copying was true or not, Packard was certainly the first firm in the world to put a V12-engined car into quantity production. It was the creation of Packard's brilliant chief engineer, Jesse G. Vincent, and its introduction in May 1915 was a master-stroke that immediately placed Packard in the forefront of luxury car constructors and spawned a host of less-successful copyists.

Jesse Vincent was a remarkable character who learned engineering by working in machine shops and through correspondence courses. At the age of twenty, he joined the Burroughs Adding Machine Company and, though he had no formal engineering qualifications, his abilities as a mechanic brought him to the attention of Alvan Macauley, who was attempting to build up the Burroughs organisation. Transferred to the engineering department, the young mechanic was promoted to chief engineer

A Fifteenth-Series Packard V12 Coupé. Note the shouldered radiator, the distinctive Packard hallmark, like the beautiful sculptured bonnet mascot. The styling of this particular car is almost subdued compared with other bodies that clothed the V12 chassis from time to time

within months, and when Macauley was offered the position of general manager of Packard in 1910, he took Vincent with him. 'Colonel Jesse G. Vincent,' commented a journalist in 1926, 'is an outstanding figure even among the brilliant engineers in the automobile field.'

Vincent's Twin-Six engine was not only the first series-production V12, it was also the first car engine in America to be fitted with aluminium pistons. And it was hugely successful: virtually half Packard's 1916 output of 18,572 cars consisted of Twin-Sixes.

The Twin-Six's slender crankshaft ran in only three main bearings, yet could rev smoothly to a maximum of 3000 rpm and was flexible to the degree that the three-speed gearbox was almost superfluous, for the car would accelerate from 3 mph (5 kph) in top gear without hesitation.

Among the advanced features of the specification were a multiplate dry clutch, pressure lubrication of the crank, built-in tyre pump and monobloc casting of each bank of cylinders.

The Twin-Six was also unashamedly expensive: for the 1918 season prices ranged from $3600 for the bare chassis to $5850 for the seven-passenger Imperial Limousine, prices only exceeded by such limited-edition luxury as the Brewster, the Cunningham and the Locomobile 48. As an indication of the market Macauley and Vincent were aiming at, the chassis price of the Twin-Six was $50 more than the most expensive closed car in the Cadillac range.

Among the rich, the royal and the famous who chose the Twin-Six as their mode of transport was the otherwise eminently forgettable Warren Gamaliel Harding, 29th President of the United States, who rode to his inauguration in 1921 aboard a Twin-Six,

the first US President to make this journey in an automobile instead of a horse-drawn carriage.

During its first and most productive association with the Twin-Six layout, which ran from 1915–22, Packard produced 35,046 V12 cars – an average of more than ten cars a week, which almost placed the Twin-Six in the mass-production league!

In fact, the V12 layout had become so associated with the Packard name that it seemed almost an anticlimax when the Twin-Six was discontinued in 1922 and replaced by the Single Eight, magnificent car though the latter model was.

But the concept wouldn't die: and when in 1930 Cadillac launched the world's first V16 car, Packard decided to hit back with a new Twin-Six designed for the 1930s. Colonel Jesse and his staff were given sufficient budget to develop alternative concepts – one front-wheel driven, and the other with a conventional transmission.

Both the engineering and styling departments were keen on the front-wheel-drive because it offered improved handling characteristics, and styling because of the low overall height that could be achieved. A novel chassis was constructed for the prototype, with a bolt-on front end that could be removed for easy access to the engine and transmission; the gearbox was mounted ahead of the engine, with the gearshift linkage passing between the banks of cylinders.

BELOW AND BELOW RIGHT *It's hard to imagine from its elegant lines that this '34 model V12 dates from the Depression years when so many exclusive car manufacturers closed*

Leading automotive stylist Count Alexis de Sakhnoffsky then created a low, purposeful sedan body for the car; it stood just 5 ft 6 in (167 cm) tall. For reasons of security, the car was fitted with a disguised radiator shell, which lacked the traditional 'shoulders' of the Packard design, and made the car look rather like a German Horch.

Bowing to the realities of the Depression, however, Macauley and his board halted the front-wheel-drive project as they feared sales resistance – and unforeseen teething troubles that could delay the new model's planned launch date at the end of 1931.

By concentrating on the familiar rear-drive technology, the development programme was in fact speeded up, and in just eleven months from the start of design work, the new Twin-Six was ready for the market.

Indeed, its arrival was so eagerly awaited that on the day of its announcement, 17 June 1931, the tickertape of the New York Stock Exchange – which, in the preceding months, had so often brought tidings of doom and disaster – hammered out news of the rebirth of the Packard Twin-Six.

Packard, of course, stood apart from the ruck of the American motor industry in turning up their nose at the annual model change which had become traditional among lesser breeds. Instead, they designated their models as 'Series' and launched them when they felt the time was right.

But the interest caused by the reintroduction of a new Twin-Six was proof enough

LEFT *Packard built V12s after the Great War and in the '20s. This is a 1922 Twin Six Town Car with stately bodywork and an early example of customised wheels*

Views of the '34 Derham-bodied Packard V12 which was sold for a record price in 1985. Values have since increased greatly, although examples of the model rarely come up for sale. Despite its impressive external dimensions, the interior was not large

that Packard's policy was correct: by distancing the announcement of the new Series from other new model announcements, they achieved maximum interest and attention. In fact, the Ninth Series Twin-Six deserved careful examination, for it was a portent of the shape of Packards to come, featuring many new concepts which would subsequently be adopted by lesser Packards.

Its radical styling included a vee-radiator whose shape was echoed in the headlamp shells and glasses, in much the same way as the optional lamps of the Edwardian Mercedes Ninety; massive bumpers incorporated oil-damped, spring-loaded harmonic stabilisers which absorbed road shock. The chromium-plated 'aircraft-type' instrument panel incorporated an automatic clock and electric fuel gauge, the brakes were vacuum servo assisted, and the starter was engaged by a solenoid.

The power unit of the new-generation Twin-Six had its twin cylinder blocks set at the unusual included angle of 67 degrees, and was fitted with aluminium cylinder heads and thermostatically-controlled dual downdraught carburettors with automatic chokes. Soaring above that elegant vee radiator was a new Packard mascot, whose origins went back to the middle ages; it was a 'pelican in her piety', inspired by the family crest of the Packard family which had been brought across to the New World from England by Samuel Packard in 1638 aboard the ship *Diligent*.

Every Twin-Six engine was carefully run in, being initially turned over by an electric motor for an hour before it was allowed to run under its own power; it was then run for six hours on the test bench, and given a 75-minute check-up on the dynamometer to ensure that it was developing the specified output – a moderately healthy 160 bhp at 3200 rpm. Quiet running was assured by hydraulic valve silencers which damped out any tapping noise from the valve gear.

Only at this stage was the 7298 cc engine fitted in the chassis, which was then taken to

the Packard proving ground, occupying a 500-acre site north of the city of Detroit where it had been constructed in 1927. Here the chassis was tested for 250 miles (400 km) at speed on the 2.5 mile (4 km) test track by racing driver Tommy Milton; during those hundred fast laps it was given its final tune-up. The tests satisfactorily completed, the Twin-Six was awarded the Packard Certificate of Approval, signed by Milton.

It would be nice to record that so much care in manufacture was rewarded with soaring sales, but the truth is that the new 1932 Twin-Six was overpriced for that black year of the Depression; as announced, it was available only with 'Individual Custom' bodywork by Dietrich – the last bodies bearing that famous nameplate to be built under Ray Dietrich's personal supervision. During 1932 he left the company he had founded in 1927 with the backing of Edsel Ford in order to help the three Graham brothers develop the stylish new Graham Blue Streak, which pioneered the use of skirted wings.

Those Dietrich Packard bodies, which were mounted on their chassis at the Murray plant, included a Sport Phaeton ($ 6500), a Coupé ($ 6600), a Convertible Coupé ($ 6750) and a Convertible Sedan ($ 6950); they were readily identifiable by their sloping vee-windscreens, short scuttles and long bonnets with six ventilators, and rear-hinged front doors. Demand for them proved to be so slow (though they were all built during the 1932 model year, they were still available on the V12 Packard chassis in 1934!) that cheaper models were added to the catalogue in January 1932, at prices ranging from $ 3895 to $ 4195; six months later, these cheaper models were all increased in price by $ 500, so presumably they had been underpriced in an attempt to boost sales! The Dietrich name itself survived only until 1936, though stockpiled bodies were still being fitted by Murray to some chassis in 1937.

Out of 16,613 cars produced by Packard

in the Ninth Series (which ran from 7 June 1931 to 7 January 1933), only 549 were V12s. When it came to marketing the new Tenth Series, announced on 5 January 1933, Packard's advertising agency, convinced that the shortfall in demand was due to the car-buying public feeling that the name Twin Six had signified that the Ninth Series V12 was merely a warmed-over 1922 design, had the model designation changed to the less romantic Twelve. Sales of the Tenth Series Twelve disproved the marketing men's theories, for they amounted to just 520 out of a Series total of 4800 (admittedly, the Tenth Series was short-lived, produced from 5 January to 21 August 1933).

Capable of accelerating from 5–30 mph (8–48 kph) in top gear in just 8.5 seconds, the Twelve backed its performance with

power brakes whose degree of servo-assistance could be controlled by a four-position selector on the dashboard.

Motor Sport tested the Tenth Series car, the Twin Six, in 1934, taking it around the Brooklands track where it reached 91 mph (146 kph). The *Motor Sport* writer was '…greatly impressed by the quiet engine, which was well-nigh inaudible' and the car's stability at speed, 'In spite of the appalling surface of Brooklands Track, the Packard was steady as a rock. The steering had been criticised on the way owing to its low ratio, but no trouble at all was experienced at high speed. A low booming sound was all that could be heard from the engine when flat out and the impression was given that the car would run at its maximum all day without overheating or showing signs of distress.'

Little was found to criticise apart from the car's tendency to roll '…when cornered fast, even with the ride control in operation, but this could be remedied by additional shock absorbers' The conclusion was that the Twin Six Packard was '…fast, amazingly smooth and silent. It handles easily and positively. A finer car for really long journeys or extensive tours would be difficult to find.'

The X-braced chassis frame was new, and would remain basically the same for all subsequent Packards for the next two decades; other new engineering features included a pressurised cooling system with a condensor on the right-hand side of the engine to convert steam to water, cooling fins on the con-rod bearing caps and an electrically-operated oil gauge on the instrument panel. Dual-coil ignition, last used in 1928, was re-introduced. For the first time on a Packard, 17 in (43 cm) wheels were used (the Ninth Series had ridden on 18 in (46 cm) wheels). The Twelve was distinguished from the lesser eight-cylinder mod-

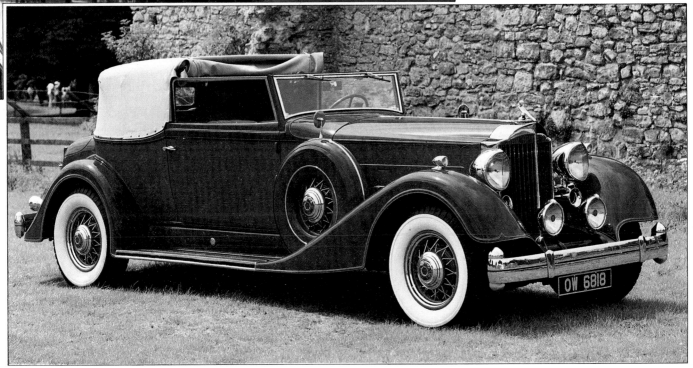

els by its painted radiator shell and chromed thermostatic radiator shutters, though for $25 extra, any combination of paint or chrome could be specified.

During the short life of the Tenth Series, the doors of the Chicago Century of Progress exhibition opened, distinguished by its outstanding automotive exhibits, with all the leading manufacturers vying for attention with specially-built coachwork. And every automotive prize at the exhibition was carried off by a very special Packard Twelve, the swansong design of Ray Dietrich at Dietrich Inc. At the Travel and Transportation Building, crowds queued for up to two hours just to see this 'Car of the Dome', a metallic bronze sport sedan with chromed wire wheels. Its interior metal brightwork was all gold-plated, from door handles to throttle pedal, while trim was in beige English broadcloth with a sheared beaver rug in the rear compartment. All the wood trim, including the rear compartment bar, was in burr Carpathian elm, and that bar, backed with a gold-mounted mirror, contained four golden goblets and two crystal glasses. After

BELOW & ABOVE RIGHT The subdued and sombre lines of a Dietrich-LeBaron-bodied V12 Sedanca de Ville
RIGHT The Sedanca de Ville's interior – note the ride control knob just below the glove box

the exhibition closed, the Car of the Dome was displayed in Packard dealerships.

Some of the styling features previewed on this show car were incorporated in the Eleventh Series, launched on 21 August 1933, but the most significant changes were hidden ones, for the engine now incorporated an entirely new lubrication system. This had an oil temperature regulator which enabled a single viscosity of oil to be used all year round, under all driving conditions, plus an oil pressure regulator which could be adjusted from the outside of the engine. There was also a self-cleaning full-flow oil filter in conjunction with larger-capacity fuel pump and galleries, plus steel-backed shell

big-end bearings.

At the Packard Proving Grounds, an Eleventh Series Twelve fitted with the new lubrication system was driven at a steady 112 mph (180 kph) for 56 hours before a big end failed and brought the run to a halt.

The Twelve, which in the Tenth Series had already carried a built-in radio reception system, now had provision for a radio control panel in the centre of the dashboard; there was also a combination speedometer/tachometer which indicated the engine speed in top gear, while reversing lights were automatically illuminated by engaging reverse gear. A redesigned ignition system had a single distributor but a separate coil

for each bank of cylinders.

Among the semi-custom built bodies available on the Eleventh Series Twelve were speedsters and sport phaetons by LeBaron; the same coachbuilder also constructed three streamlined sport coupés for show purposes, which previewed the styling of the forthcoming Twelfth Series, which was introduced on 30 August 1934. In fact, the Eleventh Series had marked a high point for the V12 Packard, for sales in the twelve months of its currency had totalled 960 cars, whilst during a similar period, the Twelfth Series Twelve sold 721 cars.

An increase in stroke to 108 mm from 101.6 mm gave a new swept volume of 7755 cc on the Twelfth Series Twelve and power output was increased to a claimed 175 bhp at 3200 rpm, 15 bhp more than the Eleventh Series (the engine, however, was capable of delivering over 190 bhp).

Though the semi-custom bodies had been discontinued due to lack of demand, the Twelfth Series Twelve was available with a wide range of special equipment. True, there were still some factory-fitted bodies which bore Dietrich or LeBaron body plates, but these were really only modified standard bodies constructed by Murray or Briggs, who respectively held the rights to those names.

Another major change for the Twelfth Series came in the shape of an announcement from the factory that the Series would also be known as '1935 Packards'. This was in line with President Roosevelt's plea that new cars should be announced in early autumn to minimise and stabilise winter unemployment, and with the Automobile Manufacturers Association campaign for the annual motor show to be held in November rather than January.

Consequently, the 36th National Automobile Show was held in November 1935, but though the new Packards on display were designated Fourteenth Series, the differences between these and the Twelfth Series were minimal, the most obvious being a steeper rake to the radiator shell. In any case, the luxury Packards were now becoming an expensive irrelevance, for the new low-priced Packard 120 launched the previous year was obviously far more in tune with the times: during the 1936 model year, 2500 of Packard's assembly staff built 5303 Senior Eights and 682 Twelves, while the remaining 2600 workers in Packard's second plant built 55,042 Packard 120 cars under the guidance of manufacturing vice-president George Christopher, a 'produc-

ABOVE LEFT *The Packard V12 engine displaced 7755 cc and developed its power in a progressive and smooth manner with little noise*

LEFT *A 1934 V12 1106 Sport Coupé with lovely smooth lines, but little rear three-quarter visibility. This car was photographed at Pebble Beach, prior to the world's most prestigious concours competition*
FAR LEFT *The heart of the matter, the V12 engine that powered so many Packards*

tion genius' hired from General Motors in 1933 to supervise the turnaround of Packard. The writing was very definitely on the wall, and Packard began a three-year phase-out of the Senior Eight and Twelve.

Nevertheless, the Fifteenth Series was the best-selling Twelve of the 1930s, with sales of 1300 representing some 20 per cent of all the Twelves built during the model's eight-year production life. Among the innovations were independent front suspension and power-assisted hydraulic brakes (all the previous Twelves had used a mechanical layout); power-assistance was also fitted to the clutch for the first time.

It was still possible to commission one-off bodywork from the steadily dwindling band of custom coachbuilders, and Murray produced a handful of Dietrich-badged phaetons to bespoke order, most notably for the White House. Other Fifteenth Series Twelve tourers were constructed by Kellner of Paris and Rollston of New York, though the latter company was less than a twelve-month from the bankruptcy court.

The last year of the V12 Packard was 1939; the Seventeenth Series Twelves were assembled against individual order only, all 446 of them, and were no different mechanically from the Sixteenth Series cars, save for the option of steering column gear change and a pushbutton radio. Among the customers for Twelves were 'Yankee Doodle Dandy' George M. Cohan, King Gustav V of Sweden and the White House. FDR's last Twelve was a very special automobile, for it was designed to resist the attack of an assassin. Like a Lincoln V12 ordered at the same time, the body and windows of the Packard were armoured to resist a direct hit from a 50-calibre machine gun bullet, while the folding hood was specially reinforced to withstand a grenade dropped from a height of 250 feet, by no means the most obvious way of effecting an assassination.

However, by August 1939, the Packard Twelve was gone for good, after a production run of 5744 cars in eight years: but Colonel Jesse wasn't quite finished with twelve-cylinder engines, for the previous spring production of a new twelve-cylinder Packard marine engine had begun, destined for the nation's wartime patrol boats, while during the war Packard built more Rolls-Royce Merlin V12 aero engines than the Rolls-Royce factories in Britain. Perhaps, since the original Twin Six had sprung from a British aero engine, this wartime reciprocation was entirely appropriate.